S0-AWY-304

# THE MYTHOLOGY OF ALL RACES

Volume VI

INDIAN
IRANIAN

Volume I. *Greek and Roman*
William Sherwood Fox, Ph.D., Princeton University.

Volume II. *Teutonic*
Axel Olrik, Ph.D., University of Copenhagen.

Volume III. *Celtic, Slavic*
Canon John A. MacCulloch, D.D., Bridge of Allan, Scotland.
Jan Máchal, Ph.D., Bohemian University, Prague.

Volume IV. *Finno-Ugric, Siberian*
Uno Holmberg, Ph.D., University of Finland, Helsingfors.

Volume V. *Semitic*
R. Campbell Thompson, M.A., F.S.A., F.R.G.S., Oxford.

Volume VI. *Indian, Iranian*
A. Berriedale Keith, D.C.L., Edinburgh University.
Albert J. Carnoy, Ph.D., University of Louvain.

Volume VII. *Armenian, African*
Mardiros Ananikian, B.D., Kennedy School of Missions, Hartford, Connecticut.
George Foucart, Docteur ès Lettres, French Institute of Oriental Archæology, Cairo.

Volume VIII. *Chinese, Japanese*
U. Hattori, Litt.D., University of Tokyo.
*(Japanese Exchange Professor at Harvard University, 1915–1916)*
Masaharu Anesaki, Litt.D., University of Tokyo.
*(Japanese Exchange Professor at Harvard University, 1913–1915)*

Volume IX. *Oceanic*
Roland Burrage Dixon, Ph.D., Harvard University.

Volume X. *American (North of Mexico)*
Hartley Burr Alexander, Ph.D., University of Nebraska.

Volume XI. *American (Latin)*
Hartley Burr Alexander, Ph.D., University of Nebraska.

Volume XII. *Egypt, Far East*
W. Max Müller, Ph.D., University of Pennsylvania.
Sir (James) George Scott, K.C.I.E., London.

Volume XIII. *Index*

## PLATE I

### Durgā

The wife of Śiva, in her dread aspect, slays the Asura Mahiṣa. Standing in an attitude of triumph on the demon, who, as his name implies, is in the shape of a buffalo, she drags his soul (symbolized in human form) from him. From a Javanese lava sculpture, probably from Prambanān, in the Museum of Fine Arts, Boston. See p. 118.

# THE MYTHOLOGY OF ALL RACES

*IN THIRTEEN VOLUMES*

LOUIS HERBERT GRAY, A.M., PH.D., EDITOR
GEORGE FOOT MOORE, A.M., D.D., LL.D., CONSULTING EDITOR

---

## INDIAN

BY

A. BERRIEDALE KEITH

D.C.L., D.LITT.

## IRANIAN

BY

ALBERT J. CARNOY

PH.D., LITT.D.

---

VOLUME VI

---

BOSTON
MARSHALL JONES COMPANY
M DCCCC XVII

Ref
BL
25
M8

Copyright, 1917
By Marshall Jones Company

Entered at Stationers' Hall, London

*All rights reserved*

Printed in January, 1917

PRINTED IN THE UNITED STATES OF AMERICA BY THE UNIVERSITY PRESS
CAMBRIDGE, MASSACHUSETTS

BOUND BY THE BOSTON BOOKBINDING COMPANY

33198

# CONTENTS

## INDIAN



## IRANIAN

# ILLUSTRATIONS

## FULL PAGE ILLUSTRATIONS

## ILLUSTRATIONS IN THE TEXT

# INDIAN MYTHOLOGY

BY

A. BERRIEDALE KEITH, D.C.L., D.Litt.

REGIUS PROFESSOR OF SANSCRIT AND COMPARATIVE PHILOLOGY
EDINBURGH UNIVERSITY

TO THE MEMORY

OF

FIELD MARSHAL THE RIGHT HONOURABLE

EARL KITCHENER OF KHARTOUM

K.G., K.P., O.M., G.C.B., G.C.S.I., G.C.M.G., G.C.I.E., LL.D.

LORD RECTOR OF THE UNIVERSITY OF EDINBURGH

(1914–1916)

# AUTHOR'S PREFACE

THE mythology of India claims unique interest by virtue of its unparalleled length of life. It is true that not even the discoveries at Boghaz Kyoi render it prudent for us to place the *Ṛgveda* at an earlier period than 1500 B.C., and in part at least that collection may come from three centuries later, so that as contrasted with the dates of Egyptian and Babylonian records the earliest monument of Aryan mythology is comparatively recent. In mass of content and in value for mythology, however, these cannot compare with the *Ṛgveda*. Of still more importance is the fact that from the period of the *Ṛgveda* to the present day, a space of some thirty-five hundred years, we have a mythology which is in constant but organic development. The high mythic systems of Teuton, Celt, and Slav, of Greek and Roman, have perished before the onslaught of a loftier faith and survive in little else than folk-lore. In India, on the contrary, though foreign invasion has often swept over the north-west of the land, though Islām has annexed souls as well as territories, though Christianity (especially in the south) has contributed elements to the faith of the people, still it remains true that the religion and the mythology of the land are genuinely their own and for this reason have in themselves the constant potency of fresh growth. Moreover, amidst the ceaseless change which is the heritage of human things, there is relative stability in the simpler thoughts of the human mind, and as in many parts of India the peasant still labours with the implements and in the mode of his ancestors in periods far remote, so his mind frames the same hypotheses to account for those phenomena of nature which in India more than elsewhere determine irrevocably his weal or his woe.

The rich variety of the mythology, despite its attraction for the student of the history of myths, renders the task of concise exposition one of peculiar difficulty. For the mythology of the present day available material is enormous: each part of the vast area of India has its own abundant store of myth and tradition, and to give detail for this period would be impossible. The same consideration applies with but slightly lessened force for the earlier epochs: the Veda, the epics, the *Purāṇas*, the literature of the Buddhists and of the Jains, each present data in lavish abundance. It has been necessary, therefore, to circumscribe narrowly the scope of the subject by restricting the treatment to that mythology which stands in close connexion with religion and which conveys to us a conception of the manner in which the Indian pictured to himself the origin of the world and of life, the destiny of the universe and of the souls of man, the gods and the evil spirits who supported or menaced his existence. Gods and demons were very present to the mind of the Indian then as they are today, and they are inextricably involved in innumerable stories of folk-lore, of fairy tale, and of speculation as to the origin of institutions and customs. The task of selecting such myths as will best illustrate the nature of the powers of good and evil is one in which we cannot hope for complete success; and the problem is rendered still more hard by the essential vagueness of many of the figures of Indian mythology: the mysticism of Indian conception tends ever to a pantheism alien to the clear-cut creations of the Hellenic imagination.

The difficult task of selecting suitable illustrations has been shared with the editor of this series, Dr. Louis H. Gray, of whose valuable assistance in this and other matters I desire to express my most sincere appreciation; and my friend Professor Charles R. Lanman, of Harvard University, has generously lent us valuable volumes from his private library. Dr. Ananda K. Coomaraswamy, with his wonted generosity and devotion to the cause of promoting the knowledge of Indian art, not merely accorded permission for the reproduction of illustrations from his *Rajput Paintings* (published by the Oxford University Press), but placed at my disposal the resources of his admirable *Viśvakarma*, a kindness for which I am deeply grateful. To the India Society and the Oxford University Press I am indebted for permission to reproduce illustrations from Lady Herringham's splendid copies of the Ajanta frescoes, published by the Press for the Society. Messrs. W. Griggs and Sons, of Hanover Street, Peckham, London, S. E., have been good enough to permit the reproduction of certain illustrations from their *Journal of Indian Art;* and I owe to the generosity of the India Office the photographs which Messrs. Griggs and Sons have made for me from negatives in the collection of that Department. Lieut.-Col. A. H. Milne, of Cults, Aberdeenshire, Scotland, kindly permitted the photographing of one of the pieces of his rich collection; the Museum of Fine Arts in Boston and the Peabody Museum in Salem, Mass., have been no less generous than he; and Mrs. Louis H. Gray placed her expert knowledge at our service in seeing the volume through the press.

To my wife I owe thanks for help and criticism.

A. BERRIEDALE KEITH.

University of Edinburgh,
22 September, 1916.

# TRANSCRIPTION AND PRONUNCIATION

THE system of transcription followed is that used by the Royal Asiatic Society and accords closely with the one adopted in the *Grundriss der indo-arischen Philologie und Altertumskunde*. The pronunciation is much as in English, but *c* is pronounced as *ch*, and *g* is always hard; the characters represented by *kh*, *gh*, *ch*, *jh*, *ṭh*, *ḍh*, *th*, *dh*, *ph*, *bh* have the *h* sounded half-separately, somewhat as in *pot-hook*, *madhouse*, *hap-hazard*, etc. Of the letters distinguished by diacritical marks *ṭ*, *ṭh*, *ḍ*, *ḍh*, and *ṇ* are pronounced very much like the ordinary dentals; *ṣ* is sounded as *sh*, and *ś* as *sh* or *s*; the *s* is always hard, never soft like *z*. The letter *ṛ* denotes the vowel sound of *r* and is pronounced approximately like *ri*; and similarly *ḷ* is almost like *li*. The letters *ṅ* and *ñ* denote a nasal assimilated to the following sound, guttural and palatal respectively, and *ṁ* indicates a nasal sound which corresponds very roughly to *ng*. The "visarga," *ḥ*, was probably pronounced like the Scottish or German *ch*. The vowels *e* (pronounced like *a* in *fate*) and *o*, which represent an original *ai* and *au*, are always long. The vowel *a* is pronounced somewhat in the manner of the *u* in English *but*; other vowels have the same value as in Italian.

# INTRODUCTION

THE earliest record of Indian mythology is contained in the *Ṛgveda*, or "Hymn Veda," a series of ten books of hymns celebrating the chief Vedic gods. The exact motives of the collection are uncertain, but it is clear that in large measure the hymns represent those used in the Soma sacrifice, which formed a most important part of the worship of the gods in the ritual of the subsequent period. It is now recognized that the religion and mythology contained in this collection are not primitive in character and that they represent the result of a long period of development of sacred poetry. Thus it is that the gods who form the subject of this poetry often appear obscure in character, though in the great majority of cases it is clear that the myths related of them refer to physical happenings. The date of the *Ṛgveda* is much disputed and admits of no definite determination; it may be doubted whether the oldest poetry contained in it is much earlier than 1200 B.C., but it is not probable that it was composed later than 800 B.C., even in its most recent portions.

Both in its mythology and in its composition the *Ṛgveda* is clearly older than the other three Vedas, the *Sāmaveda*, the *Yajurveda*, and the *Atharvaveda* — the "Chant Veda," the "Formula Veda," and the "Veda of the Atharvan Priests" — and, in point of date, these three stand much on a level with the *Brāhmaṇas*, or explanatory prose texts which are attached to or form part of them. In them are to be found many speculations of a more advanced kind than those of the *Ṛgveda*, yet at the same time the *Atharvaveda* contains a mass of popular religion which has been taken up and worked over by the same priestly classes to whose activity the other texts are due. It must, therefore, be recognized that the *Ṛgveda* gives only an imperfect impression of Indian mythology and that, in a sense, it is the work of an aristocracy; but at the same time it is impossible to regard the *Atharvaveda* as a direct complement of the *Ṛgveda* and as giving the popular side of the Ṛgvedic religion. The *Atharvaveda* was probably not reduced to its present form much, if at all, earlier than 500 B.C., and the popular worship included in it is one which is at once separated by a considerable period in time from that of the *Ṛgveda* and is presented to us, not in its primitive form, but as it was taken up by the priests. The other Vedas and the *Brāhmaṇas* may be referred roughly to a period which runs from 800 to 600 B.C. To the *Brāhmaṇas* are attached, more or less closely, treatises called *Āraṇyakas* ("Silvan"), which were to be studied by oral tradition in the solitude of the forests, and *Upaniṣads*, treatises of definitely philosophical content, whose name is derived from the "session" of the pupils around their teacher. The oldest of these works probably date from before 500 B.C. On the other hand, the *Sūtras*, or rules regarding the sacrifice both in its more elaborate and in its more domestic forms, and regulations concerning custom and law give incidental information as to the more popular side of religion.

The *Sūtras*, at any rate, and possibly even the *Brāhmaṇas*, in their later portions, are contemporaneous with the beginnings of the two great epics of India, the *Mahābhārata* and the *Rāmāyaṇa*. The first composition of these works as real epics, made up from ballads and other material, may be assigned to the fourth century B.C., and it is probable that the *Rāmāyaṇa* was practically complete before the Christian era. In the case of the *Mahābhārata*, however, there is no doubt that the original heroic epic has been overwhelmed by a vast mass of religious, philosophical, and didactic matter, and that it was not practically complete before the sixth century A.D., though most of it probably may be dated in the period from 200 B.C. to 200 A.D. These works reveal, to an extent which cannot be paralleled in the texts of the preceding periods, the religion of the warrior class and of the people generally. It cannot be assumed that the religion thus described is a later development, in point of time, than the Vedic religion, so far as the chief features of this religion are concerned; but much of the mythology is clearly a working over of the tales reported in the period of the *Brāhmaṇas*, of which, in so far, the epic period is a legitimate successor.

The epic period is followed by that of the *Purāṇas*, which show undoubted signs of the development of the religion and mythology of the epics. No doubt the material in these texts is often old, and here and there narratives are preserved in a form anterior to that now seen in the *Mahābhārata*. Yet, on the whole, it is probable that no *Purāṇa* antedates 600 A.D., and there is little doubt that portions of some of them are much later, falling within the last few centuries. Nor, indeed, is there any definite check to the continuance of this literature: at least two of the *Purāṇas* have no definite texts, and any author, without fear of positive contradiction, is at liberty to compose a poem in honour of a place of worship or of pilgrimage, and to call it a portion of either of these *Purāṇas*. This is the literature which, to the present day, contains the authoritative sacred texts of Hindu myth and worship. Yet it is essentially priestly and learned, and the popular religion which it embodies has been elaborated and confused, so that it is necessary, for a clear view of modern Hindu mythology, to supplement the account of the *Purāṇas* with records taken from the actual observation of the practices of modern India.

Besides the main stream of Hindu mythology there are important currents in the traditions of the Buddhists and the Jains. Buddhism has left but faint traces of its former glories in India itself; undoubtedly from about 500 B.C. to 700 A.D. it must be ranked among the greatest of Indian religions, and in the school of the Mahāyāna, or "Great Vehicle," it developed an elaborate mythology which displays marked original features. In comparison with Buddhism Jainism has added little to the mythology of India, but in its own way it has developed many themes of Indian mythology, with the main doctrines of which it remains in much closer contact than does Buddhism.

The subject, therefore, divides itself, in accordance with the literary sources upon which any treatment must be based, into seven divisions:

I. The Period of the *Ṛgveda* (Chapters I and II);
II. The Period of the *Brāhmaṇas* (Chapter III);
III. The Period of the Epics (Chapters IV and V);
IV. The Period of the *Purāṇas* (Chapter VI);
V. The Mythology of Buddhism (Chapter VII);
VI. The Mythology of Jainism (Chapter VIII);
VII. The Mythology of Modern India (Chapter IX).

# INDIAN MYTHOLOGY

## CHAPTER I

## THE ṚGVEDA

### GODS OF SKY AND AIR

IN his *Nirukta* (the oldest extant Vedic commentary, written about 500 B.C.) Yāska tells us that earlier students of the mythology of the *Ṛgveda* had resolved all the deities into three classes according to their position in the sky, in the atmosphere, or on the earth; and he further treats all the different members of each class as being only divergent aspects of the three great gods, Agni ("Fire") on earth, Indra ("Storm") or Vāyu ("Wind") in the atmosphere, and Sūrya ("Sun") in the sky. This apportionment of the universe is, in fact, widely accepted in the *Ṛgveda*, where, as a rule, a threefold distribution is preferred to the simpler view which contrasts the earth with all that is seen above it. To the division immediately over the earth are referred the manifestations of wind, rain, and lightning, while solar phenomena are assigned to the highest of the three parts. Each of these three classifications may again be subdivided into three: thus it is in the highest luminous space or sky that the "fathers" (the kindly dead), the gods, and Soma reside. In the atmosphere also there are three spaces, or often only two — one the heavenly and one the earthly — and in either case the highest is sometimes treated as if it were the heaven or sky itself. Like the earth it has rocks and mountains; streams (clouds) flow in it; and the water-dripping clouds are constantly compared to and identified with cows. It seems clear that the earthly as well as the heavenly portion of the atmosphere is above, not below, the earth, so that the sun does not return from west to east under the earth, but goes back by the way it came, turning its light side up to the sky and thus leaving earth in darkness. The earth, conceived as extended, broad, and boundless, is compared in shape to a wheel, but no ocean surrounds it, as in Greek and later Indian mythology. The earth has four points, or five when we include the place where the speaker stands.

An older conception is that of the earth and the sky alone as constituting the universe. In that case the idea of the shape of the earth varies, for when it is united with the sky, it is compared to two great bowls turned toward each other; while from another point of view earth and sky are likened to the wheels at the ends of an axle. So closely united are the pair that, as a deity, Dyāvāpṛthivī ("Sky and Earth") is far more frequently invoked than either Dyaus ("Sky") or Pṛthivī ("Earth"). The joint deity can claim six hymns in the *Ṛgveda*, the Earth only one, and the Sky none. Even in her solitary hymn (v. 84) the Earth is praised for sending the rain from her cloud, though that is, as a matter of fact, her husband's function. The two are called the primeval parents, who make and sustain all creatures; and the gods themselves are their children: they are the parents of Bṛhaspati ("Lord of Devotion") and with the waters and Tvaṣṭṛ ("Fashioner") they engendered Agni. Yet with characteristic impartiality they are said themselves to be created, for a poet marvels at the skill which wrought them, and others attribute their fashioning to Indra, to Viśvakarman ("All-Maker") or to Tvaṣṭṛ. They are far-extending, unaging, yielding milk, ghee (clarified butter), and honey in abundance. The one is a prolific bull, the other a variegated cow; and both are rich in seed. They are wise also, and they promote righteousness and accord protection and aid to their worshippers.

The constant problem of the fashioning of the world is expressed in many ways. With the suns Varuṇa measures the world; Indra made the wide expanse of earth and the high dome of the sky after measuring the six regions; or, again, the earth is said to have been spread out, as by Agni, Indra, the Maruts (storm-deities), and other gods. The similitude of a house leads to the question from what wood it was fashioned, and the doors of this house of the world are the portals of the east, through which comes the morning light. Both sky and earth are often said to be propped up, but the sky is also declared to be rafterless, and the marvel of its being unsupported is remarked. The earth is made fast with bands by Savitṛ (a form of the sun), and Viṣṇu fixed it with pegs. In the last and latest book of the *Ṛgveda*, however, these simple concepts are replaced by speculations in which mythology passes into philosophy. The most important of these theorizings is that contained in x. 129, which tells that nothing existed in the beginning, all being void. Darkness and space enveloped the undifferentiated waters. By heat the first existing thing came into being, whereupon arose desire, the first seed of mind, to be the bond of the existent and the non-existent. Thus the gods had their origin, but at this point the speculation concludes with an assertion of doubt. The hymn itself runs thus, in Muir's metrical rendering:[1]

"Then there was neither Aught nor Nought, no air nor sky beyond.
What covered all? Where rested all? In watery gulf profound?
Nor death was then, nor deathlessness, nor change of night and day.
That One breathed calmly, self-sustained; nought else beyond It lay.
Gloom hid in gloom existed first — one sea, eluding view.
That One, a void in chaos wrapt, by inward fervour grew.
Within It first arose desire, the primal germ of mind.
Which nothing with existence links, as sages searching find.
The kindling ray that shot across the dark and drear abyss, —
Was it beneath? or high aloft? What bard can answer this?
There fecundating powers were found, and mighty forces strove, —
A self-supporting mass beneath, and energy above.
Who knows, who ever told, from whence this vast creation rose?
No gods had then been born, — who then can e'er the truth disclose?
Whence sprang this world, and whether framed by hand divine or
no, —
It's lord in heaven alone can tell, if even he can show."

As in this hymn the gods are said to come into being after the creation of the universe, so in other philosophic hymns they are brought into existence from the waters, and in one place they are divided into groups born from Aditi ("Boundless"), the waters, and the earth. The Ādityas in particular are constantly derived from Aditi. Yet speculation is free and changes easily: Dawn is the mother of the sun and is born of Night, by reason of temporal sequence; while for local causes Sky and Earth are the all-parents. Or the greatest of a class is parent of the rest, as the storm-god Rudra ("Roarer") of the Rudras, the wind of the storm-gods, Sarasvatī of rivers, and Soma of plants. A certain mysticism and love of paradox result in a declaration that Indra produced his parents, Sky and Earth, or that Dakṣa (a creator-god) is at once father and son of Aditi. Similar vagueness prevails regarding men. They must be included in the general parentage of Sky and Earth, but the priestly family of the Aṅgirases are sprung directly from Agni, and the sage Vasiṣṭha is the child of Mitra and Varuṇa by Urvaśī, an Apsaras, or heavenly nymph. Yet they are also descended from Manu, son of Vivasvant, or from Yama, the brother of Manu, and his sister Yamī, and this pair claim kinship with the Gandharva (celestial bard) and the water-nymph.

There is too little distinction between gods and men for us to be surprised that the gods were once mere mortals, or that there are ancient as well as more recent gods. How they won immortality is uncertain: Savitṛ or Agni bestowed it upon them, or they obtained it by drinking soma, whereas Indra gained it by his ascetic practices. Yet it seems clear that they did get it and that when the gods are called unaging, it does not mean, as in the mythology of the epic, that they endure only for a cosmic age; for this latter concept is bound up with the philosophy which sees no progress in the world and which, therefore, resolves all existence into a perpetual series of growth and passing away.

Many as are the names of the gods, there is much that they

have in common as they are presented to us in a poetry which has gone so far as to recognize an essential unity among the multiplicity of the divine forms. "The bird — that is, the sun — which is but one, priest and poets with words make into many," we are told, and "Priests speak in diverse ways of that which is but one: they call it Agni, Yama, Mātariśvan." Yet this is not so much monotheism as pantheism, for we learn that Aditi is everything, gods and men, that which has been and that which shall be; and that Prajāpati ("Lord of Creatures") embraces all things within himself. From this point of view it is easy to understand the fact [2] that here and there one god is treated as if he were the highest god, or that one god can be identified with any of the others, and all the others be said to be centred in him. There is no real monotheistic strain in a declaration that "Agni alone, like Varuṇa, is lord of wealth." The same syncretism is seen in the constant addressing of prayers to groups of gods, in the stereotyping of the invocation of the gods in pairs, and in the reckoning of the gods as thirty-three, i.e. three sets of eleven each in the sky, the waters of the air, and the earth.

Normally, and subject to certain exceptions, the gods are conceived as anthropomorphic; they wear garments, carry weapons, and drive in cars. Yet their personality is very differently developed in the several cases: Indra is much more anthropomorphic than Agni, whose tongue and whose limbs merely denote his flames. The abode of the gods is in the highest realm of sky, and the offerings of men are either carried thither to them by Agni or, in a concept which is perhaps older, they are deemed to come to the straw on which the pious worshipper has set out his gifts. The food which they eat is that of man — milk, barley, butter, cattle, sheep, and goats — chosen now and then for special fitness, as when Indra, often called a bull, receives hecatombs of bulls. The drink of the gods is the soma.

Of feuds among the gods we hear little or nothing: Indra alone reveals traits of disorderliness, perhaps not unnatural in one who boasts of having drunk himself into intoxication with soma. He seems once to have fought with all the gods, to have shattered the car of Dawn, and even to have slain his father; and he actually quarrelled with his faithful henchmen, the Maruts. To their worshippers the gods are good and kind, and for them they slay the demons, with whom they wage a war which is triumphant if seemingly incessant. They richly bless the sacrificer and punish the niggard. They are true and not deceitful, although Indra again departs from the highest standard by his use of wiles, even without a good end to justify the means. Moral grandeur is practically confined to Varuṇa, and the greatness and the might of the gods are extolled far more often than their goodness. Their power over men is unlimited: none may defy their ordinances or live beyond the period allotted by them, nor is there aught that can subdue them, save in so far as they are said sometimes not to be able to transgress the moral order of Mitra and Varuṇa.

The pantheon which the *Ṛgveda* presents is essentially artificial, for as regards by far the greater part of the collection it contains hymns used in the Soma ritual, whence it gives only an imperfect conception of the gods as a whole. Thus, excepting in the tenth book, which contains a short group of hymns (14–18) constituting a sort of collection for Yama (the primeval man and the king of the departed), we learn nothing of the dead and very little of the spirits. Moreover, it is only in quite inadequate measure that we meet with the more domestic side of religion or with the belief in magic and witchcraft in their application to the needs of ordinary life. We cannot, therefore, feel any assurance that the comparative importance of the gods as they might be judged from their prominence in the *Ṛgveda* affords any real criterion of their actual position in the life of any Vedic tribe, though doubtless it does reflect their rank in the views of the group of priestly families whose traditions, united in a whole, are presented to us in the *Ṛgveda*. From the text itself it would seem that Indra, Agni, and Soma are by far the greatest gods; then come the Aśvins (the twin celestial "Horsemen"), the Maruts, and Varuṇa; then Uṣas ("Dawn"), Savitṛ, Bṛhaspati, Sūrya, Pūṣan ("Nourisher"); then Vāyu, Dyāvāpṛthivī, Viṣṇu, and Rudra; and finally Yama and Parjanya (the rain-god). Even this list, based on numerical considerations, is open to objection, for some of the deities, such as Varuṇa, are obviously greater, though less closely connected with the sacrifice, so that, despite their true rank, they are less often mentioned than others, such as the Aśvins, who are more frequently invoked in the sacrifice.

Of the gods of the sky Dyaus ("Sky") corresponds in name to Zeus, and like Zeus he is a father. Indeed, this is by far the most important characteristic of Zeus's counterpart in the *Ṛgveda*. Uṣas ("Dawn") is most often the child mentioned, but the Aśvins, Agni, Parjanya, Sūrya, the Ādityas, the Maruts, Indra, and the Aṅgirases are among his offspring, and he is the parent of Agni. Normally, however, he is mentioned with Earth in the compound Dyāvāpṛthivī, and on the solitary occasion when he is hailed in the vocative as *Dyauṣ pitar* ("Father Sky," the exact equivalent of the Greek Ζεῦ πάτερ and the Latin Iuppiter), "Mother Earth" is simultaneously addressed. Scarcely any other characteristic is ascribed to him; it is simply stated that he is a bull who bellows downward, or a black steed decked with pearls (i.e. the dark sky set with stars), that he smiles through the clouds, and that he bears the thunderbolt. Thus he is hardly anthropomorphized at all, whether named alone, or when conjoined with earth, and his worship is little removed from the direct adoration of the sky as a living being. No moral attribute belongs to him, nor is there any trace of sovereignty over the world or the other gods. The position of power and elevation which Greek mythology ascribes to Zeus is not accorded in full to any Vedic deity, but in so far as Zeus has a parallel, it is in Varuṇa, not in Dyaus.

In comparison with Dyaus Varuṇa has far more anthropomorphic traits. He wears a golden mantle and a shining robe;

with Mitra ("Sun") he mounts his shining car; in the highest heaven they abide in a golden mansion, with a thousand pillars and a thousand doors; and the all-seeing Sun, rising from his abode, goes to the dwellings of Mitra and Varuṇa to tell of the deeds of men; the eye of Mitra and Varuṇa is the sun, and Varuṇa has a thousand eyes. Both gods have fair hands, and Varuṇa treads down wiles with shining foot. Yet no myths are told of him, and the deeds ascribed to him are all intended to show his power as a ruler. He is lord of all, both gods and men — not only an independent ruler, a term more often given to Indra, but a universal ruler, an epithet used also of Indra, though peculiarly Varuṇa's. Moreover, the terms Kṣatriya ("Ruler") and Asura ("Deity") are his, the first almost exclusively, and the second predominantly. As Asura he possesses, in company with Mitra, the *māyā*, or occult power, wherewith they send the dawns, make the sun to cross the sky, obscure it with cloud and rain, or cause the heavens to rain. The worlds are supported by Varuṇa and Mitra; Varuṇa made the golden swing (the sun) to shine in the heaven and placed fire in the waters; the wind is his breath. He establishes the morning and the evening; through him the moon moves and the stars shine at night; he regulates the months of the year. He is only rarely connected with the sea, for the *Ṛgveda* knows little of the ocean, but his occult power keeps the ever-flowing rivers from filling it up. Despite this, Varuṇa and Mitra are greatly concerned with the waters of the atmosphere and make the rain to fall; they have kine yielding refreshment and streams flowing with honey.

So great is Varuṇa that neither the flying birds nor the flowing rivers can reach the limit of his dominion, his might, and his wrath. The three heavens and the three earths alike are deposited in him; he knows the flight of the birds in the sky, the path of the ships, the track of the wind, and all secret things. The omniscience and omnipotence, no less than the omnipresence, of Varuṇa receive admirable expression in a hymn which, by

# PLATE II

## Idol Car

In the worship of many deities an important occasion is their ceremonial visit to other divinities, and for this purpose elaborate vehicles are requisite for their conveyance. This car, whose wheels are of stone, has been chosen to illustrate the intricacy of Indian carving in wood. After *Architecture of Dharwar and Mysore*, Photograph L.

accident, is preserved only as degraded into a spell in the *Atharvaveda* (iv. 16), and thus rendered by Muir:[3]

"The mighty Lord on high, our deeds, as if at hand, espies:
The gods know all men do, though men would fain their deeds disguise.
Whoever stands, whoever moves, or steals from place to place,
Or hides him in his secret cell, — the gods his movements trace.
Wherever two together plot, and deem they are alone,
King Varuṇa is there, a third, and all their schemes are known.
This earth is his, to him belong those vast and boundless skies;
Both seas within him rest, and yet in that small pool he lies.
Whoever far beyond the sky should think his way to wing,
He could not there elude the grasp of Varuṇa the king.
His spies descending from the skies glide all this world around,
Their thousand eyes all-scanning sweep to earth's remotest bound.
Whate'er exists in heaven and earth, whate'er beyond the skies,
Before the eyes of Varuṇa, the king, unfolded lies.
The ceaseless winkings all he counts of every mortal's eyes:
He wields this universal frame, as gamester throws his dice.
Those knotted nooses which thou fling'st, o god, the bad to snare, —
All liars let them overtake, but all the truthful spare."

With Mitra Varuṇa is a barrier against falsehood, and in one passage he, together with Indra, is said to bind with bonds not made of rope. Mitra and Varuṇa hate, drive away, and punish falsehood, and they also afflict with disease those who neglect their worship. On the other hand, Varuṇa is gracious to the repentant sinner; like a rope he unties the sin committed and pardons the faults of the forefathers not less than those of the children. He is gracious to those who thoughtlessly break his ordinances. No hymn addressed to him fails to include a prayer for forgiveness. He can take away or prolong life by his thousand remedies; he is a guardian of immortality, and in the next world the righteous may hope to see Yama and Varuṇa. He is a friend to his worshipper and gazes on him with his mental eye.

Mention is often made of the ordinances of Varuṇa, which even the immortal gods cannot obstruct. Both he and Mitra are called "Lords of Ṛta," or "Holy Order," and "Upholders of Ṛta," an epithet which they share with the Ādityas or with the gods in general. They are also termed "Guardians of Holy Order," a term used likewise of Agni and Soma, and "Followers of Holy Order," an epithet given predominantly to Agni. This "Order" must, therefore, be regarded as something higher even than Varuṇa, and it is clearly the Asha of the Avesta. Its first aspect is cosmic order: the dawns shine in accordance with Ṛta and rise from Ṛta's abode; the sun, with the twelve spokes of his wheel (the months), moves in accord with Ṛta; it is Ṛta that gives the white cooked milk to the red raw cow. The sacrifice is under the guardianship of Ṛta; Agni is the observer of it and is its first-born. Prayers take effect in accordance with Ṛta, and the pious sacrificer claims that, discarding witchcraft, he offers with Ṛta. In the sphere of man Ṛta is a moral order and, as truth, it stands in perpetual opposition to untruth. When Agni strives toward Ṛta, he is said to become Varuṇa himself; when Yama and Yamī contend on the question whether incest may be allowed to the first pair of mankind, it is to Ṛta that Yama appeals against his sister's persuasions. The same features mark Ṛta in the Avesta, and the antiquity of the concept may be very great.[4] Unlike the Greek Moira,[6] or Fate, we never find Ṛta coming into definite conflict with the will or wish of the gods, and the constant opposition of Anṛta ("Disorder") shows that the idea is rather one of norm or ideal than of controlling and overriding fate. This may be due to the transfer of Ṛta to the moral from the physical world, or to the fact that, even as applied to the physical world, full necessity of cause and effect was not accepted.

It is perfectly clear that Varuṇa corresponds in character and in the epithet Asura too closely with Ahura Mazda, the great deity of the Iranians, to be other than in the nearest relation to him, nor can there be much real doubt that the physical basis of the god is the broad sky. Mitra is, indeed, so faint a figure apart from him that it would be difficult to be certain that he is the sun, were it not for the undoubted solar nature of the Persian Mithra.[5] Yet if Mitra is the sun, the sky is naturally the greater deity, and this not only well accounts for the connexion of Varuṇa with the waters, which, from the *Atharvaveda* onward, becomes his chief characteristic, but also accords with the attributes of a universal monarch. Nor is there anything in the name of the god to render this view doubtful. It seems to be derived from the root *vṛ*, "to cover," and to denote the covering sky, and many scholars have maintained that the name of the Greek deity Ouranos[6] can be identified with it.

The antiquity of Mitra and Varuṇa has been carried back to about 1400 B.C., when their names occur on an inscription as gods of the Mitanni in northern Mesopotamia, but whether they were then Aryan or Iranian or Vedic gods is not clear.[7] It has been suggested, however, that the peculiar character of Varuṇa is due, like the character of Ahura Mazda, to borrowing, during the Indo-Iranian period, from a Semitic people, and that he and Mitra and the other Ādityas, seven in all corresponding to the Amesha Spentas of Iran,[8] were in origin the moon, the sun, and the five planets. Yet this view does not accord well with the physical side of Varuṇa in the *Ṛgveda*, in which his connexion with night is only slight; the Indians' knowledge of the five planets is very doubtful; and the Amesha Spentas seem purely abstract and Avestan deities. Nor is it necessary to see in Varuṇa's spies the stars, or in his bonds the fetters of night; both are the necessary paraphernalia of an Indian king, and, when thought of concretely, his fetter seems to be disease, in special perhaps dropsy.

Indra occurs in the same record of the Mitannian gods, and this shows that even then he must have been a great god. In the *Ṛgveda* there can be no comparison between Varuṇa and Indra in moral grandeur, but the latter is far more often mentioned and is clearly by all odds the more popular god. Indeed, in one hymn (iv. 42) the claims of the two divinities seem to be placed before us in their own mouths, Varuṇa as the creator and sustainer of the world, and Indra as the irresistible deity of battle; and the poet seems inclined to recognize the pre-eminence of Indra. Yet there is no real evidence, save perhaps a certain diminution of mention in the tenth book of the *Ṛgveda*, that the worship of Varuṇa was on the decline in this period, and the real source of the loss of his greatness is to be traced to the growth of the conception of the creator god, Prajāpati or Viśvakarman, at the end of the period of the *Ṛgveda* and in the following epoch. Driven thus from his high functions, Varuṇa became connected with the night and the waters.

Mitra has but one hymn addressed to him alone (iii. 59), and in it he is said to bring men together when he utters speech and to gaze on the tillers with unwinking eye. The characteristics of assembling men and regulating the course of the sun confirm the view that, as suggested by the Persian evidence, he is a solar god. The name is used repeatedly to denote "friend," but it is not proved that the god is derived from that application of the term.

Mitra's indefinite character and lack of personality may be due in part to the co-existence of his rival Sūrya as the sun-god *par excellence*. Sūrya is constantly the actual solar element and is conceived in many forms, as a bird, a flying eagle, a mottled bull, the gem of the sky, the variegated stone set in the heaven. He is also the weapon of Mitra and Varuṇa, or the felloe of their car, or the car itself. He shines forth in the lap of the dawns and is the son of Aditi, and his father is Dyaus, even though many other gods are said to produce the sun. He triumphs over the darkness and the witches, drives away sickness and evil dreams, and prolongs life. His evil power as burning heat is not known to the *Ṛgveda*, unless it be hinted at in the myth that Indra overcame him and stole his wheel, which may point to the obscuration of the sun by the storm, here possibly regarded as tempering its excessive heat, though it is equally susceptible of the opposite interpretation. In another aspect Sūrya is Savitṛ, the "Impeller" or "Instigator," the golden-handed, the golden-tongued, with chariot of gold. He it is who

# PLATE III

## Sūrya

As the text-books enjoin, the Sun-God is "clad in the dress of the Northerners [i.e. Persians], so as to be covered from the feet upward to the bosom. He holds two lotuses growing out of his hands, wears a diadem and a necklace hanging down, has his face adorned with ear-rings, and a girdle round his waist." His figure thus suggests Iranian influence, especially as the sacred girdle was worn by the Magas, who traced their descent to the Magians of Persia. While the sun-cult was known in India in the Vedic period, it received new life from Iran. From a sculpture at Moḍherā, Gujarāt. After Burgess and Cousens, *The Architectural Antiquities of Northern Gujarat*, Plate LVI, No. 5. See also pp. 138–39, 183–84.

wins immortality for the gods, length of life for man, and raises the Ṛbhus (the divine artificers) to immortality. In the usual exaggeration of the poet it is declared that Indra, Mitra, Varuṇa, Aryaman, and Rudra cannot resist the will and independent rule of Sūrya. He is closely connected with Pūṣan and Bhaga, and one verse (III. lxii. 10),

> "May we attain that excellent glory of Savitṛ the god:
> So may he stimulate our prayers," [9]

has become the most famous in Vedic literature and is used to preface all Vedic study. Once he is called Prajāpati, "Lord of Offspring," or of the world; yet it seems undoubted that he is not a mere abstract god in origin, but the active power of the sun elevated into a separate deity.

Pūṣan, the "Nourisher," is also, it would seem, allied in origin to Savitṛ. His personality is indistinct: he wears braided hair (like Rudra) and a beard; and in addition to a spear he carries an awl or a goad. His car is not drawn by horses, as one would expect, but by goats; and his food is gruel. His connexion with pastoral life is shown by his epithets. He loses no cattle, but directs them; he saves and smooths the clothing of sheep; and he is also the deliverer, the guardian of the way, who removes the wolf and the robber from the path. Accordingly it is he who conducts the dead to the fathers, just as Agni and Savitṛ take them to where the righteous have gone; and he fares along the path of heaven and earth between the two abodes. Like Sūrya and Agni he woos his mother and his sister, and receives from the gods the sun-maiden in marriage, whence in the wedding-rite he is asked to take the hand of the bride and lead her away and bless her. He is often invoked with Soma and Indra, but most frequently with Bhaga and Viṣṇu. He is called glowing and once bears the name Agohya ("Not to be Concealed"), which is elsewhere Savitṛ's epithet. He is also the "Prosperer" *par excellence* and may well represent the sun in its aspect as beneficent to the flocks and herds of men, gracious to them in marriage, and the leader of their souls in death to the world of the sun and heaven. The Avestan Mithra has the characteristics of increasing cattle and bringing them back home.

Yet another form of the sun is Vivasvant, the father of Yama and of Manu, and thus in a sense the forefather of the human race. He is identical with the Avestan Vīvanghvant, the father of Yima, who first prepared the haoma,[10] and in the *Ṛgveda* also he is connected with the sacrifice. His messenger is Agni or Mātariśvan; in his abode the gods rejoice; and Soma, Indra, and the Aśvins are his close companions; yet his nature must have had a dread trait, for a worshipper prays that the arrow of Vivasvant may not smite him before old age. He shines out at the beginning of the dawn as Agni, nor is it improbable that he is no more than the rising sun. His character as sacrificer, which is not as prominent in the *Ṛgveda* as in the Avesta, can easily have been a special development, while, if he was no more in origin than the first of sacrificers like Manu in the *Ṛgveda*, his celestial character becomes difficult to explain.

Much more faint are the figures of Bhaga ("Bountiful"), Aṁśa ("Apportioner"), Aryaman ("Comrade"), and Dakṣa ("Skilful"), who with Mitra and Varuṇa are hailed in one hymn (II. xxvii. 1) as the Ādityas. Aryaman is a faint double of Mitra, but is the wooer of maidens. Aṁśa is practically a mere name, but is called bountiful. Bhaga is the giver of wealth whom men desire to share, and Dawn is his sister. In the Avesta his name is Bagha, an epithet of Ahura Mazda, and it corresponds to the Old Church Slavonic word *bogŭ*, "god." Dakṣa is born of Aditi, although he is also her father. His existence is probably due to the fact that the Ādityas are called "having intelligence" for their father, thus giving rise to the conception that Dakṣa is a person.

The Ādityas, however, are a group of uncertain number and sense. Once only in the *Ṛgveda* are they said to be seven, and once eight, the eighth being Mārtāṇḍa, the setting sun, whom

Aditi throws away and then brings back to the gods. Mitra, Varuṇa, and Indra are called Ādityas, and the same name is given to Savitṛ and to Sūrya. Sometimes the Ādityas form a group in conjunction with other gods like the Maruts, Rudras, Vasus, and Ṛbhus, or again they seem occasionally to include all the gods. From Varuṇa they appear to have derived the moral duties of punishing sin and rewarding the good; they spread fetters for their enemies, but protect their worshippers as birds spread their wings over their young. They are bright, golden, many-eyed, unwinking, and sleepless, kings with inviolable ordinances, pure, and overseers of Holy Order.

In comparison with his future greatness Viṣṇu appears of slight importance in the *Ṛgveda*, in which only five hymns and part of a sixth are given to him. His great feat is his triple stride, the third of which places him beyond the ken of man or the flight of birds. Yet it is also described as an eye fixed in heaven, where there is a well of honey, where Indra dwells, and where are the many cows desired of the worshipper. In his striding Viṣṇu moves swiftly but also according to law; he is an ordainer who, like Savitṛ, metes out the earthly spaces; or, again, he sets in motion, like a revolving wheel, his ninety steeds with their four names, who can be nothing else than the year. These traits reveal him beyond doubt as a sun-god, whether his name be explained as "the Active," from the root *viṣ*, or as "One Who Crosses the Backs of the Universe."[11] His three strides were interpreted by Aurṇavābha, one of the earliest expounders of Vedic mythology, as the rising, culminating, and setting of the sun, but Śākapūṇi, another exegete, already gave the far more probable version of earth, atmosphere, and sky.

The steps taken by Viṣṇu are for man in distress, or to bestow on him the earth as a dwelling-place, or to make room for existence, and in this conception lies, no doubt, the germ of the dwarf incarnation of Viṣṇu. His closeness to man is also attested by his connexion with Indra and the Maruts. Urged by Indra, Viṣṇu, having drunk of the soma, carried off one hundred buffaloes and a brew of milk belonging to the boar (i.e. Vṛtra), while Indra, shooting across the cloud-mountain, slew the fierce boar. In the period of the *Brāhmaṇas* Viṣṇu is conceived as assuming the form of a boar, and the way for such transformations is paved by the view of the *Ṛgveda* (VII. c. 6) that in battle Viṣṇu assumes a different shape and has to be asked to reveal his own form to the worshipper. Though, therefore, not yet in Vedic circles one of the great gods, his relation to man, his close connexion with the three worlds, and his power of change of form are traits which explain that in other circles he may have been a much greater deity.

Among the gods listed in the Mitanni inscription we find the Nāsatyas, thus confirming the early existence of the divine pair who in the Avesta have degenerated into a demon, Nāonghaithya. Their normal name in the *Ṛgveda* is the Aśvins ("Horsemen"), though they are also called "the Wonder-Workers" (Dasra), and later mythology has invented Dasra and Nāsatya as the names of the pair. They are beautiful, strong, and red and their path is red or golden. They have a skin filled with honey and touch the sacrifice and the worshipper with their honey-whip. Their chariot alone is described as honey-hued or honey-bearing, and it also has the peculiarity of possessing three wheels, three felloes, and all the other parts triple. The time of the Aśvins' appearance is at dawn; they follow dawn in their car; at the yoking of their car the dawn is born; but yet, despite this, they are invoked to come to the offering not only at the morning but also at noon and at sunset. Their parentage is not definitely decided: they are children of Sky or of Ocean, or of Vivasvant and Saraṇyū, or of Pūṣan; and though normally inseparable like the eyes or the hands, nevertheless they are once or twice said to be variously born or born here and there. They are wedded to a deity described as Sūryā, the sun-maiden, or the daughter of the Sun, and it is for her perhaps that their car has three seats and three wheels. In the marriage-rite they are accordingly invoked to conduct the bride home on their chariot, and they are also asked to make the young wife fertile, while among their feats is to give a child to the wife of a eunuch, to cause the barren cow to yield milk, and to grant a husband to the old maid. Moreover they are physicians who heal diseases, restore sight to the blind, and ward off death from the sick. The decrepit Cyavana they released from his worn-out body, prolonged his life, made him young again and the husband of maidens. By means of their winged ship they saved Bhujyu, son of Tugra, from the log to which he was clinging in the midst of the ocean. They rescued and refreshed Atri, whom demons had bound in a burning pit. At the prayer of the she-wolf they restored his sight to Ṛjrāśva, whom his father had blinded for slaying a hundred and one sheep and giving them to the wolf. They gave a leg of iron to Viśpalā when her leg was cut off in battle. They placed a horse's head on Dadhyañc, who told them in reward where the mead of Tvaṣṭṛ was; and they rescued Rebha from death, befriended Ghoṣā, who was growing old childless in her father's house, gave Viṣṇāpu back to Viśvaka, and saved the quail from the wolf's jaws. Many other names of *protégés* are mentioned, and the deeds recited may have been historical in some cases, while mythical traits doubtless exist in others.

The Indian interpreters of the early period were at a loss to decide the nature of the Aśvins, whom they regarded as heaven and earth, sun and moon, day and night, or even as two kings who were performers of holy acts. It is clear that in essence they are one with the Dioskouroi[12] and with the two sons of the Lettic god who came riding on steeds to woo for themselves the daughter of the Sun or the Moon and who, like the Dioskouroi, are rescuers from the ocean. The older identification with sun and moon has been supported, and they have been regarded merely as succouring giants who have no mythical basis, but the more probable view is either that they represent the twilight (half dark, half light), or the morning and the evening star. The latter interpretation offers the grave difficulty of the contrast between the unity of the Aśvins and the diversity of the two stars, which is only slenderly diminished by the curious traces of separate birth and worship in the *Ṛgveda.*

There is but one goddess of the celestial world, the maiden Uṣas, the most poetical figure in the whole pantheon. Decking herself in gay attire like a dancer, she displays her bosom, and like a maiden adorned by her mother she reveals her form. Clothed in light, she appears in the east and shows her charms; immortal and unaging, she awakes before the world. When she shines forth, the birds fly up, and men bestir themselves; she removes the black mantle of night and banishes evil dreams and the hated darkness. She follows ever the path of Order, though once she is asked not to delay lest the sun scorch her as a thief or an enemy. She is borne on a car with ruddy steeds or kine, and the distance which the dawns traverse in a day is thirty *yojanas* (leagues). She is the wife or the mistress of the Sun who follows her, but sometimes is also his mother; she is the sister of Bhaga, the kinswoman of Varuṇa, and the mightier sister of Night. She is likewise closely associated with Agni, as the fire of the sacrifice which is lit at dawn, and with the Aśvins, whom she is besought to arouse. Her name denotes "the Shining" and is in origin one with Aurora and Eos.[13]

Of the gods of the atmosphere by far the greatest is Indra, whose name occurs among the list of Mitannian gods. He is more anthropomorphic than any other Vedic deity. His head, his arms, and his hands are mentioned, as is his great belly in which he puts the soma; he moves his jaws after drinking soma, and his lips are beautiful. His beard waves in the air, he has tawny hair and beard. His long, strong, well-shaped arms wield the thunderbolt, which was fashioned for him by Tvaṣṭṛ or Uśanas. This is his chief weapon, and it is described as a stone, as hundred-jointed and thousand-pointed, hundred-angled, sharp, and metallic; rarely it is said to be of gold. Occasionally he bears a bow and arrows, hundred-pointed and winged with a thousand feathers, and sometimes he carries a goad. He travels in a golden chariot drawn by two or more horses, as many as eleven hundred being mentioned. He is a gigantic eater and drinker; at his birth he drank soma and for the slaying of Vṛtra he drank three lakes or even thirty. He eats the flesh of twenty or a hundred buffaloes, and when he was born the worlds quaked with fear. His mother is described as a cow and he as a bull; she is also called Niṣṭigrī, and he willed to be born unnaturally through her side. His father is Dyaus or Tvaṣṭṛ; from the latter he stole the soma and even slew him and made his mother a widow; more than this he fought against the gods, perhaps for the soma. His wife Indrāṇī is mentioned, and he is often called Śacīpati, or "Lord of Strength," whence later mythology coined a wife Śacī for him. He is closely connected with the Maruts and with Agni, and is actually identified with Sūrya.

The might and power of Indra are described everywhere in terms of hyperbole. He is the greatest of the gods, greater even than Varuṇa, lord of all that moves and of men, who won in battle wide space for the gods. Occasionally he bears Varuṇa's title of universal ruler, but more often he has his own of independent ruler. The epithet "of a hundred powers" is almost his alone, and his also is that of "very lord." The deed which wins him his high place is the feat, ever renewed, of slaying the dragon which encompasses the waters. He smites him on the head or on the back, he pierces his vitals. After slaying Vṛtra he lets loose the streams; he shatters the mountains, breaks open the well, and sets the waters free; he kills the dragon lying on the waters and releases the waters. He cleaves the mountain to liberate the cows; he loosens the rock and makes the kine easy to obtain; he frees the cows which were fast within the stone; he slays Vṛtra, breaks the castles, makes a channel for the rivers, pierces the mountain, and makes it over to his friends the cows. Again, however, he wins the light by his deed; he gains the sun as well as the waters by freeing the demons;

when he slew the chief of the dragons and released the waters from the mountain, he generated the sun, the sky, and the dawn; he finds the light in the darkness and makes the sun to shine. He also wins the dawns; with the sun and the dawn he discovers or delivers or wins the cows; the dawns again go forth to meet Indra when he becomes the lord of the kine. Moreover he gains the soma and he establishes the quaking mountains, a feat which the *Brāhmaṇas* explain as denoting that he cut off their wings. He supports the earth and props up the sky, and is the generator of heaven and earth.

Indra, however, does not war with demons only, for he attacked Uṣas, shattered her wain with his bolt, and rent her slow steeds, whereupon she fled in terror from him, this being, perhaps, a myth of the dawn obscured by a thunder-storm or of the sunrise hastening the departure of the lingering dawn. Indra also came into conflict with the sun when he was running a race with the swift steed Etaśa, and in some unexplained way Indra caused the car of the sun to lose a wheel. He also seems to have murdered his father Tvaṣṭṛ, and, though the Maruts aid him in his struggle with Vṛtra, in a series of hymns we find a distinct trace that he quarrelled with them, used threatening language to them, and was appeased only with difficulty.

Other foes of Indra's were the Paṇis, who kept cows hidden in a cave beyond the Rasā, a mythical stream. Saramā, Indra's messenger, tracks the kine and demands them in Indra's name, only to be mocked by the Paṇis, but Indra shatters the ridge of Vala and overcomes his antagonists. Elsewhere the cows are said to be confined by the power of Vala without reference to the Paṇis and are won by Indra, often with the help of the Aṅgirases. Vala ("Encircler") is clearly the name of the stronghold in which the cows are confined.

As becomes so great a warrior, Indra is a worthy helper to men on earth. He is the chief aid of the Aryans in their struggles against the Dāsas or Dasyus, and subjects the black

# PLATE IV

## Indra

The deity appears crowned as king of the gods and enthroned on his *vāhana* ("vehicle"), the elephant Airāvata. The middle one of his left hands holds the thunderbolt. He is further characterized by the multitude of marks on his body, which originally represented the *yoni* (possibly because of the fertility which the rain brings to earth), though later they were changed into eyes. The heavy beard shows the Persian influence in the painting. From an oil-painting of the Indo-Mughal school in the collection of the Editor. See pp. 32–35.

race to the Aryan; he leads Turvaśa and Yadu over the rivers, apparently as patron of an Aryan migration. Moreover he assists his favourites against every foe; and his friend Sudās is aided in his battle with the ten kings, his foes being drowned in the Paruṣṇī. To his worshippers he is a wall of defence, a father, mother, or brother. He bestows wealth on the pious man, and, as with a hook a man showers fruit from a tree, so he can shower wealth on the righteous. He is the lord of riches and at the same time is "the Bountiful One," whence in later literature the epithet Maghavan becomes one of his names. He richly rewarded a maiden who, having found soma beside a river, pressed it with her teeth and dedicated it to him. Yet he has few moral traits in his character and is represented as boasting of his drinking feats. Indeed it is most significant that we have proof, even in the Vedic period, of men doubting his existence.

It is almost certain that in Indra we must see a storm-god, and that his exploit of defeating Vṛtra is a picture of the bursting forth of the rain from the clouds at the oncoming of the rainy season, when all the earth is parched, and when man and nature alike are eager for the breaking of the drought. The tremendous storms which mark the first fall of the rain are generally recognized as a most fitting source for the conception of the god, while the mountains cleft and the cows won are the clouds viewed from different standpoints. But Indra appears also as winning the sun, a trait representing the clearing away of the clouds from the sun after the thunder-storm, with which has been confused or united the idea of the recovery of the sun at dawn from the darkness of night. That some of the terminology reflects an earlier view that Vṛtra is the winter [14] which freezes the stream, and that Indra is the sun, is not proved, nor need we hold that the poets of the *Ṛgveda* really meant only that the god freed the rivers from the mountains and did not realize that the mountains were clouds, as even the commentators on the *Ṛgveda* knew.

In the *Ṛgveda* we find a close parallel of Indra, though in a faded form, in Trita Āptya. He slays the three-headed son of Tvaṣṭṛ as does Indra; Indra impels him and he Indra, who is twice said to act for him. He is associated with the Maruts, but especially with soma, which he prepares; and this last feature associates him with Thrita in the Avesta, who was the "third man," as his name denotes, to prepare soma, the second being Āthwya. His slaying of the demon identifies him with the Thraētaona of the Avesta, who kills the three-headed, six-mouthed serpent, and he has a brother Dvita, "Second," while Thraētaona has two, who seek to slay him as in the *Brāhmaṇas* his brothers seek to murder Trita.[15] The parallelism points strongly to his identification with the lightning which is born among the waters, as his second name, Āptya ("Watery"), indicates; but he has been held to be a water-god, a storm-god, a deified healer, and the moon. In all likelihood much of his glory has been taken from him by the growth of Indra's greatness.

The lightning seems also to lie at the base of the deity Apāṁ Napāt, who likewise appears in the Avesta,[16] where he is a spirit of the waters, dwelling in their depths and said to have seized the brightness in the abysses of the ocean. He is also "Son of the Waters," born and nourished in them, but he shines and is golden, and is identified with Agni, who is often described as abiding in the waters of the air. The identification with a water-spirit pure and simple is, therefore, improbable, nor has he any clear lunar characteristics. Yet another form of the lightning is Mārariśvan ("He that Grows in his Mother"), the thunder-cloud. He is the messenger of Vivasvant and he brings Agni down to men, as the Prometheus of India; by friction he produces Agni for the homes of men. The lightning may likewise be represented by the "One-Footed Goat" (Aja Ekapād), which is occasionally mentioned among aerial deities, the goat symbolizing the swift movement of the flash and the single foot the one place of striking the earth, although this obscure god may also be a solar phenomenon. With Apāṁ Napāt and Aja Ekapād occurs the "Serpent of the Deep" (Ahi Budhnya), who is born in the waters and sits in the bottom of the streams in the spaces, and who is besought not to give his worshippers over to injury. Such an invocation suggests that there is something uncanny about the nature of the god, and his name allies him to Vṛtra, whose beneficent aspect he may represent, the dragon in this case being conceived as friendly to man.

The other great aspect of the air, the wind, is represented by Vāta or Vāyu, the former being more markedly elemental, the latter more divine. So Vāyu is often linked with Indra, being, like him, a great drinker of soma, but Vāta is associated only with Parjanya, who is, like himself, a god of little but nature. Vāyu, the son-in-law of Tvaṣṭṛ, is swift of thought and thousand-eyed; he has a team of ninety-nine or even a thousand horses to draw his car; he drinks the clear soma and is connected with the nectar-yielding cow. Vāta rushes on whirling up the dust; he never rests; the place of his birth is unknown; man hears his roaring, but cannot see his form. He is the breath of the gods; like Rudra, he wafts healing and he can produce the light. The identification with the Eddic Wodan or Odhin is still unsubstantiated.

Parjanya personifies the cloud, flying round with a watery car and drawing the waterskin downward. He is often viewed as a bull or even as a cow, the clouds being feminine. He quickens the earth with seed, and the winds blow forth and the lightnings fall; he is a thunderer and a giver of increase to plants, to grass, to cows, mares, and women. He is even called the divine father whose wife is the earth, and he is said to rule over all the world; he produces a calf himself, perhaps the lightning or the soma. He is sometimes associated with the Maruts and is clearly akin to Indra, of whom he later becomes a form. It is doubtful if the Lithuanian thunder-god Perkúnas can be identified with him.

The waters are also hailed as goddesses on their own account and they are conceived as mothers, young wives, and granters of boons. They nourish Agni and they bear away defilement and purify; they bestow remedies and grant long life. They are often associated with honey, and it may be that they were sometimes regarded as having the soma within them.

Though Rudra, the prototype of Śiva, is celebrated in only three hymns of the *Ṛgveda*, he already bears remarkable traits. He wears braided hair, like Pūṣan; his lips are beautiful, and his colour is brown. His car dazzles, and he wears a wonderful necklace. He holds the thunderbolt and bears bow and arrows; and his lightning-shaft shot from the sky traverses the earth. He generated the Maruts from Pṛśni, and himself bears the name Tryambaka (VII. lix. 12), denoting his descent from three mothers, presumably a reference to the triple division of the universe. He is fierce and strong, a ruler of the world, the great Asura of heaven, bountiful, easily invoked and auspicious, but this latter epithet, Śiva,[17] is not yet attached to him as his own.

None the less, Rudra is a very terrible deity and one whose anger is to be deprecated, whence he is implored not to slay or injure in his wrath the worshippers, their parents, men, children, cattle, or horses. His ill will is deprecated, and his favour is sought for the walking food, and he is even called man-slaying. On the other hand, he has healing powers and a thousand remedies; he is asked to remove sickness and disease; and he has a special remedy called *jalāṣa*, which may be the rain. This side of his nature is as essential as the other and lends plausibility to the view that he is the lightning, regarded mainly as a destroying and terrible agency, but at the same time as the power by which there is healing calm after storm and as propitious in that the lightning spares as well as strikes. Yet his nature has also been held to be a compound of a god of fire and a god of wind, his name denoting "the Howler" (from *rud*, "to cry"), as the chief of the spirits of the dead who storm along in the wind, and as a god of forest and mountain whence diseases speed to men.

Rudra's sons are the Maruts, the children of Pṛśni, the storm-cloud, the heroes or males of heaven, born from the laughter of lightning. All are equal in age, in abode, in mind, and their number is thrice seven or thrice sixty. They are associated with the goddess Indrāṇī, though their lovely wife is Rodasī, who goes on their car. They are brilliant as fire; they have spears on their shoulders, anklets on their feet, golden ornaments on their breasts, fiery lightnings in their hands, and golden helmets on their heads. Spotted steeds draw their chariots. They are fierce and terrible, and yet playful like children or calves. They are black-backed swans, four-tusked boars, and resemble lions. As they advance they make the mountains to tremble, uproot trees, and like wild elephants hew the forest; they whirl up dust, and all creatures tremble before them. Their great exploit is the making of rain, which they produce amid the lightning; and a river on earth is styled Marudvṛdhā ("Rejoicing in the Maruts"). They are close associates of Indra, whose might they increased when they sang a hymn; singing they made the sun to shine and clove the mountain. Not only do they help Indra to slay Vṛtra, but now and then the exploit seems attributed to them alone; yet they failed him once in the moment of struggle, whence, it seems, a quarrel arose. When not associated with Indra they exhibit, in less degree, the malevolent side of their father Rudra. Thus they are implored to avert the arrow and stone which they hurl; their wrath, which is like that of the serpent, is deprecated; and evil is said to come from them; although, again like Rudra, they have healing remedies which they bring from the rivers Sindhu, Asiknī, the sea, and the mountains.

There can be little doubt that the Maruts are the storm-gods, the winds in this qualified use. The only other view of importance is that they are the souls of the dead who go in the storm-wind,[18] but of this at least the *Ṛgveda* has no hint; nor is the etymology from *mṛ*, "to die," enough to serve as a base for the explanation, since their appellation may equally well come from a root *mṛ*, "to shine," or "to crush," either of which meanings would well enough accord with their figure. In later days they sank from their estate, as we shall see, and became the celestial counterparts of the Vaiśyas, the common folk of earth as distinguished from the two higher castes of Brāhmans (priests) and Kṣatriyas (warriors). Finally they degenerated into mere wind-godlings, their very name becoming a synonym for "wind"; and at the present day memory of them has all but vanished.

# CHAPTER II

# THE ṚGVEDA

(*Continued*)

## GODS OF EARTH, DEMONS, AND DEAD

AMONG the gods connected with earth the first place belongs to Agni, who, after Indra, receives the greatest number of hymns in the *Ṛgveda*, more than two hundred being in his honour. Unlike Indra, however, anthropomorphism has scarcely affected Agni's personality, which is ever full of the element from which it is composed. Thus he is described as butter-haired or as flame-haired, tawny-bearded, and butter-backed; in one account he is headless and footless, but in another he has three heads and seven rays; he faces in all directions; he has three tongues and a thousand eyes. He is often likened to animals, as to a bull for his strength or to a calf as being born, or to a steed yoked to the pole of the sacrifice; or again he is winged, an eagle or an aquatic bird in the waters; and once he is even called a winged serpent. His food is ghee or oil or wood, but like the other gods he drinks the soma. Brilliant in appearance, his track is black; driven by the wind, he shaves the earth as a barber a beard. He roars terribly, and the birds fly before his devouring sparks; he rises aloft to the sky and licks even the heaven. He is himself likened to a chariot, but he is borne in one and in it he carries the gods to the sacrifice. He is the child of sky and earth or of Tvaṣṭṛ and the waters, but Viṣṇu and Indra begat him, or Indra generated him between two stones. On earth he is produced in the two fire-sticks who are figured as his father (the upper) and his mother (the lower), or as two mothers, or as a mother who can-

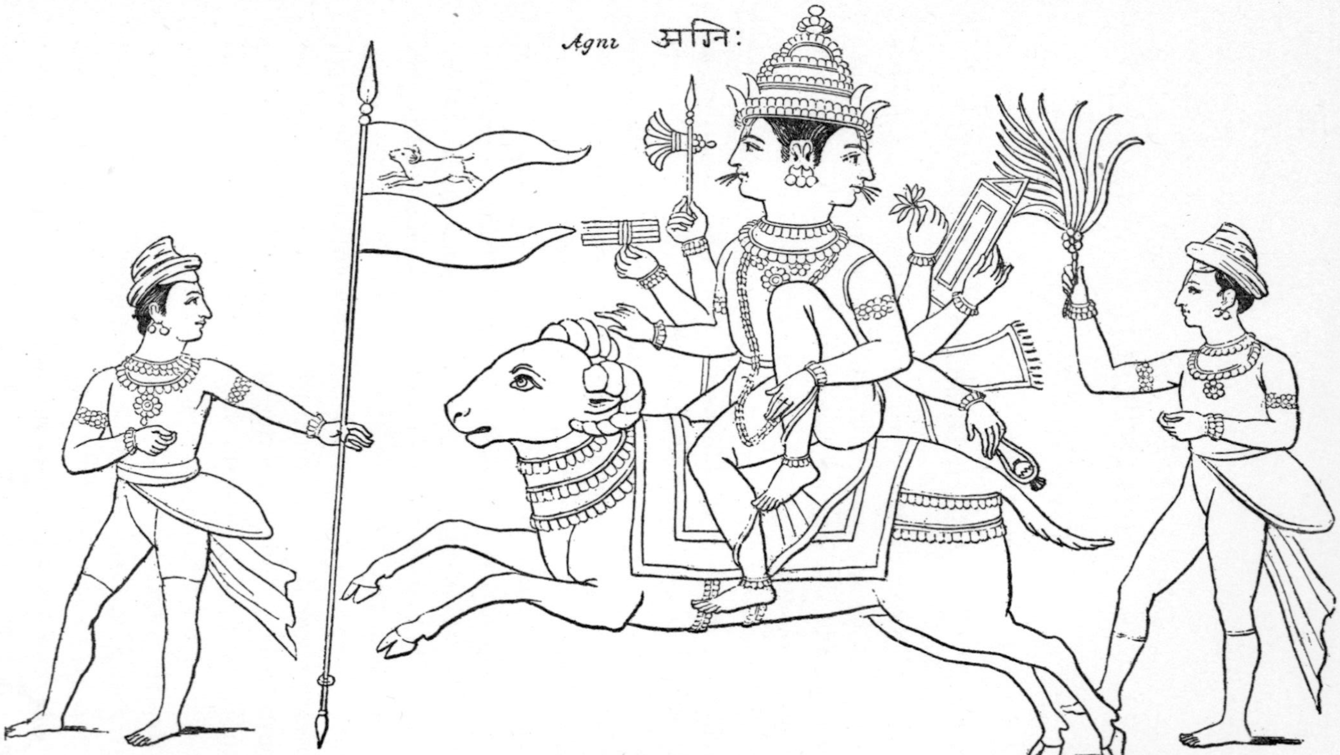


Fig. 1. Agni

The fire-god, with flames issuing from his mouths, rides his *vāhana* ("vehicle"), which is a ram. The divinity has three heads and three legs, symbolizing his triple birth and the three fires of Indian ritual, while his seven arms represent his seven rays of light. After Moor, *Hindu Pantheon*, Plate LXXX, No. 1.

not suckle. The ten maidens who generate him are the ten fingers, and as "Son of Strength" his name bears witness to the force needed to create the flame. As thus produced for the sacrifice every morning he has the title of youngest, although as the first sacrificer he is also the oldest. Or, again, he is born in the trees or the plants or on the navel of earth, the place of the sacrifice.

But Agni is born also in the waters of the atmosphere; he is Apāṁ Napāt ("Child of the Waters"), the bull which grows in the lap of the waters. Possibly, however, in some cases at least, the waters in which he is found are those of earth, for he is mentioned as being in the waters and the plants. He is born likewise from heaven in the form of lightning; Mātariśvan brought him down, doubtless a reminiscence of conflagrations caused by the lightning. He is also identified sometimes with the sun, though the solar luminary is more often conceived as a separate deity. Thus he has three births — in the sky, in the waters, and on earth, though the order is also given as sky, earth, and waters. This is the earliest form of triad in Indian religion, and probably from it arose the other form of sun, wind, and fire, for which (though not in the *Ṛgveda*) sun, Indra, and fire is a variant. The three fires in the ritual correspond with the three divine forms. On the other hand, Agni has two births when the air and the sky are taken as one; he descends in rain and is born from the plants, and rises again to the sky, whence we have the mystic commands that Agni should sacrifice to himself or bring himself to the sacrifice. Or, again, he can be said to have many births from the many fires kindled on earth. Yet the number three reappears in the conception of the brothers of Agni. Indra is said to be his twin, and from him Agni borrows the exploit of defeating the Paṇis. Mystically Agni is Varuṇa in the evening, Mitra in the morning, Savitṛ as he traverses the air, and Indra as he illumines the sky in the midst.

Agni is closely connected with the home, of which he is the

sacred fire. He alone bears the title of Gṛhapati, or "Lord of the House"; and he is the guest in each abode as kinsman, friend, or father, or even as son. Moreover he is the ancestral god, the god of Bharata, of Divodāsa, of Trasadasyu, and of other heroes. He brings the gods to the sacrifice or takes the sacrifice to them; and thus he is a messenger, ever busy travelling between the worlds. Beyond all else he is the priest of the sacrifice, and one legend tells that he wearied of the task, but consented to continue in it on receiving the due payment for which he asked. In another aspect he eats the dead, for he burns the body on the funeral pile, and in this character he is carefully distinguished from his form as bearer of oblations. He is, further, not merely a priest, but a seer omniscient, Jātavedas ("Who Knows All Generations"). He inspires men and delivers and protects them. Riches and rain are his gifts, as are offspring and prosperity; he forgives sin, averts the wrath of Varuṇa, and makes men guiltless before Aditi.

To the gods also Agni is a benefactor; he delivered them from a curse, won them great space in battle, and is even called "the Slayer of Vṛtra." His main feat, however, is the burning of the Rakṣases who infest the sacrifice, a sign of the early use of fire to destroy demons. By magic the lighting of Agni may even bring about the rising of the sun in the sky.

As Vaiśvānara Agni is the "Fire of All Men," and in him has been seen a tribal fire [1] as opposed to the fire of each householder, though the name is more normally thought to mean "Fire in All its Aspects." As Tanūnapāt ("Son of Self") Agni's spontaneous birth from wood and cloud seems to be referred to; as Narāśaṁsa ("Praise of Men") he may be either the personification of the praise of man, or possibly the flame of the southern of the three fires, which is particularly connected with the fathers. Though Agni's name, which may mean "agile," is not Avestan, the fire-cult is clearly Iranian, and the Atharvan priests of the *Ṛgveda*, who are brought into close relation with the fire, have their parallel in the Āthravans, or fire-priests, of Iran. There is also an obvious parallel to the fire of the Indian householder in the domestic fire in the Roman household and in Greece.[2]

Distinct from Agni in personality is the god Bṛhaspati, who is described as seven-mouthed and seven-rayed, beautiful-tongued, sharp-horned, blue-backed, and hundred-winged. He has a bow the string of which is "Holy Order" (Ṛta), wields a golden hatchet, bears an iron axe, and rides in a car with ruddy steeds. Born from great light in the highest heaven, with a roar he drives away darkness. He is the father of the gods, but is created by Tvaṣṭṛ. He is a priest above others, the domestic priest, or *purohita*, of the gods, and their Brahman priest; he is "the Lord of Prayer" under the title Brahmaṇaspati. He is closely connected with Agni, with whom he appears at times to be identified, has three abodes like him, and seems twice to be called Narāśaṁsa. Yet he has also appropriated the deeds of Indra, for he opens the cow-stall and lets the waters loose; with his singing host he tore Vala asunder and drove out the lowing cows; when he rent the defences of Vala, he revealed the treasures of the kine; being in the cloud, he shouts after the many cows. He also seeks light in the darkness and finds dawn, light, and Agni, and dispels the darkness. Hence he is giver of victory in general, a bearer of the bolt, is invoked with the Maruts, and bears Indra's special epithet of "bountiful." Like the other gods he protects his worshippers, prolongs life, and removes disease. As "Lord of Prayer" he can scarcely be anything more than a development of one side of Agni's character, but it is clear that the process must have been complete before the time of the *Ṛgveda*, since there is no trace of a growth of this deity in that Saṁhitā. The alternative is to lay stress on the Indra side of his nature and to regard him as a priestly abstraction of Indra, or to find in him an abstract deity, the embodiment of priestly action who has assumed concrete features from the gods Agni and Indra, but this hypothesis is unlikely.

Soma, the Avestan Haoma ("the Pressed Juice"), is the deity of the whole of the ninth book of the *Ṛgveda* and of six hymns elsewhere. The plant, which has not been identified for certain with any modern species, yielded, when its shoots were pressed, a juice which after careful straining was offered, pure or with admixture of milk, etc., to the gods and drunk by the priests. The colour was brown or ruddy, and frequent mention is made of the stones by which it was pounded, though it seems also to have been produced by mortar and pestle, as among the Parsis. As passing through the filter or strainer, soma is called pavamāna ("flowing clear"). Besides milk, sour milk and barley water were commonly added, and hence Soma is lord of the waters, who makes the rain to stream from heaven. The waters are his sisters, and he is the embryo or child of the waters. The sound of the juice as it flows is likened to thunder, its swiftness to that of a steed.

The exhilarating power of the soma doubtless explains his divinity. It is a plant which confers powers beyond the natural, and thus soma is the draught of immortality (*amṛta*), the ambrosia. The gods love it; it gives them immortality no less than men, and one hymn depicts the ecstasy of feeling produced in Indra by the drink, which makes him feel able to dispose of the earth at his pleasure. Soma is also rich in healing and lord of the plants. When quaffed, he stimulates speech and is the lord of speech. He is a maker of seers, a protector of prayer, and his wisdom is extolled. He gazes with wisdom on men and so has a thousand eyes. The fathers, no less than men and gods, love him, and through him they found the light and the cows. The great deeds of the gods owe their success to their drinking the soma, with three lakes of which Indra fills himself for the slaying of Vṛtra. When drunk by Indra, Soma made the sun to rise in the sky, and hence Soma is declared to perform the feat; he found the light and made the sun to shine. So, too, he supports the two worlds and is lord of the quarters. Like Indra he is a terrible warrior, ever victorious, winning for his worshippers chariots, horses, gold, heaven, water, and a thousand boons. He bears terrible, sharp weapons, including a thousand-pointed shaft. Again like Indra he is described as a bull, and the waters are the cows, which he fertilizes. He rides in Indra's car, and the Maruts are his friends; the winds gladden him, and Vāyu is his guardian.

The abode of Soma is in the mountains, of which Mūjavant is specially mentioned, nor need we doubt that the mountains are primarily of earth. But Soma is also celestial, and his birth is in heaven. He is the child of the sky or of the sun or of Parjanya. He is the lord, the bird of heaven, he stands above all worlds like the god Sūrya; the drops, when purified in the strainer (mystically the heaven), pour from the air upon the earth. The myth of his descent from the sky is variously told: the swift eagle brought the soma for Indra through the air with his foot; flying swift as thought, he broke through the iron castles, and going to heaven, he bore the soma down for Indra. Yet the eagle did not perform his feat unscathed, for as he fled with the soma, the archer Kṛśānu shot at him and knocked out a feather. The myth seems to denote that the lightning in the form of the eagle burst through the castle of the storm-cloud and brought down the water of the cloud, conceived as the ambrosia,[3] while at the same time fire came to earth.

Soma is also the king of rivers, the king of the whole earth, the king or father of the gods, and the king of gods and mortals; though often called a god, in one passage he is expressly styled a god pressed for the gods.

As early as the *Ṛgveda* there is some trace of that identification of the moon with Soma which is fully accomplished in the *Brāhmaṇa* period. Thus in the marriage hymn (x. 85) in which Sūryā, the sun-maiden, is said to be wedded to Soma he is spoken of as in the lap of the *nakṣatras*, or lunar mansions, and it is stated that no one eats of that soma which is known by the priest; while the same identification may be at the bottom of the expressions used in some of the more mystic hymns. The process of identification may have been brought about by the practice of calling the soma celestial and bright, as dispelling the darkness and dwelling in the water, and also by naming it the drop. This may easily enough have given rise to the concept that the soma was the drop-like moon, and so soma in the bowls is actually said to be like the moon in the waters. It has been held that Soma in the *Ṛgveda* as a deity is really the moon, the receptacle of the ambrosia, which is revealed on earth in the form of the soma that is used in the ritual. This view, however, runs counter to native tradition, which still realizes the distinction between Soma and the moon in the *Ṛgveda*, and to the clear language of the texts.

Comparison with the Avesta shows that in Iran also the plant was crushed and mixed with milk, and that in Iran, as in India, the celestial soma is distinguished from the terrestrial, and the drink from the god: it grows on a mountain and is brought by an eagle; it gives light, slays demons, and bestows blessings; but whereas in India the first preparers were two, Vivasvant and Trita Āptya, in Iran they are three, Vīvanghvant, Āthwya, and Thrita.[4] Possibly the conception goes back to an older period, to the nectar in the shape of honey mead brought down from heaven by an eagle from its guardian demon, this hypothesis being confirmed by the legend of the nectar brought by the eagle of Zeus and the mead carried off by the eagle metamorphosis of Odhin.

In comparison with the celestial waters the terrestrial rivers play little part in the *Ṛgveda*. In one hymn (x. 75) the Sindhu, or Indus, is celebrated with its tributaries, and another hymn (ii. 33) lauds the Vipāś, or Beas, and the Śutudrī, or Sutlej. The Sarasvatī, however, is often praised in terms of hyperbole as treading with her waves the peaks of the mountains, as sevenfold, best of mothers, of rivers, and of goddesses. Even a celestial origin is ascribed to her, an anticipation of the later myth of the heavenly birth of the Ganges. With the

Aśvins she gave refreshment to Indra, and she is invoked together with the Iḍā (or Iḷā), or sacrificial food, and Bhāratī, who seems to be the Iḍā of the Bharatas living along her bank. Sacrifices are mentioned as performed in the Sarasvatī and Dṛṣadvatī; and with her is invoked Sarasvant, who seems no more than a male Sarasvatī, or water-genius. The precise identification of the Sarasvatī is uncertain. The name is identical with the Harahvaiti of the Avesta, which is generally taken to be the Helmund in Afghanistan, and if the Sarasvatī is still that river in the *Ṛgveda*, there must have been Indian settlements in the Vedic period much farther west than is usually assumed to be the case. On the other hand, the description of the Sarasvatī as of great size with seven streams and as sevenfold accords better with the great stream of the Indus, and the word may have been a second name of that river. When, however, it is mentioned with the Dṛṣadvatī, a small stream in the middle country, it is clear that it is the earlier form of the modern river still bearing the same name, which at present loses itself in the sands, but which in former days may well have been a much more important stream running into the Indus. It was in the land near these two rivers that the Vedic culture took its full development, at least in the subsequent period, and it is not improbable that as early as the *Ṛgveda* the stream was invested with most of its later importance.[5]

The earth receives such worship as is hers in connexion with the sky, but only one hymn (v. 84) is devoted to her praise alone, and even in it reference is made to the rain which her spouse sends. She bears the burden of the mountains and supports in the ground the trees of the forest; she is great, firm, and shining. Her name, Pṛthivī, means "broad," and a poet tells that Indra spread her out.

Apart from the obviously concrete gods we find a certain number who may be described as abstract in that the physical foundation has either disappeared or has never been present. The great majority of these gods belong to the former type:

they represent the development of aspects of more concrete deities which have come to be detached from their original owners. Of these the most famous is Savitṛ, who is the sun, and yet is a distinct god as the stimulating power of the solar luminary. Tvaṣṭṛ represents a further stage of detachment from a physical background. He is essentially the cunning artificer, who wrought the cup which contains the ambrosia of the gods, and which the Ṛbhus later divided into four; he made the swift steed and the bolt of Indra, and he sharpens the iron axe of Brahmaṇaspati. He shapes all forms and makes the husband and wife for each other in the womb; and he also creates the human race indirectly, for Yama and Yamī, the primeval twins, are children of his daughter Saraṇyū. It seems even that he is the father of Indra, though the latter stole the soma from him and even slew him, as afterward he certainly killed his son, the three-headed Viśvarūpa. He is also closely associated with the wives of the gods. Obscure as is his origin, he presents many features of a solar character, and with this would accord well enough the view that his cup is the moon, where the ambrosia is to be found.

Much feebler personalities are those of Dhātṛ ("Establisher"), an epithet of Indra or Viśvakarman, of Vidhātṛ ("Disposer"), also an epithet of these deities, Dhartṛ ("Supporter"), and Trātṛ ("Protector"), an epithet of Agni or Indra, and the leader-god who occurs in one hymn. Of these Dhātṛ alone has a subsequent history of interest, as he later ranks as a creator and is a synonym of Prajāpati. That god's name, "Lord of Offspring," is used as an epithet of Soma and of Savitṛ, but as an independent deity he appears only in the tenth and latest book of the *Ṛgveda*, where his power to make prolific is celebrated. In one hymn (x. 121) is described a "Golden Germ," Hiraṇyagarbha, creator of heaven and earth, of the waters and all that lives. The "Golden Germ" is doubtless Prajāpati, but from the refrain "What god" (*kasmai devāya*) a deity Who (*Ka deva*) was later evolved.

"In the beginning rose Hiraṇyagarbha, born only lord of all created beings.
He fixed and holdeth up this earth and heaven. What god shall we adore with our oblation?
Giver of vital breath, of power and vigour, he whose commandments all the gods acknowledge:
Whose shade is death, whose lustre makes immortal. What god shall we adore with our oblation?
Who by his grandeur hath become sole ruler of all the moving world that breathes and slumbers;
He who is lord of men and lord of cattle. What god shall we adore with our oblation?
His, through his might, are these snow-covered mountains, and men call sea and Rasā his possession:
His arms are these, his are these heavenly regions. What god shall we adore with our oblation?
By him the heavens are strong and earth is stedfast, by him light's realm and sky-vault are supported:
By him the regions in mid-air were measured. What god shall we adore with our oblation?
To him, supported by his help, two armies embattled look while trembling in their spirit,
When over them the risen sun is shining. What god shall we adore with our oblation?
What time the mighty waters came, containing the universal germ, producing Agni,
Thence sprang the gods' one spirit into being. What god shall we adore with our oblation?
He in his might surveyed the floods, containing productive force and generating Worship.
He is the god of gods, and none beside him. What god shall we adore with our oblation?
Ne'er may he harm us who is earth's begetter, nor he whose laws are sure, the heavens' creator,
He who brought forth the great and lucid waters. What god shall we adore with our oblation?
Prajāpati! thou only comprehendest all these created things, and none beside thee.
Grant us our hearts' desire when we invoke thee: may we have store of riches in possession."[6]

This passage is the starting-point of his great history which culminates in the conception of the absolute but personal Brahmā.

Another personification of the tenth book which later is merged in the personality of Prajāpati is Viśvakarman ("All-Maker"), whose name is used earlier as an epithet of Indra and the sun. He is described as having eyes, a face, arms, and feet on every side, just as Brahmā is later four-faced. He is winged, and is a lord of speech, and he assigns their names to the gods. He is the highest apparition, establisher, and disposer. Perhaps in origin he is only a form of the sun, but in his development he passes over to become one side of Prajāpati as architect.

Another aspect of the Supreme is presented by the *Purusa Sūkta*, or "Hymn of Man" (x. 90), which describes the origin of the universe from the sacrifice of a primeval Puruṣa, who is declared distinctly to be the whole universe. By the sacrifice the sky was fashioned from his head, from his navel the atmosphere, and from his feet the earth. The sun sprang from his eye, the moon from his mind, wind from his breath, Agni and Soma from his mouth; and the four classes of men were produced from his head, arms, thighs, and feet respectively. The conception is important, for Puruṣa as spirit throughout Indian religion, and still more throughout Indian philosophy, is often given the position of Prajāpati. On the other hand, there is primitive thought at the bottom of the conception of the origin of the world from the sacrifice of a giant.[7]

Another and different abstraction is found in the deification of Manyu ("Wrath"), a personification which seems to owe its origin to the fierce anger of Indra and which is invoked in two hymns of the *Ṛgveda* (x. 83–84). He is of irresistible might and is self-existent; he glows like fire, slays Vṛtra, is accompanied by the Maruts, grants victory like Indra, and bestows wealth. United with Tapas ("Ardour"), he protects his worshippers and slays the foe. Other personifications of qualities are in the main feminine and will be noted with the other female deities.

The goddesses in the *Ṛgveda* play but a small part beside the gods, and the only great one is Uṣas, though Sarasvatī is of some slight importance. To Indra, Varuṇa, and Agni are assigned Indrāṇī, Varuṇānī, and Agnāyī respectively, but they are mere names. Pṛthivī ("Earth"), who is rather frequently named with Dyaus, has only one hymn to herself, while Rātrī ("Night") is invoked as the bright starlit night, at whose approach men return home as birds hasten back to their nests, and who is asked to keep the thief and the wolf away. Originally a personification of the thunder, Vāc ("Speech") is celebrated in one hymn (x. 125) in which she describes herself. She accompanies all the gods and supports Mitra and Varuṇa, Indra and Agni, and the Aśvins, besides bending Rudra's bow against the unbeliever. Purandhi, the Avestan Pārendi, is the goddess of plenty and is mentioned with Bhaga, while Dhiṣaṇā, another goddess (perhaps of plenty), occurs a dozen times. The butter-handed and butter-footed Iḷā has a more concrete foundation, for she is the personification of the offering of butter and milk in the sacrifice. Bṛhaddivā, Sinīvālī, Rākā, and Guṅgū are nothing but names. Pṛśni is more real: she is the mother of the Maruts, perhaps the spotted storm-cloud. Saraṇyū figures in an interesting but fragmentary myth. Tvaṣṭṛ made a wedding for his daughter with Vivasvant, but during the ceremony the bride vanished away. Thereupon the gods gave one of similar form to Vivasvant, but in some way Saraṇyū seems still to have borne the Aśvins to him, as well perhaps as Yama and Yamī, for the hymn (x. 17) calls her "mother of Yama." The fragmentary story is put together by Yāska in the following shape. Saraṇyū bore to Vivasvant Yama and Yamī, and then substituting one of like form for herself, she fled away in the guise of a mare. Vivasvant, however, pursued in the shape of a horse and united with her, and she bore the Aśvins, while her substitute gave birth to Manu. The legend may be old, for it has a curious similarity to the story of the Tilphossan Erinys,[8] though the names do not philologically tally. At any rate the legend seems to have no mythical intention, but to contain some effort to explain the name of Manu as "Son of Her of Like Shape," which appears to be known as early as the *Ṛgveda.* Perhaps she is another form of the dawn-goddess.

Other goddesses are personifications of abstract ideas, such as Śraddhā ("Faith"), who is celebrated in a short hymn (x. 151). Through her the fire is kindled, ghee is offered, and wealth is obtained, and she is invoked morning, noon, and night. Anumati represents the "favour" of the gods. Aramati ("Devotion") and Sūnṛtā ("Bounteousness") are also personified. Asunīti ("Spirit Life") is besought to prolong life, while Nirṛti ("Decease" or "Dissolution") presides over death. These are only faint figures in comparison with Aditi, if that deity is to be reckoned among the personifications of abstract concepts. She is singularly without definitive features of a physical kind, though, in contrast to the other abstractions, she is commonly known throughout the *Ṛgveda.* She is expanded, bright, and luminous; she is a mistress of a bright stall and a supporter of creatures; and she belongs to all men. She is the mother of Mitra and Varuṇa, of Aryaman, and of eight sons, but she is also said to be the sister of the Ādityas, the daughter of the Vasus, and the mother of the Rudras. She is often invoked to release from sin or guilt, and with Mitra and Varuṇa she is implored to forgive sin. Evil-doers are cut off from Aditi; and Varuṇa, Agni, and Savitṛ are besought to free from guilt before her. She is identified with the earth, though the sky is also mentioned under the name Aditi. In many places, however, she is named together with (and therefore as distinct from) sky and earth; and yet again it is said (I. lxxxix. 10): "Aditi is the sky; Aditi is the air; Aditi is the mother, father, and son; Aditi is all the gods and the five tribes;[9] Aditi is whatever has been born; Aditi is whatever shall be born." Elsewhere Aditi is made both mother and daughter of Dakṣa by a species of reciprocal generation which is not rare in the *Ṛgveda;* and in yet other passages she is hailed as a cow.

The name Aditi means "Unbinding" or "Boundlessness," and the name Āditya as applied to a group of bright gods denotes them, beyond doubt, as the sons of Aditi. Hence she has been regarded as a personification of the sky or of the visible infinite, the expanse beyond the earth, the clouds and the sky, or the eternal celestial light which sustains the Ādityas. Or, if stress be laid not on her connexion with the light, but on the view that she is a cow, she can be referred to earth, as the mother of all. In these senses she would be concrete in origin. On the other hand, she has also been derived from the epithet Aditi, the "boundless," as applied to the sky, or yet more abstractly from the epithet "sons of Aditi," in the sense of "sons of boundlessness," referring to the Ādityas. As Indra is called "son of strength," and later "Strength" (Śacī) is personified as his wife (perhaps not in the *Ṛgveda* itself), so Aditi may have been developed in pre-Ṛgvedic times from such a phrase, which would account for her frequent appearance, even though a more concrete origin seems probable for such a deity. On the other hand, from her is deduced as her opposite Diti, who occurs twice or thrice in the *Ṛgveda*, though in an indeterminate sense.

Another goddess of indefinite character is Sūryā. She cannot be other than the daughter of the Sun, for both she and that deity appear in the same relation to the Aśvins. They are Sūryā's two husbands whom she chose; she or the maiden ascended their car. They possess Sūryā as their own, and she accompanies them on their car, whose three wheels perhaps correspond to its three occupants. Through their connexion with Sūryā they are invoked to conduct the bride home on their car, and it is said that when Savitṛ gave Sūryā to her husband, Soma was wooer, while the Aśvins were the groomsmen. The gods are also said to have given Pūṣan to Sūryā, who bears elsewhere the name Aśvinī. The sun as a female is a remarkable idea, and therefore Sūryā has often been taken as the dawn, but the name presents difficulties, since it does not contain any patronymic element; and, moreover, the conception contained in the wedding-hymn of the union of Soma (no doubt the moon) and the dawn would be wholly unusual.

The constant grouping of gods in the *Ṛgveda* comes to formal expression in the practice of joint invocation, which finds its natural starting-point in the concept of heaven and earth, who are far oftener worshipped as joint than as separate deities. Even Mitra and Varuṇa are much more frequently a pair than taken individually, and this use may be old, since Ahura and Mithra are thus coupled in the Avesta. A more curious compound is Indra and Varuṇa, the warlike god and the slayer of Vṛtra united with the divinity who supports men in peace and wisdom. Indra is much more often conjoined with Agni, and the pair show in the main the characteristics of the former god, though something of Agni's priestly nature is also ascribed to them. With Viṣṇu Indra strides out boldly, with Vāyu he drinks the soma, with Pūṣan he slays Vṛtras, and to their joint abode the goat conveys the sacrificial horse after death. Soma is invoked with Pūṣan and with Rudra, Agni very rarely with Soma and Parjanya. A more natural pair are Parjanya and Vāta ("Rain" and "Wind"), and similar unions are Day and Night, and Sun and Moon. Naturally enough, these dualities develop little distinct character.

Of groups of gods the most important are the Maruts, who are numbered now as twenty-one and now as a hundred and eighty and who are Indra's followers, although as Rudras they are occasionally associated with Rudra as their father. The Ādityas are smaller in number, being given as seven or eight, while the Vasus are indeterminate in number as in character, the name denoting no more than "the Bright Ones." All the deities are summed up in the concept Viśve Devāḥ ("All-Gods"), but though originally intended to include all, the term even in the *Ṛgveda* becomes applied to a special body who are named together with other groups, such as the Vasus and the Ādityas.

An odd and curious group of deities is that of the Sādhyas,

who occur in the *Ṛgveda* and occasionally in the later literature. Neither their name nor the scanty notices of them justify any conclusion as to their real nature, though it has been suggested [10] that they may possibly be a class of the fathers (the kindly dead).

Beside the great gods the Vedic pantheon has many minor personages who are not regarded as enjoying the height of divinity which is ascribed to the leading figures. Of these the chief are the Ṛbhus, who are three in number, Ṛbhu or Ṛbhukṣan, Vibhvan, and Vāja. They are the sons of Sudhanvan ("Good Archer"), though once they are called collectively the sons of Indra and the grandchildren of Might, and again they are described as sons of Manu. They acquired their rank as divine by the skill of their deeds, which raised them to the sky. They were mortal at first, but gained immortality, for the gods so admired their skilled work that Vāja became the artificer of the gods, Ṛbhukṣan of Indra, and Vibhvan of Varuṇa. Their great feats were five: for the Aśvins they made a car which, without horses or reins, and with three wheels, traverses space; for Indra they fashioned the two bay steeds; from a hide they wrought a cow which gives nectar and the cow they reunited with the calf, the beneficiary of this marvel being, we infer, Bṛhaspati; they rejuvenated their parents (apparently here sky and earth), who were very old and frail; and finally they made into four the one cup of Tvaṣṭṛ, the drinking-vessel of the gods, this being done at the divine behest conveyed by Agni, who promised them in return equal worship with the gods. Tvaṣṭṛ agreed, it seems, to the remaking of the cup, but it is also said that when he saw the four he hid himself among the females and desired to slay the Ṛbhus for the desecration, though the latter declared that they intended no disrespect.

In addition to their great deeds a wonderful thing befell them. After wandering in swift course round the sky windsped, they came to the house of Savitṛ, who conferred immortality upon them: when, after slumbering for twelve days, they had rejoiced in the hospitality of Agohya, they made fields and deflected the streams; plants occupied the dry ground and the waters the low lands. After their sleep they asked Agohya who had awakened them; in a year they looked around them; and the goat declared the dog to be the awakener. Agohya can hardly be anything but the sun, and the period of their sleep has been thought to be the winter solstice, and has been compared with the Teutonic twelve nights of licence at that period. The nights, it has been suggested,[11] are intended to make good the defects of the Vedic year of 360 days by inserting intercalary days; and the goat and the dog have led to still wilder flights of speculative imagination. But as *ṛbhu* means "handy" or "dexterous" and is akin to the German *Elbe* and the English *elf*, and as the Ṛbhus are much more than mere men, it is not improbable that they represent the three seasons which mark the earliest division of the Indian year, and their dwelling in the house of Agohya signifies the turn of life at the winter solstice. The cup of Tvaṣṭṛ may possibly be the moon, and the four parts into which it is expanded may symbolize the four phases of the moon. They may, however, have had a humbler origin as no more than elves who gradually won a higher rank, although their human attributes may be due to another cause: it is possible that they were the favourite deities of a chariot-making clan which was admitted into the Vedic circle, but whose gods suffered some diminution of rank in the process, for it is a fact that in the period of the *Brāhmaṇas* the chariot-makers, or Rathakāras, form a distinct class by themselves.

Even more obscure than the Ṛbhus is the figure of the Gandharva; he bears the epithet Viśvāvasu ("Possessing All Good"), and this is later a proper name, while at the same time the single Gandharva is converted into many. This idea is not absolutely strange to the *Ṛgveda*, but it is found only thrice, and the name Gandharva is practically unknown to books ii–vii, the nucleus of the collection. Yet the figure is old, for the Gandarewa is found in the Avesta as a dragon-like monster.

The Gandharva is heavenly and dwells in the high region of the sky; he is a measurer of space and is closely connected with the sun, the sun-bird, and the sun-steed, while in one passage he is possibly identified with the rainbow. He is also associated with the soma; he guards its place and protects the races of the gods. It is in this capacity, it would seem, that he appears as an enemy whom Indra pierces, just as in the Avesta the Gandarewa, dwelling in the sea Vourukasha, the abode of the White Haoma, battles with and is overcome by Keresāspa.[12] From another point of view Soma is said to be the Gandharva of the waters, and the Gandharva and the Maiden of the Waters are claimed as the parents of Yama and Yamī, the first pair on earth. So, too, the Gandharva is the beloved of the Apsaras, whence he is associated with the wedding ceremony and in the first days of marriage is a rival of the husband.

The Gandharva has brilliant weapons and fragrant garments, while the Gandharvas are described as wind-haired, so that it has been suggested that the Gandharvas are the spirits of the wind, closely connected with the souls of the dead and the Greek Centaurs, with whose name (in defiance of philology) their name is identified. Yet there is no sufficient ground to justify this hypothesis or any of the other divergent views which see in the Gandharva the rainbow, or the rising sun or the moon, or the spirit of the clouds, or Soma (which he guards).

The companion of the Gandharva, the Apsaras, is likewise an obscure figure, though the name denotes "moving in the waters," and the original conception may well be that of a water-nymph, whence the mingling of the water with the soma is described as the flowing to Soma of the Apsarases of the ocean. Of one, Urvaśī, we have the record that she was the mother of the sage Vasiṣṭha, to whose family are ascribed the hymns of the seventh book of the *Ṛgveda*, and an obscure hymn (x. 95) contains a dialogue between her and her earthly lover Purūravas, whom she seems to have forsaken after spending four autumns among mortals and whom she consoles by promising him bliss in heaven. From this story has been derived the view that Purūravas is the sun and Urvaśī the dawn, which disappears at the rise of the sun.

Much less prominent than even the Gandharva and the Apsarases is the "Lord of the Dwelling" (Vāstoṣpati), who is invoked in one hymn (vii. 54) to afford a favourable entry, to bless man and beast, and to grant prosperity in cattle and horses. There can be no real doubt that he is the tutelary spirit of the house. Another deity of the same type is the "Lord of the Field," who is asked to bestow cattle and horses and to fill heaven and earth with sweetness, while the "Furrow" itself, Sītā, is invoked to give rich blessings and crops. It would, of course, be an error to conclude from the meagreness of their mythology that these were not powerful deities, but it is clear that they had won no real place in the pantheon of the tribal priests whose views are presented in the *Ṛgveda.*

So also the divinities of the mountains, the plants, and the trees are far from important in the *Ṛgveda.* Parvata ("Mountain") is indeed found thrice coupled with Indra, and the mountains are celebrated along with the waters, rivers, plants, trees, heaven, and earth. The plants have a hymn to themselves (x. 97) in which they are hailed, for their healing powers, as mothers and goddesses, and Soma is said to be their king; and the forest trees, too, are occasionally mentioned as deities, chiefly with the waters and the mountains. The "Goddess of the Jungle," Araṇyānī, is invoked in one hymn (x. 146), where she is described as the mother of beasts and as rich in food without tillage, and her uncanny sights and sounds are set forth with vivid force and power, though poetically rather than mythologically.

A different side of religious thought is represented by the deification of artificial objects, but the transition from such worships as those of the tree to articles made of it is easy and natural enough. It can be seen at work in the case of the adora-

## PLATE V

### Apsarases

The celestial nymphs, who are among the chief adornments of Indra's heaven, are shown in frescoes which are the oldest extant specimens of Indian paintings. From a fresco at Ajantā, Berār. After *Ajanta Frescoes*, Plate II, No. 3.

tion of the sacrificial post, which is invoked as Vanaspati or Svaru and which is a god who, thrice anointed with ghee, is asked to let the offerings go to the gods. The sacrificial grass (the *barhis*) and the doors leading to the place of the sacrifice are likewise divine, while the pressing stones are invoked to drive demons away and to bestow wealth and offspring. Thus also the plough and the ploughshare (Śunāsīra) as well as the weapons of war, the arrow, bow, quiver, and armour, nay, even the drum, are hailed as divine. Doubtless in this we are to see fetishism rather than full divinity: the thing adored attains for the time being and in its special use a holiness which is not perpetually and normally its own. Such also must have been the character of the image or other representation of Indra which one poet offers to sell for ten cows, on condition that it shall be returned to him when he has slain his foes.

The religion of the *Ṛgveda* is predominantly anthropomorphic in its representations of the gods, and theriomorphism plays a comparatively limited part. Yet there is an exception in the case of the sun, who appears repeatedly in the form of a horse. Thus the famous steed Dadhikrā or Dadhikrāvan, who speeds like the winds along the bending ways, is not only conceived as winged, but is likened to a swooping eagle and is actually called an eagle. He pervades the five tribes with his power as the sun fills the waters with his light; his adversaries fear him like the thunder from heaven when he fights against a thousand; and he is the swan dwelling in the light. He is invoked with Agni and with Uṣas, and his name may mean "scattering curdled milk," in allusion to the dew which appears at sunrise. No glorification of a famous racehorse could account for these epithets. Tārkṣya seems to be another form of the sun-horse, for the language used of him is similar to that regarding Dadhikrā. Perhaps, too, Paidva, the courser brought by the Aśvins to Pedu to replace an inferior steed, may also be a solar horse; nor is there any doubt that Etaśa is the horse of the sun, who bears along the chariot of the god.

After the horse the cow takes an important place in the mythology. The rain-clouds are cows, and the gods fight for them against the demons. The beams of dawn are also clouds, but it is possible that the cow in itself had begun to receive reverence, being addressed as Aditi and a goddess, and being described as inviolable, nor later is there any doubt of direct zoölatry. Indra, Agni, and rarely Dyaus are described as bulls; the boar is used as a description of Rudra, the Maruts, and Vṛtra. Soma, Agni, and the sun are hailed as birds, and an eagle carried down the soma for Indra, apparently representing Indra's lightning. The crow and the pigeon are the messengers of Yama, the god of death, and a bird of omen is invoked. The "Serpent" (Ahi) is a form of the demon Vṛtra, but there is no trace of the worship of snakes as such. Animals serve also as steeds for the gods: the Aśvins use the ass, and Pūṣan the goat, but horses are normal. Yama has two dogs, the offspring of Saramā, though she does not appear in the *Ṛgveda* as a bitch. Indra has a monkey, of whom a late hymn (x. 86) tells a curious story. Apparently the ape, Vṛṣākapi, was the favourite of Indra and injured property of Indra's wife; soundly beaten, it was banished, but it returned, and Indra effected a reconciliation. The hymn belongs to the most obscure of the *Ṛgveda* and has been very variously interpreted,[13] even as a satire on a contemporary prince and his spouse.

The same vein of satire has been discerned in a curious hymn (vii. 103) where frogs, awakened by the rains, are treated as able to bestow cows and long life. The batrachians are compared to priests as they busy themselves round the sacrifice, and their quacking is likened to the repetition of the Veda by the student. The conception is carried out in a genial vein of burlesque, yet it is very possible that it contains worship which is serious enough, for the frogs are connected with the rain and seem to be praised as bringing with their renewed activity the fall of the waters.

We have seen gods conceived as of animal form and, therefore, in so far incarnate in these animals, not indeed permanently, but from time to time. Accordingly, in the later ritual, which seems faithfully to represent in this regard the meaning of the *Ṛgveda*, the horse is not always or normally divine, but it is so when a special horse is chosen to be sacrificed at the horse-sacrifice and for this purpose is identified with the god. It is possible, too, that direct worship of the cow and the frog (at least in the rainy season) is recorded. The question then arises whether the Vedic Indians were totemists. Did they conceive a tie of blood between themselves and an animal or thing which they venerated and normally spared from death, and which they might eat only under the condition of some sacrament to renew the blood bond? We can only say that there is no more evidence of this than is implied in the fact that some tribal appellations in the *Ṛgveda* are animal names like the Ajas, or "Goats," and the Matsyas, or "Fishes," or vegetable like the Śigrus, or "Horse-Radishes"; but we have no record that these tribes worshipped the animals or plants whose name they bear. Neither do we know to what extent these tribes were of Aryan origin or religion. There may well have been totemistic non-Aryan tribes, for we know that another worship which is now accepted and bound up with the form of Śiva — the phallic cult — was practised in the time of the *Ṛgveda*, but by persons whom it utterly disapproved and treated as hostile.[14]

Beside the gods some priests and priestly families who are more than real men figure in the *Ṛgveda*. Prominent among these are the Bhṛgus, whose name denotes "the Bright," and who play the *rôle* of those who kindle Agni when he is discovered by Mātariśvan and establish and diffuse his use upon earth. They find him in the waters; they produce him by friction and pray to him. They are invoked to drink soma with all the thirty-three gods, the Maruts, the waters, and the Aśvins; they overcome the demon Makha and are foes of the historic king Sudās. They are mentioned in connexion with Atharvan, among others, and like them Atharvan is associated with the production of fire, which he churns forth. Āthravan in the Avesta denotes "fire-priest," nor is there any doubt that the Atharvan or Atharvans of the *Ṛgveda* are old fire-priests, while the Bhṛgus represent either such priests or possibly the lightning side of fire itself. Yet another set of beings connected with fire are the Aṅgirases. Aṅgiras as an epithet is applied to Agni himself, and Aṅgiras is represented as an ancient seer, but the chief feat of the Aṅgirases is their share in the winning of the cows, in which act they are closely associated with Indra; they are, however, also said to have burst the rock with their songs and gained the light, to have driven out the cows and pierced Vala and caused the sun to shine. They seem to bear the traces of messengers of Agni, perhaps his flames, but they may have been no more than priests of the fire-cult, like the Atharvans. Like the Atharvans they are bound up with the *Atharvaveda*, which is associated with that cult. The Virūpas ("Those of Various Form"), another priestly family, seem no more than they in one special aspect.

A figure of great obscurity connected with Agni is that of Dadhyañc ("Milk-Curdling"), a son of Atharvan and a producer of Agni. The Aśvins gave him a horse's head, and with it he proclaimed to them the place of the mead of Tvaṣṭṛ. Again it is said that when Indra was seeking the head of the horse hidden in the mountains, he found it in Śaryaṇāvant and with the bones of Dadhyañc he slew ninety-nine Vṛtras. Dadhyañc opens cow-stalls by the power of Soma, and Indra gives him cow-stalls. He has been interpreted as the soma because of the allusion to curdled milk in his name, which again connects him with the horse Dadhikrā, but a more plausible view is that he represents a form of lightning, the speed of which is symbolized by the horse's head, while the thunder is his speech and the bolt his bones. The legend is too fragmentary, however, to enable us to form any clear opinion of its significance. Atri, another seer, is famed for being saved from burning in a deep pit by the Aśvins, who restored him with a refreshing draught. But he also performed a great feat himself, for he rescued the sun when it was hidden by the Asura, Svarbhānu, and placed it in the sky. The same deed is also ascribed to the Atris as a family, and they are the traditional authors of the fifth book of the *Ṛgveda*, which often refers to them. Their name denotes "the eater" and may itself once have belonged to Agni, who is perhaps hidden in the guise of the blind seer Kaṇva, a *protégé* of the Aśvins, from whom he received back his lost sight.

Indra also has mythical connexions with the seers called Daśagvas and Navagvas who aided him in the recovery of the kine and whose names perhaps denote that they won ten and nine cows respectively in that renowned exploit. Still more famous is his friendship with Kutsa, to whom he gave constant aid in his struggles with Śuṣṇa; it was for him that Indra performed the feat of stopping the sun by tearing off its wheel, giving the other to Kutsa to drive on with. The myth is a strange one and seems to be a confusion of the story of the winning of the sun for men by Indra with his friendship for a special hero whom he aided in battle. Yet in other passages Kutsa appears in hostility to Indra. In the fight with Śuṣṇa, as the drought-demon, Indra also had the aid of Kāvya Uśanâs, who likewise made for him the bolt for the slaying of Vṛtra.

An independent position is occupied by Manu, who stands out as the first of men who lived, in contrast with Yama (like himself the son of Vivasvant), who was the first of men to die. He is *par excellence* the first sacrificer, the originator of the cult of Agni and of Soma, and to him indeed Soma was brought by the bird. Men are his offspring, and their sacrifices are based on his as prototype. Just as he embodies the concept of the first sacrificer, so the group of seven priests who play the chief part in the ritual are personified as the seven seers who are called divine and are associated with the gods.

Against the gods and other spirits invoked as beneficent are set the host of the demons, or more often individual spirits who are enemies both to gods and to men and whom the gods overthrow for the benefit of men no less than of themselves. The Asuras, as the demons are called throughout Indian literature subsequent to the age of the *Ṛgveda*, have not yet attained that position at the earliest period. Asura there means a spirit who is normally benignant; in four passages only (and three of those are in the tenth and latest book) are the Asuras mentioned as demons, and in the singular the word has this sense only thrice, while the epithet "slaying Asuras" is applied once each to Indra, Agni, and the sun. Much more commonly mentioned are the Paṇis, whose cows are won by the gods, especially Indra. Their name denotes "Niggard," especially with regard to the sacrificial gifts, and thus, no doubt, an epithet of human meanness has been transferred to demoniac foes, who are accused of having concealed even the ghee in the cow. Other human enemies who rank as demons are the Dāsas and Dasyus; and by a natural turn of language Dāsa comes to denote "slave" and is found in this sense in the *Ṛgveda* itself. Besides the historical Dāsas, who were doubtless the aborigines, rank others who seek to scale heaven and who withhold the sun and the waters from the gods; and the autumnal forts of the Dāsas can hardly have been mere human citadels. While, however, the transfer of name from men to demons is clear, can we go further and equate the Paṇis and Dāsas to definite tribes, and see in them Parnians and Dahae, against whom the Vedic Indians waged warfare in the land of Arachosia? The conjecture is attractive, but it shifts the scene of Vedic activity too far west and compels us to place the events of the sixth book of the *Ṛgveda* far distant from those described in book seven, the interest of which centres in the Indian "Middle Country," the home in all probability of the greater part of the Vedic poetry.

Much more common as a generic name of the adversaries of the gods is Rakṣas, either "the Injurious," or "That Which is to be Guarded Against." Rarely these demons are called Yātus or Yātudhānas ("Sorcerers"), who represent, no doubt, one type of the demons. They have the shape of dogs, vultures, owls, and other birds; appropriating the form of husband, brother, or lover, they approach women with evil intent; they eat the flesh of men and horses and suck the milk of cows. Their particular time of power is the evening and above all else they detest sacrifice and prayer. Agni, the Fire, is especially besought to drive them away and destroy them, and hence wins his title of "Slayer of Rakṣases." With the Rakṣases in later literature rank the Piśācas as foes of the fathers, precisely as the Asuras are the enemies of the gods and the Rakṣases of men, but the *Ṛgveda* knows only the yellow-peaked, watery Piśāci, whom Indra is invoked to crush. Other hostile spirits are the Arātis ("Illiberalities"), the Druhs ("Injurious"), and the Kimīdins, who are goblins conceived as in pairs.

There is no fixed terminology in the description of individual demons, so that Pipru and Varcin pass both as Asuras and as Dāsas. By far the greatest of the demons is the serpent Vṛtra, footless and handless, the snorter, the child of Dānu, "the stream," the encompasser of the waters, which are freed when Indra slays him. There are many Vṛtras, however, and the name applies to earthly as well as to celestial foes. Vala ranks next as an enemy of Indra: he is the personification of the cave in which the cows are kept, and which Indra pierces or cleaves to free the kine. Arbuda again was deprived of his cows by Indra, who trod him underfoot and cleft his head, and he seems but a form of Vṛtra. More doubtful is the three-headed son of Tvaṣṭṛ, Viśvarūpa ("Multiform"), who is slain by Indra with the aid of Trita, and whose cows are taken. In his figure some scholars have seen the moon, but his personality is too shadowy to allow of any clear result. The overthrowing of the demon Svarbhānu is accomplished by Indra, while Atri replaces in the sky the eye of the sun which that demon had eclipsed. The Dāsa Śuṣṇa figures as a prominent foe of Kutsa, a *protégé* of Indra, but his mythical character is attested by the fact that by overcoming him Indra wins the waters, finds the cows, and gains the sun. He is also described as causing bad harvests, while his name must mean either "Scorcher" or "Hisser"; and apparently he is a demon of drought. With him is sometimes coupled Śambara, the son of Kulitara, the Dāsa of ninety-nine forts, whom Indra destroys, though he deemed himself a godling. Pipru and Varcin also fall before Indra, the first with fifty thousand black warriors, and the second with a hundred thousand. As either is at once Asura and Dāsa, perhaps they were the patron gods of aboriginal tribes which were overthrown by the Aryans; but their names may mean in Sanskrit "the Resister" and "the Shining." Dhuni and Cumuri, the Dāsas, were sent to sleep by Indra for the sake of the pious Dabhīti; and their castles were shattered along with those of Śambara, Pipru, and Varcin. Dhuni means "Roarer," but Cumuri is not, it would seem, Aryan, and he perhaps, with Ilībiśa, Sṛbinda, and others of whom we know practically nothing, may be aboriginal names of foes or gods hostile to the Aryans.

A more perplexing figure and one famous in later literature is Namuci, which Indian etymology renders as "He Who Will Not Let Go." He is at once Asura and Dāsa, and in vanquishing him Indra has the aid of Namī Sāpya. The peculiarity of his death is that his head is not pierced, like Vṛtra's, but is twirled or twisted with the foam of the waters, and that Indra is said to have drunk wine beside him when the Aśvins aided and Sarasvatī cured him.

The king of the dead is Yama, who gathers the people together and gives the dead a resting-place in the highest heaven amid songs and the music of the flute. He is the son of Vivasvant, just as in the Avesta Yima is the son of Vīvanghvant, the first presser of the soma. His sister is Yamī, and a curious hymn (x. 10) contains a dialogue in which she presses her brother to wed her and beget offspring, while he urges religious objections to her suit. The story suggests what is confirmed by the later Persian record that Yama and Yima were really the twin parents of mankind. The Avesta also tells us that he lives in an earthly paradise which he rules,[15] and though this trait is not preserved in the *Ṛgveda*, it is hinted at in the epic. His real importance, however, is that he is the first man who died and showed to others the way of death. Death is his path, and he is once identified with death. As death the owl or the pigeon is his messenger, but he has two dogs, four-eyed, broad-nosed, one brindle (*śabala*) and one brown, sons of Saramā, who watch men and wander about as his envoys. They also guard the path, perhaps like the four-eyed, yellow-eared dog of the Avesta, who stands at the Cinvaṭ Bridge to prevent evil spirits from seizing hold of the righteous. Yet it may be that, as is suggested by Aufrecht,[16] the object of the dogs' watch is to keep sinful men from the world of Yama. It does not seem that the souls of the dead have (as in the epic) a stream Vaitaraṇī to cross, though it has been suggested that in X. xvii. 7 ff. Sarasvatī is none other than this river.

Though Yama is associated with gods, especially Agni and Varuṇa, and though there is an obvious reference to his connexion with the sun in the phrase "the heavenly courser given by Yama," still he is never called a god, and this fact lends the greatest probability to the view that he is what he seems to be, the first of men, the first also to die, and so the king of the dead, but not a judge of the departed. Nevertheless, his connexion with the sun and with Agni has suggested that he is the sun, especially conceived as setting, or that he is the parting day, in which case his sister is the night. The only other theory which would seem to have any plausibility is that he is the moon, for the connexion of the moon with the souls of the dead is deeply rooted in the *Upaniṣads*. Moreover, the moon actually dies and is the child of the sun. This identification, however, rests in large measure on the unproved hypothesis that the few references in the *Ṛgveda* to Soma as associated with the fathers are allusions to their abode in the moon.

It is in keeping with the belief in the heaven of Yama that the burning of the body of the dead is the normal, though not the exclusive, mode of disposing of the corpse. The dead were, however, sometimes buried, for the fathers are distinguished as those who are burned by fire and those who are not burned. The dead was burned with his clothes, etc., to serve him in the future life; even his weapons and his wife, it would seem, were once incinerated, although the *Ṛgveda* has abandoned that practice, of which only a symbol remains in placing the wife and the weapons beside the dead and then removing them from him. Agni bears the dead away, and the rite of burning is thus in part like a sacrifice; but as "eater of raw flesh" in this rite Agni is distinguished from that Agni who carries the oblations. With the dead was burned a goat, which Agni is besought to consume while preserving the body entire. On the path to the world of the dead Pūṣan acts as guide, and Savitṛ as conductor. A bundle of fagots is attached to the dead to wipe out his track and hinder the return of death to the living. Borne along the path by which the fathers went in days gone by, the soul passes on to the realm of light and in his home receives a resting-place from Yama. Though his corpse is destroyed by the flame, still in the other world he is not a mere spirit, but has what must be deemed a refined form of his earthly body. He abides in the highest point of the sun, and the fathers are united with the sun and its rays. The place is one of joy: the noise of flutes and song resounds; there soma, ghee, and honey flow. There are the two kings, Varuṇa and Yama, and the fathers are dear to the gods and are free from old age and bodily frailty. Another conception, however, seems to regard the fathers as being constellations in the sky, an idea which is certainly found in the later Vedic period.

Those who attain to heaven are, above all, the pious men who offer sacrifice and reward the priest, for sacrifice and sacrificial fee are indissolubly connected;[17] but heroes who risk their lives in battle and those who practise asceticism also win their way thither. Of the fate of evil-doers we hear very little, and it would appear that annihilation was often regarded as their fate. Yet there is mention of deep places produced for the evil, false, and untrue, and Indra and Soma are besought to dash the evil-doers into the abyss of bottomless darkness, while the prayer is uttered that the enemy and the robber may lie below the three earths. From these obscure beginnings probably arose the belief in hell which is expressed in clear terms in the *Atharvaveda* and which is later elaborated at length in the epic and in the *Purāṇas*.

But the fathers are more than spirits living in peace after the toils of life. They are powerful to aid and receive offering, while they are invoked with the dawns, streams, mountains, heaven and earth, Pūṣan, and the Ṛbhus. They are asked to accord riches, offspring, and long life; they are said to have generated the dawn and, with Soma, to have extended heaven and earth. They especially love the soma and come for it in thousands. Yet though they are even called gods, they are distinguished from the true divinities; their path is the Pitṛyāṇa, or "Way of the Fathers," as contrasted with the Devayāna, or "Way of the Gods"; and the food given to them is termed *svadhā*, in contrast with the call *svāhā* with which the gods are invited to take their portion. The fathers are described as lower, higher, and middle, and as late and early; and mention is made of the races of Navagvas, Vairūpas, Atharvans, Aṅgirases, Vasiṣṭhas, and Bhṛgus, the last four of which appear also in the *Ṛgveda* as priestly families.

In one passage of the *Ṛgveda* (X. xvi. 3) an idea occurs which has been thought to have served in some degree as stimulating the later conception of metempsychosis, of which there is no real trace in that *Saṁhitā*. It is there said, in the midst of verses providing for the dead being taken by Agni to the world above,

> "The sun receive thine eye, the wind thy spirit; go, as thy merit is, to earth or heaven.
> Go, if it be thy lot, unto the waters; go, make thine home in plants with all thy members." [18]

The conception seems natural enough as an expression of the resolution of the body into the elements from which it is derived, just as in later Sanskrit it is regularly said of man that he goes to the five elements when he dies; and it is, therefore, much more likely that the phrase is thus to be interpreted than that we are to see in it the primitive idea that the soul of the dead may go into plants and so forth. The passage is almost isolated, however, so that the sense must remain uncertain.

## CHAPTER III

## THE MYTHOLOGY OF THE BRĀHMAṆAS

WITHOUT exception the *Brāhmaṇas* presuppose the existence of a *Ṛgveda Saṁhitā*, in all probability similar in essentials to the current text, and it is more than likely that the other *Saṁhitās* — the *Sāmaveda*, the two schools of the *Yajurveda*, and the *Atharvaveda* — were composed after the formation of the *Saṁhitā* of the *Ṛgveda*. Nor can there be much doubt that, while the *Ṛgveda* shows many traces of being the product of an age which was far from primitive, the later *Saṁhitās*, in those portions which do not accord with texts already found in the *Ṛgveda*, stand generally on precisely the same level as the leading *Brāhmaṇas*, or at least the oldest of these texts. The most essential characteristic of them all from the point of view of mythology is that the old polytheism is no longer as real as in the *Ṛgveda*. It is true that there is no question of the actuality of the numerous gods of the pantheon, to whom others are indeed added, but the texts themselves show plain tendencies to create divinities of more imposing and more universal power than any Vedic deity. There are three figures in the pantheon who display the results of this endeavour, those of Prajāpati, Viṣṇu, and Rudra. Of these the first is distinguished from the other two by the essential fact that he is a creation not so much of popular mythology as of priestly speculation, and the result, as was inevitable, is that his permanence as a great god is not assured; while the two other divinities, being clearly popular deities in their essence, have survived to be the great gods of India throughout the centuries with only so much change as has proved unavoidable in the development of creed during hundreds of years.

The essential feature of Prajāpati is that he is a creator, a "Lord of Offspring," and offspring includes everything. Yet there is no consistent account of creation in the *Brāhmaṇas*, nor even in any one text. Nevertheless, the importance of the concept Prajāpati does appear in the fact that he is definitely identified with Viśvakarman, the "All-Creator" of the *Ṛgveda* (x. 81, 82), or with Dakṣa, who is at once son and father of Aditi in that *Saṁhitā* (x. 72); and the later *Saṁhitās* repeat the hymn of the *Ṛgveda* (x. 121) which celebrates the "Golden Germ," Hiraṇyagarbha, and identify with Prajāpati the interrogative Ka ("Who"), which in that hymn heads each line in the question, "To what god shall we offer with oblation?" Among the variants of the story of the creation of the world there is one which becomes a favourite and which assigns to the waters or the ocean the first place in the order of existence. The waters, however, desire to be multiplied, and produce a golden egg by the process of *tapas*, a term which, with its origin in the verb *tap*, "heat," shows that the first conception of Indian ascetic austerity centres in the process of producing intense physical heat. From this egg is born Prajāpati, who proceeds to speak in a year, the words which he utters being the sacred *vyāhṛtis*, or exclamations, "Bhūḥ," "Bhuvaḥ," and "Svar," which become the earth, the atmosphere, and the sky. He desired offspring and finally produced the gods, who were made divinities by reaching the sky; and he also created the Asuras, whereby came the darkness, which revealed to Prajāpati that he had created evil, so that he pierced the Asuras with darkness, and they were overcome. The tale, one of many, is important in that it reveals qualities which are permanent throughout Indian religion: the story of creation is variously altered from time to time and made to accord with philosophical speculation, which resolves the waters into a primitive material termed Prakṛti; but the golden egg, though spiritualized, persists in the popular conception, while the place of the creation of the god is taken by the concept of Puruṣa, or "Spirit," which is one of the names of Prajāpati, entering into the material Prakṛti. The creative power of Prajāpati exercised by himself is actually compared to child-birth and serves as the precursor of the androgynous character of the deity, which is formally expressed in the figure of Śiva as half man and half woman both in literature and in art.

Another conception of the creative activity of Prajāpati is that he took the form of a tortoise or a boar: thus in the *Śatapatha Brāhmaṇa* (VII. v. 1. 5) we learn that he created offspring after he had assumed the form of a tortoise; and that as the word *kaśyapa* means "tortoise," people say that all creatures are descendants of Kaśyapa. This tortoise is also declared to be one with the sun (Āditya), which brings Prajāpati into connexion with the solar luminary, just as he is identified with Dakṣa, the father or son of Aditi, the mother of Āditya. The same *Brāhmaṇa* (XIV. i. 2. 11) tells us that the earth was formerly but a span in size, but that a boar raised it up, and that Prajāpati, as lord of earth, rewarded him. In the *Taittirīya Saṁhitā* (VII. i. 5. 1) and the *Taittirīya Brāhmaṇa* (I. i. 3. 1) this boar is definitely identified with Prajāpati, and the later *Taittirīya Āraṇyaka* states (X. i. 8) that the earth was raised by a black boar with a hundred arms. From these germs spring the boar and tortoise incarnations of Viṣṇu in the epic and in the *Purāṇas*. Yet another avatar is to be traced to the story in the *Satapatha Brāhmaṇa* (I. viii. 1. 1) of the fish which saves Manu from the deluge, though that text does not give the identification of the fish with Prajāpati, which is asserted in the epic.

There is, however, another side to the character of Prajāpati which exhibits him in an unfavourable light. The *Brāhmaṇas* tell that he cast eyes of longing on his own daughter, reproducing here, no doubt, the obscure references in the *Ṛgveda* (X. lxi. 4–7) to the intercourse of Dyaus ("Sky") with his daughter

Uṣas ("Dawn"). The gods were deeply indignant at this deed, and Rudra either threatened to shoot him, but was induced to desist by being promised to be made lord of cattle; or actually shot him, though afterward the wound thus caused was healed. In the *Aitareya Brāhmaṇa* (iii. 33) the story takes a very mythic aspect: Prajāpati turns himself into a deer to pursue his daughter in the guise of an antelope (*rohiṇī*), and the gods produce a most terrible form to punish him, in the shape, it is clear, of Rudra, though his name is too dangerous to be mentioned; he pierces Prajāpati, who flees to the sky and there constitutes the constellation Mṛga ("Wild Animal"), while the archer becomes Mṛgavyādha ("Piercer of the Mṛga"), the antelope is changed into Rohiṇī, and the arrow is still to be seen as the constellation of the three-pronged arrow.

Despite his creative activity, Prajāpati was not immortal by birth, for the conception of the *Brāhmaṇas*, as of India in later days, does not admit of immortality won by birth alone. When he had created gods and men, he formed death; and half of himself — hair, skin, flesh, bone, and marrow — was mortal, the other half — mind, voice, breath, eye, and ear — being immortal. He fled in terror of death, and it was only by means of the earth and the waters, united as a brick for the piling of the sacred fire which forms one of the main ceremonies of the sacrificial ritual, that he could be made immortal. But at the same time Prajāpati himself is the year, the symbol of time, and by the year he wears out the lives of mortals, whether men or gods. The gods, on the contrary, attained immortality from Prajāpati; they sought in vain to do so by many sacrifices, but failed, even when they performed the piling of the fire altar with an undefined number of fire-bricks, until at last they won their desire when they followed the proper numbers of the bricks. Death, however, objected to this exemption from his control, for it left him without a portion; and the gods, therefore, ordained that thenceforth no man should become immortal without parting with his body, whether his immortality was due to knowledge or to works. Thus it happens that after death a man may either be reborn for immortality, or he may be born only to be fated to die again and again. This is but a specimen of the various means by which the gods escape death, for they are ever afraid of the Ender and must adopt rites of many kinds to be freed from his control.

Since both the gods and the Asuras ("Demons") were the offspring of Prajāpati, it becomes necessary to explain why they are differentiated as good and bad, and this is done in several ways. In one case the Asuras kept sacrificing to themselves out of insolence, while the gods sacrificed to one another; and as a result Prajāpati bestowed himself upon them, and sacrifice became theirs only. In another version the gods adopted the plan of speaking nothing but the truth, while the Asuras resorted to falsehood: because of this for a while the gods became weaker and poorer, but in the end they flourished, and so it is with man; while the Asuras, who waxed rich and prosperous, like salty ground came to ruin in the end. The gods, again, won the earth from the Asuras: they had only as much of it as one can see while sitting, and they asked the Asuras for a share; the latter replied that the gods could have as much as they could encompass, whereupon the gods encompassed the whole earth on four sides. Another legend accounts for the differences in greatness of the gods by the fact that three of them — Indra, Agni, and Sūrya — desired to win superiority, and for that purpose they went on sacrificing until in the long run they attained their aim.

Prajāpati might, it is clear, have become a much greater figure had it not been for the fact that the philosophic spirit which conceived him soon went beyond the original idea and transformed the male, as too personal for the expression of the absolute, into the neuter Brahman Svayambhū ("Self-Existent Prayer"). It still remained possible to ascribe the origin of the world to this Brahman and to account for it by ascetic austerity on its part, but the way was opened for the development of the pantheistic philosophy of the *Upaniṣads*. The change of name is significant and indicates that a new side of thought has become prominent: Brahman is the "prayer," or the "spell," which is uttered by the priest and it is also the holy power of the prayer or the spell, so that it is well adapted to become a name for the power which is at the root of the universe. When, therefore, this Brahman is converted into the subject of asceticism, it is clear that it is assuming the features of Prajāpati, and that two distinct lines of thought are converging into one. The full result of this process is the creation of a new god, Brahmā, which is the masculine of the neuter impersonal Brahman. Yet this new deity is not an early figure: he is found in the later *Brāhmaṇas*, such as the *Kauṣītaki* and the *Taittirīya*, as well as in the *Upaniṣads* and the still later *Sūtra* literature, in which he is clearly identified with Prajāpati, whose double, however, he obviously is. Was there, as has been suggested, ever a time when Brahmā was a deity greater than all others in the pantheon? The answer certainly cannot be in the unrestricted affirmative, for the epic shows no clear trace of a time when Brahmā was the chief god, and the evidence of the Buddhist *Sūtras*, which undoubtedly make much of Brahmā Sahampati (an epithet of uncertain sense), is not enough to do more than indicate that in the circles in which Buddhism found its origin Brahmā had become a leading figure. It is, in fact, not unlikely that in the period at the close of the age of the *Brāhmaṇas*, just before the appearance of Buddhism, the popular form of the philosophic god had made some progress toward acceptability, at least in the circles of the warriors and the Brāhmans. But if that were the case, it is clear that this superiority was not to be of long duration, and certainly it never spread among the people as a whole.

Of these rivals of Brahmā in popular favour Viṣṇu shows clear signs of an increasing greatness. The gods, as usual, were worsted in their struggles with the Asuras, and for the purpose of regaining the earth which they had lost they approached the

## PLATE VI

### Brahmā

In the presence of the sacred fire a worshipper presents an offering to Brahmā. The four faces of the god are said to have come into being from his desire to behold the loveliness of his daughter, who sought in vain to escape his amorous gaze. He originally had a fifth head, due to the same cause, but this was removed by Śiva, either because of wrath or because the head acquired such splendour through knowledge of the Vedas that neither gods nor demons could endure it. From an Indian painting of a *rāginī* ("sub-mode" of Indian music) in the collection of the Editor.

Asuras, who were engaged in meting out the world, and begged for a share in it. The Asuras with meanness offered in return only so much as Viṣṇu, who was but a dwarf, could lie upon; but the gods accepted the offer, and surrounding Viṣṇu with the metres, they went on worshipping, with the result that they succeeded in acquiring the whole earth. The story is further explained by another passage in the same text which refers to the three strides of Viṣṇu as winning for the gods the all-pervading power that they now possess. Besides these notices in the *Śatapatha Brāhmaṇa* (I. ii. 5; ix. 3. 9) we are told in the *Aitareya Brāhmaṇa* (vi. 15) that Indra and Viṣṇu had a dispute with the Asuras whom they defeated and with whom they then agreed to divide the world, keeping for themselves so much as Viṣṇu could step over in three strides, these steps embracing the worlds, the Vedas, and speech. Moreover, while the boar, as a cosmogonic power, is still associated with Prajāpati and not with Viṣṇu, traces of the latter's connexion with the boar occur in a legend, based on the *Ṛgveda*, which is told in the *Black Yajurveda* (VI. ii. 4): a boar, the plunderer of wealth, kept the goods of the gods concealed beyond seven hills; but Indra, taking a blade of *kuśa*-grass, shot beyond the hills and slew the boar, which Viṣṇu, as the sacrificer, took and offered to the god. This passage indicates the source of the strength of Viṣṇu in the *Brāhmaṇas:* he is essentially identified with sacrifice and with all that that means for the Brāhman. In this connexion a strange story is told of the way in which Viṣṇu lost his head. He was acknowledged by the gods to be the sacrifice, and thus he became the most eminent of the divinities. Now once he stood resting his head on the end of his bow, and as the gods sat about unable to overcome him, the ants asked them what they would give to him who should gnaw the bow-string. When the deities promised in return for such an action the eating of food and the finding of water even in the desert, the ants gnawed through the string, which accordingly broke, and the two ends of the bow, starting asunder, cut off the head of the god. The sound *ghṛm*, with which Viṣṇu's head fell, became the *gharma*, or sacrificial kettle; and as his strength dwindled away, the *mahāvīra*, or "pot of great strength," acquired its name. The gods proceeded to offer with the headless sacrifice, or *makha*, but as they did not succeed they had to secure the restoration of its head either by the Aśvins or by the *pravargya* rite. It is very curious that this should be so, for Viṣṇu takes only a small part in the ritual and is not closely connected with the Soma offering, which is, after all, the chief feature of the sacrifice; yet we must, no doubt, recognize that the god had a strong body of adherents who secured the growing attention paid to him. The same trait is seen in the relations of Viṣṇu and Indra: Viṣṇu now appears as supporting Indra in his attack on Vṛtra, and we have assurances that Viṣṇu is the chief of the gods. His dwarf shape also assimilated him in cunning to Indra, for it is doubtless nothing but a clever device to secure the end aimed at, just as Indra changes himself, in the version of the *Taittirīya Saṁhitā* (VI. ii. 4. 4), into a *sālāvṛkī* (possibly a hyena) and in that form wins the earth for the gods from the Asuras by running round it three times. Otherwise the god develops no new traits: his characteristic feature remains his threefold stride which seems to have been accepted in the sense of striding through the three worlds, though the alternative version of striding through the sky is also recognized.

The name Nārāyaṇa is not yet applied to Viṣṇu in the early texts; yet we hear in the *Śatapatha Brāhmaṇa* (XIII. vi. 1. 1) of Puruṣa Nārāyaṇa who saw the human sacrifice and offered with it, thus attaining the supremacy which he desired. Here we have, of course, a reflex of the *Puruṣa Sūkta* of the *Ṛgveda*, the Puruṣa who there is offered up being transferred into a Puruṣa who sacrifices another, and in this aspect Nārāyaṇa is closely akin to Prajāpati. As early as the *Taittirīya Āraṇyaka*, however, which can scarcely be placed later than the third century B.C., the name of Nārāyaṇa, together with those of

Vāsudeva and Narasiṁha, is ascribed to Viṣṇu, which shows that at the end of the Vedic period the conception of Viṣṇu had been enlarged to include the traits which appear in the epic, where Viṣṇu is not identified merely with Nārāyaṇa, but also with the Vāsudeva Kṛṣṇa and is revealed as the "Man-Lion," Narasiṁha.

None the less it is certain that in the *Brāhmaṇas* Śiva is really a greater figure than Viṣṇu, perhaps because he is a terrible god, an aspect never congenial to Viṣṇu. Thus he is implored to confer long life, the triple life of Jamadagni and Kaśyapa and the gods, and taking his bow, clad in his tiger's skin, to depart beyond the Mūjavants in the far north. Still more significant is the *Śatarudriya*, or "Litany to Rudra by a Hundred Names," which occurs in variant but nearly identical versions in the several texts of the *Yajurveda*. He here appears as many-coloured and as the god who slips away, even though the cowherds and the drawers of water catch a glimpse of him; he is treated as lord of almost everything conceivable, including thieves and robbers. He is a mountain dweller and, above all, is the wielder of a terrible bow; he has hosts of Rudras who are his attendants and who, like himself, are terrible; moreover he has his abode in everything. Other names are given which are not merely descriptive — Bhava, Śarva, Paśupati — as well as such as Nīlagrīva ("Blue-Necked") and Śitikaṇṭha ("White-Throated"). Of these names we find Bhava and Śarva repeatedly connected in the *Atharva-veda*, both as archers, and brought into conjunction with Rudra; while in another passage of that Veda (xv. 5) appellatives of the same deity under different forms are not merely Bhava and Śarva, but also Paśupati, Ugra, Rudra, Mahādeva, and Īśāna. In the *Śatapatha Brāhmaṇa* (I. vii. 3. 8) we are told that Rudra is Agni and that among the eastern people his name is Śarva, but that among the westerners (the Bāhīkas) he is called Bhava; and he is also termed "Lord of Cattle." Another account (VI. i. 3. 7) says that from the union of the

"Lord of Creatures" (Prajāpati) with Uṣas was born a boy, Kumāra, who cried and demanded to be given names. Then Prajāpati gave him the name Rudra because he had wept (*rud*); and he also called him Śarva ("All"), Paśupati ("Lord of Cattle"), Ugra ("the Dread"), Aśani ("Lightning"), Bhava ("the Existent"), Mahādeva ("the Great God"), and Īśāna ("the Ruler"), which are the eight forms of Agni. In slightly different order the names are given in a passage of the *Kauṣītaki Brāhmaṇa* (vi. 1 ff.) as Bhava, Śarva, Paśupati, Ugradeva, Mahādeva, Rudra, Īśāna, and Aśani; although here the origin of the being thus named is traced to the joint action of Agni, Vāyu, Āditya, Candramas (the moon), and Uṣas in the form of an Apsaras. Yet another account tells of the origin of Rudra from the deity Manyu ("Wrath"), who alone remained in Prajāpati after all the other gods left him when he was dissolved by the effort of creation. This fact explains why Rudra is so savage and requires to be appeased. He is the cruel one of the gods, and he is the boar, because the boar is wrath.

There are many other traces of the dread nature of the god. Thus in the ritual Rudra is so far identified with the Rakṣases, Asuras, and fathers that after uttering his name a man must touch the purifying waters; but, on the other hand, he is distinguished from them by the fact that his region is the north, not the south, and that the call used in his service is the *svāhā*, which is normal for the gods. While Nābhānediṣṭha, the son of Manu, was absent from home as a student, his brothers deprived him of any share in the paternal estate which they enjoyed during the lifetime of their father. When he complained of this to his parent, he was told to go to the Aṅgirases, who were sacrificing with the object of obtaining heaven, and to make good his loss by gaining from them a boon for teaching them the proper recitation on the sixth day. He did so, but, when he was taking possession of the thousand cattle which the Aṅgirases gave as the reward, a man in black raiment (Rudra) claimed the prize to be his own, declaring that whatever

## PLATE VII

### Kāla-Śiva

Śiva is represented in his dread aspect of Kāla ("Time" or "Death"). From a sculpture at Prambanān, Java. After a photograph in the Museum of Fine Arts, Boston.

was left on the place of offering belonged to him. Nābhānediṣṭha returned to his father, only to be told that the claim was just, though he was also advised how to obtain an abandonment of it in its full extent. Moreover, as we have seen, it was Rudra who was created from the dread forms of the gods in order to punish Prajāpati when he sinned against the laws of moral order. Even the gods fear him; as Mahādeva he destroys cattle; and he has wide-mouthed, howling dogs who swallow their prey unchewed. He is conceived as separated from the other gods, and at the end of the sacrifice offering of the remnants is made to him, while his hosts receive the entrails of the victim. The *Atharvaveda* attributes to him as weapons fever, headache, cough, and poison, although it does not identify him with these diseases. He seems most dangerous at the end of the summer, when the rains are about to set in and when the sudden change of season is most perilous to man and to beast. It cannot be said, however, that there is any substantial change in the character of the god from the presentation of it in the *Ṛgveda*, except that his dreadful aspect is now far more exaggerated. It is certainly not yet possible to hold that a new deity has been introduced into the conception of Rudra, whose close association with Agni is asserted at every turn, Rudra being the fire in its dread form.

In the *Yajurveda* we find that Rudra has a sister, Ambikā, and we have the assurance of the *Śatapatha Brāhmaṇa* (II. vi. 2. 9) that the name was due to the fact that he is called Tryambaka ("Three-Eyed"). It is not until the last period of the texts of the *Brāhmaṇas* (*Kena Upaniṣad*, iii. 25) that we find Umā Haimavatī, who is the wife of Śiva in the later tradition; while in the *Taittirīya Āraṇyaka*, which is still later, we find Ambikā as a wife, not as a sister, and other names, such as Durgā and Pārvatī. This, however, is merely another sign — one of many — of the contemporaneity of the later portions of the Vedic literature with the development of the epic mythology, so that in the *Āśvalāyana Śrauta Sūtra* (IV.

viii. 19) we find added to Rudra's names those of Śiva, Śaṅkara, Hara, and Mṛda, all appellatives of Śiva.

In addition to the strong evolution of monotheistic tendencies in the shape of the worship of these three great divinities, we must note the definite setting up of the Asuras as enemies to the gods. This trend is a marked change from the point of view of the *Ṛgveda*, where the term "Asura" normally applies to the gods themselves and where the conflict of the demons and the gods takes the form of struggles between individual Asuras and gods rather than between the host of the Asuras and the gods, both sprung from Prajāpati, as the *Brāhmaṇas* often declare. In this phenomenon, coupled with the fact that the Iranians treated *daēva*, the word corresponding to the Vedic *deva*, "god," as meaning "devil," it is natural to see a result of hostile relations between the Iranian reformed faith of Zoroaster and the older Vedic belief; but the suggestion is inseparably bound up with the further question whether or not the *Ṛgveda* and the *Brāhmaṇas* show traces of close connexion with Iran. In support of the theory may be adduced the fact that the Kavis who are popular in Indian literature are heretics in the Avesta; while, on the other hand, Kāvya Uśanas, who is the *purohita* of the Asuras in the *Pañcaviṁśa Brāhmaṇa* (VII. v. 20), is famed as Kavi Usan, or Kai Kāūs, in Iran.[1] Other Asuras with names possibly borrowed from Iran are Śaṇḍa and Marka (with whom is compared the Avestan *mahrka*, "death"), Prahrāda Kāyādhava, and Sṛma; but the evidence is much too feeble to afford any positive conclusion, and the other explanation of natural development of meaning in both countries is possible enough, for in the Veda *Asura* is specially connected with the word *māyā*, "power of illusion," and may well have denoted one of magic, uncanny power, a sense which would easily lead to an unfavourable meaning. The degradation of Asuras from gods to demons was doubtless helped by the apparent form of the word as a negative of *sura*, from the base *svar*, denoting "light," for by the time of the *Upaniṣads* we meet the word *sura* denoting "a god," derived by this popular etymology from *asura*, which is really connected with *asu*, "breath."

As regards the individual gods we find a clear change in the conception of Varuṇa, who, with Mitra, is now equated in several places with the night and the day respectively. Moreover in the *Atharvaveda* and the *Brāhmaṇas* there is a distinct tendency to bring Varuṇa into close connexion with the waters, who are his wives, in whom he is said to dwell, and to whom he is related as Soma to the mountains. His power of punishing the sinner, furthermore, becomes especially prominent in the final bath which terminates the sacrificial ceremony as a normal rule and by which the sacrificers release themselves from Varuṇa's noose. At the horse sacrifice this bath takes the peculiar form that a man is driven deep into the water and then banished as a scapegoat; and, since the appearance of the scapegoat is to be similar to that of the god, we learn that Varuṇa was in this connexion conceived as bald-headed, white, yellow-eyed, and leprous. The one festival which is specially his, the Varuṇapraghāsa, is again one of expiation of sin. Yet in his relation to the sacrifice Varuṇa does not appear in any of the moral splendour of the *Ṛgveda*, and he is manifestly tending, as in the epic, to sink to the level of a god of the waters, without special ethical quality.

In the other Ādityas there is little change; but the number is now usually either eight or (more often) twelve, which is to be final for later times, when the term is not as often used generically in a sense wide enough to cover all the gods, a use which leads to the epic view that every deity is a child of Aditi. One enumeration of eight gives Varuṇa, Mitra, Aryaman, Bhaga, Aṁśa, Dhātṛ, Indra, and Vivasvant. The introduction of Indra is interesting, and the *Maitrāyaṇī Saṁhitā* (II. i. 12) makes him a son of Aditi, but the connexion is not insisted upon. Mitra decidedly recedes even from the small place which he holds in the *Ṛgveda*, perhaps in accordance with

Varuṇa's loss of position. Aryaman's nature as a wooer and prototype of wooers is frequently mentioned, and two Aryamans occur in one phrase which may suggest a close alliance with Bhaga, whose character as the deity who gives good fortune seems to be definitely implied in a legend of the *Śatapatha Brāhmaṇa* (I. vii. 4. 6), according to which he is blind. Aṁśa and Dakṣa almost disappear, although the latter is once identified with Prajāpati, and the gods bear the epithet "having Dakṣa for father," where his purely abstract character is clearly seen. Vivasvant, who is several times called an Āditya, is said to be the father of men.

From the *Atharvaveda* onward there is a distinct development of Sūrya as the sun-god *par excellence*, whether under that name or under that of Āditya; and the *Aitareya Brāhmaṇa* (iii. 44) explains that there is no real rising or setting of the sun, for it always shines, though it reverses its sides, so that the shining one is now turned to and now from the earth, whence comes the discrepancy of day and night. The same *Brāhmaṇa* is responsible for the view that the distance between the earth and the heaven is that of a thousand days' journey by horse, while the *Pañcaviṁśa Brāhmaṇa* reduces it to the height of a thousand cows standing one on top of another, a mode of reckoning which has modern parallels. Naturally enough, with the growth of importance of Sūrya as such Savitṛ tends more and more to become the god of instigation, and his solar character is not marked. Pūṣan is quite often mentioned, but his nature is not appreciably altered.

Of the other denizens of the skies Dyaus is more evanescent than ever, but Dyāvāpṛthivī occupy a fair place in the ritual and receive frequent shares in the offering. Uṣas steadily diminishes in importance, thus continuing a devolution which had begun in the *Ṛgveda* itself, and no new mythology is made regarding her. On the other hand, the Aśvins are popular gods, and the references to their activity in the *Ṛgveda* are supplemented by further details, the most remarkable of these stories being that of the rejuvenating of Cyavana, which is told in the *Jaiminīya Brāhmaṇa* and elsewhere. The account of the *Śatapatha* (IV. i. 5) is that when the Bhṛgus or Aṅgirases went to heaven, Cyavana was left behind, old and decrepit. Śaryāta Mānava came to his place of abode, and the youths of the tribe mocked the old man, who in revenge brought discord among the clan; but, when Śaryāta learned this, he propitiated the seer by the gift of his daughter Sukaṇyā and hastily departed to avoid further chance of discord. The Aśvins, however, wandering among men, came upon Sukanyā, and after seeking to win her love, agreed to make her husband young again if she would tell them of a defect which she alleged in them. They made Cyavana bathe in a pool whence he emerged with the age desired, and in return she told them that they were incomplete because the gods shut them out from the sacrifice. They accordingly went to the deities, and by restoring the head of the sacrifice obtained a share in it. The reason for their exclusion from the sacrifice is interesting and is given repeatedly: they wandered too much among men to be pure, a sign of the growing decline of the physician's standing as a member of the highest class. Though the Aśvins share in the soma, the special offerings in their honour are *surā* (a kind of brandy) and honey, and the *Āśvina Śastra*, which is sung to them in the Atirātra form of the Soma sacrifice, is recited by the priest in the posture of a flying bird.

Of the gods of the atmosphere Indra is still in the height of his power and develops an elaborate mythology in which the old motives are rehandled. Of the new stories regarding him the most noteworthy is that of his struggle with Tvaṣṭṛ's son Viśvarūpa, whom he slew, and with Vṛtra, who was created by Tvaṣṭṛ from the remains of the soma left undrunk by Indra. Viśvarūpa's avenger became very powerful and mastered Agni and Soma, all sciences, all fame, and prosperity; and gods, men, and fathers brought him food. But Indra attacked Vṛtra, and having obtained the aid of Agni and Soma by the promise of a share in the cake at the sacrifice, he vanquished Vṛtra, who apparently then became his food. The story of the death of Viśvarūpa, the three-headed son of Tvaṣṭṛ, is variously told, but it is clear that Indra was afraid that this demon was likely to betray the gods to the Asuras, whence he cut off his three heads, which turned into different birds. Nevertheless by this act Indra had been guilty of the sin of slaying a Brāhman, and, since all beings cried out upon him for his deed, he besought the earth, trees, and women, each of which took to themselves a third of the blood-stain which had fallen on the deity. The slaying of Tvaṣṭṛ's son, however, is only one of the sins of Indra known to the *Brāhmaṇas:* it is said that he insulted his teacher Bṛhaspati; gave over the Yatis, who are traditionally sages, to the hyenas; and slew the Arurmaghas or Arunmukhas, of whom no further data are recorded. For these sins, according to the *Aitareya Brāhmaṇa* (vi. 28), he was excluded by the gods from the soma, and with him the whole of the warrior race; but later he managed to secure the soma for himself by stealing it from Tvaṣṭṛ, though, if we may believe one account, he paid dearly for the theft by being seriously affected by the drink and requiring to be cured by the *Sautrāmaṇī* rite.

Other new features of the Indra myth are the prominent parts played by other gods in the conflict with Vṛtra: the appearance of Agni and Soma as helpers is paralleled by the stress laid on the aid of Viṣṇu or of the Maruts. Moreover we hear now of the consequences of his slaying of the dragon, which is no longer regarded merely as a triumph. Indra himself flees to the farthest distance, thinking that he has failed to lay his opponent low, and all his strength passes from him and enters the water, the trees, the plants, and the earth; or, again, he feels that he has sinned in his action, which is parallel to his disgrace for slaying Viśvarūpa. All the gods save the Maruts abandon him at the decisive moment; and, when Vṛtra has been struck, it is Vāyu who is sent to see if he is really dead.

On the other hand, the figures of Trita Āptya, Apāṁ Napāt, Aja Ekapād, and Ahi Budhnya become fainter and fainter. Trita naturally leads to the invention of a legend according to which there were three brothers, Ekata, Dvita, and Trita, two of whom threw the third into a well. The gods of the wind also, Vāyu and Vāta, remain unchanged, but Mātariśvan assumes the distinct new feature of a wind-god pure and simple without trace of any connexion with the fire. Parjanya as the rain is still recognized just as he is in the Buddhist texts, and we find the importance of the waters duly acknowledged by the many spells of various kinds devised to secure rain, in one of which the colour black is used throughout to resemble the blackness of the clouds whence the rain must descend. In close association with the waters stand the frog, which is used in several cooling rites; the ants, who exact, in return for their action in gnawing the bow-string which cuts off the head of Viṣṇu, the privilege of finding water even in the desert; many plants; and the "Serpent of the Deep," Ahi Budhnya.

The *Śatarudriya* litanies show us the importance of the numerous Rudras, who must be propitiated no less than Rudra himself, and give them countless places of origin. They dwell on earth, as well as in the atmosphere and in the sky, and vex men on the roads and at sacred places, besides disturbing them in the platters from which they eat. The ritual of the householder provides that blood is to be offered to them in all four directions, and they are described sometimes as snakes and elsewhere as noisy eaters of raw flesh, etc. Despite their connexion with the great god, they are no more than imps and trolls, and it is no high honour for the Maruts to receive the same name as "the children of Rudra," as they are called even in the *Ṛgveda*. Besides their special association with Indra the Maruts now appear regularly as the subjects among the gods, quite like the Vaiśyas among men, and they are said to dwell in the *aśvattha*, or *Ficus religiosa*, which is the tree normally found in an Indian village enjoying the honour accorded in England to the oak. It may easily be that it was the kinship of these gods, as the common folk of heaven, to the Vaiśyas of the village that helped the theologians to locate them there, while the popular imagination could readily fancy that the storm-gods dwelt in the tree through which their winds would whistle in time of tempest.

Of the terrestrial divinities Soma has converted himself into a celestial deity by his definite identification with the moon, which begins in the latest hymns of the *Ṛgveda* and is quite common in the later Vedic literature; though of course the plant itself still remains sacred and in a sense is Soma, just as it was in the earlier period. There are few legends told regarding Soma which are of any interest, the most important being that which concerns the buying of it. It is an essential part of the ritual that the soma-plant should be represented as bought; but that the seller should be reprobated, and his price afterward even taken away from him. In this has been seen a representation, one of the beginnings of Indian drama, of the obtaining of the soma from the Gandharvas who, in the *Yajurveda*, guard it. The price is a cow, which is, therefore, called the soma-purchase cow, but in the *Brāhmaṇas* it appears that Vāc ("Speech") was the price with which the gods bought the soma from the Asuras in days gone by, when she lived with the Asuras, and that the cow is the modern representative of Vāc. The reason why the gods had to purchase soma with Vāc was that the Gandharvas were fond of women and would, therefore, prefer a woman as a price; but the divinities parted with Vāc only on the distinct secret agreement that when they desired her she would return again, and she did so. Hence in this world it is legitimate to repurchase the cow paid for the soma, though normally a cow so given could not be taken back again. It may be that the legend contains some faint indication that it was necessary to buy the plant from the hill tribes among whom it grew. But if Soma is the moon, the moon and Soma also are identified in whole or in part with the demon Vṛtra: in one passage (I. vi. 3. 17) the *Śatapatha Brāhmaṇa* divides the dead Vṛtra into two parts, one of which goes to make the moon, and the other (the belly) to trouble mankind. The conception is also found in the *Maitrāyaṇī Saṁhitā* (II. vii. 8), and it is clear proof that terror of the moon was not unknown to the Indians of the Vedic period. The moon as Candramas often appears with the sun, and the *Aitareya Brāhmaṇa* (viii. 24) — though in a passage which may be a priestly fiction rather than a genuine belief — states that the moon is born from the sun. A more important conception, which figures largely in the eschatology of the *Upaniṣads*, is that the sun is the light of the gods and the moon the light of the fathers, from which it is an easy step to the doctrine that the righteous dead dwell especially in the moon. On the other hand, in its more primitive sense Soma still figures as the heavenly drink in the story of his descent to earth, which is now attributed to the Gāyatrī metre; and since this metre is used at the morning pressing of the soma and is closely associated with Agni, we thus have a variant of the legend which is seen in the *Ṛgveda* (iv. 27) when Soma is brought down by the eagle. The Gāyatrī is shot at by the archer who guards the soma, and a nail of her left foot, being cut off, becomes a porcupine, while the goat is born of the fat that drips from the wound. The other metres, Jagatī and Triṣṭubh, failed in the effort to obtain the soma, being wearied by the long flight to heaven.

Agni does not change his essential features in the later Vedic period, but his character is more fully set out. Thus while the *Ṛgveda* mentions only one of the three fires, the Gārhapatya, the later texts name also the Āhavanīya and the Dakṣiṇāgni; and the three are brought into conjunction with the earth, the sky, and the atmosphere respectively, besides being associated with the three categories of men, gods, and fathers, and with Agni, Sūrya, and Vāyu. It is a question how far in these equations we have to see mere priestly schematism: it has been suggested that in the connexion, which is thus shown, of the fathers and the wind (Vāyu) we have a trace of the conception (which is certainly not the normal one of this period) that the fathers live in the wind; and the Narāśaṁsa has been regarded as a name of the fire for the fathers. The fire naturally and inevitably serves to show the establishment of Aryan civilization, and a famous story of the eastward movement of the Aryans in the *Śatapatha Brāhmaṇa* (I. iv. 1) tells of the fire which Videgha Māthava [2] and Gotama Rāhūgaṇa followed and which introduced the Aryan beliefs into new lands. Yet the *Brāhmaṇas* show no trace of any evolution of a public as opposed to a private fire of the king. There is, however, a new development of Agni, for his numerous aspects are frequently described by epithets, such as "Lord of Vows," "Desire," or "the Pure"; and the ritual prescribes different offerings to these several sides of his nature. This fact lends plausibility to the view that the origin of Bṛhaspati ("Lord of Devotion") lies in a feature of Agni which was developed more completely into an independent deity. Bṛhaspati himself assumes in this period two of his later characteristics. He is declared to be "Lord of the Metres," and also "Lord of Speech" (Vācaspati), which is his prominent aspect in post-Vedic literature, and he becomes the deity of the constellation Tiṣya; while in post-Vedic literature he is the regent of the planet Jupiter, although the suggestion that he is himself a planet is inadmissible.[3] The worship of the planets does not appear for certain in any Vedic text, and is clearly set forth for the first time in the law-book of Yājñavalkya in the third century A.D.

Though there is no real increase in the position of the goddesses in this period, the wives of the gods obtain a definite part in the ritual. Some importance attaches to Iḍā, the deity of the oblation, who is described as the daughter of Manu, with whom he re-created the world after the deluge, although she also passes as the child of Mitra and Varuṇa. Aditi loses anything of mystery which may have been hers in the *Ṛgveda* and is constantly identified with the cow at the sacrifice. Sarasvatī appears as in the *Ṛgveda*, and sacrifices on the banks of the Sarasvatī of special holiness are mentioned in the *Brāhmaṇas* and described at length in the ritual texts. She is also seen, however, in a new light: when Indra is compelled to resort to the Sautrāmaṇī to be cured from the ill effects of drinking soma, she, together with the Aśvins, aids his recovery; and the fact that her instrument was speech seems to have given rise to her identity with Vāc ("Speech"), as asserted by the *Brāhmaṇas*, as well as to her later elevation to the rank of a goddess of learning and culture. The prominence of the moon in the mythology of the time may explain the appearance of the names Anumati and Rākā, Sinīvālī and Kuhū as the deities presiding over the two days of full and new moon respectively.

Of the gods who may be called personifications of abstractions Tvaṣṭṛ remains active as the creator of the forms of beings and the causer of the mating of animals. His chief feature is his enmity with Indra, who steals the soma when Tvaṣṭṛ seeks to exclude him from it and slays his son Viśvarūpa of the three heads, who has been interpreted (though with little likelihood) as the moon, but who seems to be no more than proof of the cunning of Tvaṣṭṛ's workmanship. His creation of Vṛtra for vengeance on Indra is likewise a failure. His ultimate fate, as shown by the *Kauśika Sūtra*, is to be merged in the more comprehensive personality of Prajāpati, and the same doom befalls Dhātṛ, Viśvakarman, and Hiraṇyagarbha. The *Atharvaveda*, with that curious mixture of theosophy and magic which characterizes it, creates some new gods, such as Rohita ("the Sun"), Kāla ("Time"), Skambha (the "Support" which Prajāpati used for fashioning the world), Prāṇa ("Breath"), the Vrātya (possibly Rudra under the guise of non-Brāhmanical Aryans), and others. The really important figures thus created, however, are Kāma and Śrī. The former, "Desire," perhaps has its origin in the cosmogonic hymn of the *Ṛgveda* (x. 129) where Desire is said to be the first seed of Mind. This god has arrows, and though he is a cosmic power, he is to reappear as a lesser god in a *Sūtra* and in the epic period. The other deity is Śrī ("Prosperity"), who, as we know from the Buddhist sculptures, was a prominent divinity in the following age.

It is a natural sign of growing formalism that the gods should now be grouped in classes: the eight Vasus (now in connexion with Agni, not with Indra), the eleven Rudras, and the twelve Ādityas, corresponding to earth, air, and sky respectively. The *Chāndogya Upaniṣad* shows a further progress in adding two new groups — the Maruts with Soma, and the Sādhyas with Brahman. The Maruts are now usually distinguished from the Rudras, although they are still connected with them.

When we pass to the minor deities of the period of the *Brāhmaṇas*, we find a certain development clearly marked in the case of the Gandharvas and the Apsarases. The solitary Gandharva, who is only thrice made plural in the *Ṛgveda*, is now regularly transformed into a body of beings who can be placed together with the gods, the fathers, and the Asuras. Viśvāvasu, however, is still frequently mentioned, and appears to have been conceived as one of the chief guardians of the soma, by whom, indeed, in one account he was stolen. Soma is, therefore, besought to elude him in the form of an eagle in the *Taittirīya Saṁhitā* (I. ii. 9. 1), and the *Taittirīya Āraṇyaka* (I. ix. 3) tells us that Kṛśānu, the archer who shot at the eagle which carried the soma to earth, was a Gandharva. Yet in one account the gods succeed in buying the soma from the Gandharvas by means of Vāc, for the Gandharvas are lovers of women; with the Apsarases they preside over fertility, and those who desire offspring pray to them. The *Atharvaveda* declares them to be shaggy and half animal in form, though elsewhere they are called beautiful. The Apsarases now appear in constant conjunction with water, both in rivers, clouds, lightning, and stars; while the *Śatapatha Brāhmaṇa* describes them as transforming themselves into aquatic birds. Yet they have other associations also. They inhabit trees, especially the banyans and the sacred fig-tree, in which their lutes and cymbals resound; the Gandharvas live with them in these and other trees of the fig kind and are asked to bless a wedding procession as it passes them. Dance, song, play, and dicing are their sports; but they have a terrible side also, for they cause madness, so that magic is used against them.

But though the Apsarases are especially the loves of the Gandharvas, they can be won by mortal man, and among other names which are famous later are mentioned Menakā, Śakuntalā (from whom sprang the Bhārata race), and Urvaśī. The union of the latter with Purūravas is told in the *Śatapatha Brāhmaṇa* (XI. v. 1). She married him solely on the condition that she should never see him naked; but the Gandharvas, envying the mortal the enjoyment of her society, devised a stratagem which made Purūravas spring from his couch beside Urvaśī in such haste that he deemed it delay that he should put his mantle round him. Urvaśī sees him illuminated in a flash of lightning and vanishes; but he seeks her all over the earth — a theme which is developed in detail in Kālidāsa's famous drama — and finds her at last swimming in a lotus lake with other Apsarases in swan-shape. Urvaśī reveals herself to him and consents to receive him for one night a year later; and when he returns at the appointed time, he learns from her how to secure from the Gandharvas the secret of ritual by which he himself becomes one of their number.

The Ṛbhus show no such change of nature; and though they are more clearly brought into connexion with the Ṛtus, or Seasons, than in the *Ṛgveda*, they are still regarded as being not really of pure divinity, but akin to mankind, and as receiving only with difficulty a share in the draughts of soma which are reserved for the gods proper. On the other hand, we have, especially in the *Sūtras* which represent the last stage of the Vedic religion, constant references to many other minor spirits, of whom Vāstoṣpati ("the Lord of the House"), Kṣetrasya Pati ("the Lord of the Field") Sītā ("the Furrow"), and Urvarā ("the Ploughed Field") are the natural divinities of a villager. Yet the place of plants and trees is still very slight, though the *Atharvaveda* uses plants freely for medicinal and magic purposes and ascribes a divine character to them, and the blessing of trees is, as we have seen, sought in the marriage ritual, while offerings are made both to trees and to plants. In the Buddhist scriptures and stories special prominence is, on the other hand, given to tales of divinities of plants, trees, and forest. A distinct innovation is the direct worship of serpents, who are classified as belonging to earth, sky, and atmosphere, and who doubtless now include real reptiles as well as the snake or dragon of the atmosphere, which is found in the *Ṛgveda.* The danger from snakes in India is sufficient to explain the rise of the new side of the ritual: the offerings made to them, often of blood, are to propitiate them and reduce their destructive power, and Buddhism is also supplied with charms against them. Isolated in comparison with the references to the snakes are those to other vermin, such as worms or the king of the mice or ants, all of which occasionally receive offerings. A serpent-queen appears as early as the *Brāhmaṇas* and is naturally enough identified by speculation with the earth, which is the home of the snakes. Not until the *Āśvalāyana Gṛhya Sūtra* (II. iv. 1), however, do we hear in the Vedic religion of the Nāgas ("Serpents"), who are prominent in the epic. A new form of being in the shape of the man-tiger is also found, but not the man-lion. The boar is mentioned in cosmogonic myths as the form assumed by Prajāpati, who is also brought into conjunction with the tortoise as the lord of the waters. The cow is now definitely divine and is worshipped, but she is also regarded as identical with Aditi and Iḍā. Tārkṣya, the sun-horse, is named here and there, and Ariṣṭanemi, who occurs in connexion with him, is a precursor of Ariṣṭanemi as one of the Tīrthakaras of the Jains.

Many other spirits of dubious character and origin are also found, among whom Nirṛti ("Decease") is the most prominent: sacrifice is frequently made to her, and black is the colour appropriate for use in such offerings; while dice, women, and sleep, as evil things, are brought into association with her. At the royal consecration the wife who has been degraded in position is regarded as her representative, and in the house of such a woman the offering to Nirṛti is made. Other deities are much less important and appear chiefly in the *Sūtras*, which show their connexion with the life of the people. Thus the *Śāṅkhāyana Gṛhya Sūtra* (ii. 14) describes an offering which, besides the leading gods, enumerates such persons as Dhātṛ, Vidhātṛ, Bharata, Sarvānnabhūti, Dhanapati, Śrī, the night-walkers, and the day-walkers. The *Kauśika Sūtra* (lvi. 13) names Udaṅkya, Śūlvāṇa, Śatruṁjaya, Kṣātrāṇa, Mārtyuṁjaya, Mārtyava, Aghora, Takṣaka, Vaiśāleya, Hāhāhūhū, two Gandharvas, and others. The "Furrow," Sītā, is replaced by the four, Sītā, Āśā, Araḍā, Anaghā; and so on. We even find the names of Kubera,[4] the later lord of wealth, and Vāsuki, the later king of snakes, but only in *Sūtras* and, therefore, in a period later than that of the *Brāhmaṇas* proper. They serve, however, to show how full of semi-divine figures was the ordinary life of the people, who saw a deity in each possible form of action. Naturally, too, they regarded as divine the plough and the ploughshare and the drum, just as in the *Ṛgveda*, and the ritual is full of the use of symbols, such as the wheel of the sun, the gold plate which represents the sun, and the like.

In the world of demons the chief change in the *Brāhmaṇas* is the formal separation of Asuras and gods. Vṛtra, whose legend is developed, remains the chief Asura; but the story of Namuci is also elaborated, stress being laid on the use of lead in the ritual, apparently to represent the weapon (the foam of the sea) with which Indra destroyed him when he had undertaken to slay him neither with wet nor with dry. The myth of

Vala is distinctly thrust to the background, though the epic constantly celebrates the slayer of Vala and Vṛtra; Śuṣṇa now appears as a Dānava who was in possession of the soma. The Rakṣases are the more prominent fiends: they are dangerous to women during pregnancy; in the shape of dog or ape they attack women; they prowl round the bride at the wedding, so that little staves are shot at their eyes. Often, though human in figure, they are deformed, three-headed, five-footed, four-eyed, fingerless, bear-necked, and with horns on their hands. They are both male and female; they have kings and are mortal. They enter man by the mouth when he is eating or drinking; they cause madness; they surround houses at night, braying like donkeys, laughing aloud, and drinking out of skulls. They eat the flesh of men and horses and drink the milk of cows by their magic power as *yātudhānas*, or wizards. Their time is the coming of night, especially at the dark period of new moon; but in the east they have no power, for the rising sun dispels them. The Piśācas are now added to the numbers of demons as a regular tribe: they eat the corpses of the dead; they make the living waste away and dwell in the water of the villages. Magic is used both against Piśācas and against Rakṣases, the latter of whom are especial enemies of the sacrifice, and against whom magic circles, fire, and imprecations of all kinds are employed. More abstract are the Arātis, or personifications of illiberality. Other spirits, like Arbudi in the *Atharvaveda*, can be made to help against an enemy in battle. A few individual names of demons are new, and although Makha, Araru, Śaṇḍa, and Marka (the Asuras' *purohitas*) are all ancient, a vast number are added by the *Gṛhya Sūtras* — Upavīra, Śauṇḍikeya, Ulūkhala, Malimluca, Droṇāsa, Cyavana, Ālikhant, Animiṣa, Kiṁvadanta, Upaśruti, Haryakṣa, Kumbhin, Kūrkura, and so forth. None of these has individual character: the spirits of evil which surround human beings at every moment, and particularly at times like marriage, child-birth, the leaving of a spiritual teacher, sickness, and disease, are of innumerable names and forms, and the prudent man mentions all he can.

The sages of the *Ṛgveda* are, on the whole, treated more and more as mere men in subsequent literature and their mythology shows little development. Nevertheless, Manu, the son of Vivasvant, who is the hero of the tale of the deluge, is a prominent figure throughout the entire period. One day, as he was washing his hands, a small fish happened to be in the water, and at its request he spared its life in return for a promise to save him in the flood which the fish predicted. In due course the fish which Manu carefully brought up, first in a vessel and then in a trench, grew great and was allowed to go back to the sea, after warning its benefactor to build himself a ship. In course of time the flood came, and Manu made a ship which the fish dragged until it rested on the northern mountain, whereupon the flood gradually subsided, and Manu, going down from the heights, with Iḍā, the personification of the sacrifice, renewed the human race. Manu now counts also as the first lawgiver, for whatever he said was, we are told, medicine. Atri likewise remains famous for his conflict with the Asura Svarbhānu who eclipses the sun, while the Aṅgirases and the Ādityas are distinguished by their ritual disputes, in which, however, the Ādityas win the day and first attain heaven.

In the world of the dead Yama is still king, and we hear of his golden-eyed and iron-hoofed steeds; but he is also duplicated or triplicated by the abstract forms of Antaka ("the Ender"), Mṛtyu ("Death"), and Nirṛti ("Decease"), which are placed beside him; and Mṛtyu becomes his messenger. The heaven in which the virtuous dead rest is depicted in the same colours as in the *Ṛgveda:* it is made clear that in it men reunite with wives and children, and that abundance of joy reigns there. Streams of ghee, milk, honey, and wine abound; and bright, many-coloured cows yield all desires. There are neither rich nor poor, powerful nor downtrodden; and the joys of the blest are a hundred times greater than the joys of earth. Those who sacrifice properly are rewarded by unity with and identity of abode with the sun, Agni, Vāyu, Indra, Varuṇa, Bṛhaspati, Prajāpati, and Brahmā, though this identification is common only in the later *Brāhmaṇas*. On the other hand, we hear now of hell: the *Atharvaveda* tells of it as the Nāraka Loka (in contrast with the Svarga Loka, the place of Yama), the abode of female goblins and sorceresses, the place of blind or black darkness. It is described in slight detail in its horror in that Veda (v. 19) and fully in the *Śatapatha Brāhmaṇa* (XI. vi. 1), where Bhṛgu, son of Varuṇa, sees a vision of men cutting up men and men eating men. The same idea, which is clearly one of retribution in the next world for actions in this, is paralleled in the *Kauṣītaki Brāhmaṇa* (xi. 3), where we learn that the animals which man eats in this world will devour him in yonder world if he has not a certain saving knowledge, though how the reward or the penalty is accorded does not clearly appear. The *Śatapatha Brāhmaṇa* (VI. ii. 2. 27; X. vi. 3. 1) holds that all are born again in the next world and are rewarded according to their deeds, whether good or bad; but no statement is made as to who is to decide the quality of the acts. In the *Taittirīya Āraṇyaka* (VI. v. 16) the good and the untruthful are said to be separated before Yama, though there is no suggestion that he acts as judge; but the *Śatapatha* (XI. ii. 7. 33) introduces another mode of testing, namely, weighing in a balance, though by whom the man is weighed is not declared. Possibly this is a reference to some kind of ordeal.

In the *Upaniṣads* and in the legal text-books we find a new conception — that of rebirth after death in the present, not in yonder, world. It has no clear predecessor in the *Brāhmaṇas* proper, but it is hinted at in the doctrine of the later *Brāhmaṇas* that after death a man may yet die over and over again, from which the doctrine of metempsychosis is an easy step; while a further idea, also with some amount of preparation in the *Śatapatha Brāhmaṇa*, regards the man who attains true

(a)

# PLATE VIII

## A AND B

## TORTURES OF HELL

Yudhiṣṭhira, the only one of the Pāṇḍavas to attain alive to heaven, was submitted to a final test before being permitted to join his brothers and the other heroes of old. Through illusion he was caused to see the tortures of the damned, for "hell must necessarily be seen by all kings" (*Mahābhārata*, xviii. 27 ff.). Passing through the repellent horrors of decay, Yudhiṣṭhira stands aghast at the torments which he beholds. Christian influence is evident in the use of crucifixion as a punishment, and also in the figure of the hero's guide, the messenger of the gods. From a painting in the Jaipur manuscript of the *Razmnāmah* (a Persian abridgement of the *Mahābhārata*). After Hendley, *Memorials of the Jeypore Exhibition*, iv, Plates CXXXII, CXXXIII.

(b)

knowledge of the nature of the Absolute as thereby winning freedom from rebirth, and union at death with the Absolute. These teachings are mingled in the *Upaniṣads* with the older tenet of recompense in heaven and hell, and a conglomerate is evoked which presents itself in the shape that those souls which do not attain full illumination (or even all souls) go after death to the moon, whence some proceed eventually to Brahmā, while others are requited in the moon and then are born again, thus undergoing in each case a double reward. One version, that of the *Bṛhadāraṇyaka Upaniṣad* (vi. 2), refers to the existence of a third place for the evil. Later this is rendered needless by the conception that the rebirth is into a good or a bad form, as a Brāhman, warrior, or householder, or as a dog, pig, or Cāṇḍāla (member of the lowest caste). The third place mentioned in the *Chāndogya Upaniṣad* (v. 10) now becomes entirely meaningless, but that does not prevent its retention. A new effort to unite all the views is presented by the *Kauṣītaki Upaniṣad* (i. 2), which sends all souls to the moon and then allows some to go by the path of the gods to Brahmā; while the others, who have been proved wanting, return to earth in such form as befits their merit, either as a worm, or fly, or fish, or bird, or lion, or boar, or tiger, or serpent, or man, or something else. The law-books show the same mixture of ideas, for, while heaven and hell are often referred to as reward and punishment, they also allude to the fact of rebirth. The intention is that a man first enjoys a reward for his action in heaven, and then, since he must be reborn, he is reincarnated in a comparatively favourable position; while in the other instance after punishment in hell he is further penalized by being born in a low form of life.

The fathers with Yama are, no doubt, conceived as in heaven, but we hear also of fathers in the earth, atmosphere, and sky, and various classes are known, such as the Ūmas, Ūrvas, and Kāvyas. The belief that the fathers are to be found in all three worlds is natural enough as regards earth and heaven, and the souls of the dead in other mythologies are often connected with the winds. In the Veda the only other reference to this which presents itself is the possibility that the Maruts may be the souls of the dead, regarded as riding in the storm-winds, but for this there is no clear evidence. A group of the fathers, the "Seven Seers," is identified with the stars of the Bear, doubtless for no better reason than the similarity of *ṛṣi*, "seer," and *ṛkṣa*, "bear," although from time to time the idea occurs that the souls of the pious are the stars in heaven.

# CHAPTER IV

## THE GREAT GODS OF THE EPIC

IN the epic we find in developed and elaborate form a conception which is entirely or at least mainly lacking in the Vedic period, a doctrine of ages of the world which has both striking points of contrast with and affinity to the idea of the four ages set forth in Hesiod. In the Greek version, however, the four ages are naïvely and simply considered as accounting for all time,[1] while in the Indian they are only the form in which the Absolute reveals itself, this revelation being followed by a period of reabsorption, after which the ages again come into being. In the process of evolution the first, or Kṛta, age is preceded by a dawn of four hundred years and closes in a twilight of equal duration, while its own length is four thousand years.[2] This is the golden age of the world, in which all is perfect. Neither gods nor demons of any kind yet exist, and sacrifices are unknown, even bloodless offerings. The Vedas themselves have no existence, and all human infirmities, such as disease, pride, hatred, and lack of mental power, are absent. None the less, the four castes — the priest, the warrior, the husbandman, and the serf — come into being with their special marks and characteristics, though this differentiation is modified by the fact that they have but one god to worship, one Veda to follow, and one rule. In this age men do not seek the fruit of action, and accordingly they are rewarded by obtaining salvation through absorption in the absolute. On the twilight of the Kṛta age follows the dawn of the Tretā, which lasts for three hundred years, while the age itself continues three thousand and ends in a twilight of three hundred years. In

Fig. 2. The Churning of the Ocean

The gods (Śiva, Viṣṇu, and Brahmā) stand to the left of Mount Mandara, which rests on a tortoise (Viṣṇu himself in his Kūrma, or Tortoise, avatar); to the right are the demons; and with the serpent Vāsuki as the cord the two opposing sides twirl the mountain to churn the ambrosia from the ocean of milk. In the lower part of the picture are the various "gems" incidentally won in gaining the *amṛta*. After Moor, *Hindu Pantheon*, Plate XLIX.

this epoch virtue declines by a quarter from its full perfection in the golden age. Sacrifices come into existence, and with sacrifices the attaining of salvation, not as before by mere meditation and renunciation, but by the positive actions of offering and generosity. Moreover, duty is still strictly performed, and asceticism is normally practised. In the next age, the Dvāpara, the bull of justice stands on two feet only, for another quarter of virtue has departed. The Vedas are multiplied to four, yet many men remain ignorant of them altogether or know but one or two or three. Ceremonies increase, and treatises on duty multiply, but disease and sin grow rife, and sacrifice and asceticism alike are performed not, as formerly, disinterestedly, but in hope of gain. It is in this age that the need for marriage laws first makes itself felt, and the dawn and twilight alike shrink to two hundred years, while the age itself is reduced to two thousand. A dawn of only a hundred years serves to introduce the Kali and worst of the ages, when virtue has but one leg to stand upon, when religion disappears, when the Vedas are ignored, when distress prevails, and when the confusion of the castes begins. But the age lasts only a thousand years, and its brief twilight of a hundred years is a prelude to the absorption of all in the Absolute Spirit. Seven suns appear in the heaven, and what they do not burn is consumed by Viṣṇu in the form of a great fire, the destruction being made complete by a flood. A new Kṛta age cannot commence to dawn before the lapse of a period equal to the thousandfold repetition of the total of the ages, that is, twelve million years. In this complete reabsorption the gods no less than men are involved, to be reborn again in the course of the ages.

The doctrine of the ages is only an emphatic assertion of the idea which underlies all the mythology of the epic, that the gods themselves are no longer independent eternal entities, but, however glorious and however honoured, are still, like man, subject to a stronger power. Indeed, in the epic the gods are chiefly conspicuous by reason of their impotence to intervene in the affairs of men: with the exception of Viṣṇu they can merely applaud the combatants and cannot aid or succour them, in strange contrast with the gods of Homer. There are real gods, however, as well as phantoms, and their existence is clearly revealed to us in the legend of the churning of the ambrosia which is preserved in the *Rāmāyaṇa* (i. 45; vii. 1) and, in a more confused and fragmentary form, in the *Mahābhārata.* The gods and Asuras were sprung from one father, Kaśyapa Mārīca, who married the daughters of Dakṣa Prajāpati, the gods being the children of Aditi, while the Asuras (the children of Diti) were the older. They lived in happiness in the Kṛta age, but being seized with the desire to attain immortality and freedom from old age and sickness, they decided that they should seek the ambrosia which was to be won by churning the milky ocean, and accordingly they set about this task by making the serpent Vāsuki the churning rope and Mount Mandara the churning stick. For a thousand years they churned, and the hundred heads of Vāsuki, spitting venom, bit the rocks, whence sprang the deadly poison called Hālāhala, which began to burn all creation, gods, men, and Asuras alike. They fled to Rudra, "the Lord of Cattle," "the Healer" (Śaṅkara), and at the request of Viṣṇu, who hailed him as chief of the gods, he drank the poison as though it were the ambrosia. The churning then proceeded, but Mount Mandara slipped into hell. To remedy the disaster Viṣṇu lay in the ocean with the mountain on his back, and Keśava proceeded to churn the ocean, grasping the top of Mandara with his hand. After a thousand years there appeared the skilled physician Dhanvantari, then the Apsarases, who were treated as common property by the gods and the Asuras, and next Varuṇa's daughter, Surā, whom the sons of Aditi married, thus attaining the name of Sura, while those of Diti declined to marry, whence their name of Asura (here popularly etymologized as "Without Surā"). Then came out the best of horses,

Uccaiḥśravas, and the pearl of gems, Kaustubha, and the ambrosia itself. But over it strife arose between the half-brothers, so that in the end Viṣṇu by his magic power (*māyā*) secured the victory of the gods and bestowed upon Indra the sovereignty of the three worlds.

Such in essence is the attitude of the epic to the Vedic gods, who appear as feeble creatures, unable to overpower the Asuras or to effect their purpose of winning immortality by the use of the ambrosia until they are aided by Śiva and Viṣṇu, though in the genealogy these two are no more divine than the others. Indra himself who, as the god of the warrior, might have been expected to retain some degree of real authority, can hold his position only by the favour of Viṣṇu and can exercise his shadowy sway merely as a vicegerent. Beside Śiva and Viṣṇu no Vedic god takes equal rank, and the only power which can for a moment be compared with these two deities is Brahmā, the personal form of the absolute Brahman, a god, that is to say, of priestly origin and one who could never have any real hold on the mythological instinct. Viṣṇu and Śiva, on the contrary, were too real and popular to sink into the deities of priestly speculation, and round them gathers an evergrowing body of tales.

It is characteristic of the feeble personality of Brahmā that he finds a connexion with the classes of the gods only through identification with Tvaṣṭṛ, who counts as one of the twelve Ādityas, the narrower group of the children of Aditi and Kaśyapa Prajāpati. In reality, however, he is a personification of the abstract Absolute which is often described in the *Mahābhārata*. It is eternal, self-existing, invisible, unborn, unchanging, imperishable, without beginning or end; from it all is sprung, and it is embodied in the whole universe; yet in itself it has no characteristics, no qualities, and no contrasts. As all springs from it, so into it all is resolved at the end of the four ages. Thus it can be identified with Time and with Death, both of which, like itself, absorb all things and bring them to nothingness. Into the Brahman the individual self may be resolved when it casts aside even the apprehension of its own identity with the Brahman, abandons all resolves of body or mind, and frees itself from every attachment to objects of sense. When a man withdraws all his desires as a tortoise all its limbs, then the self sees the self in itself; when a man fears no one and, when none fear him, when he desires nothing and has no hatred, then he attains the Absolute. Personified as Brahmā, the Absolute appears as a creator, as Prajāpati, the maker of the worlds, the grandfather of the worlds. He creates the gods, seers, fathers, and men, the worlds, rivers, oceans, rocks, trees, etc. In other passages he created first the Brāhmans called Prajāpatis — endowed with radiance like the sun — truth, law, penance, and the eternal Brahman, customs, purifications, the Devas, Dānavas, Gandharvas, Daityas, Asuras, Mahoragas, Yakṣas, Rākṣasas, Nāgas, Piśācas, and the four castes of men. It is characteristic that the Brahman is here created by the personal Brahmā who is sprung from itself. Brahmā also appears as only one — and that the highest — of the Prajāpatis, and elsewhere we find an enumeration of seven Prajāpatis who are called his spiritual sons, Marīci, Atri, Aṅgiras, Pulastya, Pulaha, Kratu, and Vasiṣṭha, even longer lists being given elsewhere.

Beyond this creative power mythology has little to say of Brahmā. Above heaven lie his beautiful worlds, and his assembly hall stands on Mount Meru. Yet, as accords with one who created the world by virtue of his magic power of illusion, the form of his palace is such that it cannot be described: neither cold nor hot, it appears to be made of many brilliant gems, but it does not rest upon columns; it surpasses in splendour the moon, the sun, and fire, and in it the creator ever dwells. Brahmā's wife is Sāvitrī, and swans are harnessed to his chariot, which is swift as thought. His altar is called Samantapañcaka, and it was from a great sacrifice which he performed on the top of Mount Himavant (roughly to be iden-

## PLATE IX

### Trimūrti

The Trimūrti ("Triad") is a relatively late development of Indian thought. It represents the union of Brahmā (the Creator), Viṣṇu (the Preserver), and Śiva (the Destroyer). Here Śiva faces front, the bearded head to the left being Brahmā. From the cave of Elephanta, Bombay. After a photograph in the Library of the India Office, London.

tified with the Himālayas) that there came into being a creature with the colour of the blue lotus, with sharp teeth and slender waist, of enormous strength, at whose birth the earth trembled, and the ocean rose in great waves. This being was Asi ("the Sword"), born to protect the gods, and it was given to Rudra by Brahmā. Rudra handed it on to Viṣṇu, and he to Marīci, whence it came to the seers, from them to Vāsava and the world guardians, and then to Manu in the shape of the law.

As contrasted with the Vedic gods Brahmā shows some of the features of the greatness of a creator. Thus in time of distress the gods are apt to turn to him and to seek his advice, but he yields in importance to the two great gods, Śiva and Viṣṇu, even though here and there in the *Mahābhārata* phrases occur which suggest that these gods owed their origin to him, or rather to the Absolute, of which he is the personal form. When worshipped as the greatest of gods, he himself responds by adoration of Viṣṇu, who, though sprung from the Brahman, has created him as a factor in the process of world creation; and it is stated that Brahmā was born from the lotus which came into being on the navel of Viṣṇu as he lay sunk in musing. Once only in the epic is the doctrine of a triad of Brahmā, Viṣṇu, and Śiva laid down in a passage of the *Mahābhārata* (iii. 18524), where it is said: "In the form of Brahmā he creates; his human form [i.e. Viṣṇu] preserves; in his form as Rudra [i.e. Śiva] will he destroy; these are the three conditions of Prajāpati." This view, however, is foreign to the epic as a whole and to the *Rāmāyaṇa*, and the creator-god is at most regarded as one of the forms of the two great sectarian divinities.

It accords well with the faded position of the creator-god that the account of Indian religion which we owe to the Greek writer Megasthenes (about 300 B.C.) makes no mention of him as a great god, even when it tells us of two deities who are identified with Dionysos and Herakles and in whom we must recognize Śiva and Viṣṇu, rather than, as has also been suggested, Viṣṇu and Śiva, though the possibility of the double identification reminds us that there is much in common in the two Indian as in the two Greek gods themselves. The divinity whom Megasthenes calls Dionysos was at home where the vine flourished in the Aśvaka country, north of the Kabul river, in the north-west country north of Delhi, and further north in Kaśmīr; and his worship also extended east to Bihār and even as far as Kaliṅga in the south-east, and was prevalent round Gokarṇa in the west. Herakles again was worshipped in the Ganges valley and had as chief seats of his cult the towns of Methora and Kleisobora, in which have been seen (doubtless rightly) Mathurā and the city of Kṛṣṇa, both on the Jumnā, the former being the capital of the Yādavas, among whom Kṛṣṇa ranked as hero and god. Consistent with this is the fact that Megasthenes ascribes to Herakles a daughter Pandaie, for this accords with history, since the Pāṇḍyas of southern India, whose connexion with the Pāṇḍavas of the epic was recognized, were worshippers of Kṛṣṇa, and in their country a second Mathurā is found.

In the epic Śiva, the ten-armed, dwells on the holy Himavant, on the north side of Mount Meru, in a lovely wood, ever full of flowers and surrounded by divine beings; or, again, he lives on Mount Mandara. He is said to be born of Brahmā, but also from the forehead of Viṣṇu. His hair flashes like the sun, and he has four faces which came into being when he was tempted by Tilottamā, a beautiful nymph created by Brahmā from all that was most precious in the world. As she walked round the great god, a beautiful countenance appeared on each side: of the four, those facing east, north, and west are mild, but that which faces south is harsh; with that which faces east he rules, with that which faces north he rejoices in the company of his wife Umā; that which faces west is mild and delights all beings, but that which faces south is terrible and destructive. He has three eyes which shine like three suns, while, again, it is said that the sun, moon, and fire are his three eyes. His third eye he owes to the playful act of Umā. One day in jest she suddenly placed her hands over his eyes, whereupon the world was plunged in utter darkness, men trembled from fear, and all life seemed to be extinct, so that, to save the world, a third eye flamed forth on the god's forehead. His neck is blue, whence his name Nīlakaṇṭha, either because in the churning of the ocean he swallowed the poison produced by the biting of the rocks by the teeth of the serpent Vāsuki when he was being used as the churning string, or because Indra hurled his thunderbolt at him, or because he was bitten by the snake which sprang from Uśanas's hair.

Śiva is clothed in skins, especially those of the tiger; but his garments are also described as white, while his wreaths, his sacred cord, his banner, and his bull are all said to be white, and on his head he bears the moon as his diadem. His steed is his white bull, which serves likewise as his banner and which, according to one legend, was given to Śiva by Dakṣa, the divine sage; it has broad shoulders, sleek sides, a black tail, a thick neck, horns hard as adamant, and a hump like the top of a snowy mountain. It is adorned with a golden girth, and on its back the god of gods sits with Umā. Śiva's weapons are the spear — named Pāśupata because of his own title of Paśupati, or "Lord of Creatures" — the bow Pinäka, the battle-axe, and the trident. With the spear he killed all the Daityas in battle and with it he destroys the world at the end of the ages; it is the weapon which he gave to the heroic Arjuna after his contest with him. It was with his axe, which he gave to Rāma, that Paraśu-Rāma ("Rāma of the Axe") annihilated the race of warriors. His bow is coloured like the rainbow and is a mighty serpent with seven heads, sharp and very poisonous teeth, and a large body; and the weapon never leaves his hand. The trident served to slay king Mandhātṛ and all his hosts; it has three sharp points, and from it Śiva derives his names of Śūlin, Śūlapāṇi, and Śūladhara ("Owner of the Spear," "With the Spear in his Hand," and "Spear-Holding").

As a ruler over Mount Himavant Śiva is rich in gold and is

hailed as a lord of gold, wearing mail of gold, and golden-crested, and is a close friend of Kubera, lord of treasures.

The names of Śiva are countless and his shapes many: of the former now one thousand and eight, now one thousand, are mentioned, but names and forms alike simply illustrate either the mild or the terrible aspect of his nature. The terrible form is declared to be fire, lightning, and the sun; the mild form is Dharma (or "Justice"), water, and the moon; or, again, the terrible form is fire, and the mild is Soma as the moon. His sovereign power gives him the name Maheśvara ("the Great Lord"); his greatness and omnipotence cause him to be styled Mahādeva ("the Great God"); and his fierceness, which leads him to devour flesh, blood, and marrow, is the origin of the name Rudra; while his desire to confer blessings on all men makes him to be termed "the Auspicious" (Śiva), or "the Healer" (Śaṅkara). As the devastating power which finally destroys the universe he is Hara ("the Sweeper Away" of all beings). Moreover he sends disease and death; the deadly fever is his deputy, and he is actually personified as death and disease, destroying the good and the bad alike. As Kāla ("Time") he is lord of the whole world, and as Kāla ("Death") he visits impartially the young, children, the old, and even those yet unborn. As Kāla he is the beginning of the worlds, and the destroyer; on the instigation of Kāla everything is done, and all is animated by Kāla. He created the whole world indeed, but at the end of the ages he draws it in and swallows it; yet all that is thus absorbed is born again, save only the wise who understand the origin and disappearance of all things and so attain full union with him. He is the "Lord of Creatures" (Paśupati), a term not merely denoting "the Lord of Cattle" as a pastoral deity, but signifying also the complete dependence of all human souls upon him.

Other epithets which proclaim his might are Īśāna ("the Ruler"), Īśvara ("the Lord"), Viśveśvara ("the Lord of All"), Sthāṇu ("the Immovable"), and Vṛṣa ("the Bull"), a name which is also significant of the close connexion and partial identification of the god with the beast which he rides. The terrible aspect of his character is likewise reflected in the nature of his appearance: his ears are not merely large, but are shaped like spears or pegs (*śaṅku*), or basins (*kumbha*); his eyes and ears are frightful; his mouth is mis-shapen, his tongue is like a sword, and his teeth are both large and very sharp.

On the other hand, in his mild form as Śiva or Śaṅkara, he is friendly to all beings, bears a mild countenance, and rejoices over the welfare of men. He is gay and is fond of music, song, and dance; indeed, he is said to imitate the noise of the drum with his mouth and to be skilled in song and dancing and music, arts to which his followers are also addicted.

In the *Mahābhārata* (xiii. 7506) part of his mild form is reckoned to be his practice of the asceticism of a *brahmacārin*, or chaste Brāhmanical scholar, but his self-mortification is distinctly of the horrible type and sets an example for the worst excesses of the Indian fakir. The most fit place for sacrifice which he can find in his wanderings over all the earth is none other than the burning ghat, and he is believed to be fond of ashes from the funeral pyre and to bear a skull in his hand. He lives in burning ghats, goes either shaved or with uncombed hair, is clothed in bark or skins, and is said not only to have stood on one foot for a thousand years, but also to endure heavy penances on Mount Himavant. All this is done for the good of the world, but it affords a precedent for the most painful renunciation and the most appalling austerities, features which endear Śiva to the Brāhman as the ideal of the true *yogin*, or ascetic.

It is characteristic of the god that the tales of him dwell rather on his power than on his gentleness, although there is a striking exception in a legend told in the *Mahābhārata* (xii. 5675 ff.) which shows both Śiva and his consort in a tender light. After a long time a Brāhman had been blessed with a son, but the child soon died and was carried to the burning place. A vulture, attracted by the lamentations of the relatives, bade them depart, saying that no useful purpose would be served by their staying, since all must die; but just as they were preparing to follow his advice, a black jackal appeared, and declaring that the child might perhaps revive, asked them if they had no love for it. They went back, and while the two animals continued their dispute Śaṅkara, instigated by Umā, appeared on the scene with eyes full of tears of pity, and as a boon bestowed on the child a hundred years of life, rewarding the vulture and the jackal as well. In striking contrast with this is the famous tale of Dakṣa's sacrifice. At the end of the Kṛta Yuga the gods sought to perform a sacrifice and prepared it in accordance with the prescriptions of the Vedas, while Prajāpati Dakṣa, a son of Pracetas, undertook the offering and performed it on Himavant at the very place where the Ganges bursts forth from the mountains. The gods themselves decided how the sacrifice was to be apportioned, but as they did not know Rudra well they left him without a share. In anger Rudra went to the place of offering, bearing his bow, and straightway the mountains began to shake, the wind ceased to blow, and the fire to burn, the stars quenched their light in fear, the glory of the sun and the beauty of the moon departed, and thick darkness filled the air. Śiva shot right through the sacrifice, which took the shape of a hart and sought refuge in heaven together with Agni; in his wrath he broke the arms of Savitṛ and the teeth of Pūṣan, and tore out the eyes of Bhaga. The gods hastily fled with the remains of the preparations for the sacrifice, pursued by Śiva's mocking laughter. The string of his bow, however, was rent by a word spoken by the gods, and the deities then sought him and strove to propitiate him. Mahādeva suffered his anger to be appeased, hurled his bow into the sea, and restored to Bhaga his eyes, to Savitṛ his arms, and to Pūṣan his teeth, and in return received the melted butter as his share of the offering. Such is the tale in its simplest form (*Mahābhārata*, x. 786 ff.), but it is a favourite theme of the priests and is related elsewhere with differing details, while both epics often refer to it.

Not only was Śiva wedded to Umā, the younger daughter of Himavant, but he was fated to be connected with her elder sister Gaṅgā, the sacred Ganges. King Sagara of Ayodhyā (the modern Oudh) sought to perform a horse sacrifice as symbol of his imperial sway; but the horse was stolen, and his sixty thousand sons sought for it. In their wanderings they came upon the sage Kapila, whom they unwisely accused of having been the thief, whereupon in just anger he transformed them into ashes. Kapila was really Viṣṇu, who had undertaken the duty of punishing the sons of Sagara for piercing the earth in their efforts to find the horse which Indra had taken away. When the sons did not return, Sagara sent his grandson by his first wife, Keśinī, to seek them, and he discovered their ashes; but, just as he was about to sprinkle them with water as the last funeral rites, he was told by Suparṇa that he must use the waters of the Ganges. He returned with the horse, thus enabling Sagara to complete his sacrifice, but the king died after a reign of thirty thousand years without having succeeded in his quest for the water. His grandson and great-grandson likewise failed to accomplish the task, but his great-great-grandson Bhagīratha by his asceticism secured from Brahmā the fulfilment of his desire, subject to the condition that Śiva would consent to receive the stream on his head, since the earth could not support its weight. By devotion to Śiva Bhagīratha then proceeded to win his consent to this, and at last, after a long period, the god granted him the boon which he desired. When, however, the deity received the stream in his hair, it sought to hurl him into the lower world, and in punishment for its misdeed Śiva made it wander for many years through his long locks, until finally, at the earnest request of Bhagīratha, he allowed it to descend on earth in seven streams, the southernmost of which is the earthly Ganges. The gods flocked to see the wonderful sight of the descent of the river and to purify themselves in the waters.

The stream on earth followed the chariot of Bhagīratha until it came to the offering place of Jahnu, who swallowed it and was induced by the gods to allow it to issue forth again through his ears only on condition that it should count as his daughter. Bhagīratha then conducted the river into the underworld, where he sprinkled the ashes of the sons of Sagara with it and received the praise of Brahmā for his great deed.

Śiva performed another mighty feat when he made the deity of love to lose his body. As the lord of the gods was engaged in deep meditation, Kāma approached him to induce him to beget with Pārvatī a son powerful enough to overthrow the Daitya Tāraka, who had conquered the worlds. In deep anger Śiva with a glance of his eye burned Kāma to ashes, whence the god of love is called Anaṅga, or "Bodiless." The incident is only briefly referred to in the *Mahābhārata* (xii. 6975–80) and owes its fame to its handling by Kālidāsa in the famous epic *Kumārasaṁbhava*, which tells of the birth of the war-god as the result of the love excited by the hapless Kāma in Śiva, despite the penalty paid by him.

The first in rank among Śiva's martial exploits was his destruction of the three citadels of the Asuras in the wars which they waged against the gods. These citadels are already known to the *Brāhmaṇas* as made of iron, silver, and gold, one in each of the three worlds, but the epic places them all in heaven, and makes Vidyunmālin, Tārakākṣa and Kamalākṣa their respective lords. Even Indra could not pierce these citadels, wherefore the gods sought the aid of Rudra, who burned the forts and extirpated the Dānavas. Among the Asuras he had one special foe in Andhaka, whom he slew; and he also had an encounter with the sage Uśanas, who by means of his ascetic power deprived Kubera of his treasure. In punishment Śiva swallowed him and not only refused to disgorge him until he had long been entreated to do so, but even then would have slain him had it not been for the intervention of Devī. A more poetic tale is the encounter of Śiva with Arjuna: Arjuna, the

FIG. 3. THE PROPITIATION OF UMĀ, OR DEVĪ

The goddess is seated in her temple on the summit of a mountain and is adored by (1) Śiva, (2) Viṣṇu, (3) Brahmā, (4) Indra, (5) Agni, and another deity. Above to the left is Sūrya ("the Sun") with his charioteer Aruṇa, and to the right is Candra ("the Moon"). The mountain, which is shown to be the haunt of wild beasts, is the home of various kinds of ascetics. After Moor, *Hindu Pantheon*, Plate XXXI.

noblest of the five Pāṇḍavas, by his ascetic practices created panic among the gods, so that Śiva, assuming the form of a mountaineer, or Kirāta, went to Arjuna and picked a quarrel with him over a Rākṣasa in boar-form whom Arjuna killed without permitting the Kirāta to share in the booty. The two fought, finally wrestling with each other, and Arjuna fainted in the god's embrace, to be revived by the deity and to receive from him the divine weapons which were to stand him in good stead in the great war which forms the main theme of the *Mahābhārata*. At Śiva's bidding Arjuna was borne to the heaven of Indra, where he remained for five years, learning the use of the celestial weapons.

Closely akin to Śiva is his wife Umā, the younger daughter of Himavant, whose gift of her to Rudra cost him the loss of all his jewels through a curse of Bhṛgu, the sage of the gods, who came too late to seek her in marriage. As "Daughter of the Mountain" she is also Pārvatī, and Gaurī ("the Radiant White One"), and Durgā ("the Inaccessible"). The fancy of the poet, however, derives this last epithet from the fact that she guards her devotees from distress (*durga*), and she is proclaimed as the refuge for those lost in the wilds, wrecked in the great ocean, or beset by evil men. Yet her normal aspect is terrible: she lives in trackless places, she loves strife and the blood of the Asura Mahiṣa, and in battle she conquers Dānavas and Daityas. She is Kālī or Mahākālī, as her spouse is Kāla, and she is called the deep sleep of all creatures. She is also said to live on Mandara or the Vindhya, and to be of the lineage of the cowherd Nanda, a daughter of Yaśodā and a sister of Vāsudeva, a descent which is clearly intended to connect her closely with Viṣṇu. Like her husband she has four faces, but only four arms, she wears a diadem of shining colours, and her emblem is the peacock's tail.

In the *Mahābhārata* sectarian influence has exalted both Śiva and Viṣṇu at the expense of the other: it seems clear that the Vaiṣṇavas first exercised their influence on the text, but

## PLATE X

### Marriage of Śiva and Pārvatī

The union of the deities is honoured by the presence of the chief divinities. Viṣṇu and Lakṣmī stand on the left; on the right the Trimūrti ("Triad") of Brahmā, Viṣṇu, and Śiva is seen. Gandharvas and Apsarases float above in the sky, and among the gods Viṣṇu (riding on Garuḍa), Vāyu (on an antelope), Agni (on a ram), Indra (on an elephant), and Kāma (on a dolphin) are clearly recognizable. From the Dumār Leṇa cave at Elura, in His Highness the Nizam's Dominions. After a photograph in the Library of the India Office, London.

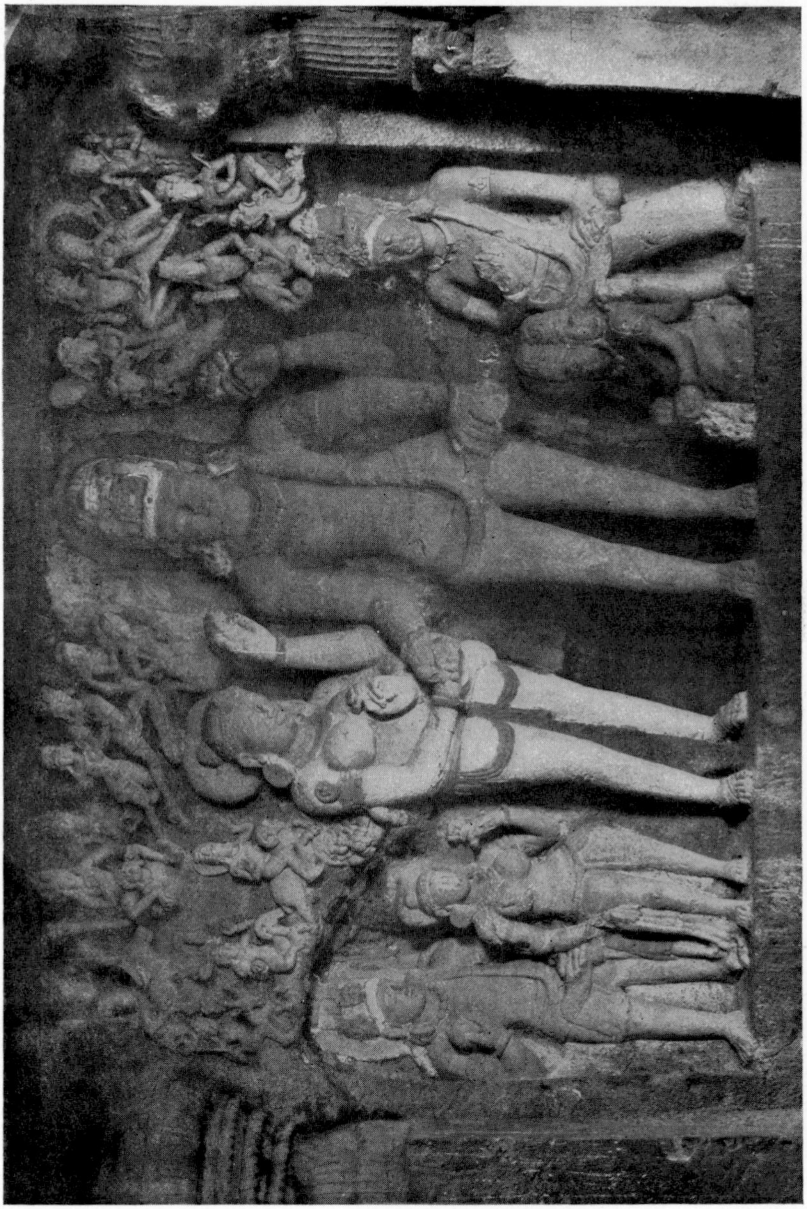

the Śaivas later made amends by freely interpolating passages in which Śiva is exalted to the position of all-god in a manner too strikingly parallel to the encomia of Viṣṇu to leave much doubt as to the deliberate character of the change. Thus Śiva is praised by Viṣṇu himself (vii. 2875 ff.) in terms of the highest laudation; and elsewhere (vii. 9461 ff.) he is lauded as the unborn, the inconceivable, the soul of action, the unmoved; and he who knows him as the self of self attains unity with the absolute. Quite apart from this sectarian glorification it is clear that in the earliest epic Śiva already enjoyed the position of a great god, and this is borne out even by the *Rāmāyaṇa*, which, in its present form, is a Vaiṣṇava text. This is in perfect accord with the growing greatness of his figure in the age of the *Brāhmaṇas*, but in the epic a new motive in his character appears undisguisedly: in addition to the dark and demoniac side of his nature, in addition to his aspect as the ideal ascetic, he is seen as a god of fertility whose worship is connected with the phallus, or *liṅga*, and whose ritual, like that of Dionysos, is essentially orgiastic. It is uncertain to what origin we should trace this feature in his character:[3] the *Ṛgveda* already reprobates the phallus-worshippers (*śiśnadeva*), and there is no evidence of a phallic cult in the *Brāhmaṇa* literature. There is, therefore, reason enough to believe that the phallic element in the Śiva-cult was foreign to Vedic worship and that it probably owed its origin to the earlier inhabitants of the land, though it is possible that it may have been practised by another stock of the Aryan invaders and rejected by the Vedic branch. At any rate it seems certain that Śiva, as he appears in the epic, includes the personality of a vegetation-god.

In Umā, the wife of Śiva, we have, no doubt, a goddess of nature and a divinity likewise foreign to the old Vedic religion, since her name appears only in the last strata of the period of the *Brāhmaṇas*. But though she was, we may well believe, an independent deity in the beginning, in her development she has evolved into a female counterpart of Śiva and has lost her own personality in great measure in becoming a feminine expression of her husband's character, especially in its dark and sinister aspect. As her descent from Himavant denotes, like her husband she was particularly a goddess of the north and of the earth in its mountainous, and not in its peaceful, aspect, which explains in part her wild and ferocious character. She seems also to have been identified with a goddess of the non-Aryan tribes of the Vindhya.

While Śiva and his consort represent the ascetic side of Indian religion, Viṣṇu and his spouse display the milder and more human aspects of that faith. Like Indra he is reckoned as one of the Ādityas, and the youngest, but he is also the only Āditya who is enduring, unconquerable, imperishable, the everlasting and mighty lord. Though Indra's younger brother, it was he who secured Indra in the kinship over the worlds. His abode is on the top of Mount Mandara, to the east of Meru, and to the north of the sea of milk. Higher even than Brahmā's seat is his place, in everlasting light, and thither they only go who are without egoism, unselfish, free from duality, and with restrained senses. Not even Brahmarṣis or Maharṣis attain to it, but Yatis alone, that is, men who have completely overcome the temptations of sense. He has four arms and lotus eyes, and bears on his breast the *vatsa* ("calf") mark which he received when the great sage Bharadvāja threw water at him because he disturbed him at prayer. From his navel, when he lay musing, sprang a lotus, and in it appeared Brahmā with his four faces. His raiment is yellow, and on his breast he bears the Kaustubha gem which came forth on the churning of the ocean. He has a chariot of gold, eight-wheeled, swift as thought, and yoked with demons, and the couch on which he lies as he muses is the serpent Śeṣa or Ananta, who holds the earth at Brahmā's command and bears up the slumbering god. His standard is the bird Garuḍa. His weapons are a *cakra*, or discus, with which he overwhelmed the Daityas, a conch, a club, and a bow.

## PLATE XI

### Birth of Brahmā

Viṣṇu rests, absorbed in meditation, on the cosmic serpent Ananta ("Infinite"), who floats on the cosmic ocean. Lakṣmī, the wife of the god, shampoos his feet. From his navel springs a lotus, on which appears the four-headed deity Brahmā. From an Indian water-colour in the collection of the Editor.

Like Śiva Viṣṇu must have a thousand names, which the *Mahābhārata* enumerates and in part explains, ascribing the name Viṣṇu to the greatness (*vṛhattva*) of the god. Sectarian enthusiasm raises him to the position of all-god and subordinates to him not only Brahmā but even Śiva himself. As Brahmā is born from the lotus on Viṣṇu's navel, so Śiva is born from his forehead. A favourite name of his is Hari, and at the very close of the epic period the *Harivaṁśa* commemorates the equality of the two great gods of the epic in the compound Harihara, Hara, as we have seen, being an epithet of Viṣṇu. Another name with mystic sense is Nārāyaṇa, which is used to denote the god in his relation of identity with man.

While Śiva is the ascetic in his gruesome aspect, the performer of countless years of hateful austerities, Viṣṇu also is a *yogin*, though in a very different way. When all the world has been destroyed and all beings have perished, then Viṣṇu muses on the waters, resting on the serpent, thus personifying the state of absorption of the soul in the Supreme Being. This, however, is the less important side of his being, which expresses itself in the desire to punish and restrain the bad and to reward and encourage the good. He is represented as deliberately deciding for this purpose to assume such forms as those of a boar, a man-lion, a dwarf, and a man; and these constitute his avatars, or "descents," which in ever increasing number reveal Viṣṇu in his character of the loving and compassionate god, and which, by bringing him into close contact with humanity, distinguish him from Śiva, whom the epic never regards as taking human shape.

The incarnations of Viṣṇu known to the *Mahābhārata* are as a boar, a dwarf, a man-lion, the head of a horse, and Kṛṣṇa, of which the first three only are normally reckoned among his avatars. The boar incarnation was assumed when all the surface of the earth was flooded with water, and when the lord, wandering about like a fire-fly in the night in the rainy season, sought some place on which to fix the earth, which he was fain to save from the deluge. The shape which he took was ten *yojanas* (leagues) broad and a hundred *yojanas* long, like a great mountain, shining with sharp tusks, and resembling a dark thunder-cloud. Assuming it, he descended into the water, and grasping the sinking earth with one of his tusks, he drew it up and set it back in its due place. In the dwarf incarnation Viṣṇu was born as a son of Kaśyapa and Aditi, his original parents, in order to deprive Bali, son of Virocana, of the sovereignty of the three worlds which he had attained. He came into being with matted hair, in the shape of a dwarf, of the height of a boy, bearing staff and jar, and marked with the *vatsa.* Accompanied by Bṛhaspati, he strode to the Dānavas' place of sacrifice, and Bali, seeing him, courteously offered him a boon. In reply Viṣṇu chose three steps of ground, but when the demon accorded them, Viṣṇu, resuming his true shape, in three great strides encompassed the three worlds, which he then handed over to Indra to rule. The myth is clearly only a variant of the three steps of Viṣṇu in the *Ṛgveda*, and the boar incarnation also has a forerunner in that text in so far as Viṣṇu is represented in close connexion with a boar.

The episode of the man-lion is only briefly related in the *Mahābhārata:* Viṣṇu assumed the form half of a lion and half of a man and went to the assembly of the Daityas. There Hiraṇyakaśipu, the son of Diti, saw him and advanced against him in anger, trident in hand and rumbling like a thunder-cloud, only to be torn in pieces by the sharp claws of the lion-man. This double form is a new motive in Indian mythology and has no Vedic parallel.

The incarnation with a horse's head has a faint Vedic predecessor in the legend that the doctrine of the Madhu ("Mead") was told by a horse's head. In the epic story we are informed that two Dānavas, Madhu and Kaiṭabha, stole the Vedas from Brahmā and entered the sea, whereupon the deity was cast into deep sorrow and bethought himself of seeking the aid of Viṣṇu. The latter, gratified by his adoration, assumed the

## PLATE XII

### Varāhāvatāra

Viṣṇu, incarnate as a boar, raises from the flood the Earth, who, in the figure of a woman, clings to his tusk. From a sculpture at Eran, Sagar, Central Provinces. After Coomaraswamy, *Viśvakarma*, Plate XCIII.

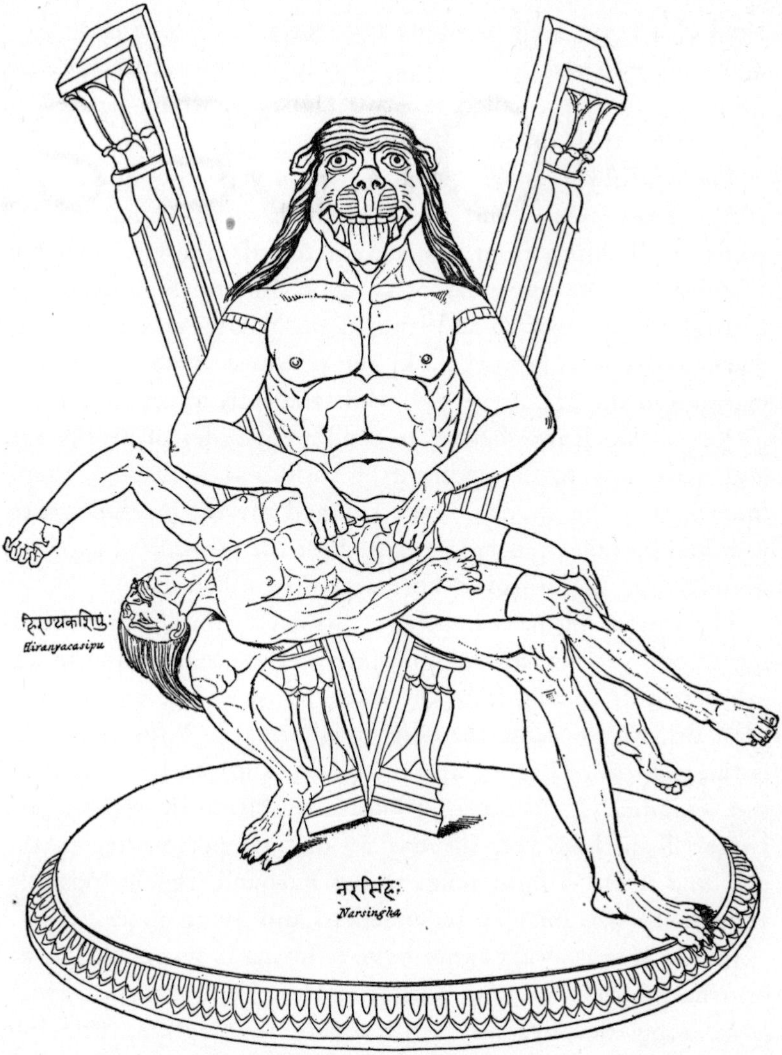


FIG. 4. THE NARASIṂHA ("MAN-LION") AVATAR OF VIṢṆU

Through his austerities the Daitya Hiraṇyakaśipu had obtained the boon that he should be slain neither by man nor by animal. His son, Prahlāda, was a devout worshipper of Viṣṇu, whom Hiraṇyakaśipu hated. Told by Prahlāda that Viṣṇu is omnipresent, Hiraṇyakaśipu asked scornfully whether he was in a certain pillar of the palace, and when told that he was even there, he struck it to destroy the deity. Immediately Viṣṇu appeared from the pillar in the guise of a being part man and part lion and tore the unbeliever asunder. After Moor, *Hindu Pantheon*, Plate L.

head of a horse, and plunging into the sea, rescued the Vedas and restored them to Brahmā, after which he returned to his proper form and assailed the two Dānavas, whom he slew in revenge for their insult to Brahmā.

The *Mahābhārata* (iii. 12746 ff.) has a version of the famous story of the deluge, but the fish which saves Manu and the seeds of all things from destruction reveals himself, when the vessel which he supports rests upon Mount Naubandhana, as Brahmā rather than as Viṣṇu, as in the later accounts of the *Purāṇas*. These, however, like the previous avatars, are mere episodes in the life of the god, while the embodiments of Viṣṇu as Kṛṣṇa and Rāma belong to a different order of myths and add materially to the godhead of Viṣṇu. It is through them, indeed, that the ancient Vedic sun-god attains his full greatness and becomes specially adapted for the position of supreme divinity and the object of keen sectarian worship.

The wife of Viṣṇu is Lakṣmī or Śrī, who came forth, according to one version, at the churning of the ocean, while in another a lotus sprang from the forehead of Viṣṇu, whence was born Śrī, who became the wife of Dharma, or "Justice." She is the goddess of beauty and prosperity and can boast that no god, Gandharva, Asura, or Rākṣasa is able to overpower her. Unlike Kālī, however, she has no distinct personality in the epic and is but a faint reflex of her husband, though possibly enough she was once an independent and living goddess.

In the *Mahābhārata* as we have it Kṛṣṇa is recognized as an incarnation of Nārāyaṇa Viṣṇu, and the *Bhagavadgītā*, which is his song, declares his identity with the supreme principle of the universe. He was, we are told, born in the family of the Yadus as the son of Vasudeva and Devakī, and throughout the body of the epic he plays the *rôle* of a partisan and most energetic supporter of the Pāṇḍavas. His character is decidedly unsatisfactory and is marked by every sort of deceit and trickery. It was he who gave the advice how to secure the overthrow of Droṇa and who proved to Arjuna that truth must

## PLATE XIII

### Lakṣmī

The Goddess of Wealth and Beauty, whose birth at the churning of the ocean is represented in Fig. 2, is here shown in her usual form as a lovely woman seated on a lotus. On either side stands an elephant holding a canopy over her head. The small, separate figures have no mythological significance. For another conception of her see Plate XXI. From a painted alabaster group in the Peabody Museum, Salem, Mass.

not always be told, and against the reproof of Yudhiṣṭhira he defended the action of Bhīma in unfairly defeating Duryodhana in the final duel. Subsequently he saved Bhīma from the fate prepared for him by Dhṛtarāṣṭra by substituting an iron statue for him. Because of his share in the ruin of the Kauravas he was cursed by Gāndhārī, their mother, and he admitted that the doom was fated to be accomplished in the destruction of himself and his race. He was present at the horse sacrifice by which Yudhiṣṭhira proclaimed his complete sovereignty, and then retired to his country of Dvārakā. There strife broke out among the Yādavas, this being followed by the death of Kṛṣṇa, who was accidentally pierced in the sole of the foot (where alone he was vulnerable) by an arrow shot by a hunter with the significant name of Jarā ("Old Age"). Later, in the *Harivaṁśa* and the *Purāṇas* we have details of the early days of Kṛṣṇa, and there is evidence that these stories were known even in the second century B.C., although, disregarding interpolations which are obviously late, it is certain that the epic normally considers Kṛṣṇa as essentially heroic. It is, however, equally clear that his association with Viṣṇu is not primitive, but that it has been introduced into the epic in the course of time: indeed, it is doubtful if the *Bhagavadgītā* itself was originally Vaiṣṇavite in tendency, but even if that were the case, it is certain that the Kṛṣṇaite redaction was an afterthought.

The origin of this new and most important deity is obscure and probably insoluble. In the opinion of E. W. Hopkins [4] Kṛṣṇa was the chief god of the invading tribe of the Yādavas-Pāṇḍavas who came from the hill country north of the Ganges and overthrew the Kurus in the stronghold of Brāhmanism in the holy land about the present Delhi. But the conquerors, as often, were merged in the Brāhmanic society which they had conquered, while the priests identified their divinity, who — as in the case of most of the hill tribes of the Gangetic region — was the tribal hero as a sun-god, with Viṣṇu, the

Vedic and Brāhmanic solar deity. Kṛṣṇa, son of Devakī, is mentioned in the *Chāndogya Upaniṣad* (III. xvii. 6) as having a teacher named Ghora Āṅgirasa, who taught him a doctrine which is summed up by Hopkins as showing the vanity of sacrifice and inculcating the worship of the sun-god; and in this record may be seen a trace of a deity whose name in the native tongue of the invaders may have been sufficiently close to the Sanskrit Kṛṣṇa to render the identification possible and easy. On the other hand, R. Garbe[5] insists that from the first Kṛṣṇa was nothing more than a man, and that his deification was a process of euhemerism, carried out at an early date, since the excavations at Rummindei indicate that the predecessors of the Buddha worshipped Rukmiṇī, the wife of Kṛṣṇa. The early date of his cult is clearly proved by the Herakles of Megasthenes, who can certainly be none other than this god. So far as it goes, the earliness of the date of the divinity of Kṛṣṇa seems rather to tell against the theory of his deification and to suggest that he was always a god and, probably enough, not so much a sun-god — a conception which ill fits his name, which means "Black" — as a representation of the spirit of the dark earth, a vegetation-god. For this hypothesis a definite support is given by a notice in the *Mahābhāṣya*[6] of Patañjali (written about 150–140 B.C.), from which it appears that Kṛṣṇa and Kaṁsa, who in the later accounts of the *Harivaṁśa* appears as his cruel uncle, were protagonists in a ritual contest which is precisely parallel to the combats which in many parts of Europe have symbolized the death of the old and the victory of the new spirit of vegetation, and from which the Greek and perhaps the Indian drama have grown. The human character of the vegetation-spirit is a marked characteristic of that spirit in all lands, and hence we may readily understand how the god of the Pāṇḍavas was conceived as aiding them in bodily presence even at the expense of some diminution of his divinity, of which, however, the epic never loses sight. His identification with Viṣṇu was doubtless

## PLATE XIV

### Kṛṣṇa

The deity is represented in characteristic pose with crossed legs and playing his pipe, which is lost in the carving here shown. From an old Orissan ivory. After Watt, *Indian Art at Delhi*, Plate LXXVI.

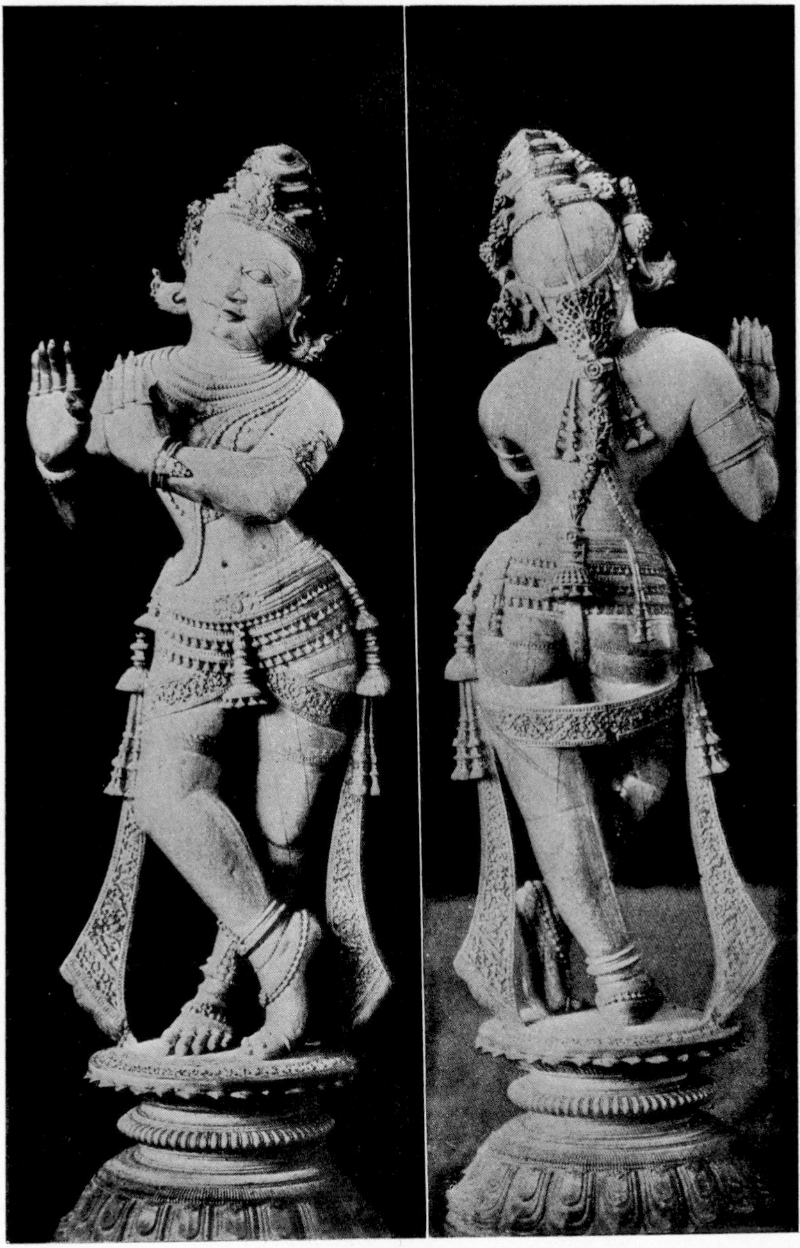

effected easily enough, for in all times the Brāhmans have found no difficulty in finding a place for new gods. In the epic the home of Kṛṣṇa in his latter days figures as Dvārakā in Gujarāt, but it is difficult to say whether this is safe ground for inferring that his godhead was first recognized there; it is at least clear that it was among the Pāṇḍavas and in the vicinity of the Gangetic valley that his greatness grew.

In the epic the wife of Kṛṣṇa is Rukmiṇī, but she shows no divine features: she refused to survive her husband's death and perished by fire with Gāndhārī and others.

The other great incarnation of Viṣṇu is that as Rāma, whose story, as told both in the *Rāmāyaṇa* and in a long episode in the *Mahābhārata*, presents him as none other than Viṣṇu. Daśaratha, king of Kosala, with his capital at Ayodhyā, was a wise and powerful ruler, but he had no sons, wherefore, to obtain children, he performed the horse sacrifice with the aid of the sage Ṛśyaśṛṅga. At the time the gods were in fear of the demon Rāvaṇa, to whom Brahmā had granted the gift of invulnerability, and they sought a means of killing him. This, they found, could be accomplished only by a man, and for this end they begged Viṣṇu to take human form. Viṣṇu accordingly came to life as Rāma, the son of Daśaratha by Kausalyā, while Kaikeyī and Sumitrā, the other wives of the king, bore Bharata and the twins Lakṣmaṇa and Śatrughna respectively. Rāma grew up to a glorious youth and won the hand of Sītā, who had sprung from the earth when King Janaka of Videha ploughed the ground. Daśaratha, feeling that his life was drawing near its close, contemplated the performance of the ceremony of appointing Rāma to be heir apparent, but at this moment Kaikeyī intervened and demanded from the King the execution of a promise which he had made long before. The monarch felt that he must keep his word, in which resolve he was strengthened by Rāma's readiness to aid him to fulfil his promise, so that Rāma was banished for fourteen years, the post of heir apparent being conferred on

Bharata. The separation from his son broke the heart of Daśaratha, who soon passed away, whereupon Bharata, hastily seeking Rāma, endeavoured to persuade him to return to rule the state, and when he refused, regarded himself as no more than his vicegerent. In the meantime Rāma, accompanied by the faithful Sītā and Lakṣmaṇa, proceeded to the Daṇḍaka forest, where Sītā was stolen from him by Rāvaṇa and carried away to Laṅkā, which (in later times at least) is reckoned as Ceylon. Rāma makes alliance with the apes under Sugrīva, who is at variance with Vālin, his elder brother; and with the ape army, and especially Hanumān, the son of Māruta by Añjanā, succeeds after great struggles in reaching Laṅkā and in slaying Rāvaṇa. By passing through the fire Sītā proves that her purity has been uninjured despite her captivity in Laṅkā, and husband and wife are united. Later, however, Rāma is again troubled by the popular dissatisfaction at his action in taking Sītā back after her abduction and dismisses her; she departs and stays at the hermitage of Vālmīki, to whom the *Rāmāyaṇa* is ascribed, and there gives birth to the children Kuśa and Lava, in whose names can be seen a popular etymology of the word *kuśīlava*, the name of the wandering minstrels who sang the epic songs to princely courts and even to the people. Rāma prepares a horse sacrifice, and his two sons, at the instigation of Vālmīki, appear at the place of sacrifice and recite to him the story of his deeds. Learning the identity of the boys, the king sends to Vālmīki, desiring to arrange that Sītā should prove her purity by an oath before the whole assemblage; and when Vālmīki presents himself accompanied by Sītā and declares her spotlessness, Rāma admits that he is now convinced. Then the gods all manifest themselves to lend their authority to the oath of Sītā, but she, asserting her chastity, asks the divinity Mādhavī to receive her in proof of it. The goddess Earth then appears, embraces Sītā, and vanishes with her under the ground to the wonder of the assembled gathering, while Rāma's despair at her loss

# PLATE XV

## Hanumān

The monkey-god, the great ally of Rāma, is here shown in mild and attractive form. From a Ceylonese copper figure in the Indian Museum, London. After Coomaraswamy, *Viśvakarma*, Plate C.

is lessened only by assurances of future reunion. This second doubt of Sītā and her tragic departure, is, however, like the assertion of the identification of Rāma and Viṣṇu, clearly no part of the earlier form of the *Rāmāyaṇa* legend. Taking what remains, it falls into two parts, the first of which is quite a simple story of the intrigues which must have troubled many a royal family, while the second is definitely mythical in nature. By far the most probable explanation of the story is that suggested by H. Jacobi.[7] Sītā, it is clear, is no mere mortal woman, for in the *Ṛgveda* (IV. lvii. 6–7) she is worshipped as the furrow made by the plough, and this conception was a popular one, since in the much later and more popular texts, the *Adbhutādhyāya* of the *Kauśika Sūtra* and the *Pāraskara Gṛhya Sūtra* (ii. 17), she appears as the genius of the ploughed field and is described as a being of wonderful beauty, wife of Indra or Parjanya. The rape of Sītā at once presents itself as the parallel to an agricultural population to the Paṇis' theft of the cows in the shape of the waters, and he who wins them back can be none other than a form of Indra, while the thief must be Vṛtra. This again finds support in the fact that a son of Rāvaṇa's is called Indra's foe or vanquisher, and one of his brothers, Kumbhakarṇa, dwells, like the Vedic Vṛtra, in a cave. Further confirmation from the position of Hanumān is also forthcoming. That god in modern India is essentially the guardian god of every village settlement, and it may well be that in origin he was the genius of the monsoon. This conception would be quite in harmony with his birth from the wind-god, his power of assuming shape at will like the clouds, his long journeys over the sea in search of Sītā, and the bringing back of Sītā from the south (whence the monsoon comes) with the help of the apes, that is, the rain-clouds. In the deeds of Hanumān there may actually be a reflex of the journey of Saramā in the Veda across the Rasā to seek the clouds when they were stolen by the Paṇis. Rāma may have been a local god similar in character to Indra, but representing the views of a society which was essentially agricultural and not pastoral; and his identification with Viṣṇu was doubtless instigated by the same motives which led to the identification of Kṛṣṇa with that great god and which has in the course of time brought many other deities into the fold of Viṣṇu.

Efforts have been made to find a mythological background for the *Mahābhārata* in the conception of a struggle of the five seasons of the year, represented by the Pāṇḍavas, against the winter, which is thus supposed to be typified by Duryodhana, but this interpretation can scarcely be maintained in face of the extremely human characteristics of the figures of the great epic, which in this respect stands in marked contrast to much of the *Rāmāyaṇa*.

## CHAPTER V

## MINOR EPIC DEITIES AND THE DEAD

MANY as are the deities recognized in the epic, no one of them has any real supremacy in comparison with the great gods, Śiva and Viṣṇu. The tradition of the greatness of Indra survives indeed in the epithets which are freely bestowed upon him, but in nothing else. He is called "the Head of the Suras," "the God of the Gods," "the King of the Gods," "the Lord of All the Gods," and "the Powerful" (Śakra); he is also said to have attained Indraship by surpassing all the gods in sacrifice and to have become the overlord of the gods through slaying Daityas and Dānavas, while after the killing of Vṛtra he won the title of Mahendra ("Great Indra"). His abode is "Heaven" (Svarga), and at the entrance stands his elephant Airāvata, with its four tusks like Mount Kailāsa. After his conflict with Śiva in the form of a mountaineer, Arjuna was conducted thither by Mātali in Indra's chariot, the ascent being made from Mount Mandara in the Himavant range. The grove in Svarga is called Nandana ("the Place of Joy"), and Indra's city itself is termed Amarāvatī. It has a thousand gates and is a hundred *yojanas* in extent, is adorned with jewels, and yields the fruit of every season. There the sun does not scorch, and neither heat nor cold nor fatigue torments the dwellers. There there is neither grief, nor despondency, nor weakness, nor anger, nor covetousness. In his assembly hall, which he himself built and which can move where it wills, sits Śakra with his wife Śacī, wearing his crown and with a white screen held over him. Old age, fatigue, and fear are forgotten in that abode of bliss; and thither come those who sacrifice, those who perform penance, and above all those warrior heroes who meet their death in battle.

Besides Airāvata, Indra has a steed named Uccaiḥśravas, which came forth at the churning of the ocean. His chariot is drawn by ten thousand reddish-yellow horses who are as swift as wind; the lightning and the thunderbolt are on the car, and as it cleaves the sky it scatters the dark clouds. The flagstaff, Vaijayanta, is bright blue and is decorated with gold. The charioteer is Mātali, councillor and friend of Indra, of whom a pretty story is told. His daughter by Sudharmā was of exceeding beauty, and neither among gods, demons, men, nor seers could Mātali find one whom he thought worthy of her. Accordingly, after taking counsel with his wife, he decided to go to the world of Nāgas, or Serpents, in search of a son-in-law, and by permission of Varuṇa he went thither with Nārada, in due course finding the handsome Sumukha who became the husband of Guṇakeśī. The weapons borne by the god are the thunderbolt, which Tvaṣṭṛ made from the bones of the seer Dadhīca and with which he struck off the head of Vṛtra and cleaves even mountains, the spear Vijaya, and the conch Devadatta.

As in the Veda, Indra is ever distinguished by his conflicts with demons. He was engaged in the great struggle of the Suras with the Asuras which broke out after the churning of the ocean, but his weakness is shown by the fact that the victory could be achieved only by the aid of Viṣṇu, who on the overthrow of the demons gave the rule of the three worlds to Indra. Then followed for a time a golden age, when Indra, seated on Airāvata, gazed on a prosperous world, flourishing towns and villages, kings devoted to their duty, and happy and contented people. Śrī came and dwelt with him, and Indra wrought great deeds, such as the slaying of numbers of the Asuras, the freeing of Bṛhaspati's wife Tārakā, and the rescue of the daughter of Puloman. But prosperity led Indra to fall into evil courses: he set his desire upon Ruci, the wife of

Devaśarman, and seduced Ahalyā; and, worst of all, he slew the son of Tvaṣṭṛ, Viśvarūpa Triśiras. Failing to tempt this pious being by the wiles of an Apsaras, he smote him with his thunderbolt and ordered a wood-cutter to chop off his head. In revenge Tvaṣṭṛ created Vṛtra and commanded him to slay Indra. Then ensued a long war, and the gods sought the advice of Viṣṇu in order to secure peace. Vṛtra, however, would not consent to any reconciliation unless he were promised immunity from dry or wet, stone or wood, sword or javelin, by day or by night. On these terms peace was made, but Indra kept to his resolve to slay his rival, and meeting him on the seashore, at the junction of wet and dry, at the twilight between day and night, he killed him with the foam of the sea and the thunderbolt into which Viṣṇu had entered. Soon, however, he realized the enormity of his own deed in slaying a Brāhman and fled in terror to the remotest part of the earth, where he lived concealed in a lotus stalk in a lake. Then the earth became desolate, the forest withered, the rivers ceased to flow, and creatures perished for lack of rain; wherefore the gods and seers went to Nahuṣa and persuaded him to accept the kingship, seeing the evils caused by the lack of a monarch. He consented, but after receiving the new rank he abandoned himself to idle enjoyment, and seeing Śacī, the wife of Indra, he desired her. Śacī, loyal to Indra, sought the protection of Bṛhaspati, but Nahuṣa replied that as Indra had been allowed to seduce Ahalyā, he also should be permitted to take Śacī. Śacī in despair obtained a postponement by insisting that Indra might still be discovered, and in the meantime the gods sought the advice of Viṣṇu, who promised that Indra should regain his position by performing a horse sacrifice to him. Indra did so and thus was purified from the sin of Brāhman-slaying. Śacī then besought him to return and slay Nahuṣa, whereupon he bade her induce the sage to cause himself to be drawn in a chariot by the seven Ṛṣis. The advice proved successful, for, while Nahuṣa carried out the wish of Śacī, he foolishly allowed himself to be drawn into an argument with Agastya as to the lawfulness of the eating of meat, and indignant with him, the seer, whom he had kicked on the head, hurled him from heaven to dwell in snake form for ten thousand years. Indra was then restored to the kingship. Other demons were also slain by Indra, the most important of them being Namuci, whose story is a variant of that of Vṛtra, of whom he is only another form.

Indra has a famous wish-cow who is the daughter of Surabhi and is called Sarvakāmadughā or Nandinī. She is fat, and the potency of her milk is such that the mortal who drinks it will be like a strong youth for a thousand years. Vasiṣṭha, son of Varuṇa, obtained her as a sacrificial cow, but for a time she was stolen by Dyaus, so that in atonement of his crime he was doomed to a long sojourn on earth among mortals. Her mother, Surabhi, was the daughter of Dakṣa Prajāpati, and her home is the seventh layer under the earth, Rasātala; but by her asceticism she received from Brahmā immortality and a world, Goloka, above the three worlds. She created daughters, four of whom — Surūpā, Haṁsikā, Subhadrā, and Sarvakāmadughā — support the east, south, west, and north corners of the heavens, but she weeps because her son is tormented by the ploughman with his goad.

Indra has a thousand eyes since, according to one version, when Tilottamā walked round him and the other gods, producing the four heads of Śiva, a thousand eyes burst forth on his back, sides, and front; although another legend says that Gautama cursed Indra for his inability to restrain his passions and as punishment caused a thousand marks to appear on his body which afterward in compassion he allowed to disappear.

Indra's wife is Indrāṇī, Mahendrāṇī, or Śacī ("the Powerful"). She proved her devotion to her husband and her quickness of wit in the efforts which she made to repulse Nahuṣa.

In the epic Indra is constantly a god of rain, and in this aspect he has completely swallowed up Parjanya, who is indeed mentioned separately from him in the lists of the Ādityas, but who is no more in reality than another name for Indra. Thus, when Agastya sacrificed liberally and the Thousand-Eyed One still did not rain, the sages could say, "Agastya offers generously in sacrifice, yet Parjanya does not rain; how, then, can there be food?" Both epics have the most vivid descriptions of the effects of the rain on the earth after the drought, and of the misery caused by the failure of the rain to fall; but the storm no longer produces mythology, and the treatment is poetic.

Another god who has fallen on evil days in an age in which the mere physical element is not enough to support a real divinity is Vāyu ("Wind"), who bears also the names of Marut, Vāta, Anila, and Pavana ("the Purifying"). It is said indeed that neither Indra nor Yama nor Varuṇa is his peer in strength, and his pleasant, comfort-bearing breath is mentioned, as well as his friendship for Agni, but the deification is merely formal.

Agni has survived with more reality, though not simply as fire, his continued importance, such as it is, being due to the fact that he represents on the one hand the sacrificial flame, and on the other the cosmic fire. He is the eater of the oblations, the mouth by which the god and the fathers partake of the sacrifice; he upholds the sacrificial ceremonies and purifies from sin; his wife is the Svāhā call uttered at the sacrifice; and he himself is the sacrifice. On the other hand, in his cosmic aspect he is the creator of all the worlds and the ender of them. Nevertheless, traces of his earlier nature still exist: he is the lightning in the clouds, he hides within the *śamī*-wood, and though he fears the water which quenches him, still he is said to have been born in the waters, and in case of need (as when Indra had fled after the slaying of Vṛtra, and the gods were anxious to find him to overthrow the wicked Nahuṣa) he can be persuaded to enter them once more. From a higher point of view he is the real cause of the existence of water, and the waters are said to be deposited in him. Again, Agni is the internal fire within each man, and as such he knows everything and is Jātavedas. He is, as of old, lord of Vasus and is said to be a child of Brahmā.

As in the Veda, Agni was apt to disappear, and on one occasion this was due to the curse of Bhṛgu. That sage had succeeded in marrying Pulomā, who had formerly been betrothed to the Rākṣasa Puloman, but whom her father had later given in due form to Bhṛgu. While the latter was absent the Rākṣasa came to his dwelling, where he was received hospitably by Pulomā, who was disclosed to him by Agni; but not knowing whose wife she was, Puloman abducted her. In revenge for Agni's action Bhṛgu cursed him, and as a result the divinity withdrew from the sacrifice and disappeared into the *śamī*-tree. Much disturbed, the gods sought him, and at their request he returned, so that the sacrifices were resumed once more. Another story tells that Agni fell in love with King Nīla's beautiful daughter, whose lot it was to tend her father's sacred fire. In the form of a Brāhman he wooed and with difficulty won the maiden, and rewarded her father in his struggle with Sahadeva by causing the horses, chariots, army, and even the body of the latter to burst into flame, Sahadeva and the other rivals of Nīla being thus destroyed and eaten by the god of fire.

Soma also ranks, like Vāyu and Agni, as a Vasu: his father was Atri, and in the epic he is the moon pure and simple, so that at times he bears the names Candramas, Candra, or Indu, all meaning simply "Moon." His fame rests on his marriage with twenty-seven of the daughters of Dakṣa Prajāpati, the twenty-seven Nakṣatras, or lunar mansions. Soma unhappily conceived an excessive affection for Rohiṇī alone of his wives, wherefore her sisters, going to their father, asked him to redress their grievance. Thereupon Dakṣa, by a curse, brought sickness on Soma, who appealed to his father-in-law, only to be told that he had acted unfairly. Nevertheless, the seers directed him to effect a cure by bathing at Hiraṇyatīrtha in the western region by the sea, and Soma did so, whence the place won the name of Prabhāsa ("Splendour"). On account of the curse, however, the moon is still hidden when it is new, and at its full shows a body covered by a line of clouds, whence is derived the view that there is a hare in the moon. Another trial of Soma's is his enmity with Rāhu, a demon who ever seeks to swallow him and who thus causes eclipses.

With Varuṇa Soma comes into close relation: by drinking all his six juices he is born to kill the darkness at the beginning of the light half of the month, and his daughter Jyotsnākālī married Puṣkara, Varuṇa's handsome and clever son. Trouble arose, however, over his daughter Bhadrā. Soma found for her a suitable husband in the Brāhman Utathya, but since Varuṇa had long desired her, one day he came to the forest where she lived and stole her after she had entered the water in order to bathe. On hearing the news Utathya sent Nārada to demand the restoration of his wife, but Nārada's embassy was fruitless. Utathya then drank up all the waters; and since even this drastic procedure had no effect, he caused the lakes on earth, to the number of six hundred thousand, to dry up and the rivers to disappear in the desert, whereupon Varuṇa at last repented of his action and restored his wife to Utathya.

In this legend Varuṇa appears, just as in early days, as a god of the waters, and this is essentially his character throughout the epic. Here and there, in company with Mitra, mention is made of his radiance and his light hue, and both are Ādityas; but, unlike the Vedic concept of these two deities, neither stands in any relation with the light of day or night. Varuṇa, on the contrary, bears many aqueous epithets, such as "God of the Waters," "Lord of Water," "Lord of the Rivers," and "Lord of Every Stream"; and it is as "Lord of the Waters" that he is said to rule over the Asuras. To this supremacy he was unanimously appointed at the beginning of the Kṛta age. His realm is in the west, and he dwells in the ocean, filled with Nāgas, aquatic monsters, precious stones, and fire, and rich in salt; and in the sea is also an egg whence flames will burst forth at the end of the world and destroy the whole of the three worlds. His city is full of palaces and Apsarases, and his own palace is made wholly of gold, while cooling waters drip from his royal canopy. He sits with his wife, Siddhi, or Gaurī, or Vāruṇī, in his hall of assembly, which Viśvakarman built in the midst of the waters and which contains divine trees consisting of pearls and producing every kind of fruit. He himself is dark blue in colour and like Yama he bears a noose, while his conch was fashioned for him by Viśvakarman from a thousand pieces of gold. It was from him that Arjuna obtained the bow Gāṇḍīva, as well as chariots and other gifts. Besides his son Puṣkara he had another, who was named Bandin and was the *sūta* of King Janaka. Defeated by the young boy Aṣṭāvakra in a competition because of his inability to enumerate things which made up thirteen, Bandin proved his connexion with his father by plunging into the waters and thus uniting himself with him.

The sun-deity of the epic is Sūrya or Āditya, son of Aditi, the ruler of the flaming lights, the light of the world, the father of beings who sustains them with his heat, the entrance to the ways of the gods. In him are summed up the many aspects of the Ādityas, as Pūṣan, Bhaga, Savitṛ, Aryaman, Dhātṛ, and Vivasvant. The sun is described as being as yellow as honey, with large arms and with a neck like tortoise-shell, and as wearing bracelets and a diadem. His ear-rings were the gift of Aditi. A single Nāga draws his chariot, which has but one wheel, though elsewhere seven steeds are mentioned. He has a special place in the epic in that he was the god whom Kuntī summoned to wed her and to whom she bore Karṇa, who was thus the eldest brother of the Pāṇḍava Yudhiṣṭhira. His wife is called Suvarcalā ("the Resplendent") and is mentioned as taking the form of a mare. His daughter is married to Bhānu, i.e. to himself in another form, and his son is Yama

Vaivasvata. Like Soma he lives at enmity with Rāhu, by whose swallowing of him he is at times eclipsed.

Two other forms of the sun are to be seen in Aruṇa and Garuḍa, the sons of Kaśyapa by Vinatā, daughter of Dakṣa Prajāpati. Aruṇa ("the Ruddy") was made the charioteer of the sun because, in anger at the misery inflicted upon him by Rāhu, he threatened to burn the world, and the gods desired to restrain his fury. It is even possible that the *Ṛgveda* alludes to him. He is, however, but a faint figure, while his younger brother, Garuḍa, figures in a great achievement, the stealing of the ambrosia from the gods. His mother Vinatā had a sister Kadrū who like herself was married to Kaśyapa, who gave each a boon: Kadrū received as progeny a thousand serpent sons, against Vinatā's two children. In both cases the offspring were produced as eggs, from which the snakes were born in five hundred years; but Vinatā unwisely broke one of the two eggs and found Aruṇa only half grown. He doomed her to become a slave until she should be set free by her second son, Garuḍa, and his curse was soon fulfilled. Kadrū and Vinatā staked their freedom [1] on the question whether the horse Uccaiḥśravas, which came into being at the churning of the ocean, was partly black or pure white. They crossed the ocean to decide the wager, and as Kadrū had induced her sons, the snakes, to fasten themselves on to the horse, it was found to have a black tail, and Vinatā fell into bondage. Then Garuḍa came to life from the egg and shared his mother's fate. He learned, however, that he could free himself by obtaining the ambrosia, and after many adventures he defeated the gods, extinguished the fire which surrounded the ambrosia, penetrated the whirling wheel of blades, and slaying the snakes which guarded the soma, he bore it away without drinking of it. In reward for this great deed Viṣṇu gives him immortality, sets him on his standard, and chooses him for his steed. Indra, however, hurls the thunderbolt against him, but Garuḍa lets only a single feather fall. Indra then makes peace with him and seeks to obtain the soma from him. Garuḍa refuses to give it to Indra, but the deity steals it after Garuḍa has gone to bathe, having set it out on *kuśa*-grass for the snakes. The serpents lick the place where the soma has lain, and thus their tongues become forked.

The legend shows clear traces of the Vedic tale of the bringing down of the soma to earth by the Gāyatrī: like the Gāyatrī Garuḍa is regarded as a bird and is called both Garutmant ("the Winged") and Suparṇa ("the Fair-Feathered"). With the wind of the motion of his wings he can stay the rotation of the three worlds, and his strength is so great that he seems to drag the earth after him as he goes. Viṣṇu indeed once had to check his boast of his might by laying on him the weight of his right arm. The main object of Garuḍa, however, as of his six sons and their offspring, is to prey on the snakes.

An essentially new deity is Skanda, who ranks both as the son of Agni and of Śiva, although as a matter of fact he was brought to life in a mysterious way in order to create for Devasenā, daughter of Prajāpati, a husband stronger than gods and men alike. He was thought to be the son of the six wives of the Seven Seers, Arundhatī being omitted; and the seers having repudiated their spouses for their apparent infidelity, they became stars in the constellation Kṛttikās ("Pleiades"). Skanda is six-faced, but has only one neck; he always wears red garments and rides on a peacock. His prowess in war is great and marks him as the real war-god in the later epic: he becomes the general of the army of the gods, who are defeated in his absence, while the Asura Mahiṣa seeks to grasp the chariot of Viṣṇu; but Skanda returns, and, slaying him, reestablishes Indra in his position. He also killed Tāraka, and his spear never misses the mark, but, once thrown, returns to him after slaying thousands of his foes. When a boy, he thrust his spear into the ground in contempt for the three worlds and challenged the whole world to remove it; the Daitya Prahlāda, Hiraṇyakaśipu's son, fainted at the attempt, but, when Viṣṇu

## PLATE XVI

### Garuḍa

The mythic bird Garuḍa is the *vāhana* ("vehicle") of Viṣṇu. He is the lord of birds, the brother of Aruṇa, the charioteer of Sūrya ("the Sun"), and the implacable foe of snakes, who are his half-brothers. From an ebony carving in the collection of Lieut.-Col. A. H. Milne, of Cults, Aberdeenshire, Scotland.

moved it with his left hand, the earth and its hills shook. With his arrows Skanda split the rock Krauñca in Himavant; yet he is not merely a war-god, for sometimes he is celebrated in terms applicable to Śiva himself as all-god and he seems to be no more than a specialized form of Śiva. The other form of Śiva, Gaṇeśa, though prominent in the *Purāṇas*, is not known in the epic save in interpolated passages.

Another new god is Kāma, who is called also Manmatha ("the Confusing"), Madana ("the Intoxicating"), and Kandarpa ("the Proud"), or Anaṅga ("the Bodiless"), who lost his corporeal shape by his rash action in inspiring love in the heart of Śiva. He is the son of Dharma and has arrows like Cupid. There can be little historical connexion between this somewhat dilettante god of passion, who is a late comer in the epic, and the Kāma of the *Atharvaveda* (iii. 25), though both have arrows. It is possible that Greek influence is here to be seen at work, and it has even been suggested that it was the fame of Alexander the Great that brought the name of Skanda into prominence as a war-god.

The Aśvins remain little changed: their old names of Nāsatya and Dasra have been turned into proper names of the pair, but they are still the physicians of the gods and the healers of mankind. Their origin is variously described. In one passage they are called the children of Mārtāṇḍa, one of the Ādityas born from the nose of his wife Sañjnā, whence the name Nāsatya, since in Sanskrit *nāsā* means "nose." In another they are Guhyakas, born of Savitṛ and the daughter of Tvaṣṭṛ; in yet another account they are sprung from the tears of Agni. Despite their great beauty, they were Śūdras, or members of the lowest caste, and Indra would not allow them to share the Soma offering. One day, however, they came across Sukanyā, daughter of Śaryāti and wife of Cyavana, as she was bathing and sought her in marriage; but when she refused to listen to their advances, in reward they promised to make her aged and decrepit husband fair and young. She then went and brought

Cyavana, who entered the water with the Aśvins, all three emerging in the same youthful and lovely condition. She managed, however, to choose her own husband from among them, and in delight he secured for the Aśvins a share in the soma drink. In the epic special interest is given to them by the fact that they were born as Mādrī's two sons Nakula and Sahadeva, the youngest of the Pāṇḍavas.

The Maruts, who have sunk to mere names, serve to aid Indra in his conflicts with his foes. In one passage they are said to be descended from the Seven Seers, and in another place Marīci is said to be the chief among them, which brings them into connexion with the Prajāpatis, of whom Marīci is the most important.

The Rudras form an indeterminate group, either eleven or eleven thousand in number. They are children of Dharma, and Śiva is their protector, but they are effectively swallowed up in his omnipotence. One list ascribes to their ranks Mṛgavyādha, Sarpa, Nirṛti, Aja Ekapād, Ahi Budhnya, Pinākin, Dahana, Īśvara, Kapālin, Sthāṇu, and Bhaga, a curious conglomerate of epithets of Śiva and the ancient Vedic gods.

The Vasus number eight, and are sons of Dharma or of Prajāpati Manu. In one list they appear as Dhara, Dhruva, Soma, Aha, Anila, Anala, Pratyūṣa, and Prabhāsa, but in another Sāvitra replaces Aha, and in the *Harivaṁśa* Āpas takes his place. They sinned against the great sage Vasiṣṭha by stealing his cow to please the wife of Dyaus, and were doomed by him to be born on earth. Accordingly they became the children of Gaṅgā, who for another fault had been condemned to assume mortal form, and King Śāntanu. But their mother cast the first seven into the water, and Śāntanu succeeded in saving only the eighth, who became Bhīṣma, the famous sage and warrior of the epic. The Vasus, however, showed their realization of their kinship with Bhīṣma by cursing Arjuna for slaying him.

The Ādityas number, as usual, twelve, but the lists of them

differ: one gives Indra, Viṣṇu, Bhaga, Tvaṣṭṛ, Varuṇa, Aṁśa, Aryaman, Ravi, Pūṣan, Mitra, Manu, and Parjanya; while another has Dhātṛ, Aryaman, Mitra, Varuṇa, Aṁśa, Bhaga, Indra, Vivasvant, Pūṣan, Tvaṣṭṛ, Savitṛ, Parjanya, and Viṣṇu, making thirteen. Of these Aṁśa, Aryaman, Pūṣan, Bhaga, Mitra, Ravi, Vivasvant, and Savitṛ are all equivalents of the sun-god; Parjanya and Indra have no real solar character; and Dhātṛ, Tvaṣṭṛ, and Manu are synonyms of the creator-god Brahmā.

The Gandharvas as heavenly musicians are often mentioned as playing on their lutes and as singing, while the Apsarases dance. They reside near Lake Mānasa and also on Mount Niṣadha. Two of their leaders, Viśvāvasu and Tumburu, are mentioned, and the Kinnaras and Naras are classed with them. The mystic connexion of the Gandharva with birth has, however, disappeared; and the Apsarases have also lost all mystery and have sunk to be the dancers of the gods, beautiful with lotus eyes, slender waists, and swelling hips, who enchant mortals with their gestures and their honeyed words. They serve Śakra in heaven and consort with the Gandharvas. It is they who are called upon to interrupt from time to time the devotions of saints when they threaten to acquire too much sanctity. Yet they are often unsuccessful in these errands, and even Urvaśī herself failed when she sought to attract the love of Arjuna on his visit to the heaven of Indra. Repulsed, she cursed him to become a eunuch, but her malediction was only nominally fulfilled. Long lists of names of Apsarases are given, among which are Rambhā, Menakā, Puñjikasthalā, Viśvācī, Ghṛtācī, Sahajanyā, Pramlocā, Miśrakeśī, and Irā. Some of these are Vedic, and Irā is none other than the Iḍā, or sacrificial food in the Vedic offering. It is a curious fate which brings the holy consecrated essence of the offering into the rank of a dancing girl.

The Cāraṇas, wandering minstrels or troubadours, are mentioned with the Gandharvas, and the Siddhas and Sādhyas also occur as blessed spirits, though without mention of their special functions. The Siddhas, however, are said to dwell on the south of the Nīla Mountain and the northern side of Meru in the realm of the Uttara Kurus. In that land trees yield fruits at pleasure, milk, and six kinds of food tasting like ambrosia; the trees bear clothing, and in their fruits are ornaments. The men there are beautiful and live ten thousand and ten hundred years; children are born as twins and intermarry; at death birds called Bhāruṇḍas come and carry away the dead, throwing them into mountain caves.

The Vidyādharas live in the Himavant on Mount Krauñca; their chief is Cakradharman, but their only function is to rain flowers down on the warriors as they fight with one another.

Still less definitely divine are the Ṛṣis, or seers, of whom many classes are mentioned. The greatest are the Seven Seers, normally given as Aṅgiras, Atri, Kratu, Pulastya, Pulaha, Marīci, and Vasiṣṭha. The names, however, vary, and in the legend of the drawing of the chariot of Nahuṣa by the Seven Seers it is Agastya who plays the chief *rôle* and hurls Nahuṣa from heaven. Another famous story,[2] which in its main lines must have been known as early as the *Aitareya Brāhmaṇa* (v. 30) and which is preserved in variant versions in the *Jātaka*, tells of an adventure of Atri, Vasiṣṭha, Kaśyapa, Gautama, Jamadagni, Bharadvāja, and Viśvāmitra, with Arundhatī. Once upon a time the seers found themselves threatened with famine, and in the midst of it Śaibya Vṛṣādarbhi, who had been given to them as an offering by his royal father, died. The king offered them large sums to prevent them eating human flesh, but these they declined to take as transgressing the rule which forbade the acceptance of presents, and wandered away. The king performed a sacrifice whence sprang a terrible demon named Yātudhānī, whom he sent after the seers. As they went along, they were joined by a man with a dog, and finally they came to a lake guarded by the Yātudhānī, who allowed them to enter it to pluck lotuses for the sake of the edible fibre on condition that they should declare their identity. They all gathered the lotuses, and then laying them down, went to bathe, only to find them vanished on their return. Thereupon the seers invoked terrible curses on him who had stolen the fibres, but their new friend wished that man good luck, thus revealing himself as the thief. He then declared himself to be Indra and rewarded the seers by according heaven to them.

The seers are also classed as "Divine Seers" (Devarṣis), "Brāhman Seers" (Brahmarṣis), and "Royal Seers" (Rājarṣis). Bṛhaspati figures as the sage and protects Śacī against Nahuṣa. He was the son of Aṅgiras and acted as Indra's charioteer. Bhṛgu was of higher origin, being a son of Brahmā; and among his feats were his curse of Agni, through whom Puloman abducted his wife Pulomā, and his curse of the Himālaya. Nārada and his friend Parvata play a certain part in the *Mahābhārata*, where they appear as high in honour among sages: Nārada gave to King Śaibya Sṛñjaya a son Suvarṇaṣṭhīvin, whose evacuations were all gold. Great riches thus accumulated in the home of the king, but robbers seized the boy and slew him, only to find no gold within. Finally Nārada comforted Suvarṇaṣṭhīvin's father and restored the lad to life. Nārada also cursed the Yādavas and so brought about their final destruction, which culminated in the death of Kṛṣṇa, who was already doomed by Gāndhārī's curse.

Gautama plays his part in a foolish tale which tells how he rejuvenated his faithful pupil Utaṅka and gave him his daughter in marriage; but for his mother-in-law Ahalyā Utaṅka had to seek the ear-rings of the wife of Saudāsa, who had become a man-eater. He succeeded in doing this, though only after a quest in hell for the ear-rings which he had accidentally lost. Ahalyā has an evil notoriety through being seduced by Indra.

More interesting is the strife of Vasiṣṭha with Viśvāmitra, now king of Kanyakubja (the modern Kanauj). Viśvāmitra seeks from Vasiṣṭha his famous cow, Nandinī, and on his refusal endeavours to take her by force, but his troops are defeated by hosts of Mlecchas ("Barbarians") which the cow produces. He therefore devotes himself to asceticism, and at last attaining Brāhmanhood, he revenges himself on his rival by getting Kalmāṣapāda to eat Vasiṣṭha's son Śakti and other sons. In despair Vasiṣṭha seeks to slay himself, but the river into which he casts himself bound rejects him and hence acquires its name of Vipāś, or "Unbound" (the modern Beas). At last he is comforted by finding that Śakti's wife is to bear a son Parāśara. Viśvāmitra also distinguished himself by devouring a dog's flesh when in hunger and by debating with a Cāṇḍāla, or outcaste; by the Apsaras Menakā he was the father of the famous Śakuntalā. Vasiṣṭha, whose wife was Arundhatī, cursed the Vasus and made them be born as men, and he also cursed Hiraṇyakaśipu.

Of Agastya wild legends are related. He created Lopamudrā to be his wife, but gave her as an adoptive daughter to the king of Vidarbha (Berār), a tale doubtless meant to explain the mixed marriage of persons of the Brāhman and warrior castes. To win treasure for her he made a pilgrimage to various kings, but took nothing from them, since he found that they spent their wealth in good deeds. Finally, however, he came to king Ilvala, who had already destroyed many Brāhmans by causing them to eat, in the form of flesh, his brother Vātāpi, who then emerged from them, rending their bodies and killing them. Ilvala sought to destroy Agastya in like manner, but by his wondrous power of digestion the sage succeeded in assimilating Vātāpi, who could not, therefore, come forth at his brother's call, whereupon Ilvala richly rewarded the seer. The story of the theft of the lotuses is narrated of him also, and it was he who prevented the Vindhya, which was growing up to heaven, from actually reaching the sky. He had a son Dṛḍhasyu, who was of incomparable strength; and he drank up the ocean and burnt the Asuras, besides bringing Nahuṣa to ruin.

Vāmadeva is the hero of a curious episode: in a thicket one day King Parikṣit comes upon a fair maiden who consents to marry him on condition that she shall never see water. After a time, however, she unhappily beholds a tank of water and vanishes while bathing in it; the water is let out, and only a frog is found. Parikṣit orders the massacre of the frogs, whereupon their king, Āyu, appears and explains that the maiden is his daughter, who is then united in marriage to the king, but whose offspring are fated by their grandfather's curse to be foes of Brāhmans. The children of Parikṣit, Śala, Dala, and Bala, grow up, and in hunting one day Śala borrows from Vāmadeva two horses which he refuses to return, even though the seer causes a Rākṣasa to tear him to pieces. Dala aims a poisoned arrow at Vāmadeva, but kills only his own son; and Dala's wife, at last propitiating the sage, returns the horses to him.

Manu plays a comparatively small *rôle:* he is the son of Vivasvant, the brother of Yama, and the hero of the tale of the deluge. On the advice of the fish he builds a ship and places in it the seeds of all beings,[3] so that he restores the world again when, after the deluge, the ship rests on Naubandhana. The fish reveals itself as Brahmā, not (as in the later legend) as Viṣṇu. One of his children, Ila, was of double character, now man now woman, and he was the father of Purūravas, who oppressed the Brāhmans. With Ila's androgynous nature there is a parallel in the *Mahābhārata* (xiii. 528 ff.) in the tale of Bhaṅgāsvana who, with his sons, was turned into a woman and who preferred to retain that sex. Later Śiva is often androgynous, and in the Vedic mythology Prajāpati is, it would seem, occasionally so conceived, but this double character of Ila cannot be traced earlier in the Vedic legend of Purūravas.[4]

Another Vedic story appears in an altered form in the tale of Śunaḥśepa. As in the *Mahābhārata*, Viśvāmitra is engaged in rivalry with Vasiṣṭha and after the repulse of his effort to seize the cow of his rival he practises asceticism, rising through the states of royal seer, great seer, and finally Brāhman seer, even Vasiṣṭha recognizing his position. In the course of this process he has two adventures without a parallel in the *Mahābhārata.* Triśaṅku, a king who sought to attain heaven with his own body by means of the sacrifice, found that Vasiṣṭha would not help him to this end. Nevertheless, by a mighty offering to which all the seers were invited, but from which Mahodaya and the Vasiṣṭhas kept away, Viśvāmitra raised Triśaṅku aloft toward the sky. Indra, however, struck him downward, but Viśvāmitra arrested his flight in mid-air, where he hangs in the southern sky, head down, among other stars and constellations which Viśvāmitra made to accompany him. The second experience was his encounter with Ambarīṣa, a king whose sacrificial victim had been carried away by Indra from the altar. As a substitute he decided to offer a human victim to appease the god, and after long search was able to purchase Śunaḥśepa, the second son of Ṛcīka, for a thousand cows. On being sold by his father, however, Śunaḥśepa entreated Viśvāmitra to help him, and the seer did so by giving him a couple of *gāthās*, or verses, which saved him from death.

There is a curious exception to the rule that the Vedic gods appear as of little account in the epic. In one passage in the *Mahābhārata* (iii. 15457 ff.) we are told that in the world of Brahmā, which lies above the worlds of the Vedic gods, are the seers and others, including the deities of the gods, the Ṛbhus, whom even the divinities worship. They are described as being exempt from old age, from death, from pain or happiness, from love or hate, as living without sacrifice and without ambrosia; and — what is yet more wonderful — they do not perish with the ages like the other gods, who accordingly seek in vain to attain their rank. The passage is as remarkable as it is isolated, and it contrasts strongly with the somewhat lowly position occupied by the Ṛbhus in the Vedic pantheon.

Diverse as are their natures, there are certain things which the gods have in common: they are all immortal, though this must be taken with the qualification that they are subject to the periodic absorption of the universe at the end of the cycle of ages. They move freely in the air; and their place of life is normally the heaven, whence they descend to earth at will. Their pleasure-ground is Mount Meru in the Himālaya between Mālayavant and Gandhamādana. This mountain, which shines like the morning sun, is of gold and is as round as a ball; it is eighty-four thousand *yojanas* high and as far below the earth does it penetrate. The birds on it have golden feathers, for which reason Sumukha, one of the six sons of Garuḍa, refused to stay there because the ranks of the birds were not distinguished. Round the mountain go the sun, the moon, and Vāyu, and on it gods, Gandharvas, Rākṣasas, and Asuras play with bevies of Apsarases. There are lovely forests on its top, and it rings with the songs of female Kinnaras.

Many signs distinguish the gods from mortals, these being enumerated in the story of Nala, where Damayantī recognizes the deities by their exemption from perspiration, their unwinking eyes, their unfading garlands, their freedom from dust, and their standing without touching the earth. Yet there is no absolute division between gods and men, and the *Mahābhārata* can tell us that the Rudras, Vasus, Ādityas, Sādhyas, and royal seers have all attained heaven by their devotion to duty.

While the epic has little to say of the old *quasi*-abstract deities, such as Aditi, who figures merely as the mother of the Ādityas, or Nirṛti, who appears simply as a Rudra, there is an abstraction which has a real existence and which develops a slight mythology. This is Dharma, the personified conception of law, who married ten of the daughters of Dakṣa, but who is more closely connected with the heroes of the epic by the fact that by Kuntī he was the father of Yudhiṣṭhira, the chief of the Pāṇḍavas. On three occasions he tempted Yudhiṣṭhira in order to test his true worth; and every time Yudhiṣṭhira proved his character, refusing to enter the celestial realms without his faithful dog, which alone arrived with him at the entrance to Indra's heaven, and preferring to live in hell with his kindred than to dwell in heaven when he was told that they could not share its pleasures with him. Dharma also made proof of the virtue of other heroes, but his dealings were severely criticized by the sage Māṇḍavya. This seer, while engaged on a penance which included complete silence, was wrongly believed guilty of the theft of property which thieves in their flight deposited in his place of abode, and was impaled as a penalty. Nevertheless, he did not die, and the king, recognizing the wrong done to him, had him removed from the stake, a part of which, however, remained in his body. The sage sought Dharma in order to learn for what atrocious crime in his earlier life he had thus cruelly been punished, and was told by Dharma that it was because, in his childhood, he had stuck a thorn into the back of an insect. Naturally enraged at the ridiculous disproportion between the offence and the punishment, Māṇḍavya cursed Dharma to be born as the son of a Śūdra woman, and accordingly he came to life as Vidura, being born through the union of Vyāsa with a slave woman, instead of with Ambikā, one of the widows of Vicitravīrya, who was too frightened to submit to marriage with the sage, even for the purpose of securing a son for her dead husband in accordance with the ancient practice of the levirate. Vidura proved a wise councillor of Dhṛtarāṣṭra as well as a protector of the Pāṇḍavas, and at the end, when the Kuru family had fallen into ruin, it was he who accompanied to the forest the aged Dhṛtarāṣṭra, and there by his power of *yoga*, or mystic union, he gave up life and was united with Yudhiṣṭhira. Contrary to custom, his body was not burnt.

Just as in the period of the *Brāhmaṇas*, the Asuras stand over against the gods in a compact body and ever wage war with them. The conflict is one which has no ending, despite the constant slaying of the demons by the gods; for as often as the fiends are routed, others arise to take their place. Demon after demon is mentioned as causing fear to the gods, and though unquestionably the deities have the superiority, just as they have in the

*Brāhmaṇas*, the ascendancy is only that of one set of immortals against another. In so far as the triumph of good is secured in the universe, it is not in the sphere of the empirical world with its apparatus of gods and demons, but in the absolute as personified in the sectarian divinities. Moreover, the Asuras are the elder brothers of the gods, being, like them, children of Kaśyapa Prajāpati and of thirteen of the daughters of Dakṣa Prajāpati; the children of Diti are the Daityas, and those of Dānu the Dānavas; and since Diti was the eldest daughter of Dakṣa, the Daityas were older even than the gods. The enmity of the gods and the Asuras commenced at the churning of the ocean for the sake of the ambrosia and is briefly related in the *Rāmāyaṇa* (i. 45 ff.) in concluding its account of that great event. The *Mahābhārata* (i. 1103 ff.) has a fuller version of the struggle. When the moon, Lakṣmī, the white steed, the Kaustubha gem, and Dhanvantari had appeared — the latter bearing the nectar in his hand — and when the dread poison had been swallowed by Śiva, the Asuras were filled with despair and decided to war with the gods for the possession of Lakṣmī and the ambrosia. Thereupon Nārāyaṇa called to his aid his bewitching power of illusion (*māyā*) and in ravishing female form coquetted with the Daityas, who placed the nectar in her hand. Then, with his counterpart Nara, Nārāyaṇa took away the *amṛta*, but Rāhu, a Dānava, was drinking it in the form of a god. The nectar, however, had reached only his throat when the sun and the moon discovered his theft and told the gods, whereupon Nārāyaṇa with his discus clove the head of Rāhu, which leapt to the sky, where it ever wars with the sun and moon, swallowing them and causing their eclipse. Nārāyaṇa then laid aside his female form and attacked the demons; and after an appalling conflict Nārāyaṇa and Nara defeated their foes, securing the ambrosia for the gods.

The Asuras have strongholds and haunts in the mountain caves, and they dwell in the depths in Pātāla, where are the cities of Nirmocana, Prāgjyotiṣa, and Hiraṇyapura. Or they are within the sea, having been cast there and placed in the keeping of Varuṇa. In heaven they made three fortresses, one of gold, one of iron, and one of silver, and thence they assailed the three worlds, only to fail in their attempt and to be cast from heaven. It is characteristic, however, of the constant relationship in which they stand to the gods that on the divine Mount Meru itself Asuras and Rākṣasas mingle in friendly contact with gods and Gandharvas; and, demons though they are, Viśvakarman, who serves as divine architect, having fallen to this humble position from his late Vedic rank, builds for them, to plans devised by Maya, their town Hiraṇyapura. It is equally significant that it was Dharma who bound the demons and handed them over to Varuṇa to guard in the sea; and Varuṇa's loss of rank is shown with special clearness by the fact that it was with the nooses of Dharma, doubtless the very ones which had been his own in the Vedic period, that Varuṇa bound the Daityas and Dānavas, while both Dharma and Varuṇa act under the orders of the supreme lord.

Evil as they are, the demons are formidable fighters: Mahiṣa attacks the gods with a mountain as his weapon; Keśin snatches a mountain-peak for an assault. Not only are they numberless, but they are skilled in sorcery and in every magic art, transforming themselves into all manner of shapes, such as those used by Rāvaṇa in the abduction of Sītā, and spreading universal terror by their appalling roars. The Daityas and Dānavas become invisible and must be met with invisible weapons. An episode in the *Mahābhārata* (iii. 11903 ff.) tells in detail of the exploits of Arjuna against the demons: on the instigation of Indra he attacks the Nivātakavacas in their fortress beneath the sea, and though they strive against him with magic arts, at last they are defeated, notwithstanding the fact that they had taken their city from the gods and had held it despite them. He then proceeds to destroy the city of Hiraṇyapura, which was occupied by the Paulomas and Kālakañjas and which Brahmā had given to Pulomā and Kālakā as the reward of asceticism. The practice of asceticism by individual Asuras reminds us that they had once been virtuous, had practised righteousness, and had sacrificed; with them Śrī ("Fortune") dwelt at the beginning of the world. But as they grew in numbers they became proud and wicked, they ceased to sacrifice or to visit Tīrthas (holy places), and they set themselves in defiance of the gods. That they sometimes won partial victory is sufficiently proved by the tale of Bali, from whom Viṣṇu had to win back the earth by his three steps, but Śrī definitely forsook them because of their lack of righteousness, and thus their successes were never lasting.

The names of the Asuras, whether classed as Daityas or as Dānavas, are curiously mixed. Some are clearly ancient Vedic demons sunk to a lower level: Vṛtra and Vala, Śambara, Namuci, and Triśiras are all old enemies of Indra. It is more surprising to find among them the pious Vedic sage Uśanas, who is identified with Śukra after emerging from Śiva's body when that god had swallowed him. He was the *purohita*, or domestic priest, of the Asura Vṛṣaparvan and was chiefly noted for his skill in bringing the dead to life, a feat performed by him for Kaca, and by Kaca for him. Sunda and Upasunda, children of Nikumbha, by their ascetic practices obtained from Brahmā the boon that they should be vulnerable only by each other; but the god then induced Viśvakarman to create in Tilottamā a woman of wondrous beauty, and she was revealed one day to the two brothers as they amused themselves in the Vindhya, with the fatal result that, casting aside their ancient love, the two brothers slew each other. Prahrāda was defeated by Indra, Madhu by Viṣṇu, and Mahiṣa by Skanda; while Vātāpi, after killing many Brāhmans, was devoured and digested by Agastya. Maya the architect also appears as an Asura, and it has been conjectured that in him we have a faint reflex of the supreme god of Iran, the influence of Persian architecture having been claimed to exist at Pāṭaliputra, but the suggestion seems to rest on no assured foundation. Other names are those of Kamalākṣa, Kālanemi, Jambha, Tārakākṣa, Tālajaṅgha, Daṁśa, Naraka (apparently a personified hell), Nahuṣa (the rival of Indra, overthrown by Agastya), Pāka, Mada, Virocana, Vīra, Vegavant, Saṁhlāda, Sālva, and Hiraṇyakaśipu, the latter of whom was slain by Viṣṇu in his man-lion avatar.

The old Vedic Dasyus, who were often enough nothing but human foes, but who were also doubtless demons, at least in part, are practically mere men in the epic, where it is said that Indra invented armour, arms, and the bow for their destruction. On the other hand, great importance now attaches to the Nāgas, who are described as serpents and also enumerated with them. Many and various are their dwelling-places: they live in Nāgaloka ("Snake-World") in the depths of the earth, where are many palaces, towers, and pleasure gardens, but their home is also called Pātāla and Niraya. Their chief town is Bhogavatī, where the serpent king, Vāsuki, lives. Yet they are found also in caves, in inaccessible mountains, in the valleys, in Kurukṣetra, on the banks of the river Ikṣumatī, in the Naimiṣa forest, on the shores of the Gomatī, on the northern banks of the Ganges, and in the Niṣadha district. The strength of the snakes is great; they are huge in size, very violent, swift to strike, and full of deadly poison; but they are also said to be handsome and of many shapes, and to wear ear-rings. There are many kinds: of Vāsuki's race some are blue, some red, and some white; some have three, some seven, and some ten heads.

The most famous episode connected with the snakes is the sacrifice of them by Janamejaya in revenge for his father's death. When pursuing a wounded gazelle Parikṣit met an ascetic named Śamīka, but since the latter could not help him to know its path, he threw a dead snake on the hermit's neck. In anger the son of Śamīka cursed the king to die in seven days from the bite of the serpent ruler Takṣaka. Displeased with this action, Śamīka warned the king of his fate, and Parikṣit

## PLATE XVII

### Vāsuki

Vāsuki, the king of the Nāgas ("Serpents"), is represented, like his subjects generally, in human form, the only trace of his original nature being his serpent crest. This fact reflects the belief that the Nāgas assume human form at will. For the true serpent shape of Vāsuki, see Fig. 2. From the temple rail at Bhārhut, Baghelkhand. After Cunningham, *The Stūpa of Bhārhut*, Plate XXI.

retired into a carefully guarded palace raised on pillars. Kāśyapa, who came to heal him from the threatened bite, was bribed by Takṣaka to depart, and the latter introduced himself into the palace in the shape of a worm in fruits presented by snakes in Brāhman guise as a gift to the sovereign. Then appearing in his true form, he bit the king; but Parikṣit's son, Janamejaya, in his anger made so huge a sacrifice of the snakes that even Takṣaka would have perished if it had not been for the intervention of Āstīka, who induced the young monarch to spare him.

Śeṣa lies underneath the earth and supports it. He is the son of Kadrū and at the churning of the ocean he performed the important task of tearing out Mount Mandara so that it might be placed on the great tortoise in preparation for the churning. Vāsuki also served as churning string at the churning and was grandfather of Kuntī, the mother of the Pāṇḍavas. He healed Bhīma when the latter was poisoned. Another snake is Arbuda, who is reminiscent of a figure of the *Atharvaveda;* and Dhṛtarāṣṭra appears as a serpent king, as in the *Śatapatha Brāhmaṇa.* Others are Karkoṭaka, Kālapṛṣṭha, Jaya, Mahājaya, and Padmanābhi.

The snakes take part even in the epic conflict, and we are told that the great serpents were for Arjuna and the little for Karṇa. There is still a Nāga people in India, and it may be that the epic refers to the Nāga tribes of the Ganges valley. Doubtless many causes have combined to produce the belief in Nāgas. The cloud-snake is Ṛgvedic, and the serpent is closely connected with rivers and streams as the *genius loci.* Similarly it is a representative of the earth spirit, while, again, the snake in itself is a dangerous animal and worthy of worship for its own sake. It may well be that, in part at least, the worship was totemistic and was accompanied by a belief in the ancestorship of the snake and in its kinship with the worshippers, though the epic says nothing directly on these points.

The Rākṣasas are of particularly terrible aspect: they have

red hair and eyes and a mouth stretching from ear to ear, the latter being pointed like spears. Large and strong, they wander in the darkness and are unconquerable at midnight, and they are skilled sorcerers and wizards, changing shape at will. They haunt the woods and the lonely mountains, but they also lie in wait for the pious at places of pilgrimage and worship. They delight in destroying the sacrifice and are cannibals, desiring human flesh; yet they can appear in beautiful form when they wish to deceive the unwary.

Of individual Rākṣasas by far the greatest is Rāvaṇa, the enemy of Rāma, though perhaps he was originally an Asura, rather than a mere Rākṣasa. His son Indrajit performed great deeds of strength before he finally fell in battle; his brothers Khara and Vibhīṣaṇa also fought on his side, and his sister Śūrpanakhā assisted him. Mārīca aided him in his plot to steal Sītā and finally was killed in the form of a golden gazelle by Rāma. In the *Mahābhārata* (i. 5928 ff.) Hiḍimba, a Rākṣasa, made an attack on the Pāṇḍavas, but was brought low by Bhīma; his sister fell in love with the slayer of her brother and bore to him Ghaṭotkaca. More interesting is the tale of Jarā. King Bṛhadratha had no son, but through the favour of Caṇḍakauśika each of his two wives bore a portion of a boy. These fragments were thrown away as monstrosities, but when Jarā approached and placed them together in order to carry them away, they formed a complete child who called out, whereupon his parents came to see what had happened and found him. Jarā then explained that she had refrained from devouring the child because as the house-deity she had dwelt in painted form on the walls, surrounded with offerings; and she declared that this was an infallible mode of securing prosperity.

Closely akin with such female Rākṣasas as Jarā are the Mātṛs, or "Mothers," who appear in the *Mahābhārata* in close connexion with Skanda. They dwell in cemeteries, at cross-roads, or on the mountains, and practise witchcraft.

## PLATE XVIII

### Yakṣī

This sculpture of the Yakṣī Sirimā Devatā well illustrates the Indian ideal of feminine beauty as represented in sculpture and painting, and as described in Sanskrit literature. From the temple rail at Bhārhut, Baghelkhand. After a photograph in the Library of the India Office, London.

They are mentioned together with the Grahas, or "Seizers," spirits which afflict men and which are both male and female: one class is dangerous to children up to the sixteenth year, and others are perilous from then to the age of seventy, after which the fever demon is alone to be dreaded. Their effects are various and range from mere foolish and mischievous sports, like those of fairies, to gluttony or lust. From the point of view of religion the presence of the Grahas is significant; but despite the identity of their name with the word for "planet," it does not seem that they have astrological connexions, and at times they are classified with Piśācas, Yakṣas, and similar minor beings.

The Piśācas are closely akin with the Rākṣasas and often occur with them: like them they drink blood and rend human flesh, and their appearance is hideous and revolting. Their very name has been interpreted as "Eaters of Raw Flesh," and their origin traced to cannibal tribes,[5] but this suggestion is not convincing.

On the other hand, the Yakṣas are free from savage traits, and their lord Kubera stands on the verge of divinity. Their duty is to guard him, and they are often mentioned along with the Guhyakas, with whom they are sometimes identified. In the first chapter of the *Mahābhārata*, which is of late origin, the Yakṣas, Sādhyas, Guhyakas, Piśācas, and fathers are reckoned as manifestations of Śiva.

Kubera has a history. He was, it is said, originally an Asura, his father being the sage Viśravas, and his mother Ilavilā, and his half-brothers being Rāvaṇa, Kumbhakarṇa, and Vibhīṣaṇa, all of whom figure in the legend of Rāma. His half-brothers were the children of Kaikasī, and his grandfather was Sumāli, who lived in Pātāla, while Kubera dwelt in Laṅkā. Incited by Sumāli, however, Rāvaṇa drove Kubera forth from his kingdom, and he departed thence with a train of Gandharvas, Yakṣas, Rākṣasas, and Kimpuruṣas, Vibhīṣaṇa accompanying him and being given in reward the charge of the

Rākṣasa and the Yakṣa armies. He went to the Himālaya range, to the mountain Gandhamādana, and to Kailāsa with the lively Mandākinī River, while Rāvaṇa entered Laṅkā with those Rākṣasas who had espoused his cause, attacked both gods and demons, and won his name by the roars of grief which he caused.

On Kailāsa and Gandhamādana Kubera now dwells, enjoying a quarter of the treasure of the mountain and giving one sixteenth to man. Rākṣasas, Gandharvas, and Kinnaras, as well as Guhyakas and Yakṣas, are in his service and attend him amid scenes of the utmost beauty. His great forest is called Nandana, and his grove is Caitraratha. The waters of his river, the Mandākinī, are covered with golden lotuses; and his lake, Nalinī or Jambūnadasaras (also known as Alakā), is full of golden lotuses and lovely birds, is surrounded by dense trees, has cool water, and is guarded by the Krodhavaśa Rākṣasas under their king Maṇibhadra. In his city of Alakā flags ever flutter, and women dance. In his assembly hall he sits in solemn state, surrounded by his retainers; and Lakṣmī, Śiva, and Umā all visit him there. His chariot Puṣpaka was wrought, like his palace, by Viśvakarman and was given to him by Brahmā, but Rāvaṇa took it from him on his defeat, only to be cursed in consequence. His favourite weapon is a mysterious one called Antardhāna, with which Śaṅkara once destroyed the three fortresses of the Asuras. He has, ever guarded by poisonous snakes, a jar of honey, and if a mortal might taste of it, he would win immortality, a blind man would regain his sight, and an old man would become young again.

Besides these groups of minor divine powers, more or less well defined, the epic is full of worship of anything that can be regarded as charged with mysterious potency. Prominent among these lesser beliefs is that in trees, which are deemed to be not merely homes of spirits, but actual living beings, a relic of an older stratum of thought. Thus in the days of Pṛthu Vainya the trees were not only good, so that clothes pleasant to

## PLATE XIX

### Kubera

Kubera, lord of the Yakṣas and guardian of treasures, was originally king of the gnomes who hide metals and jewels in the mountains. As a mountain-god, he is also a deity who promotes fertility. It is not impossible that Kubera is the Indian counterpart of the Greek Kabeiroi, even in name. From the temple rail at Bhārhut, Baghelkhand. After Cunningham, *The Stūpa of Bharhut*, Plate XXII.

touch could be made from all of them, but they themselves came and had speech with Pṛthu Vainya, a culture hero of great antiquity. Or, again, two wives desirous of children embrace trees, which, unfortunately, are interchanged, so that the wife who seeks a heroic obtains a priestly son, and *vice versa*. Many trees are sacred in the extreme: the worship of the *Ficus religiosa* is equal to the worship of a god, and there are five heavenly trees of special sanctity. The mountains, too, are full of life, and the Vedic legend of their wings is still remembered. Vindhya seeks the sky and is restrained only by the cunning of Agastya; Maināka is famed because when the other mountains lost their pinions, it retained its own; and Krauñca is renowned for being pierced by Skanda. All the mountains were once reduced to ashes by a saint Dhanuṣākṣa as the only means to destroy Medhāvin, son of Vāladhi, who had secured from the gods the promise that his son's life should last as long as the mountains endured.

The lord of the dead is Yama Vaivasvata, even as in the Vedic epoch; and he ranks as one of the four Lokapālas, or "World-Protectors," who are normally reckoned as Indra, Agni, Varuṇa, and Yama, though in one version Kubera takes the place of Agni, while Rāvaṇa claims that he himself is the fifth world-guardian. As his name denotes,[6] Yama "restrains" men and thus is often nearly identified with Dharma, so that when the sage Māṇḍavya goes to question the latter he seeks his place of judgement just as if it were Yama's. Yama is also the king of the Pitṛs, or "Fathers," who live in his realm, this being in the south under the earth at a distance of eighty-six thousand *yojanas*, along which the dead must travel. In it are the Vaitaraṇī River and the Raurava Hell. His assembly hall is an abode of bliss which sages and kings attend to pay homage to Yama, and there Gandharvas and Apsarases sing and dance. He himself is of majestic appearance, red-eyed and of dark hue, but he is also terrible to look at and with noose in hand he strikes dread into the hearts of men. His messengers wear dark apparel, and thus are unlike their master, whose clothes are red; their eyes are red, their hair bristles, and their legs, eyes, and noses are like a crow's; Yama carries the staff of justice and a noose, and his charioteer is Roga ("Disease"). He has two four-eyed dogs, the offspring of Saramā.

Two aspects are inextricably blended in the character of Yama: he is the ender of the life of man, and therefore is accompanied by death and hundreds of dreadful diseases, and his messengers drag the weary dead through a region with neither water nor shade. On the other hand, he is also the just judge, before whose throne all must go without friend or kin to aid, save only their own deeds. As a ruler of the realm of the dead he executes righteous punishment on the evil and rewards the good, and his staff metes out just judgement to all mortals. Pleasant places are reserved for the good, while hell awaits the bad, and the terrors of the infernal world are vividly described: the evil man is threatened with a hell where he sinks in the hot stream Vaitaraṇī, where the forest of sword-leaves wounds his limbs, and where he is bound to lie on axes. Another torture is that described by Agastya, who found that his ancestors were hanging head downward in a cave until such time as he should perform the sacred duty of rearing a son to continue the race.

The Vedic views as to the future of the dead still survive in parts of the epic. In one of the finest episodes of the *Mahābhārata* (iii. 16616 ff.) we are told of the marriage of Sāvitrī, the daughter of Aśvapati of the Madras, to Satyavant. Though the sage Nārada approved the choice, nevertheless he foretold the death of the husband in a year, but Sāvitrī would not alter her choice. With Satyavant she lived in happiness in the hermitage where he dwelt, for his royal father had lost his kingdom to his foes. One day when he was cutting wood, he fell asleep, wearied out, with his head on her lap. Then she saw Yama approaching, noose in hand, and the dread deity, saying he had come for the soul of her husband, drew it forth with his cord and went his way. Sāvitrī, however, followed him and would not go back until he gave her as successive boons the restoration of her father-in-law's kingdom, a hundred sons for her own father, and the life of her husband as a reward for her devotion.

In this tale it is assumed that all men must yield their lives to Yama and go to the realm of the dead. Yet there is an increasing tendency to confuse this simple picture by the growth of the doctrine that the good depart at once to joy in the world of Indra, while only the bad go to Yama, who thus becomes not a judge of right and wrong, but a punisher of sin. By a further development of thought the judicial or retributive functions of the god usurp his part of ender of the lives of men, this latter *rôle* being given to Mṛtyu ("Death") as an independent power. With these ideas blends the philosophic doctrine of release through true knowledge, which makes the function of Yama wholly meaningless for the few who attain freedom. A further complication arises from the cross-current of the doctrine that retribution takes the form of rebirth in a less fortunate life and reward that of reincarnation in a more fortunate existence; and these views are variously and tentatively fitted into the scheme of retribution in hell and reward in the delights of paradise. The same problems had presented themselves to the philosophers who wrote the *Upaniṣads*, who were as little able to evolve a harmonious system as were the sages and saints of the epic.

## CHAPTER VI

# THE MYTHOLOGY OF THE PURĀṆAS

THERE is no essential difference between the mythology of the *Purāṇas* and the mythology of the epic. Tradition is strong in India, and the fame and popularity of the great epics would in any case have served to make much of their mythology a permanent inheritance of later ages. There is, therefore, for the most part no substantial change in the myths affecting the well known features of the epic pantheon: details vary, and the outline of the stories tends to be further confused by contamination of legends and by free invention and rearrangement, but these divergencies, while not without interest for literary history and folk-lore, seldom have mythological significance.

The most noteworthy feature of the Paurāṇic mythology is the deepening of the sectarianism of the worship of the two great gods. That worship is sectarian as early as the epics, in the latest parts of which there is a free use of language which goes as far as anything in the *Purāṇas;* but there is a difference in degree in the devotion when the main body of the epic is compared with these poems, and sectarianism develops more and more conspicuously the later the *Purāṇa* is. At the same time these texts show a steadily increasing tendency to deal with questions of philosophy and to dress out their doctrines as far as practicable in the garments of that compound of the Sāṁkhya and the Vedānta philosophical systems which is seen in the *Bhagavadgītā* and in the long disquisitions of the didactic books of the *Mahābhārata.* They unite with this adoption of theory the rules of *yoga* practice which they find in the Yoga philosophy; and on the other hand they direct polemics against the Buddhists, Jains, and more especially the Cārvākas, who are held to be the leading and most dangerous school of materialists, preaching a life of self-indulgence.

Of the two great gods Viṣṇu has the greater number of *Purāṇas* as directed in the main in his honour, including the *Viṣṇu*, the *Bhāgavata*, the *Brahma*, the *Brahmavaivarta*, the *Brahmāṇḍa*, the *Varāha*, the *Vāmana*, the *Kūrma*, the *Padma*, the *Garuḍa*, and the *Nārada*. Śiva can claim only the *Vāyu*, the *Agni*, the *Liṅga*, and perhaps the *Matsya*, though the latter has much to say on Viṣṇu. The *Mārkaṇḍeya* treats both deities without prepossession for either, and the *Bhaviṣya*, with the *Bhaviṣyottara*, is not markedly sectarian. Yet despite the vast number of legends contained in the *Viṣṇu* and the *Bhāgavata*, which are *par excellence* the text-books of Vaiṣṇavism, few of them are more than quaint or foolish. The depth of the devotion of his followers can, however, be gathered from a tale in the "Uttarakhaṇḍa" of the *Padma Purāṇa*. The sage Bhṛgu was sent by the seers to ascertain which god possessed the quality of goodness, in the highest degree, so that they could decide whom to worship. The sage found Śiva so deeply engrossed in his sport with his wife that he did not receive his visitor, while Brahmā was surrounded by seers and so taken up with himself that he had no attention to pay to Bhṛgu. The latter then went to find Viṣṇu, who was asleep, whereat the angry sage aroused him with a kick. Instead of showing anger at this rude awakening, the deity gently stroked the foot of the seer and expressed the honour which he had felt at his unusual method of calling his attention. It is not surprising that, overjoyed at this condescension, Bhṛgu declared that Viṣṇu was by far the most worthy of worship of all the gods. The *Nārada Purāṇa*, however, goes further. This late and worthless tract tells us a vapid tale of the daughter of a king who obtained from her father a promise that he would grant her anything she desired and who then insisted on her parent either breaking one of the fast-days of Viṣṇu or slaying his son, whereupon the monarch chose the latter alternative as being the lesser sin. On the whole the *Viṣṇu Purāṇa* is less absurd in its legends, although it has extravagances enough. The great name of Bharata is now degraded by a foolish story (ii. 13–16) of how one day a frightened antelope died near him, leaving a young fawn, which Bharata took home and brought up, devoting his whole life to meditation upon it. Justly enough in the next birth he was reincarnated as an antelope, but by his practice of asceticism in this state he was able to be born in his following reincarnation in the position of the son of a pious Brāhman. Nevertheless, though fully acquainted with the knowledge of the self, he was heedless of all mundane things, spoke indistinctly and confusedly, performed no rites, went about dirty and in rags, and generally so conducted himself as to earn the name of Fool Bharata. He was accordingly engaged on the meanest tasks and in this way came to be employed in the service of King Sauvīra. This opportunity being afforded him, he displayed himself as a skilled and most learned teacher by telling a story which showed emphatically the unity of the whole of existence and the lack of any real individuality amongst men. All this Bharata won through his devotion to Viṣṇu. In contrast the demerits of such heretics as the Buddhists and the Jains are revealed by the story of King Śatadhanus (iv. 18). On one sacred moment this true worshipper of Viṣṇu, moved by courtesy, said a few words to a heretic; and all his goodness could not avail to prevent his being born successively as a dog, a jackal, a wolf, a vulture, a crow, and a peacock, until the devotion of his wife Śaibyā succeeded in securing his rebirth into his royal rank. On the other hand, devotion to Viṣṇu sustains men through appalling trials, this being the case with Prahlāda, the pious son of Hiraṇyakaśipu (i. 17–20). Uninstructed by his teacher, the lad proclaimed before his father the deity and supremacy of Viṣṇu and would not desist. Every

## PLATE XX

### Viṣṇu Slays the Demons

While Viṣṇu slumbered on Ananta (see Plate XI), two demons, Madhu and Kaiṭabha, sprang from his ear and sought to destroy Brahmā; but the deity awakened and slew them. From a painting in a Sanskrit manuscript. After Hendley, *Ulwar and its Art Treasures*, Plate LXIII.

effort was made to slay him: the snakes, Kuhaka, Takṣaka, and Andhaka bit him in vain; elephants' tusks were harmless against him; fire could not overcome him; cast down from the palace, he survived the shock; thrown fettered into the sea, he rose on the waters. Finally Viṣṇu revealed himself and justified Prahlāda, who begged for his father's life, but ultimately Hiraṇyakaśipu was slain by the god in his man-lion incarnation. Another tale is that of Dhruva (i. 11–12). He was the son of Uttānapāda by his second wife, and for that reason his father did not take him up on his lap as he did Uttama, his son by his first wife, whom he was unwilling to annoy. Though only four or five years old, the younger lad resented this inferiority, but his mother explained to him that it was due to the fact that his brother was more meritorious than himself through reason of accumulated goodness. Dhruva then resolved, despite his tender years, to attain a virtue which should surpass even that of his own father, and learning from some seers the mode to venerate Viṣṇu, he gave himself to this task. Disturbed by the deepness of his devotions, the gods attempted to terrify or cajole him to desist, but Viṣṇu appeared, calmed the fears of the deities, and duly rewarded Dhruva by elevating him to the position of the pole-star. The story is the more interesting since many of the *Purāṇas* merely say that Brahmā raised Dhruva to the skies, showing that Viṣṇu has taken over from Brahmā this feat as he has other of his great deeds.

A further tale (i. 13) tells that Death had a daughter Sunīthā, who married Aṅga and by him had a son who was named Vena. This king unhappily inherited the evil disposition of his grandfather, and when he was established in the realm he forbade the paying of sacrifice to Hari (Viṣṇu) on the ground that all the gods were effectively present in the person of the king. The Brāhmans strove to obtain permission at least to offer to Hari, but the monarch proved so obdurate that at last in deep wrath they slew him with the blades of the sacred grass. Shortly afterward, however, the sages saw clouds of dust, which, they were told, were raised by hordes of robbers hastening to steal, now that the strong arm of the king was removed. They accordingly rubbed the thigh of the corpse, whence sprang a man with flattened countenance and of dwarf size, representing the Niṣādas, or aboriginal inhabitants of the country, by whose production the guilt of the sin was carried away. The sages then rubbed Vena's right arm, from which came Pṛthu, at whose birth sacrifice the Sūta ("Herald") and Māgadha ("Minstrel") were brought forth, and they sang of the future deeds which he was to do, since they could not tell of the achievements that a newly born child had wrought. Pṛthu found that the earth was withholding all vegetation because of the period of anarchy and with his might he compelled her to submit to being milked. He is the culture hero of India: he made the earth level by lowering the mountains; he divided out the land and established boundaries; and he introduced agriculture.

Another tale (iv. 2) is of King Yuvanāśva. Since he was childless, the seers left on the altar a specially consecrated draught which they meant his queen to swallow, but by error he drank it instead, the result being that a boy was born from his side who won the name Māndhātṛ from the fact that he was nourished by sucking the thumb of Indra.[1] The daughters of this emperor were sought in marriage by the sage Saubhari, who had spent a prolonged period of asceticism, but was aroused to a desire for the joys of life by gazing at the gambols of the great fish Sammada in the pool in which he was performing penance. By his magic might he assumed a lovely form so that all the daughters of the king insisted on being wedded to him, and by this same power he made each believe that he was constantly with her. But from this dream of happiness he awoke one day to the inutility and unending character of human joy and with his wives assumed his old ascetic practices in devotion to Viṣṇu, finally attaining liberation.

Fig. 5. The Matsya ("Fish") Avatar of Viṣṇu

When the world had been destroyed by a deluge which spared only the ship containing Manu, the seven Ṛṣis ("Sages"), and their wives, Viṣṇu assumed the form of a fish and kept the vessel safe until the waters had subsided. Viṣṇu has here taken the place of Prajāpati or Brahmā in earlier myth (see pp. 74, 124). After Moor, *Hindu Pantheon*, Plate XLVIII, No. 1.

The list and the details of the avatars naturally begins to expand, and a very interesting account is given in the *Matsya Purāṇa* (ccxxxi-ccxxxv). In the interminable wars of the gods and demons Śukra left the Asuras and went to the gods, but was entreated by his former associates to return to their aid. He finally did so and undertook to obtain from Śiva spells which would make him more powerful than Bṛhaspati, the priest of the gods. Mahādeva imposed on him the horrible penance of hanging for a thousand years head downward over a fire of chaff, and while he was engaged in this the gods attacked the Asuras, whom Śukra's mother sought to protect. She rendered Indra powerless, and to prevent the complete discomfiture of the divinities Indra had to seek aid from Viṣṇu, who with great hesitation cut off her head, for which deed he was cursed by Śukra to be born seven times on earth for the good of the world when unrighteousness should prevail; therefore is Viṣṇu born in this world. After Śukra's thousand years of penance were over, he was beguiled for ten years by Jayantī, daughter of Indra, to live with her concealed from all. In this period Bṛhaspati took advantage of Śukra's absence to palm himself off on the Asuras as Śukra, so that at first they rejected Śukra when he came back to them. Finally they succeeded in pacifying him and after a thousand years of war they won a victory over the gods, although this was soon undone when the deities seduced the demons Śaṇḍa and Marka from their allegiance; and thus the Asuras were finally driven from heaven.

The list of avatars is then given by the *Matsya* as ten in all, the last seven of which represent the results of the curse of Śukra. They are a part sprung from Dharma, the man-lion, the dwarf, Dattātreya, Mandhātṛ, Paraśurāma, Rāma, Vedavyāsa, Buddha, and Kalki. The *Bhāgavata* (I. iii. 24) gives twenty-two, namely, Puruṣa, the boar, Nārada, Nara and Nārāyaṇa, Kapila, Dattātreya, the sacrifice, Ṛṣabha, Pṛthu, the fish, the tortoise, Dhanvantari (counting as two), the man-lion, the dwarf, Paraśurāma, Vedavyāsa, Rāma, Balarāma, Kṛṣṇa, Buddha, and Kalki, the two latter being ascribed to the future. It adds, however, that, like rivulets flowing from an inexhaustible lake, the incarnations of Viṣṇu are innumerable, and seers, Manus, gods, sons of Manus, and Prajāpatis are all but portions of him. Of these varied avatars, which are differently given in other *Purāṇas*, that of Buddha is a curious example of the desire to absorb whatever is good in another faith: so far as the Buddha was divine, it is argued in effect that he must have been Viṣṇu. He is said to have manifested himself as Buddha in order to encourage wicked men to despise the Vedas, reject caste, and deny the existence of the gods, and thus to bring about their own destruction. As Kalki he will appear at the end of the Kali age, seated on a white horse, carrying a drawn sword, and blazing like a comet for the final destruction of the wicked, the renovation of creation, and the restoration of purity. The avatar as Paraśurāma recalls a hero famous in the *Mahābhārata* and mentioned also at some length in the *Rāmāyaṇa*. He was a son of Jamadagni, at whose bidding he struck off the head of his own mother, Reṇukā, as a punishment for her impurity; but as a reward for his obedience his father revived Reṇukā in purity and gave Rāma invincibility in war. King Kārtavīrya came to Jamadagni's hermitage and, dissatisfied with his reception, took away the sacrificial cow. In revenge Rāma slew Kārtavīrya, whose sons then killed Jamadagni, only to be themselves slain by Rāma, who in his anger annihilated the Kṣatriyas twenty-one times and filled five lakes in Samanta-pañcaka with blood. He also gave the earth to Kaśyapa and made his own dwelling on Mahendra. His relations with the younger Rāma were unfortunate: enraged when the latter broke Śiva's bow, he came against him, but after a contest was defeated and suffered spiritual degradation, though not death. In his personality the tradition sees the action of Viṣṇu to humble the Kṣatriyas, or warrior caste, when they became unduly proud. Balarāma, another of the incarnations, is the brother of Kṛṣṇa, and in this capacity alone is considered a representative of Viṣṇu, especially when Kṛṣṇa is regarded not as a mere partial incorporation, but as the full incarnation of the deity. The avatar as Dattātreya was due to a penance performed by Atri, as a result of which the three gods, Brahmā, Viṣṇu, and Śiva, became incorporated in part in his three sons, Soma, Datta, and Durvāsas.

All these additions and modifications of the avatar theory are in keeping with Indian tradition: just as the older attribution of the fish, the tortoise, and the boar incarnations to Brahmā or Prajāpati gradually yields to the tendency to confer them on a real living deity, so it was only natural that other greater beings should be definitely ranked as incarnations of Viṣṇu, though originally no such character attached to them. The process was gradual, as can be seen from the increase in the number of the avatars in the later *Purāṇas*, and needs no explanation by external influence. Every trend in Indian religion told toward the process of recognizing a series of such "descents." From the *Ṛgveda* onward the identification of one god with another was normal and of increasing frequency, nor can we suppose that these identifications were meaningless. On the other hand, it was the natural aim of the Brāhmans to admit into their pantheon, in such a manner as to meet their views, the great gods of tribes which fell under the influence of their culture. Again, quite apart from these two motives, from the first the gods are powerful beings who can assume a multitude of shapes at will and who may for their own purposes be present in strange places; and, furthermore, we must not exclude the possibility that the animal incarnations point to totemism and to the incorporation of inferior gods into the Hindu pantheon. But while the motives of the avatars cannot be assigned with certainty, it is wholly needless to seek to impute them to the influence of Christianity. There was indeed in the births of

## PLATE XXI

### Lakṣmī

The Goddess of Wealth and Beauty is shown with her characteristic emblem, the lotus. This is particularly appropriate, not merely because of the beauty of the flower, but because it is a water-plant, while Lakṣmī herself is sprung from the waters, having come into being at the churning of the ocean (see Fig. 2). For another conception of her see Plate XIII. From a bronze statuette in the Museum of Fine Arts, Boston.

the Buddha, the tradition of which is undoubtedly long anterior to the Christian era, a form of incarnation which, springing immediately from the Hindu tenet of reincarnation, would have been sufficient to render reference to any external source superfluous, but it is doubtful whether even this doctrine is necessary to explain the incarnation of deities, which is already presaged in texts older than Buddhism.

On the other hand, a new influence does seem to be at work in the tales of the child Kṛṣṇa, which are wanting in the genuine portions of the epic and are first recorded in the *Harivaṁśa* (before 500 A.D.) and then appear in the *Viṣṇu* and *Bhāgavata Purāṇas* in full detail, and more or less fully in the *Brahma*, the *Brahmavaivarta* and other *Purāṇas.* Nārada, the sage, warned King Kaṁsa of Mathurā (the modern Muttra), the land destined to be the holy state of the Kṛṣṇa cult, that death awaited him at the hands of the eighth child of Devakī and Vasudeva. To avert this evil, Kaṁsa kept Devakī under strict watch, and six of her children were duly slain. The seventh, however, was saved by the goddess Sleep, who removed it before birth from the womb of Devakī to that of Rohiṇī, the other wife of Vasudeva, of whom it was born as Balarāma or Baladeva. The eighth child had to be saved in a different way. A herdsman called Nanda had come with his wife Yaśodā up to the town to pay tribute to Kaṁsa, and so immediately after the birth of the child Vasudeva bore it across the deep and dangerous Jumnā, which in regard to him rose no higher than his knee, and exchanged the infant for the daughter just born from Yaśodā. The tiny girl was at once cruelly slain by the King's order, while Nanda returned to his home with the youthful Kṛṣṇa and with Balarāma also, for Kaṁsa, in his anger at discovering that the child which he had put to death was not the one destined to kill him, but was really a form of the goddess Sleep, had given orders for the slaughter of all male children which showed signs of special vitality.

The two boys grew up together, and Kṛṣṇa early gave signs of his prowess. He slew the demon Pūtanā, who came to offer him suck with intent to slay him; he overturned a cart and broke the pots and pans; when tied with a rope round his waist, he dragged the mortar, to which it was fastened, between two trees, and after it had thus become wedged fast, by hard pulling he overthrew both trees. Not content with these miracles, according to the *Harivaṁśa* he created hundreds of wolves from his body until he persuaded the herdsmen to settle in the Vṛndāvana, where he desired to be. Arrived there, he leaps into the Jumnā and defeats the great serpent Kāliya, whom he bids depart to the ocean; he destroys the demon Dhenuka, who was in ass form; he causes Rāma to slay the Asura Pralamba. When the time comes for the festival of Indra, he persuades the cowherds to abandon the practice of worshipping Indra, inculcating instead the adoration of the mountains and of their own cattle as means of success. In anger at his thus diverting sacrifice from him Indra sends a terrible storm on the cattle, but Kṛṣṇa upraises Mount Govardhana and thus protects the kine and the herdsmen until after seven days the storm dies away, and Indra recognizes the greatness of the boy, who, however, declines to admit his divine character to the herdsmen, with whom he continues to live, enjoying sports of all kinds and in special indulging in dances with the Gopīs, or milkmaids. Here arose the Rāsa or Hallīśa dances performed in honour of Kṛṣṇa in many parts of India, even to the present day. On one occasion a demon Ariṣṭa attacked Kṛṣṇa in the midst of his dance, but was slain.

Learning of the deeds of Kṛṣṇa, Kaṁsa determines to fetch him to his capital and there to procure his death, if he cannot slay him before. He accordingly sends Akrūra to fetch Kṛṣṇa and his brother to Mathurā, and Keśin to attempt his life; but Keśin, who attacks in horse shape, is destroyed by Kṛṣṇa. The boys accompany Akrūra to Mathurā, and they enter the town, killing Kaṁsa's washerman who shows them disrespect, but conferring a benediction on a flower-seller who pays reverence to Kṛṣṇa. They also meet a crooked woman, Kubjā, who is made straight by Kṛṣṇa. Kaṁsa sets two skilled wrestlers to work to slay the brothers, but the bravoes are themselves laid low, while Kaṁsa, who, throwing aside all pretext in anger at the sight of the death of his men, seeks to have their conquerors killed, is seized and dies at the hands of Kṛṣṇa. The hero then places a new king on the throne and proceeds to Ujjayinī (Ujjain), where he becomes the pupil of Sāndīpani and recovers from the sea the son whom his teacher had lost there; and he also kills the marine demon Pañcajana and makes himself a conch from his shell. A new danger now arises: Jarāsandha of Magadha, the father-in-law of Kaṁsa, determines to avenge his daughter's husband, and a long struggle breaks out, ending in the failure of the attacks of Jarāsandha. In the course of this conflict, however, a king named Kālayavana, "the dark Yavana" (or "Greek"), advances against Mathurā, and as a result Kṛṣṇa decides, in view of the strength of his enemy, to establish the Yādavas at Dvārakā (Gujarāt). Nevertheless, he succeeds in overthrowing Kālayavana by leading him into a cave where the ancient king Mucukunda, awakened from the sleep which, at his own request, the gods had bestowed upon him, destroys the Yavana and praises Kṛṣṇa, who takes the army and treasure of his enemy and repairs to Dvārakā. His next important exploit is the wedding of Rukmiṇī against the wishes of her brother, whom he finally conquers, but whose life he spares at Rukmiṇī's entreaty. By this wife he has a son Pradyumna, in whom the mystic interpretation of Kṛṣṇaism sees Mind (*Manas*). When six days old, this boy was stolen by the demon Śambara, who foresaw that he would cause his death, and who therefore cast him into the deep. Here Pradyumna was swallowed by a great fish which, being captured, was cut up in the presence of Śambara's queen, Māyādevī, who found the boy and reared him. When he grew to manhood, she manifested her love to him and explained that he was not her son, whereupon, in anger with Śambara, he slew him and carried Māyādevī as his wife to Dvārakā, being received there with great joy, since in reality he was none other than the god of love, reunited to his wife Rati under the form of Māyādevī. From this marriage was sprung young Aniruddha, who ranks as Egoism to the mystics and who married Rukmin's granddaughter; but the wedding-feast ended in bloodshed, for Rukmin challenged Baladeva to dice, played him false, and was slain by him.

Then one day Indra came to Kṛṣṇa and told him of the vile deeds of Naraka of Prāgjyotiṣa, who had robbed Aditi of her ear-rings and had insulted Varuṇa and the other gods. After a valiant fight Kṛṣṇa destroyed Naraka and returned to Aditi her ear-rings. This visit to the celestial world, however, leads him to another adventure, for Satyabhāmā, one of his other sixteen thousand one hundred wives, sees the Pārijāta tree in heaven and desires him to take it home with them. He agrees to do so in order to lessen her jealousy of his favourite Rukmiṇī, though for this purpose he has first to overthrow Indra and the gods; but finally with the permission of Indra he takes the tree to Dvārakā and marries the princesses held in captivity by Naraka. A greater struggle now awaited him: Ūsā, the daughter of Bāṇa, the Asura king, became enamoured of Pradyumna's son Aniruddha, but Bāṇa strongly opposed his daughter's wish, and being a devotee of Śiva, secured that god's aid. Bāṇa managed to find Aniruddha in his palace, where he had come in secret, and bound him; and a terrible struggle then ensued between Kṛṣṇa, Balarāma, and Pradyumna on the one side, and Bāṇa, Śiva, and Skanda on the other. Finally the might of Kṛṣṇa prevailed, and he was about to slay the Asura king when Śiva intervened and asked for his life, which Kṛṣṇa graciously granted, as Śiva had acknowledged his supreme position. In the *Harivaṁśa* the scene ends differently: the two gods are reconciled by the intervention of Brahmā, who points out their identity; and the whole ends with a hymn asserting their unity. The version of the *Viṣṇu Purāṇa*, however, clearly asserts a victory of the Vaiṣṇavas and doubtless has some semi-historical basis. Here the *Harivaṁśa* ends, but the *Viṣṇu Purāṇa*, after one or two more legends, narrates the death of Kṛṣṇa on the model of the *Mahābhārata*.

The study of Kṛṣṇa's youth at once raises irresistibly the question whether we have here a real growth of Indian religion, derived from native sources, or whether we must look for foreign, and particularly Christian, influence. The facts as to Christianity in India are unhappily open to grave doubt: the legend of the working of St. Thomas in western India, much discussed as it has been,[2] can and will yield no clear proof of any actual contact of Christianity with India in the apostolic period. The statement that in 190 A.D. Pantaenus found Indians who were Christians depends upon the interpretation to be given to the vague word "India" in a notice of Eusebius, which may with more probability be assigned to South Arabia. The assertion of Dio Chrysostom that Christian texts were turned into their native tongue by Indians may equally well be referred to the same source, if indeed it is anything but a rhetorical exaggeration. Yet it is probable that by the middle of the fourth century of the Christian era Christians fleeing from Persian persecution had come to a land which was to be guiltless of intolerance until the advent of Muhammadanism, and we have the conclusive evidence of the Egyptian traveller Cosmas that about 525–530 A.D. there were Christian communities on the Malabar coast and that at Kalliana, which is doubtless Kalyāṇ near Bombay, there was a bishop appointed from Persia. This proves that by that date the Indian Church had become Nestorian, and probably enough the event was of recent origin, for it was only in the latter part of the fifth century that the Persian king Pērōz declared that Nestorianism should be the only legitimate form of Christianity and in 498 A.D. the Bishop of Seleukia formally declared his independence of the Bishop of Antiochia.

The fate of the Nestorian Church was a chequered one: it was very loosely connected with the parent body and in the ninth century it seems to have evolved into a practically autonomous communion at a time when those who professed the faith were gaining political independence or semi-dependence. Christian influence was also becoming more pronounced in the north. There it can be fully assumed in 639 A.D., when we have the first record of the visit of a body of Syrian Christians to the court of the Chinese emperor and of their setting forth their doctrines;[3] and in 781 A.D. a Nestorian joined with a Buddhist in a translation of a Buddhist text in China. The dates are of importance, for they enable us to judge the external probabilities of the introduction into Indian mythology of conceptions taken from Christianity.

The influence of the Gospels has been sought in detail in the *Bhagavadgītā*, but though the parallelisms of thought and language are sometimes remarkable enough, they cannot be said to prove borrowing, nor, as we have seen, is there any need to assume that the idea of incarnation was borrowed from Christianity. There is, however, one passage in the epic which seems to hint at knowledge of the Christian faith. Here we are told (xii. 12696 ff.) that Nārada once journeyed to the Śvetadvīpa ("White Island"), where he learned the Pāñcarātra doctrine, a mystic form of Vaiṣṇavism; and it is also said that three sons of Brahmā, Ekata, Dvita, and Trita ("One," "Two," and "Three"), went to the same place, which is at a distance of thirty-two thousand *yojanas* north or north-west of Mount Meru on the north bank of the sea of milk. There dwell men without organs of sense, white in colour, and of a brilliance which dazzles the eyes of the sinful. They ever revere God in muttered prayer and with folded hands; but their deity, for whom they are filled with the deepest love, cannot be seen. None of them has a higher rank than the others, but all are equal. Laying aside the fabulous part of the tale, which probably belongs to one of the latest parts of the epic, it is not improbable that we have here a record of a Christian community, not of Alexandria, but in the vicinity of the Balkash Sea, which by its physical characteristics may have suggested the milky ocean of the epic. The episode is, however, of little importance in Indian religious history and has at most a faint echo in a story, preserved in the *Kūrma* and *Vāyu Purāṇas*, that Śiva proclaimed the Yoga system to four pupils of his, Śveta, Śvetāśva, Śvetaśikha, and Śvetalohita, in the Himālaya. Nor is it possible to see any real Christian influence in the legend of the death of Kṛṣṇa, which bears not the slightest real similarity to the motives of the Gospel narrative, nor in the story (i. 4305 ff.) of the impaling of Māṇḍavya. It is also needless to seek any such influence in the account (xii. 5742 ff.) of the Śūdra Śambuka, who, the epic tells us, was slain for confusing the castes by seeming to raise himself to an equality with the gods by the use of ascetic practices allowed only to the Aryan classes. The idea might indeed be Christian, but it is equally Indian.

It is at first a more attractive theory that the child god in India is borrowed from the youthful Christ. This hypothesis, however, cannot be maintained in face of the evidence of the *Mahābhāṣya*[4] (of about 150 B.C.), which shows that at that time Kaṁsa and Kṛṣṇa were deadly foes, and that the former was the cruel uncle of the latter. That notice suggests irresistibly the fact that there must have been some ground for the enmity of uncle and nephew, and that basis can scarcely have been other than the attempts made by Kaṁsa to slay the child. Again, one feature of Kṛṣṇa's life, his dances with the Gopīs,[5] is already alluded to in an early passage of the *Mahābhārata* (ii. 2291), and for that reason alone, as well as for other considerations of probability, cannot be regarded as a translation into terms of flesh and blood of the mystic doctrine of the unity of Christ and the Church. Nevertheless, there is evidence that the Christian religion did not fail to affect the theology and cult of Kṛṣṇa, whose name is pronounced as

Kṛṣṭa in many parts of India at the present day and whose bright and cheerful religion with its pronounced theism and its doctrine of faith was naturally akin to Christianity in far greater degree than Buddhism, Jainism, or Śaivism with its especial devotion to ceremonies and ascetic practices. For the most part, though not without important exceptions, including the *Bhāgavata*, the *Purāṇas* describe the festival of the birthday of Kṛṣṇa in great detail: the essential feature is that the child is represented as being born in a cow-stall and as lying on the breast of his mother Devakī in indubitable imitation of the Madonna Lactans. The change from the orthodox story of the exchange of the children by Vasudeva is significant of the new influence. The same factor betrays itself in the traditions of the *Viṣṇu Purāṇa* that Nanda was going to Mathurā to pay his tribute to the king in accordance with the Gospel of Luke, and of the healing of the crooked Kubjā, who presents him with a vessel of salve, in which seem to be blended events recorded by Matthew (ix. 20; xv. 30–31) and by Luke (vii. 37–38). To the borrowing may be added the tale of the bringing to life of the son of Duḥśalā which is recounted in the *Jaimini Bhārata*, a work not later than the thirteenth century. Later texts add other small points of resemblance, but on the whole the influence of Christianity extends to details, not to principles.

In comparison with the richness of the mythology which has grown up round the person of Viṣṇu it is astonishing that Śiva remains so poor in legends, though he is given twenty-eight incarnations to enable him to compete with his rival. The strength of his worship, however, lies in cult, not in theory, and the centre of that cult is formed by the sacred *liṅga*. Many of these are described by the *Purāṇas*, and they represent the god in his creative capacity, while with them are connected the traditions of Śiva's activity, such as that recorded in the story of Dakṣa. In a late Paurāṇic passage the *Mahābhārata* (xii. 10208 ff.) tells us that when Dakṣa was sacrificing, but ignoring Śiva, Umā incited the deity to secure a part of the offering, and he then created a terrible being called Vīrabhadra, while Umā assumed her form as Bhadrakālī, and together the pair upset the sacrifice. In the result Dakṣa recognized his error, and Vīrabhadra, who showed the gentle as well as the terrible side of Śiva's nature, took him to Benares, where he erected a *liṅga* and by meditation entered into it. In the *Saura Purāṇa*, a work which is not later than 1200 A.D., this episode is so narrated as to bring out in great clearness the anxiety of the supporters of Śiva to prove that he was superior to Viṣṇu, and this indeed seems to be a trait of all the Śaiva *Purāṇas*, which seek to make good the importance of the god whom they worship. As in the later additions to the epic, Śiva is set off against Viṣṇu, and it is insisted that he is the father of both Brahmā and Viṣṇu: he created the first from his right side and the second from his left, while from his heart he sent forth Rudra, the first deity being formed to create, the second to protect, and the third to destroy the world. The popular view, which the *Purāṇa* itself expresses, that Śiva was born of Brahmā is refuted by a proof which demonstrates to Brahmā that the only real creator is Śiva and that by his power of illusion he has brought about the apparent birth of himself as the son of Brahmā. Like Viṣṇu, Śiva is the all-god, and the tenets of the Vedānta and the Sāṁkhya are fitted to him with as much skill as they are adapted to Viṣṇu, subject to the fact that he has no sons like Pradyumna and Aniruddha to identify with Mind and Egoism in the process of the descent of the Absolute into empirical reality. As a creator, however, Śiva has one advantage over Viṣṇu, for at times he is clearly conceived as being androgynous. This idea is not new, for it is perhaps found on coins of the so-called Scythian kings, probably about the beginning of the Christian era,[6] but stress now begins to be laid on it. From the female side of his nature Śiva created his consort Śivā, who serves as his feminine counterpart and who in the philosophic interpretation of the deities represents Prakṛti, the material out of which the whole universe develops; while Śiva himself is the eternal Puruṣa, or spirit, for which Prakṛti unfolds itself in its unreal display. Like her husband, Śivā is a terrible foe of the demons: the *Saura Purāṇa* (xlix) tells how Indra in fear of them is fain to go to beg her aid, and then with her three heads and twenty arms she attacks the Daityas, slays them in enormous numbers, despite the feats of their leaders Raktākṣa and Dhūmrākṣa, and dances a wild dance of victory, a reminiscence of the dance of Śiva which is recorded as early as Megasthenes.

As in the case of Viṣṇu, great rewards await the pious devotee of Śiva. Thus we are told (iii. 14 ff.) of a king who in his previous birth had been a robber and hunter, a man without the slightest tincture of virtue or culture. On his death he comes before Dharma, who takes the place of Yama as judge of the dead, the ancient lord of the departed being relegated to the duty of punishment. Dharma's spy, Citragupta, cannot relate a single virtuous act consciously done by the robber, but he reveals the fact that day by day, while plying his nefarious craft, he has been unwittingly invoking Śiva as Hara in the words *āhara*, "bring the booty," and *prahara*, "strike"; and this is enough to wipe out every other one of his sins and to secure his ultimate birth in the royal palace. One Pulaha, who had the fortune to be a fly in the temple of Śiva, is for that cause alone reborn as the son of Brahmā (lxvii. 14 ff.). Even a dog-eater who reveres Śiva ranks above a Brāhman who does not. Still more striking is the story of the origin of Kubera, lord of riches (xlvii. 45 ff.). A Brāhman in Avantī left home in greed of gain, and his wife, deserted by him, formed a connexion with a Śūdra, bearing to him a son named Duḥsaha, who was disregarded by all his kinsfolk because of his low origin. He turned to ways of wickedness and finally broke into the temple of Śiva to plunder it; but since the wick of his lamp failed during his efforts to find the treasure, he had to light no fewer than ten more, thus unconsciously paying honour to the god. At last one who was sleeping in the temple awoke and stunned the intruder with a blow from a club, and the temple guards put him to death. He was born again as an unrighteous and vile-living king, Sudurmukha of Gāndhāra, but with a remnant of recollection of his deeds in his former birth he maintained well-lighted lamps in Śiva's temple. He was ultimately slain by his foes, but by this time all his evil deeds had been wiped out by his piety, and he was next born as Kubera.

The other gods are of importance and interest only in so far as they are closely connected with Śiva. Thus Skanda is frequently mentioned, and indeed is more and more brought into the likeness of his father. His position as compared with the older gods is significant: Indra foolishly seeks to war with him, but is defeated with humiliation. Importance also attaches to Nandin or Śailādi, who guards the door of Śiva's palace; to the Rudras, who act as his hosts; and to the Pramathas, his familiar spirits. Another deity who is really Śiva himself is Gaṇeśa, the lord of the troops who serve Śiva; but as Gaṇeśa's figure has been developed in the mythology he has a distinctive character and a cult of his own. In the *Mahābhārata* he is mentioned as undertaking the task of writing down the great work, but he is really foreign to it, and it is only in the *Purāṇas* — and there sporadically — that his importance is acknowledged, though in course of time he becomes recognized as a great divinity. This is probably due to the protection which he gives to learning, for he is the god of wisdom and the remover of obstacles. As a deity his worship is known in the legal textbook of Yājñavalkya (i. 291 ff.), which perhaps dates from 300 A.D.,[7] and it seems that Bardesanes had heard of him. The legends which concern him are mainly intended to account for his abnormal physical appearance: he was short and stout, with protuberant stomach and four hands, and in place of a human head he had that of an elephant with only one tusk. The loss of his real head is variously explained: one story tells that his mother Pārvatī, from the scurf on whose body some believed him to have been born, asked Śani, the planet Saturn, to look upon him, forgetful of the effect of his glance. When Śani obeyed, he burned the child's head to ashes, and Pārvatī, on Brahmā's advice, replaced it with the first head she could find, this happening to be an elephant's. Again it is said that Pārvatī, when bathing, placed the boy at the door to guard her privacy; but Śiva sought to enter and in his anger at the child for attempting to stay him cut off his head, for which he then substituted an elephant's to propitiate his wife. Another version attributes it to the punishment inflicted on Śiva for slaying Āditya (the sun), Gaṇeśa losing his head as a result and receiving in its place that of Indra's elephant. The loss of the one tusk is explained by a further legend: Paraśurāma once came late to see Śiva, but since the deity was asleep, his son Gaṇeśa sought to prevent the visitor from disturbing his father. Enraged as usual, Rāma then attacked him, and while at first the god had the advantage, his enmity was disarmed by seeing flung at him the axe which his father had given to Rāma, so that he submissively allowed the weapon to tear away one of his tusks. A further peculiarity of this deity is that he is said to ride on the rat. Possibly enough some local variety of the earth or corn spirit has been amalgamated with the conception of the lord of Śiva's hordes. A counterpart to Gaṇeśa as patron of learning and literature is Sarasvatī, who can trace her origin to the Vedic Vāc; but in striking contrast to Gaṇeśa she is always depicted as a woman of great beauty, seated on a lotus and with a crescent on her brow.

Among the other gods Agni shares a certain importance, though merely because he is connected with the birth of Skanda, who is produced by him and Śiva; and in the *Saura Purāṇa*, curiously enough, Varuṇa is somewhat often mentioned. Indra, on the other hand, appears only as in constant need of help and presents almost a comic figure. Himavant as the father of

## PLATE XXII

### Gaṇeśa

The deity Gaṇeśa is especially honoured as being the god who averts obstacles, whence he becomes a divinity of good fortune, who should be worshipped before each new undertaking. Various legends, hard to reconcile with each other, are told of his parentage and to explain his elephant's head, which is apparently a symbol of wisdom. He is probably a god of some aboriginal tribe who was adopted by Hinduism. From a bronze in the Peabody Museum, Salem, Mass.

Gaurī is of some consequence, and Kāma is inseparably connected with the Śiva legend through his part in bringing about the wedlock of Pārvatī with Śiva, from which Skanda was fated to spring. The literature also shows other traces of the prominence of this god, whose *rôle* in the epic is small enough.

More important than these survivals of the old mythology is the new stress laid on the cult of the sun. Sun-worship has indeed from all time been practised in India, and we hear of three classes of worshippers who adored the rising, the setting, and the midday sun; while one form of the triad, or Trimūrti, was the veneration of the whole three forms of the sun. The record of Hüan Tsang shows what importance at his time attached to the cult of the sun in India. It appears, however, that fresh life in that worship was derived from Persian influence. In a story told in the *Bhaviṣya Purāṇa* (cxxxix) we learn that Sāmba, the son of Kṛṣṇa, was afflicted by leprosy as a result of the curse of the irascible sage Durvāsas, and that in order to secure healing he decided to apply himself to devotion to Sūrya, of whose power Nārada had told him much. Having obtained the permission of his father, he left Dvārakā, crossed the Indus and the Candrabhāgā (the modern Chenab), and arrived at the grove of Mitra, where he was freed from his disease. In gratitude he returned to the Chenab, having sworn to erect a temple there in honour of the god and to found a city. When he had done this, however, he was in doubt in which form to worship the god until an image was miraculously found by him when bathing; but since he was still in need of priests to tend the idol, and as Brāhmans were not available for such a duty, he was advised to seek "Magas" from over the sea. By Kṛṣṇa's aid and by using Garuḍa he succeeded in finding the Magas and inducing eighteen families to come with him to Sāmbapura and to settle there. The Persian origin of these Magas is proved by many details given regarding them: they observed the vow of eating in silence, were afraid of contamination by the dead, wore the sacred girdle of the Parsis, covered the mouth at worship, etc.[8] Moreover they are found in Śākadvīpa, which suggests that the legend lays hold of the historic fact of the flight of Parsis to India. The *Saura Purāṇa*, which is a purely Śaivite work, though it purports to be revealed by the sun, contains some references to practices of Saura sects, and here and there it identifies Śiva with the sun. It is, however, significant for the inferior position of the sun that to it is given the duty of destroying the world at the end of a period, while the complete annihilation of the universe is reserved for the great god himself.

In close connexion with the cult of Śiva we find a development of the Tantric rites and of their accompanying demonology. For the history of religion in its lower phases the *Tantras*, the dates of which are still wholly uncertain, but which doubtless represent a form of literature belonging to the latter part of the first millennium, are of great importance; but mythologically they are of little value. The worship inculcated is that of the female side of Indra, his Śakti, which philosophically is regarded as Prakṛti and as Māyā, or the Delusion which created the apparent world and which is identified with Śivā under her various names as Kālī, Durgā, Aghorī, and many others. She is Satī, daughter of Dakṣa, whose sacrifice Śiva destroyed, whereupon in anger she departed to be reborn as Umā and thus to be reunited to her husband. In the ritual of the Śākta sects human sacrifice has apparently been usual from the earliest times and has prevailed down to the present day, though in later years sporadically and by stealth. The other feature of the cult is the grave immorality which it exalts as a sacred duty, at least among the votaries of the "left-hand" sect, who are the more numerous, though the Tantric texts veil the ceremonies in a mass of pseudo-mysticism. The character of the rites can only be explained, not by any adoration of an abstraction, but by the continued practice of a worship of a vegetation or earth spirit who is identified with Śiva's wife, this nature cult being transformed and altered by being taken up into the Śaivite faith. The primitive type of the worship further shows itself in the fact that drunkenness is an essential feature of its Bacchanalian orgies, and that the immorality is evidently a refinement on the old fertility magic of simple and primitive communities, dignified — or degraded — by being brought into connexion with mystic principles. Even when human sacrifice is abandoned, blood-letting is practised by the votaries, and the common phenomenon of interchange of garments by the two sexes is found.

Not essentially distinct from the Śākta cult of Śiva is the form in which it has been adopted by certain of the adherents of Rāma, and in particular by the Rādhā Vallabhīs. In accordance with the genial character of the worship of Viṣṇu in his various forms the bloodthirstiness of the Śaivite cult is wanting, but, on the other hand, the legend of Kṛṣṇa and the Gopīs is considered to be the fullest justification for the extreme of licence. The curious blend of mysticism with sensuality which pervades this cult is preluded, though not equalled, by Jayadeva's famous poem, the *Gītagovinda*, written in the twelfth century A.D.

Another side of the worship of female divinities or demons is the growing importance which attaches to such hideous personalities as that of Pūtanā, the ogress who kills children after birth by giving them suck and who is slain by the infant Kṛṣṇa. The Mātṛs, or "Mothers," who are connected with Skanda, are of increasing rank in an age which is nothing if not catholic in its worship and which recognizes the power of these disease-demons. It is also clear that the Gandharvas and Apsarases, the more attractive forms of an earlier mythology, are sinking to mere names.

The *Purāṇas* show no change of view as to the position of the dead. Among their miscellaneous and confused contents many of them include instructions on the just mode of offering to the dead, and they reveal the same mixture of eschatology which marks earlier Hinduism. The chief development is in the doctrine of hells, of which the *Mārkaṇḍeya Purāṇa* describes seven in full detail, and with a certain power enumerates with care the tortures of the inhabitants of these abodes. On the other hand, it gives a tale of remarkable beauty (xv). It is that of the old king Vipaścit ("the Wise"), who dies and, much to his amazement, is dragged down to hell by the retainers of Yama, who is still more completely identified with Dharma than even in the epic. He inquires in wonder why this treatment is inflicted upon him and learns that it is a brief and slight penalty for the omission of a trifling domestic duty during his lifetime. When, however, he is about to depart from hell, the souls in torment ask him to stay, since from him a refreshing breath emanates which lessens their pains; and on learning this he refuses to obey the bidding of Yama's attendants and will not leave. Dharma himself and Śakra come to see him and point out that the sinners in hell suffer for their evil acts, while his good deeds have earned him celestial bliss, and urge him to go forth from his temporary place of punishment. He declares, however, that he will not do so without obtaining freedom from anguish for the souls in hell, and eventually the gods give way and relieve the damned of all their pain at the moment when the king goes to heaven. The last book of the *Mahābhārata* appears to be an echo of the tale.

# CHAPTER VII

## BUDDHIST MYTHOLOGY IN INDIA AND TIBET

CAREFUL analysis of the texts of the Buddhist Pāli[1] Canon, which at the present day represents the sacred scriptures of the Buddhists in Ceylon, enables criticism to establish a picture of the life and teaching of Gotama Śākyamuni, the Buddha, or "Enlightened One," which deprives him of all save human attributes. According to this view, which is most brilliantly represented by the writings of H. Oldenberg, Gotama was a purely human personage who, building on the foundation of the thought of the *Upaniṣads* and on contemporary religious and philosophic movements, arrived at a theory of human life which, recognizing and accepting as its basis the fact of human suffering, saw clearly that the attainment of full self-control and the suppression of passion were the true ends of mankind. Holding these views, he inculcated them by teaching among a wide circle of pupils, founded a religious order, and in due course died of a perfectly simple disease, produced by indigestion, which acted fatally on the constitution of the old man. A variety of historical considerations lead to the conclusion that the death of the Buddha fell in the third decade of the fifth century B.C., or possibly a few years earlier, though it is admitted that this date is not absolutely free from suspicion. Rigorously followed out, but without real alteration of their principles, the teachings of the "Enlightened One" show that not only are all life and striving merely unhappy, but that the true end of existence is the termination of that existence and the breaking of the chain of action which keeps in perpetual motion and which the Buddhists substituted for the conception of self which they had inherited from the current philosophy. The Buddha also inculcated a simple form of monastic discipline and a method of life which involves a strict morality and a steady process of mental culture.

This version of early Buddhism, which reveals it as a faith of extraordinary simplicity and purity of origin, laying aside all futile belief in gods, abandoning outworn beliefs in souls, and carrying to a logical conclusion the reasoning of the *Upaniṣads*, which elevates the subject of thought into a meaningless Absolute, may possibly correspond with historical reality, for we have not, and never can expect to have, any conclusive proof as to the actual views and teachings of Gotama. It is true that high age has been ascribed to the earliest texts of the Pāli Canon, but the evidence for that date is conjectural and doubtful, and we have no assurance that a single Buddhist text which has come down to us is even as early as two hundred years after Gotama had departed. There is, therefore, abundant room for alteration and change in the tradition. If the Buddha were but a simple mortal, there was time for him to be transformed into something more than human, and we may, if we please, cite in favour of this view the opinion of Sir R. G. Bhandarkar [2] and Professor R. Garbe [3] that the Kṛṣṇa myth has arisen from the personality of a simple head of a clan and religious teacher who at an early, if uncertain, date, though still long before the Buddha, taught a religion in which *bhakti*, or faith in and devotion to God, played a most important part, and who in the course of time was himself regarded as being a form or incarnation of the divinity whom he preached. On the other hand, it is equally legitimate as a matter of hypothesis to suppose that the rationalistic treatment of the Buddha shown in part of the texts of the Pāli Canon represents a deliberate effort to place on a purely philosophic basis the fundamental portion of his creed. Neither is it possible to ignore the force

## PLATE XXIII

### The Great Buddha

The Buddha here appears as in his youth, when he was simply Prince Siddhārtha and before he had deserted all for the sake of salvation. His portrayal is an admirable example of the Indian ideal of manly beauty. From a fresco at Ajantā, Berār. After *Ajanta Frescoes*, Plate XI.

of the argument that even if the supposed origin of the divinity of Kṛṣṇa be granted, yet it was clearly more easy for a preacher of faith in a personal god to become regarded as himself a god than to deify a man who *ex hypothesi* was no god and had no real belief in the gods.

Whatever be the truth, it is at least certain that the Pāli Canon does not fail to reveal to us traces that Gotama was more than a mere man. It is indeed clear that the system of the Pāli Canon, the Hīnayāna, or "Little Vehicle," has no place for devotion to a personal divinity, for the Buddha is not such a divinity: no prayers can be addressed to him to be answered, and no act of grace performed. Yet, on the other hand, the way to salvation requires meditation upon the Buddha as an indispensable part of it, as necessary as the Dharma, or "Law," itself or the Saṅgha, or "Congregation." This is very far from constituting the Buddhism of the Pāli Canon essentially a religious system, but undoubtedly it must have had some influence in this regard.

What is more important, however, is that from the first in the sacred books of the Hīnayāna school itself obvious traces appear that the "Enlightened One" is much more than a mere man, despite all the homely traits which mark his life. Nor is there any sign in that literature that the legend regarding the person of the Buddha is of slow and gradual growth, so that we could trace its development step by step and see how humanity is merged in divinity. This fact does not preclude the possibility that the legend did so develop, especially if the Pāli Canon is placed at a much later date than that assigned to it by the majority of authorities, but it unquestionably tells against the theory of an original humanity. At least it proves that no such humanity was sufficient to satisfy the Buddhists even of the Hīnayāna.

Moreover the period in which the Buddha preached was essentially one in which his qualities were such as to be reckoned divine. As early as the time of the *Brāhmaṇas* the gods of India had definitely become subject to the need of accounting for their existence by some exploit of merit. These texts are full of explanations of the reasons why the gods gained immortality, of how they became gods, and why individual gods have their functions and being. As in the religion of ancient Rome, as in the religion of modern India, a deity is not a creature which exists from birth or from all time and continues to be, irrespective of his actions: the gods must create their divinity by the sacrifice or by ascetic feats, and the epic is full of tales of sages of all kinds who seek to become divine and whose efforts the gods strive to restrain by inducing them to abandon their asceticism under temptation. These sages are as powerful as gods and mingle freely with them: when Indra is hurled from his throne and flees into hiding, and when Nahuṣa usurps his place, it is no divine power that restores him to his kingdom, but the anger of the seer Agastya, with whom Nahuṣa had rashly entered into a theological disputation. Indeed it must be remembered that the *Brāhmaṇas* assert in all seriousness that the Brāhmans are the gods on earth, their location being the point of distinction between them and the gods in the skies above, and the whole sacrificial conception of the *Brāhmaṇas* is based on the view that by the sacrifice the priests hold complete control over the gods. It was inevitable that under these circumstances the Buddha, with his triple perfection of knowledge, of virtue, and of austerity, should be regarded by his followers as a being of a divine character, and that a mythology should rapidly develop round his person.

It might, however, be thought that, though the mythology did grow, yet in that mythology it would not appear that the Buddha himself ever made any claim to more than human nature, that he was in his own opinion a simple man, and that as a preacher of a system of rationalism any claim of divinity or superiority in kind to other men would not be asserted by him. Here again the expectation is disappointed: the texts not

# PLATE XXIV

## The Buddha and Sujātā

Before attaining enlightenment (Bodhi) the Buddha sought to win salvation by Brāhmanic precepts. While thus engaged, he was mistaken for a deity by Sujātā, the wife of a landholder, who sought of him a boon and presented him an offering of milk, giving him likewise a bowl of water to wash his hands. Touched by her homage, he blessed her and granted her request. After this he bathed, and when the golden cup in which Sujātā had brought the milk floated up-stream, he knew that he was soon to gain Buddhahood. From a painting by the modern Indian artist Abanindro Nath Tagore. After *International Studio*, XVIII, Plate facing p. 26.

merely ascribe to Gotama traits which are mythological, but they attribute to him claims which are incompatible with humanity. Many as are the notices of the Buddha, we find that at the most important periods of his life the non-human characteristics have a practice of appearing, whether because the fancy of the disciples then thought it fit to insert them or whether from the beginning the Buddha felt himself to be more than a man.

In the *Saṁyutta Nikāya* and elsewhere a comparison occurs between the Buddha and the flowers: as the lotus grows up in the water from which it is born, rises above it, and ceases to be sullied by it, thus the Buddha grows above the world and is no longer defiled by it. In itself the analogy might be satisfied by the view that the Buddha rises from the world into the way of deliverance from all desire of any kind in Nirvāṇa, that is, he becomes an Arhat. This interpretation, however, is forbidden by an important dialogue in the *Aṅguttara Nikāya* (ii. 37), in which the Buddha himself answers the question as to his humanity and divinity. A certain Brāhman named Doṇa, seeing on the feet of the "Blessed One" — for the Buddha often bears the title of "Blessed" (*Bhagavant*), which is peculiarly that of Kṛṣṇa — thousands of wheels with their spokes and their naves, cries out in wonder that, being but a man, he should have these marks. He then proceeds to question the Buddha and asks if he is a god. To this the Buddha responds, "No." He then asks, "Art thou a Gandharva?" and receives the same reply, which is repeated in answer to his next inquiry whether the "Blessed One" is a Yakṣa, a term denoting a sort of demoniac being, which (sometimes at least) is conceived as of mysterious and heavenly beauty. The questioner therefore resorts to the only hypothesis which seems available and suggests that, after all, the Buddha must be a man; but this conclusion is at once rejected by Gotama, who finally explains that from him have vanished the passions which could bring about his being a Gandharva, a Yakṣa, or a man, and that, like the lotus, he has passed out from the world and is not affected by the world; in sum, he is a Buddha. It is impossible to explain away this passage as a mere reference to the condition of an Arhat, for Arhats as men have no such remarkable physical features as the wheels on the feet of the great god. Similarly, though the Buddha is fain to eat and drink like other men, and though we have the full details of his last days and of the efforts to heal him made by human means, the texts can tell us without hesitation that he is the first of beings, the controller and the sovereign of the whole world and of everything which is contained in it, of Māra who tempts him, of Brahmā, of all the generations of living beings — men and gods, ascetics and Brāhmans. When in the *Aṅguttara* Ānanda rejoices to know that the Buddha is able to spread his glory and make his voice heard in countless worlds, Udāyin questions the value of such a power; but the "Blessed One," far from reproving Ānanda's admiration, declares that if Ānanda should fail to secure emancipation in the present existence, he will, by reason of his acquiescence in the Buddha's wonderful power, be born for seven existences to come as king of the gods and for other seven as king of Jambudvīpa, or the world. Again, when the deities of the sun and moon are assailed by the terrible demon Rāhu, who swallows them and thus from time to time causes their eclipse, it is to the Buddha that they go seeking shelter. "Rāhu," says Śākyamuni, "the deity of the moon has had recourse to me; let go the moon, for the Buddhas pity the world"; and the demon departs in terror, reflecting that had he harmed the moon, his head would have flown into seven parts.

While various Buddhas may have their earthly life from time to time, it is characteristic of these beings in all texts, both early and late, that in this world there cannot be more than a single Buddha at any one time, even as in the view of the Brāhmans the god Brahmā exists and must exist alone. There is, however, a distinction between the Brāhmanical view and

## PLATE XXV

### The Buddha on the Lotus

The Buddha, seated on his lotus-throne, is represented in the "teaching attitude," expounding the Law to the multitude who surround him. The small figures in the upper corners show him in the "contemplative attitude," and the second from the top on the right portrays him in the attitude of benediction (cf. Plate XXIV). The "witness attitude" is shown in Plate XXVI. The principal other "attitude" is reclining on the right side with the head to the north, this representing the Buddha's death. From a Gandhāra sculpture now in the Lahore Museum. After *Journal of Indian Art*, viii, No. 62, Plate V, No. 2.

the Buddhist as regards the question of time. In the former, Brahmā's existence endures throughout a cosmic age, or *kalpa*, at the end of which, he, like all things else, is absorbed for the time in the Supreme Spirit or the Absolute. On the contrary, like the Jains and like the Vaiṣṇavas, it is an article of faith with the Buddhists that the Buddhas come into being only at irregular intervals, when there is special cause for their presence, and that they depart again when they have fulfilled the purpose for which they came, have set in motion the wheel of the gospel which they preach, and have founded an order destined to last for some period of time. Nevertheless, the influence of the former conception breaks forth strongly in the account given of the last days of Gotama. As he felt the end approaching, he said to his favourite disciple, Ānanda, that the Buddha could remain in the world for a whole age or to the end of the present age, and thrice he repeated these words. Unhappily the heart of Ānanda was possessed by the wicked Māra, who had not forgiven his defeat by the "Blessed One," and he took no notice of an occasion so favourable to secure the prolonged life of the Buddha: when the moment came that he realized the force of the words, it was too late, for the "Enlightened One" had decided not to live beyond the limit of human life. This story, so significant of the Buddha's belief in his own superhuman nature, is recorded in all the canons. Moreover his divine character is attested by the transfiguration which awaits his body upon death: it becomes brilliant like a god, and the brocade in which it has been clothed by Pukkusa fades in contrast. In the life of the Buddha this event twice takes place, once when the future Buddha becomes a Buddha and on the occasion of attaining Nirvāṇa. But in addition to this, the same text, the *Mahāparinibbāna*, ascribes to the Buddha himself the claim that he changes his form in accordance with his audience, be it Brāhmans, nobles, householders, ascetics, gods of the *entourage* of the four world-guardians, gods of the thirty-three gods, or gods of the heaven of Brahmā, and that, after he has finished his discourses, his hearers wonder whether he be god or man. It is not surprising if the obsequies of such a man were marked not merely by the honours due to an earthly supreme king, but by miracles of different kinds, testifying rather to his immortal nature than to a merely human character.

The birth of the Buddha is no less remarkable than his death. The "Buddha To Be," or Bodhisattva, had for some centuries been living in glory in the world of the Tuṣita, or "Happy," gods, which he had attained by the only possible means, that of good deeds in earlier births. In the fullness of time, and after mature consideration of the time and place, and of the caste, family, and personality of the mother, he selected for this honour Māyā, the wife of the Śākya king, and while she slept he entered her womb in the guise of a six-tusked elephant. Four celestial beings guarded the infant before birth, and he eventually saw the light in the Lumbinī grove while his mother held in her hand a branch of the sacred *sāl*-tree. The parallelism with the myth of Leto [4] is made yet more striking in the legend as told of another Buddha, Dīpaṁkara, which signifies either "Maker of Light" or "Island-Maker," who was born on a mystic island in the Ganges. There is no tradition in the early canon that Māyā was a virgin, but although a single passage in the Tibetan literature[5] suggests a natural conception, that appears to be a blasphemy. Moreover the mysterious nature of the birth is heightened by the fact that Māyā dies seven days afterward.

It is, of course, possible to see in all this a distorted version of actual facts: death of the mother of the Buddha in childbirth is as legitimate an explanation of the tale of the death of Māyā as any interpretation based on the theory of a sun-myth. Yet in the Pāli Canon we have the authority of the Buddha himself for his abode in the Tuṣita heaven and his descent from it, and it is not easy to explain the six-tusked elephant which Māyā in vision saw entering her womb. The most plausible hypothesis is to refer the dream to the Indian belief that a child before its conception already exists in an intermediate condition, as follows naturally from the doctrine of rebirth, and to find that the six tusks of the elephant arise from a misunderstanding of a phrase denoting "one who has the six organs of sense under control."[6] These hypotheses, however, ingenious as they are, seem needless in face of the natural explanation that the Buddha, like his followers, regarded himself as really divine.

The same difficulty presents itself in a new form regarding the marks which can be seen on the body of the Buddha, thirty-two of which are primary and eighty secondary. Can these be resolved into the products of the Indian conception of physical perfection combined with the historical tradition of certain somatic peculiarities of Śākyamuni? These signs are eagerly noted on the body of the infant Buddha by the soothsayers, and they are found there without lack or flaw. Yet the legend tells that they could not decide whether the boy would become a universal monarch or a Buddha, although one sage declared that the signs showed that if the prince stayed in the secular life, he would be a universal monarch; but if he abandoned this world, as he would do, he would be a Buddha. Moreover the marks are described as being those of a Mahāpuruṣa, or "Great Male"; and their abnormal character is clearly shown by the description given of some of them: thus the feet of the Buddha are covered, as we have seen, by wheels of great beauty, his hands have the fingers united by a membrane, between his eyebrows extends a circle of soft, white hair which emits marvellous rays of light, his spine is so rigid that he cannot turn his head, and so forth.

In these features of the Buddha there is strong reason to see mythology, for the marks are those of the "universal monarch," the Cakravartin, as he is described freely in the Buddhist scriptures. The *Mahāsudassana Sutta* of the *Dīgha Nikāya* gives us a picture of such a king in the shape of Śākyamuni in an earlier birth as a Cakravartin. As he walks on the terrace of his palace, the divine wheel appears; and the king, after paying it due honour, bids it roll on and triumph. The wheel rolls to the east, followed by the king and his army, and the east yields to him; the wheel rolls then south, then west, then north, and all the lands submit and accept the Buddhist doctrine; after which it comes back to rest on the terrace of the palace with its sevenfold rampart of gems. It is difficult to doubt that the conception of the wheel owes its origin to sun-worship, for as early as the *Brāhmaṇas* the wheel is freely used in the ritual to represent the solar luminary. This hypothesis receives increased force when it is remembered that the term Mahāpuruṣa is applied in Brāhmanical literature to Nārāyaṇa, that form of Viṣṇu which recalls the Puruṣa of the *Ṛgveda* and the *Brāhmaṇas*, the primeval being from which the world was created, and the spirit which is eternal and unique. The later northern Buddhist text, the *Lalitavistara*, actually identifies Nārāyaṇa with the Buddha. Further the Brāhmanic character of the marks is interestingly shown by a piece of ancient evidence — a *Sutta* in the *Suttanipāta* which tells how the Brāhman Sela was convinced of the truth of the nature of the Buddha, not by any preaching of the "Blessed One," but by the argument that he bore the special marks, a demonstration of which he gave to the Brāhman, including the miracle by which he covered the whole of his face with his tongue.

It is not surprising that such a saint as the Buddha should have been subject to temptation, for, despite the fact that one of the commandments laid down for his order is to avoid asceticism as a means to secure Nirvāṇa, it is certain that it was by a great feat of self-mortification that he attained to his Buddhaship. For six years he practised ascetic rites and wore himself nearly to a skeleton, though at the end of this time he became satisfied that starvation was not the due means of securing the desired end. Yet before Buddhaship is won he has a severe contest with the evil Māra, the Vedic Mṛtyu, or "Death," who

# PLATE XXVI

## Temptation of the Buddha

The Buddha, seated in the "witness attitude" (i. e. touching the earth to call it to witness his rights), is assailed by the powers of evil, led by Māra. The assailants adopt both frightfulness and seduction. Demons in threatening human shape and also in hideous animal guise endeavour to terrify him; Māra's wanton daughters seek to divert his attention to life's evils; but his thoughts remain fixed on Bodhi ("Enlightenment"), and the fiends of every sort are routed. From a fresco at Ajantā, Berār. After Griffiths, *The Paintings in the Buddhist Cave-Temples of Ajantâ*, Plate VIII.

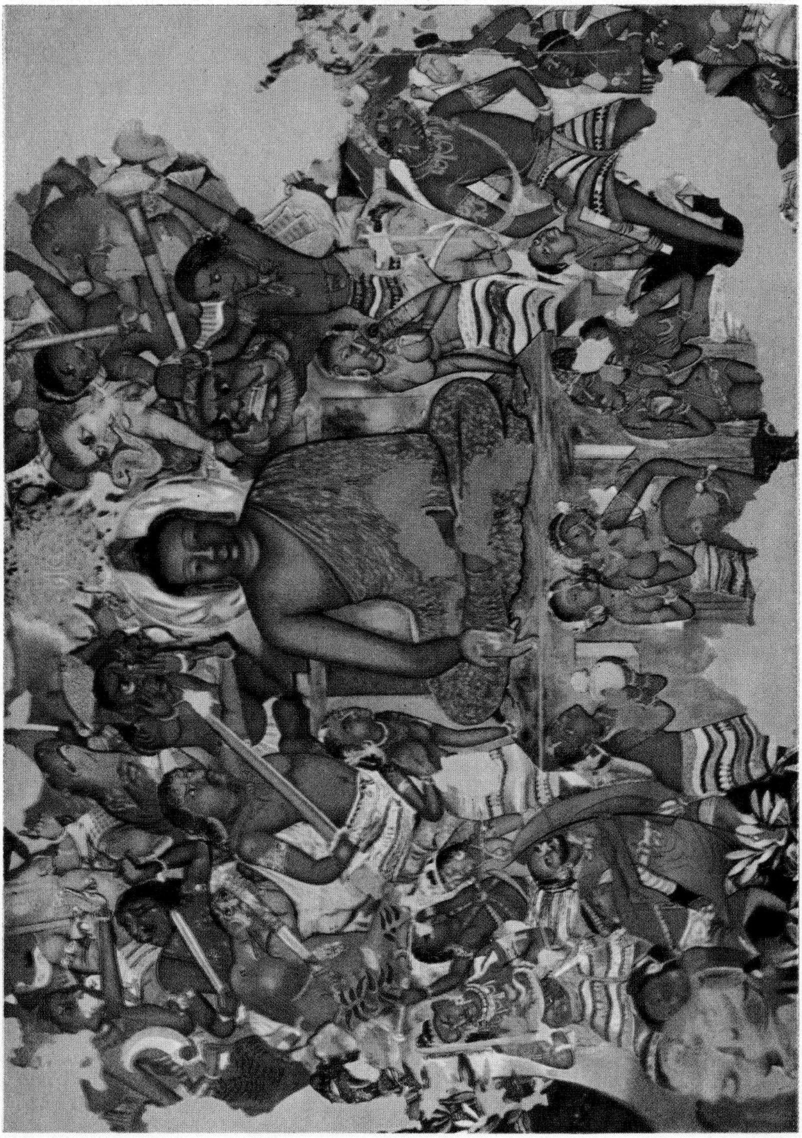

assails him with all his host as he sits under the tree of knowledge, beneath which he is to attain to Buddhahood. The gods flee before the terrors of Māra, but the prince remains unmoved; the mountains and other weapons hurled at him turn to garlands in his honour; and the enemy is forced to parley with him and to claim that his liberality in past days has won him the right to the seat under the tree usurped by the prince. His hosts support their master's claim with loud approbation, but when the "Buddha To Be" appeals to the earth, she asserts his right to his place with such vehemence that in affright the hosts of Māra are discomfited, and the elephant on which Māra rides kneels in homage to the "Blessed One." The tree and the *bodhi* (the "knowledge" which makes the Buddhas) now become the property of Gotama, and the serpent Mucalinda celebrates his victory by covering him with its coils. A further legend states that Māra endeavoured to retrieve his defeat by the use of three daughters, Desire, Pining, and Lust, but these damsels failed wholly to have any effect upon the sage.

Rationalized, the story means no more than that, after realizing the futility of fasting as a means to salvation, in one moment of insight the truth which he was to teach as his lifework came home to the future Buddha as he sat, like many another ascetic or student, under a fig-tree. Among his variant names Māra has not only that of Namuci, one of Indra's enemies in the *Ṛgveda*, but also that of Kāma ("Desire"), who, akin to Death, is an enemy of that renouncement and enlightenment which it is the main object of the life of the Buddha to attain. Did the episode stand alone, the suggested account might be acceptable, but amid so much mythology it seems unfair to reject the obvious conclusion that the tree is no ordinary tree, but the tree of life, and that the conflict with Māra represents a nature-myth, and not the inner struggles of an Indian ascetic.

Yet another fact attests the religious character of the Buddhist tradition: in the *Cakkavattisutta* of the *Dīgha Nikāya* Śākyamuni predicts the coming of Metteya, the future Buddha, and this is confirmed by the *Buddhavaṁsa*, for though the verse (xxvii. 19) which gives his name is late, it is clear that his existence is implied, since the text mentions three Buddhas who have lived in this happy world-period before Gotama, and a happy period is one in which there must be full five Buddhas. Metteya, in whose name is recorded the Buddhist *metta*, or the "friendship" of the Buddha for all beings, is later a subject of special reverence. Moreover the "Enlightened One" himself tells of six prior Buddhas, a conception hard to reconcile with the idea of a simple human doctrine.

The divine or supernatural character of the Buddha is indeed adequately proved by the signs of extreme devotion to his relics which appeared immediately after his death, and which are incompatible with the mere interest taken in the remains of a famous teacher. The fact that only symbols, such as the tree, the feet, or the wheel, are chosen for representation in the sculptures of Sānchī, Bhārhut, and Bodh Gayā, which afford the oldest examples of Buddhist religious art, shows that the Buddha was still the centre of the devotion, though it was not yet considered seemly to portray his bodily figure. It is true that many of his followers adopted a rationalist attitude, held that a Mahāpuruṣa was merely a great man, asserted that this was the Buddha's own interpretation of the term, denied the mysterious conception and birth, and explained the reference of the "Blessed One" to his power to live to the end of the age as meaning merely that he might have lived to the full age of a hundred years, instead of dying at eighty, as he actually did. At the same time, however, there were schools of supernaturalists who held that the Buddha was something remarkable and far from merely human: thus some of the faithful asserted that the fact was that Śākyamuni had never truly lived in the world of men, that during his alleged stay on earth he was in reality dwelling in the Tuṣita heaven, and that a mere phantom appeared to gods and men. This doctrine, if we may believe the tradition, was already current by 256 B.C., and was condemned by the Council which was held in that year.

Whatever may have been the date of the rise of docetism in the Buddhist community, the simple, human side of the "Enlightened One" has entirely disappeared when we find the Mahāyāna, or "Great Vehicle," system set forth in the literature, as in *The Lotus of the Good Law* (*Saddharmapuṇḍarīka*); and we see instead a deity of singular greatness and power. This Buddha came into being at the beginning, it may be presumed, of the present age, but he can boast of having taught the true law for endless millions of years. He possesses a body of delight (*sambhoga*), which has the famous thirty-two marks, including the marvellous tongue, which now can reach forth to the world of Brahmā. This, however, is reserved for the vision of beatified saints, and to men he shows only an artificial body, which is a derivative, in far inferior nature, of the true body. It was in this appearance that Śākyamuni appeared on earth, entered Nirvāṇa, and left relics of himself in a Stūpa; but in reality his real body dwelt and dwells in a celestial sphere and will, when his true Nirvāṇa shall come, be changed into a divine Stūpa (of which the earthly Stūpa is but a reflex), where the "Blessed One" will repose after having enjoyed the pleasures of instruction. Nevertheless, he will sometimes arise at the desire of one of the other Buddhas, for the number of Buddhas now increases to infinity, just as space and time are similarly extended. The oldest stage of the Buddhist canon knew six earlier Buddhas, and they grew to twenty-four before the Pāli Canon was complete. In the Mahāyāna there is no end to the numbers, for the heaping up of huge figures is one of the most conspicuous features of the school. Thus the "Blessed One" can remember having honoured eight thousand Buddhas named Dīpaṁkara, five hundred called Padmottara, eighteen thousand Māradhvājas, eighty thousand

Kaśyapas, and so on up to three hundred million Śākyamunis. His seeming entrance upon Nirvāṇa while yet on earth is explained by the great eagerness of the god to benefit men and is illustrated by the example of the physician who, being anxious to persuade his sons to take medicine which they would not receive so long as they had him to look to for help, withdrew himself from them, so that, thinking him lost to them, they made use of the healing agency. The path of salvation, too, is a very different one from the old conception of moral discipline: it is true that this is still a means of deliverance, but to hear the preaching of the Buddha, to honour relics, to erect Stūpas, to set up statues of gems or marble or wood, to offer flowers or fragrant essences, all these will bring the supreme reward; nay, even the children who in play build Stūpas in the sand or scrawl figures of the Buddha on the wall, and those who by accident utter the words, "Reverence to the Buddha," are equally fortunate. The parallelism with the legends of the *Purāṇas* is clear and convincing, and renders it probable that the Mahāyāna texts (at least as they are preserved to us) are not to be dated earlier than the third or fourth centuries of the Christian era, even though mention is made of Chinese translations of some of the important documents at surprisingly early times.

Śākyamuni is not, however, the greatest figure of the Mahāyāna faith: a certain monk, Dharmākara by name, in ages long passed addressed to the then reigning Buddha, Lokeśvararāja, an intimation of his determination in due course to become a Buddha who should be the ruler of a world in which all were to be free from any trace of suffering and should be saints. It is through this resolve of Dharmākara that he now exists as Amitāyus or Amitābha ("With Infinite Life" or "With Infinite Glory") in the Sukhāvatī heaven, contemporaneously with the Buddha known as Śākyamuni. The glories of this heaven are described in the *Sukhāvatīvyūha*, which was translated into Chinese between 148 and 170 A.D., and in the

*Amitāyurdhyānasūtra*, works which have had great influence in China and Japan. The heaven is entirely flat, no mountains being there; streams of water give lovely music, and trees of beautiful gems abound. There is no hell, nor animal kingdom, nor ghosts, nor demons; neither is there distinction between men and gods, for all the beings in that land are of exceptional perfection of mind and of body. Day and night are not, because there is no darkness to create the difference between the two. Those who dwell in that happy realm are not born in any natural manner, but are miraculously conceived in the heart of lotuses, where they grow into maturity, nourished by the echo of the teaching of the Buddha, until in course of time they come forth when the fingers or the rays emanating from the Buddha have brought the flowers to ripeness. Nevertheless, the heaven can be attained even by those who speak Amita's name in blasphemy, so sacred is that utterance.

Another figure of high importance in this pantheon of Buddhas is that of Avalokiteśvara, to whose devotion is directed the *Kāraṇḍavyūha*, one version of which was translated into Chinese by 270 A.D. We know also that this worship was a real one by 400 A.D., for when the Chinese pilgrim Fa Hien met with a storm on the journey from Ceylon to China, he had recourse to Avalokiteśvara, whose representations in art, moreover, are dated in the fifth century A.D. He it is who has decided to remain a "Buddha To Be," a Bodhisattva, until such time as he has secured deliverance for all mankind. In return for this he is the patron of those in shipwreck and of those who are attacked by robbers; the sword of the executioner is arrested by calling on his name, fetters drop when he is invoked, a woman who seeks a fair son or daughter need only pray to him to secure her desire. He descends into the dreadful hell Avīci to aid the sufferers there and converts it into a place of joy; the appalling heat changes to agreeable coolness; the kettle in which millions of the damned are boiling becomes a lotus pond. In the world of the Pretas, which he next visits, he comforts these hungry and thirsty hosts with food and drink. In Ceylon he converts man-eating Rākṣasīs; and as the winged horse, Balāha, he rescues from disaster men who have been shipwrecked and are troubled by evil demons; while in Benares he preaches to those creatures who are embodied as insects and worms. He ranks as the first minister of Amitābha, for it is part of the Mahāyāna doctrine that each Buddha has two Bodhisattvas as his attendants who visit the hells, carry souls to paradise, and take care of the dying. For some reason or other Avalokiteśvara ranks high above Maitreya (or Metteya), who is the only Bodhisattva recognized by the Buddha of the Hīnayāna canon. Curiously enough, Chinese piety has converted this Bodhisattva into a woman, a view which is contrary to both schools of Buddhism, though the Mahāyāna acknowledges the Tārās as feminine deities of maternal tenderness, a point in which it shows agreement with the *śakti*-worship of Śaivism. After Avalokiteśvara the most important Bodhisattva is Mañjuśrī, celebrated in the *Gaṇḍavyūha*, which was translated into Chinese between 317 and 420 A.D.

It is not surprising that from this mass of speculation and religion should be evolved the conception of an Ādibuddha, that is, a Buddha who should, in the fullest sense of the word, be without beginning, and not merely (like the other Buddhas) go back to an infinitely distant period in time. This figure was probably developed as the view of some of the faithful by the end of the fourth century A.D., for the *Sūtrālaṁkāra* of Asaṅga refutes the idea, which at least suggests that it was a current belief, and not merely a possible position, although it cannot be said ever to have become orthodox or established.

The net result of the Mahāyāna tradition was to add to the divine powers the Buddhas, raised to countless numbers, and to swell the hosts of the deities by the Bodhisattvas in like abundance, since not for a moment did either school abandon belief in the ordinary gods. If we may trust the Hīnayāna

## PLATE XXVII

### Avalokiteśvara

The Bodhisattva ("Buddha To Be") Avalokiteśvara bears the expression of calm and benevolence, which is in conformity with his love for mankind. In his left hand he bears a lotus, and his right hand is held in the position which conventionally expresses favour to suppliants. From a Nepālese jewelled figure of copper gilt in the collection of Dr. Ananda K. Coomaraswamy. After Coomaraswamy, *Viśvakarma*, Plate XI.

canon, the Buddha himself was completely satisfied of the existence of the gods, both the higher, of whom Brahmā and Indra are by far the most active and prominent, and the lower, such as the horde of Nāgas, Garuḍas, Gandharvas, Kinnaras, Mahoragas, Yakṣas, Kumbhāṇḍas (a species of goblin), Asuras, Rākṣasas, and so forth. The Pretas, the ghosts of the dead, occupy a somewhat prominent place in Buddhist imagination, and the Yakṣas also are frequently mentioned, though the word itself is sometimes applied even to a god like Indra, or to Śākyamuni, in the more ancient sense of a being deserving worship, or at least a powerful spirit. To the surprise of Buddhaghoṣa, the great commentator of the Pāli Canon, the Buddha himself recommended that due worship should be paid to these spirits to secure their good will. The Nāgas fall into several classes, those of the air, of the waters, of the earth, of the celestial regions, and of Mount Meru; they are conceived as half human, half snake in form. The point of view of the Hīnayāna is shown to perfection in the methods used to guard the monks against the evil beings around them. Thus the *Āṭānāṭiya Sutta* portrays the deities of the four cardinal points as coming to the Buddha with their retinues and as declaring to him that among the divine spirits some are favourable to the Buddha and some unfavourable, since he forbids murder and other wickednesses, and that, therefore, the monks need some protection from these beings. Accordingly they offer a formula which all the faithful should learn by heart, and which, enumerating the creatures in the various quarters, declares that they join whole-heartedly in the cult of the Buddha, ending with a list of the chiefs of the spirits who are to be invoked if any of their subjects improperly attack the monks despite the assurances of the formula. Similarly the *Khandaparittā* prevents danger from snakes by declaring friendship for their various tribes, and in the *Mora Jātaka* an old solar charm is converted into a Buddhist spell to secure safety from all evils. It is not unnatural that, when the Hīnayāna school is so closely associated with the ordinary religion of the day, the Mahāyāna is still more open to such influences. The "Great Vehicle" is especially fond of bringing some *quasi*-divine figure into connexion with its Buddhas, the most striking of these being Vajrapāṇi ("the Thunderbolt-Handed") who aids in converting the doubtful, drags such demons as Māra-Namuci before the Buddha, and assists in deep grief at the funeral of the "Blessed One." His thunderbolt brings him into close relation with Indra, the troops who attend him are like the Gaṇas of Śiva, and he has affiliations with Kubera. For the Mahāyāna he is a great Bodhisattva, but though he ranks high among the future Buddhas, he is nothing more in origin than a Yakṣa by race and a Guhyaka by caste. Another instance of the steady working of the Indian pantheon is the fact that in this period Nārāyaṇa becomes definitely identified with the Buddha.

It is clear, nevertheless, that at first this adoption of closer connexion with the ordinary deities had no substantial effect upon the theology of the Mahāyāna school nor upon its practice, which was inspired with the conception of benevolence which differentiates it from the individualistic and less emotional Hīnayāna, whose aim is personal attainment of Nirvāṇa, and whose ideal is the Buddha, not the Bodhisattva. But the development of the worse side of the Paurāṇic religion had its influence on the theology of the Mahāyāna, and apparently from the sixth century A.D. onward the whole system began to be seriously altered by the effect of the Tantric doctrines. At any rate, as early as the eighth century we find in Padmasaṁbhava, the converter of Tibet, no orthodox Buddhist, but a sorcerer who defeats the magicians of Tibet on their own ground and who, when he has accomplished this task, changes himself into a horse in order to convert the people of some other land. Both the literature and the art reveal a vast horde of terrible forms, largely female, such as Piśācīs, Mātaṅgīs, Pulkasīs (the last two named after debased castes), the Parṇaśabarī (or "Savage Clad in Leaves"), the Jāṅgulī (or Snake-Charmer), the "Maidens," the "Mothers," the "Sisters," the four, six, eight, or even twenty-five Yoginīs, or "Sorceresses," and the naked Ḍākinīs. Above these in rank are the five Tārās, who preside over the senses and the elements and are especially suited for incantations, and the gods He, Hūm, and "He of Seven Syllables," who are made to emerge from these syllables. Naturally Śiva and his wife, as Mātaṅgī or Cāṇḍālikā or some one of her many other names, are present, and (what is perhaps more important) the Bodhisattvas are moulded into the likeness of Śiva and associated, as he with his wife, with the Tārās as their female counterparts. The epithets of Śiva are freely transferred to the Bodhisattvas: thus Avalokiteśvara is called "the Lord of the Dance," "the God of the Poison" or "of the Blue Neck," "the Lord of the Worlds," and so forth. A further development of this new theology prefixes to the names the mystic word *vajra* ("thunderbolt") and places at the head of the pantheon the Vajrasattva, who is little else than an Ādibuddha, and then ranges below it the Vajrabodhisattvas, down to the Vajrayoginīs and other demoniac beings. At the same time the Tantric cult is developed to the full with its devotion to wine and women, its revolting ritual, and its exaltation of magic, which leads the teacher of this agreeable cult to arrogate to himself the position of the Vajrasattva himself.

It is of course inevitable that the question should have presented itself how far the growth of the system of the Mahāyāna can be explained by internal causes, and how far it owes its development and its missionary force to outside elements. With much ingenuity Dahlmann has sought to show that the change in the spirit of the Mahāyāna as compared with the Hīnayāna — its marked theism and its charity — is a reflex of the Christian religion and that in its success it really was indebted to elements which cannot be regarded as truly Buddhistic. Yet if, as seems likely, there was from a very early period a theistic element in the Buddhism of the time, it becomes unnecessary to seek the theistic stratum of the Mahāyāna from an external source; and, as we have seen, the Pāli Canon already refers to Metteya as a "Buddha To Be." Nor indeed, unless we can accept the legend of St. Thomas as referring to actual mission work in the north-west of India, is there any clear proof of Christian influence there before the third century. It would be idle to deny that the negative argument is not complete, but, on the other hand, we must admit that there is no conclusive ground to seek for any Christian modification to explain the rise of the Mahāyāna. That in later times some borrowing may have taken place is certainly possible: thus in the late Mahāyāna texts we find the comparison of the Buddha to a fisher, which is not Buddhistic, and the art exhibits the influence of the Madonna with the Christ, but these facts do not affect the main body of the mythology.

It has, on the contrary, been contended that the legends of the earlier Hīnayāna school penetrated to the west and influenced in detail the Christian Gospels. As the claim is put forward by its ablest expositors, it does not amount to more than a belief that Buddhist legends had penetrated in some shape to the east of the Mediterranean and were known in the circles in which the Gospels of the Church were composed. The best example adduced in support of this hypothesis is the parallelism of the story of Simeon in the Gospel of Luke (ii. 25–35) with the tale of Asita, which is found as early as the *Sutta Nipāta* and may, therefore, be presumed to be older than the New Testament. In both cases the old man hears of the birth of the child and worships it, but realizes that he must die before the things which he foresees come to pass. There is also a certain similarity in the account of the temptation of the Buddha by Māra and that of the Christ by the devil. In this instance the evidence for the Buddhist story must be pieced together from portions of the Tipiṭaka, and the analogy is not very convincing. Other parallels which are alleged are those of the miracle of the feeding of the five thousand

(Matthew xiv. 15–21, Mark vi. 35–44, Luke ix. 12–17) and Peter's walking on the sea (Matthew xiv. 25–33), but the Buddhist source from which these stories are cited is only the introduction to two legends in the Pāli *Jātaka*. That text is a collection, as we now have it, of five hundred forty-seven stories of the adventures of the present Buddha of the Hīnayāna in previous births, and it is a mine of treasures, though for folklore rather than for mythology. The verses which it contains are of uncertain date, but the prose commentary and the introductions are not, as they stand, older than the fifth century A.D. It is matter of conjecture to what extent the prose represents the older tradition,[7] and the occurrence of the legends in question in the *Jātaka* prose is of no value as proof of borrowing on the part of the Gospels. Some scholars hold that in the stories of the *Jātaka* we must seek the originals of the legends of Placidus (who is canonized as St. Eustathius), of St. Christopher, and of the attempts of the devil to assail saints under the guise of the Holy One; and it has also been suggested that it is to Buddhism that we must look for the origin of the Christian community of monks, for the requirement of celibacy, the custom of the tonsure, the veneration of relics, the use of church bells and of incense, and the actual plan of church building. The proofs of borrowing in these cases are still to seek, and the essential fact remains that neither Buddhism nor Christianity appears to have contributed essentially toward the mythology or the religion of the other.

The Buddhism of Tibet is an offshoot of the Mahāyāna school of Indian Buddhism, but it represents the faith of that sect in a form of marked individuality. In all its types, despite considerable differences of tenets among the several schools which have appeared from time to time, the Buddhism of Tibet is penetrated with Hinduism, especially Śaivism, and by the aboriginal worship of the land, which, though compelled to assume a Buddhist garb, retains much of its primitive force and nature.

To King Sroṅ-btsan-sgam-po, in the period from 629 to 650 A.D., belongs the credit of introducing Buddhism into Tibet, for he sent T'on-mi Sambhoṭa to India to collect books and pictures pertaining to the Buddhist faith, being assisted in his work by his two wives, one the daughter of the king of Nepāl and one the daughter of the Chinese emperor. He transferred the seat of government from Yar-lun to Lha-sa, and when he died at an advanced age, he took up his abode with his spouses in a statue of the Bodhisattva Avalokiteśvara, which is still exhibited at Lha-sa. The legend is quite typical of the faith, as is the story that both his wives were incarnations of the goddess Tārā, for the embodiment of the divinities in human form is a marked characteristic of Tibetan mythology. These features appear fully developed in the account of Padmasambhava, who in the eighth century A.D. gave the Tibetans the decisive impulse to the Buddhist faith. He was apparently a native of Udyāna, which, like Kaśmīr, was the home of magic arts, and he appears as *par excellence* a magician who claimed to excel Gotama himself in this dubious accomplishment. The legendary account of his life makes him a spiritual son of Amitābha, produced for the conversion of Tibet, and he was born from a lotus as the son of the childless, blind king Indrabhūti, whence his name, which means "Lotus-Born." Educated as the heir of the monarch, he surpassed all his equals in accomplishments and was married to a princess of Ceylon; but a supernatural voice urged him to abandon worldly things, and by killing some of his father's retainers, whose past lives had earned them this punishment, he succeeded in obtaining banishment from the kingdom. Ḍākinīs and Jinns brought him the magic steed Balāha, on which he went away. After resorting to meditation in cemeteries, and there winning supernatural powers through the favour of Ḍākinīs, he travelled through all lands, and despite the fact that he was, as a Buddha, already omniscient, he acquired each and every science, astrology, alchemy, the Mahāyāna, the Hīnayāna, the *Tantras*, and all languages. He likewise converted the princess Mandāravā, the incarnation of a Ḍākinī, who thereafter accompanied him in all his wanderings, now in human form with a cat's head, now in other shapes. Then he set himself to the conversion of India and accomplished this by promulgating in each part the doctrine corresponding to the local faith, to which he gave an external coat of Buddhism. At last, on the invitation of the king of Tibet, K'ri-sroṅ-lde-btsan, he proceeded there to contend with the demons who hindered the spread of the faith in that land; and though Māra himself sought to frustrate his success, the fiend was defeated, and the evil powers were forced to yield, Padmasambhava's victory being marked by the building of the monastery of bSam-yas, thirty-five miles from Lha-sa, the oldest of Tibetan monasteries. On the completion of his mission he departed on the steed Balāha from the sorrowful king in order to carry the doctrine to the land of the western demons, among whom he still dwells and preaches his faith.

It is probably in large degree from the form of Buddhism promulgated by this teacher that the magic part of modern Buddhism in Tibet is derived, although the present faith represents a reform due to the monk Tsoṅ-k'a-pa, who was born in 1355 A.D., and among whose pupils were the two heads of the monasteries at rNam-rgyal-c'os-sde and bKra-shis-lhun-po (Ṭa-shi-lhun-po), whose successors are known as the Dalai and Ṭashi Lamas. These dignitaries, the first of whom has always held the highest rank in the Tibetan hierarchy, are reputed to be incarnations of the Bodhisattva Padmapāṇi and the Buddha Amitābha respectively.[8] On the death of the temporary incarnation of the Bodhisattva the spirit of the latter passes over to a child who must be born not less than forty-nine days after the departure of the soul of the last Lama, the identity of this child being decided by divination, and the diviner being the Dharmapāla of gNas-c'un (near Lha-sa), who is regarded as an incarnation of the god Pe-har.

The child denoted by the oracle is taken with his parents to a temple east of the capital; at the age of four he is brought to Potala and made a novice, and at seven or eight becomes a monk and the titular head of the two great monasteries of Lha-sa. The control exercised by China over Tibet led formerly to the taking of steps to prevent any Dalai Lama reaching maturity, doubtless in order to obviate the growth of a power hostile to Chinese claims. The same doctrine of successive reincarnation applies to the Ṭashi Lama, and the tenet is widely applied to other spiritual heads, especially among the Mongolians.

Naturally enough, the Tibetans have added to their mythology not merely the priests of Tibetan Buddhism proper, but also the masters of the Mahāyāna school, from which the Buddhism of Tibet is ultimately derived. Thus the great masters of the Mahāyāna, Nāgārjuna, Āryadeva, Asaṅga, and Vasubandhu, are all elevated to the rank of Bodhisattvas. Other saints of later origin than these are included in the group of eighteen Arhats and of eighty-four Mahāsiddhas; while additional famous individuals include Dharmakīrti, a contemporary of the king in whose reign Buddhism was first brought into Tibet, and Abhayākara, a sage of the ninth century born in Bengal, who is said to have assumed the form of a Garuḍa to rout an army of Turuṣkas and to have rescued a large number of believers from slaughter by an atheistic king, a huge snake appearing above the head of the saint as he interceded for the captives and terrifying the ruler into compliance with his request.

In Tibet the Indian practice of placing oneself under the protection of a special god is carried to the furthest extent, and each monk adopts some divinity as his patron, either generally or for some special period of life or for a definite undertaking. Such gods make up the class of guardian deities, or Yi-dam, and these are of various kinds. On the one hand there are the Dhyānibuddhas, and on the other divinities who are manifestations of Buddhas or Bodhisattvas; both these classes are marked out from other kinds of guardian deities in that they are regularly represented in art as holding in their arms their *śaktis*, or energies in female form, this mode of presentation being most characteristic of the influence of Śaivism on the Buddhism of Tibet.

It is also significant of the change in the faith that Gotama plays a comparatively slight part in the religious life of Tibet. A much more important place is taken by the five Dhyānibuddhas, or "Meditative Buddhas," Vairocana, Akṣobhya, Ratnasambhava, Amitābha, and Amoghasiddha. They correspond to the five Mānuṣibuddhas of the present period, Krakucchanda, Kanakamuni, Kāśyapa, Śākyamuni, and the future Buddha, Maitreya. There are also five Dhyānibodhisattvas, of whom the chief are Samantabhadra, the Bodhisattva of Vairocana, and Vajrasattva, that of Akṣobhya. Of the Dhyānibuddhas the chief is Amitābha, whose paradise, Sukhāvatī, is as famous in Tibet as in China and Japan; nor is it improbable that in the development of this deity, as in that of the Dhyānibuddhas, Iranian influences may be seen, since the Iranian Fravashis, or spiritual counterparts of those born on earth,[9] have some affinity to the conception of Dhyānibuddhas. Along with Amitābha, or Amitāyus, which is his name in his perfect, or *sambhoga*, form, we frequently find representations of a Buddha called Bhaiṣajyaguru ("Master of Healing"), whose effigies his worshippers use as fetishes, rubbing on them the portions of their persons affected by disease.

Of the forerunners of Gotama, the first, Dīpaṁkara, and the six immediately preceding, Vipaśyin, Śikhin, Viśvabhū, Krakucchanda, Kanakamuni, and Kāśyapa, are often mentioned, although neither they nor Maitreya, the future Buddha, play any considerable part in the mythology. Of Maitreya, however, is related a legend with Iranian affinities. In the hill Kukkuṭapada, near Gayā, lies the uncorrupted body of Kāśyapa, whether one of the pupils of Gotama or his predecessor. When Maitreya has abandoned his home and made the great renunciation expected of all Buddhas, he will proceed to the place where Kāśyapa lies, the hill will miraculously open, Maitreya will take from his body the Buddha's dress, and a wondrous fire will consume the corpse of the dead man so that not a bone or ash shall remain over.[10]

Much more prominent than Maitreya is the Dhyānibodhisattva of Gotama, the spiritual son of Amitābha, Padmapāṇi, or Avalokiteśvara. In one of his forms this deity bears the name Siṁhanāda ("Lion's Roar"), and in this aspect he has the half moon as his crest jewel, a sign of the Śaivite origin of this manifestation of the god. The old Buddhist legend of Siṁhanāda is doubtless the source of the mediaeval story preserved in the *Physiologus*, which tells how the lion by its roar vivifies its lifeless young after their birth, a parable applied to the Redeemer, who lies in the grave for three days until called to life by the voice of His heavenly Father. Another Śaivite form of the god is that as Amoghapāśa, and the same influence appears in two other aspects of the deity as Nāteśa ("Lord of the Dance") and Halāhala, the name of the poison whence Śiva derives his name of Nīlakaṇṭha, or "Blue Neck." In yet another manifestation he appears with eleven heads, whose origin is traced to the grief felt by the sage when, after his unwearying work for the freeing of creatures from ill, he found that the hells were once more becoming full. Because of his sorrow his head fell off, and from its fragments his spiritual father, Amitābha, created ten heads, to which he added his own as the eleventh.

Another Bodhisattva of high rank is Mañjuśrī, who is reputed to have been a missionary of Buddhism in north China, and into whose complex composition the record of a historic teacher may perhaps have entered. He was born out of a lotus without father or mother, and from his face a tortoise sprang. This and other traits of the legends affecting him suggest that he has been assimilated to the Hindu Brahmā. While Avalokiteśvara is incarnated in the Dalai Lama, the Chinese Emperor was an embodiment of Mañjuśrī, as were the envoy to India of Sroṅ-btsan-sgam-po and the king who patronized Padmasambhava. His *śakti* is Sarasvatī, just as she is the wife of Brahmā, and hence one of his forms is that of Dharmadhātuvāgīśvara, while he appears also as Mañjughoṣa and Siṁhanāda. Like other Bodhisattvas, however, he has also a fierce form, in which he appears as a foe of the enemies of the faith under the names of Vajrabhairava, Yamāntaka, or Yamāri, the last two names (both meaning "Foe of Yama") celebrating his conquest over Yama, the demon of death who was depopulating the land. It is characteristic of him that in his effigies he bears a sword, and this feature of his nature seems connected with his repute as founder of the civilization of Nepāl, where he is credited with emptying the valley of water.

Vajrasattva or Vajrapāṇi is a Bodhisattva whose title, "the Bearer of the Thunderbolt," clearly denotes his origin from Indra. In the later period of Tibetan Buddhism this god supplants Samantabhadra as the representative of the Ādibuddha, a conception which, however, never became generally accepted, even in Tibet. Vajrapāṇi often forms one of the triad with Padmapāṇi and Mañjuśrī, although Amitābha is frequently substituted for Mañjuśrī. From Vajraṣattva the Dhyānibuddhas are supposed to emanate. On the other hand, there is a terrible side to the character of the god. In his benevolent aspect he serves as one of the Yi-dam, or guardian deities, but in his dread form as one of the Dharmapālas, or "Protectors of Religion," who are Hindu or local Tibetan gods brought into the Buddhist system as protectors of the true faith against the demons of their several spheres. The device is obviously an ingenious one, and apparently the same principle of distinguishing the two sides of the divine character was generally adopted. The Dharmapālas are represented as beings of ferocious aspect, with broad and hideous heads, protruding tongues, huge teeth, and hair erect. Their limbs are enormously strong, but short, and their bodies are misproportioned; they are surrounded with flames or smoke, and on their forehead they bear a third eye; their appearance is that of readiness to fight.

The hate of Vajrapāṇi for the demons is explained by the fact that at the churning of the ocean he was entrusted with the duty of guarding the ambrosia, but being deceived by the demons, he became their deadly foe. Like his prototype Indra, he is a god of rain and in this capacity protects the Nāgas, who send rain, from the onslaught of the giant Garuḍa birds. The legend tells that when the Nāgas came to hear the preaching of Gotama, Vajrapāṇi was given the function of guarding them, when thus engaged, from the attack of the Garuḍas. Yet this special position does not prevent the close association of Vajrapāṇi and the Garuḍas, and in one form he appears with the wings of a Garuḍa and the head of a Garuḍa above his own.

Another Dharmapāla, who is also a Yi-dam, is Acala ("Immovable"), whose main characteristic is the fact that in his effigies he always bears a sword, while his wrathful temper is reflected in his name of Mahākrodharāja ("Great-Wrath-King"). Better known than he is Hayagrīva ("Horse-Neck"), a god with a horse's head arising from his hair. He is described as generally friendly to men, but he terrifies the demons by neighing and by the same means he announces his presence when he is summoned by the appropriate spell. The Mongols regard him as the protector of the horse, and his name and character suggest that an animal origin is not improbable.

Hayagrīva ranks as the first of the eight dreadful gods united by the Tibetans in the group of Drag-gšhhed. The second in this list is the war-god lCam-sriṅ, whose Indian prototype is possibly Kārttikeya, the son of Śiva, but who may also be a purely Tibetan divinity. The third is Yama, the old deity of death and punisher of sin. Now, however, he is of diminished importance, for the pains of hell will not endure forever, and in the end he will be freed from his task; while again he himself is one of the damned and, according to one legend, must swallow molten metal every day. His sister Yamī reappears beside him, charged with the duty of taking away the clothes of the dead. As of old, Yama bears the noose to grasp the souls of the dead and he has retainers, two of whom are represented with the heads of a bull and a stag. Next to Yama comes his enemy, Yamāntaka, one form of Vajrabhairava or Mañjuśrī. He is followed by the one female figure among the dreadful gods, Devī, who rides on a mule over a sea of blood which flows from the bodies of the demons which she slays. She is accompanied by two Ḍākinīs, Siṁhavaktrā and Makaravaktrā, who have the heads of a lion and a *makara* (a sort of dolphin) respectively. Other Ḍākinīs also appear with Siṁhavaktrā, two of whom have the heads of a tiger and a bear.

It is obvious that this goddess, though in part she approximates to the artistic type of Sarasvatī, is nothing but the dread aspect of the wife of Śiva, and appropriately enough two forms of Śiva are enumerated among the dreadful deities, the white Mahākāla and the six-armed protector. His essential characteristic in Tibet is that of the guardian god and the giver of inspiration, a feature which connects him closely with the Indian legends attributing to him the patronage of grammar and of learning generally. He is not only a Dharmapāla, but also a Yi-dam, and his form is likewise to be recognized in the two Yi-dam Śambara and Hevajra.

The eighth of the dreadful gods is a special white form of Brahmā or, more normally, Kubera or Vaiśravaṇa, the god of wealth. The latter, however, more commonly and more properly appears as one of the four Lokapālas, or "World-Guardians." These four great kings are thought to dwell round Mount Meru, ruling the demon hordes which live about that mountain, the reputed centre of the Buddhist world. They are Virūḍhaka, lord of the Kumbhāṇḍas in the south; in the north Kubera, lord of the Yakṣas; in the west Virūpākṣa, lord of the Nāgas; and in the east Dhṛtarāṣṭra, lord of the Gandharvas.

Apparently sometimes identified with this group is another of local origin, five in number, one of whom serves as their head and the other four as the Lokapālas. The chief of these deities is reputed to be incarnate in the head of the monastery of gNas-c'un, who is the giver of oracles and in especial of the one which determines on whom the spirit of the dead Grand Lama has descended. The incorporation of this remarkable body of divinities into the Buddhist pantheon is ascribed, doubtless rightly, to Padmasambhava, who undertook the difficult but essential task of assimilating the local deities to his teaching, following the model adopted at an earlier date by Asaṅga in introducing the Śaivite pantheon into the Buddhism of the Mahāyāna school. Another of these local divinities is Dam-can rDo-rje-legs, who seems to stand in close relation to the group of five gods.

Tibet has also borrowed directly from India its chief and its minor deities in various forms. Thus from Indra are derived not merely Vajrapāṇi of the Mahāyāna as an attendant of Gotama, but also the Bodhisattva Vajradhara, the Dhyānibodhisattva, the Yakṣa Vajrapāṇi, and even Indra *eo nomine*. Brahmā, again, is not merely reproduced in part in Mañjuśrī, but enters the pantheon independently; Rudra appears beside Mahākāla; deities like Agni, Varuṇa, Vāyu, and Vasundharā ("Earth"), which are closely connected with natural phenomena, are often mentioned. More interesting than these are the minor deities who possess a special affinity for Tibetan imagination. The Nāgas are very conspicuous: they have human forms with snakes appearing above their heads, or are figured as serpents or as dragons of the deep. They have castes and kings and can send famine and epidemics among men. Their enemies are the Garuḍas, beings with the heads and wings of birds, but with human arms and stout, semi-human bodies. Among the snakes the chief are Nanda, Upananda, Sāgara, Vāsuki, Takṣaka, Balavant, Anavatapta, Utpala, Varuṇa, Elāpattra, and Śaṅkhapāla.

The Rākṣasas, Yakṣas, and Gaṇas are presented in two aspects: in the one they are assimilated to the appearance of the Dharmapālas, while in the other they are regarded as the victims of the dreadful gods, who destroy them and drink their blood. The Vetālas, as in Hindu legend, serve in conjurations in cemeteries.

The female element plays a great part in the mythology of Tibet. In addition to the *śaktis*, which are inseparable from the great gods, there exist separate female deities, the Tārās and the Ḍākinīs. The term Tārā is rendered in Tibet as "Saviour," and the Tārā *par excellence* is the *śakti* of the Bodhisattva of Avalokiteśvara, which has two forms, the white and the green. The two wives, the Chinese and the Nepālese princesses, of King Sroṅ-btsan-sgam-po are held to have been incarnations of these two aspects of the Tārā, and the distinction may be traced to the pale colour of the Chinese on the one hand and the *śyāmā* colour of the Hindu lady on the other, if (as is possible) "green" is an erroneous version of that difficult term. In her artistic form the Tārā borrows much from the goddess Śrī, who has a prominent *rôle* in the iconography of early Buddhism, but her main features are, like the other elements of Tibetan Buddhism, rather Śaivite. Additional aspects of the Tārā, who are regarded also as separate deities, are Marīcī, Mahāmayūrī, Mahājāṅgulītārā, Ekajaṭā, Khadiravanatārā, and Bhṛkuṭī, though the latter is much more prominent as a separate goddess, who is represented in company with the Tārā and Avalokiteśvara. Another very important divinity is Uṣṇīṣavijayā, whose ancient fame is attested by the fact that a *dhāraṇī*, or spell, bearing her name is among those preserved in the old palm-leaf manuscripts of the Japanese monastery at Horiuzi, where they have been kept since 609 A.D. Another favourite deity is Sitātapattra Aparājitā, who is distinguished by the possession of eight arms. Much more savage is the goddess Parṇaśabarī, who is also called Pukkasī, Piśācī, and Gāndhārī; her dress of leaves and her names justify her claim to be the lady of all the Śabaras, or wild aboriginal tribes of India. Kurukullā ranks as the goddess of wealth and is closely connected with Vaiśravaṇa; it was her help which secured great wealth for the Dalai Lama who first held that office. She is the wife of Kāmadeva and is clearly nothing else than the Hindu Rati, the goddess of sexual love.

The *śakti* of the Bodhisattva Mañjuśrī is Sarasvatī or Vāc, who is represented, in accordance with her Indian prototype, as a beautiful woman with but one face and two arms, playing on an Indian *vīṇā*, or lute. She has a great part in the *Śrīvajrabhairavatantra* because she is the wife of Mañjuśrī in his aspect as Vajrabhairava.

A less reputable group of female divinities is composed of the Ḍākinīs, who are all held to be the wives of a deity Ḍāka, and whose Sanskrit name, of unknown meaning, is translated in Tibetan as "Wanderers in the Air." These goddesses are multiform, but while they can confer supernatural powers on their worshippers, they are also prone to wrath and must be assiduously cultivated to win their regard. Those who seek from them their lore must expect to find them in hideous human or animal shapes. They form two groups, those who have already left this earth and those who still remain on it. To the first belong Buddhaḍākinī, Vajraḍākinī, Padmaḍākinī, Ratnaḍākinī, and Karmaḍākinī. The most important of all Ḍākinīs is Vajravarāhī, incarnate in the priestess who is the head of the monastery bSam-ldin; she is not permitted to sleep at night, but is supposed to spend that time in meditation. A legend tells that a Mongolian raider who, in 1716 A.D., sought to enter the monastery in order to satisfy himself as to whether the priestess bore the characteristic mark of the goddess whose incarnation she was, found nothing within the walls but a waste space in which a herd of swine wandered, feeding under the leadership of a large sow. When the danger was over, the swine changed their shape and once more became monks and nuns under the control of their abbess, while the Mongol, converted from his misbelief, richly endowed the monastery. In Nepāl this goddess seems to count as a form of Bhavānī, the wife of Śiva. Her representations are characterized by the presence of the snout of a hog, and her incarnate form must bear a mark having a similarity to this.

Other Ḍākinīs figure as attendants upon Devī in her aspect as one of the eight dreadful gods. In all likelihood many of these Ḍākinīs are local spirits of Tibet, though naturally enough they do not differ materially from the similar spirits of Hindu mythology.

## CHAPTER VIII

# THE MYTHOLOGY OF THE JAINS

WHATEVER be the relative antiquity of the Jain and the Buddhist sects and the trustworthiness of the tradition which makes the founder of the Jain faith, as we now have it, a contemporary of the Buddha, and whether or not he merely reformed and revised a religion already preached in substance by his predecessor Pārśvanātha, there can be no doubt that the mythology of the Jains has a great similarity with that of the Buddhists and that it also shows close relations to the ordinary mythology of India. The question is rendered more complex by the fact that the Jain scriptures of the older type, the Pūrvas, are confessedly lost, that the sacred texts which we now possess are of wholly uncertain date, and that even if the comparatively early date of the third century B.C. be admitted for the substance of their contents, nevertheless it is certain that the documents were not finally redacted until the time of Devarddhigaṇa in the middle of the fifth century A.D., up to which period they were always subject to interpolation in greater or lesser degree. In their present form the Jain beliefs are schematized to an almost inconceivable extent, and their mythology, which centres in the personalities of the twenty-four Tīrthakaras, is connected with their remarkable views on the formation of the world and on the nature of time. Thus the number of Tīrthakaras, or perfected saints, is increased to seven hundred and twenty by the ingenious device of creating ten worlds or continents, in each of which are twenty-four Tīrthakaras, and three ages for each. The worlds are all modelled on the continent of Jambudvīpa, which is the continent on which we live, and are separated from it by impassable seas. It has two parts, the Bharata and the Airāvata, and the number ten is made up by the divisions of Dhātakīkhaṇḍa and Puṣkarārdha, each of which has the sections Airāvata and Bharata, while these are subdivided into east and west. In time again the Jains delight, like the Mahāyāna Buddhist texts, in huge numbers: thus one year alone of the type described as "former" (*pūrva*) embraces seven thousand five hundred and sixty millions of normal years, a conception which has been compared with the belief of advancing age that the earlier period of life was the happier and the longer. To the Jain time is endless and is pictured as a wheel with spokes, perhaps with six originally corresponding to the six seasons, but at any rate normally with twelve, divided into two sets of six, one of which belongs to the *avasarpiṇī*, or "descending," and the other to the *utsarpiṇī*, or "ascending." In the first of these eras good things gradually give place to bad, while in the latter the relation is reversed. Of these eras the fifth "spoke," or *ara*, of the *avasarpiṇī* is that in which we live.

The real gods of the Jains are the Tīrthakaras of the present *avasarpiṇī* period, and the names of the whole twenty-four are handed down with a multitude of detail. Yet the minutiae are precisely the same for each, with changes of name and place, and with variations in the colour assigned and the stature, as well as in the designations of the attendant spirits, who are a Yakṣa and a Yakṣiṇī, of the Gaṇadhara, or leader of disciples, and of the Āryā, or first of the female converts. A minor alteration here and there is quite remarkable: thus the twentieth Tīrthakara, Munisuvrata, and the twenty-second, Neminātha, are said to have been of the Harivaṁśa, and not, like all the others, of the Ikṣvāku family. Nearly all the Tīrthakaras obtain consecration and saving knowledge at their native place, though Ṛṣabha is said to have become a Kevalin, that is, one possessed of the highest knowledge, at Purimatāla, Neminātha at Girnār, and Mahāvīra (the last) on the Ṛjupālikā River.

Twenty of them attained final release on Sametaśikhara, or Mount Pārśvanātha, in the west of Bengal, but Neminātha enjoyed this bliss at Girnār, Vāsupūjya at Campāpurī in north Bengal, Mahāvīra at Pāvāpurī, and Ṛṣabha himself at Aṣṭāpada, which is identified with the famous Śatruṁjaya in Gujarāt. Ṛṣabha, Nemi, and Mahāvīra agree also in the fact that they attain release when seated on the lotus-throne and not, like the others, in the *kāyotsarga* posture, that of a man standing with all his limbs immovable, by which he fortifies himself against any sin. The Tīrthakaras all differ, however, in two further respects: the mark or cognizance which appertains to them and which appears sculptured on their images, and the tree under which they are consecrated. Nevertheless, for the most part the economical Jains adopt the sage device of narrating precisely the same wonders attending their birth, their determination to become devotees of the life of a Tīrthakara, the obtaining of release, and so forth, so that, as handed down, the canonical texts consist of fragments which may be expanded, as occasion requires, from notices of other persons contained in them.

The life of the last Tīrthakara, Mahāvīra, is characteristic of all. At a time precisely defined, though we cannot absolutely ascertain it, Mahāvīra descended from his divine place and, assuming the shape of a lion, took the form of an embryo in the womb of Devānandā of the Jālandharāyaṇa Gotra, wife of the Brāhman Ṛṣabhadatta of the Gotra of Koḍāla. The "Venerable One" knew when he was to descend and that he had descended, but not when he was descending, for the time so occupied was infinitesimally small. The place of his descent was Kuṇḍagrāma, which is now Basukund near Besārh. Indra, however, was dissatisfied with this descent, since he reflected that it was improper for a Tīrthakara to be born in a poor Brāhmanical family; and accordingly, with the full knowledge of Mahāvīra, he reverently conveyed the embryo from the womb of Devānandā to that of Triśalā of the Vāsiṣṭha

## PLATE XXVIII

### Tīrthakara

The gigantic statues of the Jain Tīrthakaras ("Perfected Saints") are invariably represented with an expression of superhuman calm. As becomes the oldest Jain sect, the Digambara ("Sky-Clad," i. e. naked), they are nude. The elongated ears are interesting as recurring in images of the Buddha. From a statue at Sravana Belgola, Mysore. After a photograph in the Library of the India Office, London.

Gotra, wife of the Kṣatriya Siddhārtha of the Kāśyapa Gotra and of the clan of the Jñātṛs, and transferred the foetus in the womb of Triśalā to that of Devānandā. In that night Triśalā beheld fourteen wonderful visions, and similarly the mother of a Tīrthakara always sees these dreams on the night in which the Arhat enters her womb. She tells her husband, and soothsayers predict the greatness of the child to be. When it is born, the gods come in vast numbers, and the rites connected with its nativity are performed with the utmost splendour, out of all keeping with the real position of the father of Mahāvīra; while from the time of the conception of the child the prosperity of the house is so augmented that the babe is given the name Vardhamāna ("He that Increases"). At the age of thirty, with the permission of his elder brother Nandivardhana, his father having died, Mahāvīra gave himself up to asceticism and after a prolonged life of religious teaching, during which he was for a period closely associated with the Ājīvika sect under Gosāla, he passed away. The gods descended at his death as at his birth, and in the shape of a heap of ashes a great comet appeared which has been rashly identified with the horn-shaped comet that, according to Pliny, was seen at the time of the battle of Salamis.

This narrative leaves no room for doubt that the Tīrthakara was deemed to be a divine being by his followers and, probably enough, by himself as well. But what is to be made of the story of the interchange of the embryos? Professor H. Jacobi,[1] to whom we are indebted for the effort to make history from the legend of Mahāvīra, sees in the account an endeavour to explain away a fact which told against the advancement of Mahāvīra. In his opinion Devānandā never had any other husband than Siddhārtha, and the alleged Ṛṣabhadatta is a mythical person. In reality the boy was the child of Devānandā, a Brāhman woman by origin, and the attempt to connect him with Triśalā was in order to obtain for him the powerful protection of the noble relatives of Triśalā, who was a Kṣatriya lady. The story would gain more ready credence since the parents of Mahāvīra were dead before he revealed himself as a prophet, but as the facts could not be wholly forgotten, the story of the exchange of embryos was invented. Yet on the other hand, as Jacobi himself notes, the exchange is an open borrowing from the similar account of the birth of Kṛṣṇa, and we must recognize that it is idle to seek any such rational explanation as that proposed. From whatever cause — most probably the Kṛṣṇa legend — it had become a doctrine of the school of the Jains that the high nature of a Tīrthakara required this transfer, possibly to heighten the importance of the birth, and it is not impossible that the belief was borrowed from the Ājīvika sect, who have been brought into connexion with the worship of Nārāyaṇa.[2]

The same close association with the Kṛṣṇa sect is shown to us by the biography of Ariṣṭanemi (or Neminātha), the twenty-second of the Tīrthakaras, which is set forth at length in the Jain *Antagaḍadasāo*. In connexion with it we learn of the life and the death of Kṛṣṇa, the son of Devakī, with (on the whole) slight change, though of course the facts selected are only a small number from the entire life of that hero. The interchange of embryos is specially mentioned, and we hear of the futile births of six children to Devakī who, as in the *Purāṇas*, are destroyed by Kaṁsa and whose death she mourns. As a result of the intervention of Kṛṣṇa with Hariṇegamesi an eighth child, Gaya Sukumāla, is born, but his fate is somewhat unfortunate. His brother Kṛṣṇa arranges for his marriage to Somā, the daughter of the Brāhman Somila and his wife Somasirī, but in the meantime the prince hears a discourse of Ariṣṭanemi and determines to abandon the worldly for the ascetic life. In this desire he persists, despite every effort to hold him back, and in the end is allowed (as always in these tales) to have his own will after he has enjoyed the royal state for only a single day. Now he obtains the permission of the Arhat to perform meditation in the graveyard of Mahākāla for one night, and while thus engaged he is seen by Somila who, deeming him to be devising evil, in anger slays him. Next day the fact is made known to Kṛṣṇa, while by a parable the sage shows him that the dead man has really been profited greatly by death; but the evil-doer is driven by the terrors of a guilty conscience to come before Kṛṣṇa and to fall dead in his presence. Some interest attaches likewise to the prediction of the death of Kṛṣṇa, for the Arhat tells him that when Dvārakā is burnt, he shall go with Rāma and Baladeva to the southern ocean to Paṇḍumahurā, to the Pāṇḍavas, where in the Kosamba forest he will be wounded in the left foot by a sharp arrow which Jarākumāra will shoot from his bow. Paṇḍumahurā is doubtless Madurā of the south, where the Pāṇḍyas were kings, and the text assumes the identity of the Pāṇḍavas and the Pāṇḍyas.[3] Moreover it makes Kṛṣṇa have as a companion not merely Baladeva, who is his comrade in the *Purāṇas*, but also Rāma, who is not directly associated with Kṛṣṇa in the ordinary mythology. The close connexion of the Kṛṣṇa mythology and the Jain is further illustrated by the fact that in the same period as the twenty-four Tīrthakaras twelve Cakravartins are born, including the well-known Bharata, Sagara, Maghavan, and Brahmadatta; nine Vāsudevas, including Puruṣottama, Puruṣasiṁha, Lakṣmaṇa, and Kṛṣṇa; nine Baladevas, including Rāmacandra and Balarāma; and nine anti-Vāsudevas, including Rāvaṇa and Jarāsandha.

The story of the first Tīrthakara, Ṛṣabha, leads us to the very beginning of the first *ara* of the *avasarpiṇī* era. In those days the land was level, men were good and extremely tall and strong, and lived for long periods of time, receiving from wish-trees whatever they needed. This was the *yugalin* ("pair") period, for sons and daughters were born as pairs and intermarried, but there was no pressure on the means of subsistence, and contentment reigned, a picture of society and life obviously similar to that of the Uttara Kurus in the epic. As time went on the people increased, and at length the Kulakaras, the first lawgivers, appeared, the last of whom was Nābhi. To his wife was born a son called Ṛṣabha ("Bull, Hero"), because she had dreamt of a lion. He it was who taught, for the benefit of the people, the seventy-two sciences, of which writing is the first, arithmetic the most important, and the knowledge of omens the last; the sixty-four accomplishments of women; the hundred arts, including such as those of the potter, blacksmith, painter, weaver, and barber; and the three occupations. To him tradition also attributes the discontinuance of the *yugalin* system of intermarriage. In due course he bestowed kingdoms on his sons and passed into the ascetic life.

Of the legends regarding Pārśvanātha special interest attaches to one told to show why he has Dharaṇendra and Padmāvatī as his attendants. Two brothers, Marubhūti and Kamaṭha, were born as enemies in eight incarnations, the last being as Pārśvanātha and Śambaradeva respectively. Once, while felling a tree for his fire-rite, an unbeliever, despite the protest of the Jina, cut to pieces two snakes in it, but these the Jina brought to life by a special incantation. When, therefore, Śambaradeva attacked Pārśvanātha with a great storm while he was engaged in the *kāyotsarga* exercise and was standing immovable and exposed to the weather, much as Māra assailed the Buddha at Bodh Gayā, then the two snakes, who had been born again in the Pātāla world as Dharaṇendra and Padmāvatī, came to his aid from their infernal abode, Dharaṇendra holding his folds over the Jina and the Yakṣiṇī spreading a white umbrella over him to protect him. Thereafter they became his inseparable attendants, just as Śakra in Buddhist legend accompanies the "Blessed One." Hence in the figures of the Jina Pārśvanātha in the Jain sculptures at Bādāmi, Elurā, and elsewhere he is often represented with the folds of a snake over him. Curiously enough, the Digambara Jains, who follow the stricter rule of the sect advocating nudity and who have, therefore, nude statues, assign to the seventh Tīrthakara a smaller set of snake hoods.

# PLATE XXIX

## Dilwāra Temple

The wealth of detail in sculpture is strikingly shown in the white marble temple of Dilwāra (Delvāḍa or Devalvāḍa) on Mount Ābū, Sirohi, Rājputāna. The temple was built in 1032 A.D. in honour of the first Jain Tīrthakara, Ṛṣabhadatta, whose statue is seen in the niche. After a photograph in the Public Library, Boston (copyright, H. C. White Co., New York).

Beside the real deities, the Tīrthakaras, the ordinary divinities are minutely and carefully subdivided into classes. In the thirty-sixth chapter of the *Uttarādhyayana Sūtra* they are enumerated as follows: there are four kinds, Bhaumeyikas (or Bhavanavāsins), Vyantaras, Jyotiṣkas, and Vaimānikas. Of the first category there are ten subdivisions, the Asura-, Nāga-, Vidyut-, Suparṇa-, Agni-, Dvīpa-, Udadhi-, Dik-, Vāta-, and Ghaṇika-Kumāras. Of the second class there are eight kinds: Piśācas, Bhūtas, Rākṣasas, Yakṣas, Kinnaras, Kimpuruṣas, Mahoragas, and Gandharvas. The moons, the suns, the planets, the Nakṣatras, and the stars are the dwellings of the Jyotiṣkas. The Vaimānika gods are of two kinds: those born in the *kalpas* and those born above the *kalpas*. The former category of divinities falls into twelve classes who live in the *kalpas* after which they are named: Saudharma, Īśāna, Sanatkumāra, Māhendra, Brahmaloka, Lāntaka, Śukra (or Mahāśukra), Sahasrāra, Ānata, Prāṇata, Āraṇa, and Acyuta. The gods born in the regions above the *kalpas* are again subdivided into those who live in the "neck," or upper part, of the universe, Graiveyakas, and the Anuttaras ("With None Higher"), above whom there are no higher gods. The first group consists of three sets of three, ascending from lowest to highest, and the Anuttaras are classed as the Vijayas, the Vaijayantas, the Jayantas, the Aparājitas, and the Sarvārthasiddhas. The text proceeds to state the duration of the lives of these deities, which in the case of the highest gods, those of the Sarvārthasiddha Vimāna, increase to inconceivable numbers, but still the divinities are subject to *saṁsāra*, or transmigration, and cannot endure for ever.

Twelve *yojanas* above this Vimāna is the place called Īṣatprāgbhāra, shaped like an umbrella, where go souls which are finally perfected. It is four million five hundred thousand *yojanas* long, as many broad, and rather more than thrice as many in circumference, with a thickness of eight *yojanas* in the middle, decreasing until at the ends it is only the size of the wing of a fly. Above Īṣatprāgbhāra, which consists of pure gold, is a place of unalloyed bliss, the Śilā, which is white like a conch-shell, and a *yojana* thence is the end of the world. The perfected souls penetrate the sixth part of the topmost *krośa* of the *yojana* and dwell there in freedom from all transmigration. Individually each soul thus perfected has had a beginning but no end; collectively, however, there has not been even a beginning. They have no visible form, they consist of life throughout, and have developed into knowledge and faith.

On the other hand, the Jains provide for a series of hells which lie below our earth, the Ratnaprabhā, Śarkarāprabhā, Vālukāprabhā, Paṅkaprabhā, Dhūmaprabhā, Tamaḥprabhā, and Mahātamaḥprabhā. With due precision it is specified that in the lowest hell all the inmates have a stature of five hundred poles, which decreases by half with each ascending step.

Apart from its truly remarkable schematism, the most wonderful things about Jain mythology are the prominence which it gives to the minor divinities whom it classes as Vyantaras and who are described as wood-dwellers, and the importance which it attaches to the sphere of thought corresponding to the belief in fairies, kobolds, ghosts, spooks, and so forth. These godlings are present in the *Ṛgveda*, though naturally they are not salient there, and doubtless they have always been essential items in the popular belief of India. Another notable figure in the pantheon is the god Hariṇegamesi,[4] who figures in the *Kalpa Sūtra* as the divine commander of the foot troops of Indra and who is entrusted with the unmilitary duty of effecting the transfer of the embryo of Mahāvīra, while in the *Antagaḍadasāo* he appears as a god who has power to grant the desire for children. In art he is represented with an antelope's head, seemingly due to a false rendering of his name, which is Sanskritized from the original Prākrit as Hariṇaigamaiṣin, though he is scarcely known to the Brāhmanical books. An additional deity who is practically — though not entirely —

confined to the Jain texts is Nalakūvara, the son of Vaiśravaṇa or Kubera, who (in the Tibetan view at least) is regarded as a great general of the Yakṣas. These latter beings play a conspicuous part, as in Buddhism, and a Yakṣa and a Yakṣiṇī form the attendants on every Tīrthakara.

This close connexion with Brāhmanical theology was characteristic of the Jain attitude to the Brāhmans. They allowed the Brāhmans to perform for them the ceremonies of birth, marriage, and death, and used Brāhmans in their temple worship, in which Brāhmanical deities are to be found side by side with the saints of Jainism. Ultimately it is clear that this close contact with the Brāhmans had its inevitable effect in bringing the mythology of the Jains into closer association with that of Brāhmanism. The figure of the Jina begins to bear the appearance of the deity whom Jainism theoretically refuses to recognize, though the Jina still remains bereft of the powers of creation or destruction, of punishment or forgiveness of sins, for the working of action is without exception and fully explains all existence. The Tamil poem *Śindāmaṇi*, in the twelfth or thirteenth century A.D., can already speak of a god, uncreated and eternal, who can be represented with four faces like Brahmā, seated under an *aśoka*-tree, and shaded by a parasol. In theory, indeed, every man may become a Jina, but there is a sensible difference between the actual conception of a Jina and that of the potential alteration which may be produced by the full knowledge which gives the status of perfect enlightenment. The theistic conception which is so widely developed in Buddhism thus attains, though in modest and simple form, a foothold in Jainism and assimilates that faith to the theism which constitutes the basis of Indian religion.

## CHAPTER IX

# THE MYTHOLOGY OF MODERN HINDUISM

THE religion of India as manifested to us in literary history has been a constant process of the extension of the influence of the Brāhmanical creed over tribes, whether Aryan or (more often) non-Aryan, who lay outside its first sphere of control. Brāhmanism has, on the whole, proved itself the most tolerant and comprehensive of religions and has constantly known how to absorb within its fold lower forms of faith. In doing so it has received great assistance from the pantheistic philosophy which has allowed many of its ablest supporters to look with understanding and sympathy, or at least with tolerance, upon practices which, save to a pantheist, would seem hopelessly out of harmony with the Divine. Thus the doctrine of Devī as the female side of Śiva has enabled Brāhmanism to accept as part of its creed the wide-spread worship of Mother Earth, which is no real component of the earlier Vedic faith; the Vaiṣṇava can regard as forms of Viṣṇu even such unorthodox persons as the Buddha himself. Of course, in thus incorporating lower religions Brāhmanism has done much to transform them and has greatly affected the social practices of the tribes which had become Hinduized, but it is still easy to find among these peoples stages of the earliest forms of primitive religion, much less developed than any type recorded for us in the Vedic texts. In the result the pantheon of Hinduism is a strange and remarkable thing: on the one hand, there are the great gods Viṣṇu and Śiva with their attendants and assistants, who are in one aspect regarded as nothing more than forms of the Absolute and subjects of a refined philosophy, but who at the same time are wide enough in character to cover deities of the most primitive savagery. On the other hand, we have innumerable petty deities (*deotās*), godlings as contrasted with real gods, whose close connexion with nature is obvious and who belong to a very primitive stratum of religion. Many of these minor deities represent the same physical facts as the great Vedic gods, but the mythology of these divinities has perished, and folk-lore makes a poor substitute.

During this period Vaiṣṇavism passes through an important period of deepening of the religious interest as a result of the reforms of Rāmānuja in the twelfth century and those of Rāmānanda in the fourteenth, which emphasized the essence of faith which had been a vital feature of the worship of Viṣṇu, but which now assumed a more marked character, perhaps under Christian influence from the Syrian church in South India.[1] The worship of Rāma as the perfect hero has been finally established by the *Rāmcaritmānas* of Tulasī Dās (1532–1623 A.D.); but, on the other hand, the cult of Kṛṣṇa on its erotic side has been developed by such sects as the Rādhā Vallabhīs, who have sometimes brought the worship into as little repute as the excesses of the votaries of the *śaktis* of Śiva. The worship of these *śaktis*, the personifications of the female aspect of Śiva's nature, is the chief development of the Śaivite cult, and it forms the subject of the new literary species which comes into prominence after the tenth century of the Christian era, the Tantric text-books, of which the greater part are modern, but which doubtless contain older material. The worship which they seek to treat as philosophy is in itself made up of very primitive rites, much of it seemingly at the best fertility magic, but the philosophic guise into which these books seek to throw it is not proved to be early. While the cult of Śiva, as of Viṣṇu, has continued to extend by the process of amalgamating with itself the deities of ruder faiths, that of the *śakti* has grown to such a degree as to place the god in the inferior position, the Absolute now being conceived in the *Tantras* as essentially feminine in character, a curious overthrowing of the older Indian religion, which, on the whole, gives very little worship to the female deities. Brahmā has of course disappeared more and more from popular worship and at the present day has but two shrines dedicated to him in the whole of India.

Of the celestial deities the sun, Sūrya or Sūraj Nārāyaṇ, still has votaries and is worshipped at many famous sun temples. The Emperor Akbar endeavoured to introduce a new character into his cult, providing that he should be adored four times a day, at morning, noon, evening, and midnight, but this exotic worship naturally did not establish itself. There is a Saura sect which has its headquarters in Oudh, while the Nimbārak sect worships the sun in a *nīm*-tree (*Azidirachta indica*) in memory of the condescension of the luminary who, after the time of setting, came down upon such a tree in order to afford light for an ascetic to enjoy the meal to which he had been invited, but which his rule of life forbade him to eat in the night-time. In the villages of North India the villagers refrain from salt on Sundays and bow to the sun as they leave their dwellings in the morning, while the more learned repeat the famous Gāyatrī in his honour. In comparison with the sun the moon has little worship, and that usually in connexion with the sun. Yet it serves of course to suggest stories to account for the marks on its surface, which are generally explained as a hare and attributed to the punishment inflicted on the moon for some sin; its different phases are used to guide operations of agriculture; and there are many superstitions regarding lucky and unlucky days. The demon Rāhu, whose function it is to eclipse the sun and moon, and Ketu, representing his tail, once turned into constellations, have fallen on evil days: the latter is a demon of disease, and the former is the divinity of two menial tribes in the eastern districts of the North-Western Provinces, whose worship consists in a fire-offering at which the priest walks through the fire, this ceremony being clearly a device to secure abundance of sunlight and prosperity for the crops. A further degradation reduces Rāhu to the ghost of a leader of the Dusādh tribe; while the Ghasiyas of Mirzāpur hold that the sun and moon once borrowed money from a Ḍom but did not pay back, whence a Ḍom occasionally devours these two heavenly bodies. Eclipses are, as everywhere, of bad omen and are counteracted by various ceremonials, including the beating of brass pans by women to drive Rāhu from his prey.

Of the minor luminaries of the sky popular religion knows for purposes of worship practically only the Navagrahas ("the Nine Seizers"): the sun and moon, Rāhu and Ketu, regarded as the ascending and descending nodes, and the five planets. The other signs of the zodiac and the Nakṣatras have some astrological interest, but are not objects of worship, though in Upper India it is still the popular view that the stars are shepherded as kine by the moon. The bright and picturesque figures of Uṣas and the Aśvins have passed away without leaving a trace.

Indra still exists, but has ceased to be anything but a name, a god who lives in a heaven of his own, surrounded by his Apsarases as of old; no real worship is accorded to him. As a rain-god he is replaced in Benares by Dalbhyeśvara, who must be carefully arrayed to prevent disturbance of the seasons. Prayer is no longer addressed to Indra to procure rain, which is now obtained by many magic rites or by offerings made to the sun or to Devī, although here and there we find traces of the old place of Indra as the god of rain *par excellence*. The whirlwind and the hail once associated with the gods are now produced by demons who are to be propitiated. Aerolites, however, are still divine, and one which fell in 1880 at Sītāmarhi in Bengal is worshipped as Adbhut Nāth ("Marvellous Lord").

Though the fire is no longer the great deity that it was in the early Vedic period, it is still produced in the old-fashioned way from the fire-sticks by certain Brāhmans, and Agnihotri Brāhmans are exceedingly careful to preserve the sacred flame. In imitation of the Hindu fire-cult the Muhammadans of Gorakhpur have maintained for over a century a sacred fire unquenched, and its ashes are, like those of the fire of Indian Yogīs, believed to have magic qualities. Volcanic fire is also revered, but the lightning is now attributed to demoniac agency. The earth, however, has a fuller share of worship than in the earlier faith: she is essentially "the Mother who Supports" (Dhartī Māī), and her sanctity is so great that the dying are laid upon her, as are women at child-birth. The dust of the earth has powerful curative properties. Hindu cooking-vessels are regularly cleansed in this way, and in the crisis of the engagement the Hindu troopers at the battle of Kāmpti took dust from their grooms and cast it over their heads, thus doubtless gaining courage from close contact with Mother Earth. Among many tribes dust is also flung upon the dead. The worship of the earth is very marked among the Dravidian tribes and is beyond question most primitive in character.

Of the rivers the most holy is Gaṅgā Māī ("Mother Ganges"), to whom temples have been raised all along the bank of the stream. Her water is holy and is in great demand as a viaticum, as pure for use in sacrifice, and as valuable for stringent oaths. The full efficacy of the stream is, however, best obtained by bathing in it during the full moon or at eclipses, and on these occasions the ashes of the dead are brought from afar and cast into the river. The Jumnā is also sacred, but since, according to modern legend, she is unmarried, she is not of the highest sanctity, and so the water is heavy and indigestible. The union of the two sacred streams is especially holy at the modern Allahābād. The great rival of the Ganges is the Narmadā, which tore through the marble rocks at Jabalpur in anger at the perfidy of her lover, the Son, who was beguiled by another stream, the Johilā. In the opinion of her supporters the Narmadā is superior to the Ganges, for both its banks are equally efficacious for bathing, and not — as in the case of her rival — only the northern shore. The *Bhaviṣya Purāṇa*, in-

## PLATE XXX

### SHRINE OF BHŪMIYA

The earth-deity of the aborigines is Bhūmiya, who is gradually being incorporated into the Hindu pantheon. The shrine is of interest as showing the humble character of the temples of the primitive godlings, who are frequently represented merely by rough stones and do not enjoy the honour of any shrines whatever. After Crooke, *The Popular Religion and Folk-Lore of Northern India*, Plate facing i, 105.

deed, is credited with the prophecy that after five thousand years of the Kali age, i.e. in 1895 A.D., the sanctity of the Ganges should depart and the Narmadā take her place, but this has not yet come to pass. Most other rivers are sacred in some degree, but there are ill-omened streams. The Vaitaraṇī, located in Orissa, is the river which flows on the borders of the realm of Yama and over whose horrible tide of blood the dead must seek the aid of the cow. The Karamnāśā, which for part of its course traverses the Mirzāpur district, is said to represent the burden of the sins of the monarch Triśaṅku, which Viśvāmitra sought to wash away with holy water from all the streams, or an exudation from the body of that king as he hangs head downward in the sky where Viśvāmitra placed him. Even to touch it destroys the merit of good deeds,[2] so that people of low caste can make a living by ferrying more scrupulous persons across it. Yet although rivers as a rule are benevolent deities, many dangerous powers live in them, such as the Nāgas (or water-serpents) and ghosts of men or beasts drowned in their waters. Whirlpools in particular are held to harbour dangerous spirits who require to be appeased, and floods are believed to be caused by demons who are elaborately propitiated. Boatmen have a special deity called Rājā Kidār, or in Bengal Kāwaj or Bīr Badr, who is said to be the Muhammadan Kwāja Khiḍr [3] and who has also the curious function of haunting the market in the early morning and fixing the price of grain, which he protects from the evil eye.

Wells are sacred if any special feature marks them, such as is the case with hotsprings, and waterfalls are naturally regarded as holy, a famous cataract being where the Chandraprabha descends from the plateau of the Vindhya to the Gangetic valley. Lakes are at once more common and more renowned. At Pokhar in Rājpūtāna, where Brahmā's shrine and temple stand, there is a very sacred lake, which, according to tradition, was once inhabited by a dragon. Still more famous is Mānasarovara, which, formed from the mind of Brahmā, is the abode not only of him, but of Mahādeva and the gods, and from which flow the Sutlej and the Sarjū. The Nainī Tāl Lake is sacred to Devī. In Lake Taroba in the Chānda district of the Central Provinces all necessary vessels used to rise out of the water at the call of pilgrims, but since a greedy man took them home, this boon has ceased to be granted. Other objects of reverence are the tanks at certain sacred places, as at Amritsar. Some tanks have healing power, and others contain buried treasure.

Mountains are likewise the object of worship both by the Aryanized and the Dravidian tribes. The Himālayan peak Nanda Devī is identified with Pārvatī, the wife of Śiva, and the goddess of the Vindhya is worshipped under the style of Mahārāṇī Vindhyeśvarī and was once the patron divinity of the Ṭhags. The Kaimūr and the Vindhya ranges are fabled to be an offshoot from the Himālaya: they were composed of rocks let fall by Rāma's followers when they were returning from the Himālaya with stones for the bridging of the way to Laṅkā; but before they had reached their destination Rāma had succeeded in his aim and he therefore bade them drop their burdens. Another famous hill is Govardhana, the peak upraised by Kṛṣṇa for seven days to protect the herdsmen from the storm of rain sent by Indra to punish them for withholding his meed of sacrifice.

In addition to these deities, and more important than they for popular religion, must be reckoned the village deities. Of these a notable figure is Hanumān, whose rude image is to be found in most Hindu villages of the respectable class. He is adored by women in the hope of obtaining offspring and he is the favourite deity of wrestlers. He is a very popular divinity among the semi-Hinduized Dravidian races of the Vindhya range and he bears his old name of "Son of the Wind." This, coupled with the fact that in the Panjāb appeal is made to him to stop the whirlwind, suggests that the theory that he is connected with the monsoon has a good deal of probability. What is most extraordinary is that the apes in India are regarded as sacred, and weddings of apes are still occasionally performed at great cost as a religious service. Bhīmasen, who has a certain amount of popularity in the Central Provinces, has apparently borrowed his name mainly from the Bhīma of the epic, but the Bhīṣma of the epic has a real worship as a guardian deity.

Another divinity of the village is Bhūmiya, who is either masculine or feminine, in the latter case having the name Bhūmiyā Rāṇī. This is clearly the earth god or goddess in a local form, and the nature of the worship is shown by the fact that reverence is especially paid when a village site is consecrated, when a marriage takes place or a child is born, or at the harvest. In the Hills he is a deity of benevolent character and modest pretensions, being quite satisfied with simple cereal offerings; but in Patna he is being elevated into a form of Viṣṇu, in the hills he is becoming identified with the aspect of Svāyambhuva worshipped in Nepāl, and in the plains a Mahādeva Bhūmiśvara and his consort are being created, so that the figure of the earth god or goddess is being taken up into the bosom of the Vaiṣṇava and Śaiva systems.

Similarly the local god Bhairon is metamorphosed into Bhairava, a form of Śiva, but his epithet Śvāśva ("Whose Horse is a Dog") indicates his real character, for in Upper India the favourite way of appeasing this deity is to feed a black dog until surfeit. In Benares he figures as Bhaironnāth ("Lord Bhairon") or Bhūt Bhairon ("Ghost Bhairon") and serves as guardian to the temples of Śiva. In Bombay he is Bhairoba or Kāla Bhairava, in which aspect he is terrible. Elsewhere, however, he is called "Child Bhairon" and Nanda Bhairon, names which suggest a connexion with the Kṛṣṇa cycle of legends.

In close fellowship with Śiva stands Gaṇeśa, who is often depicted in Śaivite shrines, and whose elephant head continues to be the subject of conjecture and suggestion, while his association with the rat seems to imply some humble origin for this deity. The "Mothers," who appear as early as the epic in company with Skanda, have a steadily increasing worship. Their number ranges from seven to sixteen, and their names vary, but in Gujarāt the total exceeds one hundred and forty. Some of these "Mothers" are no more than disease-demons, and some are angry spirits of the dead, whereas others appear to have a more exalted origin. Thus Porū Māī of Nadiyā seems clearly to be the goddess of the jungle, and in the North-Western Provinces the title Vanaspati Māī declares her to be "the Mother of the Forest." Mātā Januvī (or Janamī) is a goddess of birth, as her name implies, while Bhūkhī Mātā ("the Hunger Mother") is a personification of famine. The Rājpūts have a supreme "Mother Deity," Māmā Devī, the mother of the gods, who is presumably a representation of Mother Earth. In the plains Māyā, the mother of the Buddha, is often accepted as a village deity, and even the famous Buddhist poet Aśvaghoṣa has thus received adoration; while in similar fashion the Gond deity Gansām Deo has been metamorphosed, according to one theory, into Ghanaśyāma ("Black Like the Rain-Cloud"), an epithet of Kṛṣṇa.

The belief in the tree-spirit which is found in the *Ṛgveda* is prominent throughout the popular religion. The Maghs of Bengal would fell trees only at the instigation of Europeans and in their presence: on cutting down any large tree one of the party used to place a sprig in the centre of the stump when the tree fell as a propitiation to the spirit which had been displaced, pleading at the same time the orders of the strangers for the work. Another example of the same belief in the life of the tree is the constant practice of the performance of marriage ceremonies with trees for the most various purposes, either, as often, to enable a man to marry a third wife without incurring ill luck or to prevent a daughter from remaining unwed beyond the normal time of marriage. In many places people object to the collection of toddy from the palm-trees because it necessitates cutting their necks. Folk-lore is full of

## PLATE XXXI

### Bhairon

Originally a village godling of the aborigines, Bhairon has become identified with Bhairava ("the Fearful"), one of the dread forms of Śiva. His animal is the dog. He is essentially a deity whose function is to keep guard and thus to give protection. Accordingly he is usually represented as armed with club or sword, while his terrible aspect appears in the bowl of blood which he carries. After Crooke, *The Popular Religion and Folk-Lore of Northern India*, Plate facing ii, 218.

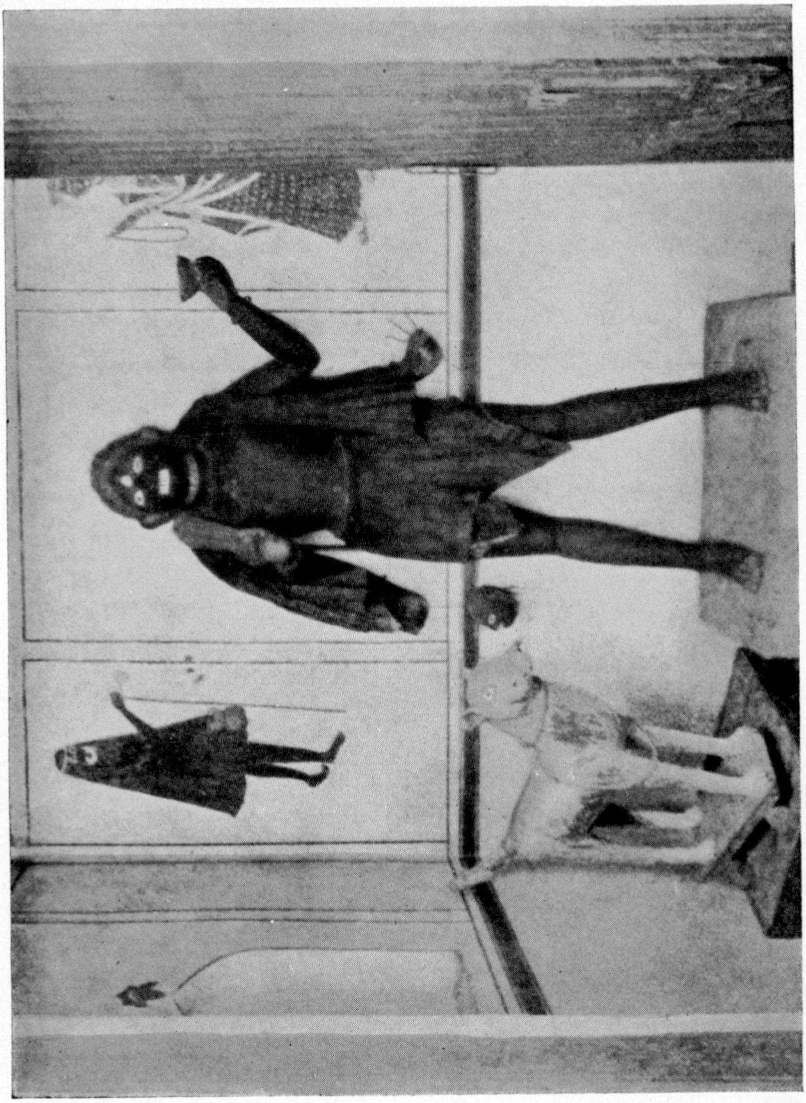

stories of tree-spirits, and there is no doubt that in many cases trees have become closely connected with the souls of the dead; groves of trees are often set aside and treated as sacred, being a dwelling-place of the spirits of the wild when cultivation has limited their sphere. The *pippala* or *aśvattha* (*Ficus religiosa*) is said to be the abode of Brahmā, Viṣṇu, and Śiva; but the cotton-tree is the home of the local gods, who can more effectively watch the affairs of the village since they are less occupied than these great deities. The *nīm*-tree harbours the demons of disease, but its leaves serve to drive away serpents. The coco-nut is revered for its intoxicating qualities as well as for its similarity to the human skull. The *tulasī*-plant, or holy basil (*Ocymum sanctum*), has aromatic and healing properties, and in myth it figures as wedded to Viṣṇu, by whose ordinance its marriage to the infant Kṛṣṇa in his image is still performed. The *bel* (*Aegle marmelos*) is used to refresh the symbol of Śiva, and its fruit is fabled to be produced from the milk of the goddess Śrī. The *palāśa* (*Butea frondosa*), bamboo, sandal, and many other trees are more or less sacred and are applied to specific ceremonial uses or avoided as dangerous, just as in the *Brāhmaṇas* we find many injunctions regarding the due kinds of wood to be used for the sacred post, the fire-drill (for which the hard *khair*, or mimosa [*Acacia catechu*], and the *pippala* are still used), and the implements of sacrifice.

As in the *Ṛgveda* also, there is much worship of the work of human hands. The pickaxe fetish of the Ṭhags was wrought with great care, consecrated, and tested on a coco-nut: if it failed to split it at one blow, it was recognized that Devī was unpropitious. Warriors revere their weapons, tanners their hair-scrapers, carpenters their yard-measures, barbers their razors, scribes their writing materials. So, in accordance with Kṛṣṇa's advice to the herdsmen, in the Panjāb farmers worship their oxen in August and their plough at the Dasahra festival, and shepherds do reverence to their sheep at the full moon of July. Among other implements the corn sieve or winnowing basket, the broom used to sweep up the grain on the threshing-floor or in cleaning the house, the plough, and the rice pounder are all marked by distinct powers, as in many other lands.

Stones too are often worshipped, whether for their own sake or for their connexion with some spirit or deity. The most famous is the curiously perforated *śālagrām*, or ammonite, found in the Gaṇḍak River and said to be Viṣṇu's form as a golden bee, for the god, when wandering in this shape, attracted such a host of gods in the guise of bees that he assumed the form of a rock, whereupon the gods made each a dwelling in the stone. Viṣṇu's footsteps are also revered at Gayā, and those of his disciple, Rāmānand, at Benares. A fetish stone in each village represents the abode of the village deities; legends are told of the stone statues of older gods and spirits found in the great shrines, or of uncanny or weird-looking natural rocks; while here and there even the tombs of modern English dead receive some degree of worship.

As regards animal cults far more evidence of the characteristic signs of totemism is available than in the Vedic period, but these data are mainly to be found among the aboriginal tribes which have been Hinduized. Thus many families are named after the wolf, cat, rat, heron, parrot, tortoise, weevil, frog, or other animal. Stories of animal descent are not rare, as in the case of the royal family of Chotā Nāgpur, who use as their seal a cobra with a human face under an expanded hood, invested with the insignia of royalty. Some tribes refrain from eating the animals which are their totems, though in many cases they have different explanations of their refusal; and other tribes observe exogamy as regards the totem of the family, such as those of Berār, where the totems are trees and plants. In Bombay the *devak*, or guardian deity, is held to be the ancestor or head of the house: families with the same *devak* do not intermarry; and if the *devak* is an animal, they do not eat its flesh, though if it be a fruit-tree, the use of the fruit is not generally forbidden. Similar reasons may underlie the noneating of various kinds of food by different tribes, and hence the suggestion has been made that the avatars of Viṣṇu and the animals which are regarded as the vehicles of the gods are traces of totemism grafted upon an original non-totemistic cult, or even proofs of primitive totemism. Neither view, however, can be regarded as more than a speculation, the demonstration of which cannot be attempted with any prospect of success in the absence of material bearing on early beliefs.

The Nāgas, or "Snakes," are the reputed ancestors of a people about whom much mythical history has been created, but who were doubtless and still are a Himālayan tribe claiming descent from Nāgas. These snakes are often considered as being controllers of the weather, especially of rain, and thus they reveal, in part at least, an aerial origin: Karkoṭaka is their king, but Śeṣnāg, the old Śeṣa, is still worshipped, and there are tales of Nāga maidens as well as of Nāgas. Vāsuki survives as Bāsuk Nāg, and Takṣaka is still known. Serpents again are often connected with the souls of the dead, especially the domestic snake, which is the kindly guardian of the family and its goods and which is naturally thought to be the spirit of an ancestor returned to watch over the family fortunes. In the Panjāb dead men often become *sinhas*, or snake spirits, which must be propitiated. Some snake-gods are legendary persons who performed favours to serpents, like Gūga and Pīpa in northern India. Snakes are also, perhaps as embodying human spirits, the great guardians of treasure, which in India is constantly hidden and lost. On the other hand, much of the worship of the serpent is doubtless due to fear of the uncanny and dangerous beast, and in no small degree the ceremonials in its honour partake of exorcisms. Inevitably Śiva has grown to be regarded as the sovereign of the snakes, and Devī is often represented with the cobra.

Of other animals the tiger, as is natural from his ferocity, comes into due honour, being worshipped in many parts of India, though other tribes spare no effort to kill him. He is believed to be amenable to control by sorcerers; in Hoshangābād the Bhomkas, who are priests of Bāgh Deo ("the Tiger-God"), can by offerings to the deity restrain the tigers from appearing for a certain period; and if a tiger is addressed as "uncle," he will spare his victim. Men may easily turn into tigers, who can be recognized by lacking a tail. The horse and the ass both have worshippers, and the dog, curiously enough, enjoys a good deal of reverence, both from wild tribes (where it is the wild dog which is respected) and from those which are more civilized. His connexion with death, his useful characteristics, and his uncanny power of recognizing spirits and barking at them are doubtless among the qualities which give him fame. The Bedd Gelert legend, as told in India, applies in its normal form to the ichneumon who slays the cobra which would devour the child; in its application to the dog it runs that it is mortgaged by a Banyā or Banjārā to a merchant, that his goods are stolen, and that it recovers them. The merchant dismisses it to its home with a paper round its neck containing a release of the mortgage debt, but the owner foolishly slays it in anger for failing in its duty. The bull and the cow receive worship, the latter very widely, and the rule against the slaying of a cow is in force in orthodox Hindu states like Nepāl to the present day. The wandering Banjārā tribe reveres the bull. Because of his wisdom the elephant is inseparably associated with Gaṇeśa, and men are also thought to become elephants. The cat has demoniacal qualities; it is the vehicle of the goddess Ṣaṣṭhī and is fed at dinner as part of the orthodox Hindu rite. The rat is the vehicle of Gaṇeśa, and his sacredness leads to the difficulty of exterminating plague-bearing rats. Among birds the peacock, the crow, the hoopoe, and many others are occasionally revered. Alligators are quite frequently worshipped in tanks, perhaps because of their dangerous qualities, which prevent their destruction except in pursuance of a blood feud for the killing of a near relative. Fish occasionally enjoy adoration, so that the Muṇḍāri Kols revere the eel and tortoise as totems. Even insects like the silk-worm are sometimes treated as divine. Much of this adoration of animals seems clearly to be accorded to them in their own right, but in other cases the devotion may be no more than a trace of the temporary entry of the corn spirit into the body of the animal in question.

No distinction of principle separates the reverence paid to animals from the worship of saints, and it is still less distinct from the cult of holy men after their death. The Hindu saint is often venerated at the spot where he lies interred, for his sanctity is so great that it is not necessary that he should be burned, as ordinary people are, while other holy men are buried in the Ganges enclosed in coffins of stone. The worship takes place at a shrine or tomb, which is generally occupied by a disciple (if not by an actual descendant) of the sage, and there prayers are made and offerings are presented. The grounds for according the honours due to a saint are many and various. One holy man is actually said to have won his rank at Meerut on the strength merely of a prophecy that a mill belonging to a Mr. Smith would cease shortly to work. Many saints, however, won their rank by harder means than that. Harṣu Pānre, the local god of Chayanpur, was, according to tradition, a Brāhman whose house and lands were confiscated by the local Rāja on the instigation of one of his queens, who was jealous of his influence with the Rāja and insinuated that the priest proposed to oust the prince from his throne. In revenge the Brāhman performed *dharṇā*, that is, he starved himself to death at the palace gate in 1427 A.D., but only to arise as a *brahm*, or malignant ghost of a Brāhman, and he brought to ruin the family of the Rāja, save one daughter who had befriended him in his misfortunes. He now exorcizes evil spirits who cause disease, but who cannot resist his Brāhmanical power. There are other such spirits, while Nāhar Khān of Mārwār is revered because, in his duty to his chief, he was willing to sacrifice his life for him in expiation for his prince's crime. Vyāsa, the editor of the *Mahābhārata*, Vālmīki, the author of the *Rāmāyaṇa*, Dattātreya, an authority on Yoga or an incarnation of Viṣṇu, Kālidāsa, Tulasī Dās, Vasiṣṭha, Nārada Muni, and Tūkarām are among those whose divinity is due to their learning. The Pāṇḍavas, the heroes of the *Mahābhārata*, receive honour, but so does their teacher Droṇa, who was their rival in the actual fighting. The Banjārās have a saint named Mitthu Bhūkhiya, whom they worship and whom they consult before committing a crime. A famous Kol deity is Rāja Lākhan, who is apparently none other than the son of Rāja Jaichand of Kanauj, a strange hero for a Dravidian race. Belā, the sister of this prince, has a temple at Belaun on the banks of the Ganges, though her only claim to renown is that she was the object of the dissension of the Rājpūt princes which preceded the Mussulman invasion. Many of the Muhammadans have holy men who seem nothing more than Hindu saints thinly veneered. An important class of women saints are the *satīs* who have burnt themselves with their husbands on the funeral pyre: offerings are paid to the memorials erected to them, and they are credited with saving power. The tombs of saints, moreover, are deemed to work miracles, and a new holy man will not receive full acceptance until the account of his marvellous deeds has been spread abroad and more or less generally admitted to be true.

The demons of modern India are many and varied, but it is characteristic that the Asuras should show little of their former greatness; while it is on a par with this that the Devas, their old rivals, have sunk to the rank of mere cannibal demons who would be a serious danger, were it not for their stupidity, which renders them liable to being hoaxed with ease. There are, as of old, Dānos, who represent the Dānavas, but they are no more than the Bīrs, or heroes, who are malignant village demons. The Daits bear the name of the old Daityas, but are mere goblins who are fond of residing in trees. Far more important are the Rākṣasas, who have retained much of their primitive character. They are tree-dwellers and cause indigestion to those who wander into their domain at night. They are the constant enemies of the gods, and from the blood shed in these conflicts is derived the Lohū, or "Blood-Red River," and the red ferruginous clay which is occasionally observed in the Hills. The Rākṣasas often take the form of old women with long hair, but their malignity is much lessened by their stupidity, which causes them to be easily fooled by those who fall into their power. They are fond of eating corpses and travel through the air, but are powerful only at night. Both they and the Asuras pass for the builders of old temples and tanks. There are also female Rākṣasas who take the form of lovely women and lure young men to destruction. Many Rākṣasas have a human origin: not only are the souls of some Muhammadans supposed by the Hindus to become Rākṣasas, but there are cases of Hindus whose cruelty in life has brought them that fate after death. One of these is Vīsaladeva, king of Ajmer, who, turned into a Rākṣasa as retribution for his oppression of his subjects, resumed in that form the kingly task of devouring his subjects until one of his grandchildren was patriotic enough to offer himself as a victim, when the Rākṣasa, recognizing the victim, departed to the Jumnā. A temple at Rāmtek in the Central Provinces is connected in popular tradition with the Rākṣasa Hemādpant, who is believed to have been the minister of Mahādeva, the Yādava king of Devagiri in the thirteenth century. The Piśāca, which is closely allied in earlier literature with the Rākṣasa, is now often regarded as the evil spirit produced by a man's vices, the ghost of a liar, adulterer, madman, or criminal of any kind.

One class of evil beings of special importance in a country so ridden by disease as India is the category of disease-demons. The most noteworthy of all these is Śītalā ("the Cool"), a word euphemistically applied to the divinity, since she is the demon which brings smallpox. She has, of course, many forms: thus at Kankhal near Hardwār she is reputed to be a Muhammadan lady who took up her abode there on the bidding of

Badarināth, who rewarded her for her piety, as evinced by her desire to interest herself in the gods of Hinduism, by making her the incarnation of Śītalā and the guardian goddess of children. In another shrine in the Dehra Dūn district she is a Satī named Gāndhārī, the wife of Dhṛtarāṣṭra, the father of the Kauravas in the epic. Yet she does not stand alone, for according to one version of the story there are seven "Mothers" who represent and control diseases similar to smallpox. Inevitably she is recognized as a form of Devī, and Mahākālī, Bhadrakālī, and Durgā, as well as Kālī, appear as names of the seven "Mothers." In Bengal escape from the ravages of smallpox is the purpose of the worship of the goddess Ṣaṣṭhī ("Sixth"), apparently a personification of the spirit presiding over the critical sixth day after the birth of a child. Śītalā again is one form of Mātaṅgī Śakti, a modification of the power of Devī as the female side of Śiva. This deity is of horrible aspect, with projecting teeth, a hideous face with wide-open mouth, and ears as large as a winnowing fan. She also carries such a fan and a broom together with a pitcher and a sword. In the Panjāb the disease is directly attributed to Devī Mātā, who is honoured in order to secure the departure of the malady. It is clear, however, that the disease is considered to be a manifestation of the entry of Devī into the child, and thus, owing to the holiness produced by the inward presence of the deity, the bodies of those who die are, like those of saintly persons, buried, and not cremated.

Cholera has its female divinity, Marī Bhavānī, but it is also represented by a male deity, Hardaul Lāla, in the region north of the Jumnā. According to the legend, he is the ghost of a prince who was murdered in 1627 A.D. by his brother, Jhajhār Singh; and at one time he was so important that in 1829 it is said that the village headmen were incited to set up altars to him in every village at Hoshangābād in order to preserve the cultivators, who were apt to run away if their fears of epidemics were not calmed by the respect paid to local gods.

Cholera is also sacred to Devī, and in addition to prayers the ceremony of the formal expulsion of the demon is often performed. Besides the deities of the great diseases, we find gods of minor maladies, such as he of the itch, who is solemnly propitiated.

Other evil beings are the ghosts of the dead, the *bhūts*, in so far as they are malignant. Such a spirit is that of a man who has died a violent death, whether by suicide, accident, or capital punishment; and the malevolence of a ghost of this type is inevitably increased greatly if he has been denied due funeral rites. Indeed, if a man otherwise free from sin dies without offspring to perform the *śrāddha* for him he is liable to become a *gayāl*, or sonless ghost, especially dangerous to the young sons of other people. Many Bīrs are men killed by accident, as by a fall from a tree, by a tiger, and so on. The *bhūts* are particularly feared by women and children, and at the time of marriage, and a woman who weds a second time must take steps to propitiate the spirit of her first husband. *Bhūts* never rest on the ground, which is inimical to them. Hence their shrines are provided with a bamboo or other place to allow them to descend upon it; whereas, on the other hand, people anxious to avoid ill from *bhūts* lie on the ground, as do a bride and bridegroom, or a dying man at the moment of dissolution. Three signs of the nature of a *bhūt* are his lack of shadow, his fear of burning turmeric, and his speaking with a nasal accent. A person beset by them should invoke Kālī, Durgā, and especially Śiva, who is the lord of *bhūts*. The vampire of Europe has a parallel in the *vetāl*, who enters corpses, often being the spirit of a discontented man who chooses such a home instead of retaining his own body.

The *pret* is in some degree allied to the *bhūt* in that it often denotes the ghost of a deformed or crippled person or one defective in some member, or of a child which dies prematurely owing to the omission of certain of the ceremonies prescribed for its good during its life as an embryo. In another sense, however, a *pret* is a spirit after death and before the accomplishment of the funeral rites. It wanders round its old home, in size no larger than a man's thumb, until it is gradually raised through the intermediate stage of a Piśāca to that of a "father."

One form of ghost with many European parallels is the headless Dūnd, who is, according to one account, derived from the wars of the great epic. He roves about at night and calls to the householder, but it is dangerous to answer such a summons. When he visited Agra in 1882, much terror was caused, and houses were shut at night. Other such demons are not rare, and at Faizābād there is a road which country folk will not travel at night, since on it marches the headless army of Prince Sayyid Sālār. In like manner Abū'l-Faḍl tells of the ghosts of the great slaughter at Pānīpat, and in modern times there are the ghosts of the hard-fought field of Chiliānwāla. The spirits who haunt burning grounds are styled *masān* from the Sanskrit *śmaśāna* ("cemetery") and are dangerous to children, whom they afflict with consumption. Among the *bhūts* of the Hills is Airi, the ghost of a man killed in hunting, who goes about with a pack of belled hounds and to meet whom is death. The *acheri* are the ghosts of little girls, living on the mountain-tops, but descending for revels at night. The *baghauts* are the ghosts of men slain by tigers, for whom shrines are erected on the spot of their sad end. Such spirits are dangerous and require careful treatment. Still more perilous is the *churel*. In origin the name seems to have denoted the ghosts of some low caste people, whose spirits are always especially malignant, and whose bodies — like those of suicides in England in former times — are buried face downward to hinder the easy escape of the evil spirit. The modern acceptance of the *churel*, however, is that it is the ghost of a woman who dies while pregnant or in child-birth or before the period of ceremonial impurity has elapsed. Such a ghost may appear beautiful, but it can be recognized by the fact that its feet are turned round. She is apt to captivate handsome young men and take them to her abode, where, if they eat the food she offers, they fall under her power and will not be dismissed until they are grey-haired old men. All sorts of spells are adopted to prevent the ghost of a dead woman from becoming a *churel* and to avert the spirits which threaten evil to children and to mothers.

Ghosts are accustomed to haunt the deserts, where they can be seen and heard at night. They also live in old dwellings, whence the unwillingness in India to demolish ruinous buildings, because the spirits which dwell there may be annoyed and punish the man who destroys their home. Excavators in their explorations have constantly found this difficulty in the way of their work. Other places frequented by *bhūts* are the hearth of the household, the roof of the house, cross-roads, and boundaries; while empty houses and even flowers may be infested by them.

The Hindu idea of the dead remains quite unchanged. The spirit of the departed is still to be worshipped after death, and it is clearly believed that the ghost expects these offerings and cannot be at peace without them. Nor is there any reason to doubt that the same view applies to the non-Aryan tribes, whose worship differs (in so far as it does differ) in detail rather than in principle. Thus the Dravidian tribes are, as a rule, convinced that the souls of the dead are mortal, or at any rate that after a couple of generations there is no need to trouble about remote ancestors, so that worship can be restricted to the later ones. The Goṇḍs go the length of propitiating souls for only a year, unless the deceased has been one of the important people of the tribe, in which case a shrine will be erected to his memory and annual offerings will be made. In contrast in detail only is the Hindu ritual proper with its due care and elaboration, which becomes more and more marked with the passing of time. It is interesting to note that in practice the last three ancestors of the offerer alone are taken into account in the performance of *śrāddhas*, and that the modern conception regards the oblations made during the first period after death as being intended to create a body for the deceased, which converts his spirit from a mere *preta*, or ghost, into a real individual, capable of experiencing either the pleasures of heaven or the pangs of hell. Heaven, however, is by no means difficult of access to the man who believes in one of the sectarian divinities: the mere repetition of the name of the god at the moment of death secures a favourable result, and similar effects are predicated of the use of sacred water (especially that of the Ganges) and of the employment of various plants at the moment of death; while the same idea has led to the wide development of the custom of casting the ashes of the dead into the Ganges or some other holy river.

# IRANIAN MYTHOLOGY

BY

ALBERT J. CARNOY, Ph.D., Litt.D.

PROFESSOR OF LINGUISTICS AND OF IRANIAN PHILOLOGY,
UNIVERSITY OF LOUVAIN

RESEARCH PROFESSOR, UNIVERSITY OF PENNSYLVANIA

# AUTHOR'S PREFACE

THE purpose of this essay on Iranian mythology is exactly set forth by its title: it is a reasonably complete account of what is mythological in Iranian traditions, but it is nothing more; since it is exclusively concerned with myths, all that is properly religious, historical, or archaeological has intentionally been omitted. This is, indeed, the first attempt of its kind, for although there are several excellent delineations of Iranian customs and of Zoroastrian beliefs, they mention the myths only secondarily and because they have a bearing on those customs and beliefs. The consequent inconveniences for the student of mythology, in the strict sense of the term, are obvious, and his difficulties are increased by the fact that, with few exceptions, these studies are either concerned with the religious history of Iran and for the most part refer solely to the older period, or are devoted to Persian literature and give only brief allusions to Mazdean times. Though we must congratulate the Warners for their illuminating prefaces to the various chapters of their translation of the *Shāhnāmah*, it is evident that too little has thus far been done to connect the Persian epic with Avestic myths.

None the less, the value and the interest presented by a study of Iranian mythology is of high degree, not merely from a specialist's point of view for knowledge of Persian civilization and mentality, but also for the material which it provides for mythologists in general. Nowhere else can we so clearly follow the myths in their gradual evolution toward legend and traditional history. We may often trace the same stories from the period of living and creative mythology in the Vedas through the Avestic times of crystallized and systematized myths to the theological and mystic accounts of the Pāhlavī books, and finally to the epico-historic legends of Firdausī.

There is no doubt that such was the general movement in the development of the historic stories of Iran. Has the evolution sometimes operated in the reverse direction? Dr. L. H. Gray, who knows much about Iranian mythology, seems to think so in connexion with the myth of Yima, for in his article on "Blest, Abode of the (Persian)," in the *Encyclopædia of Religion and Ethics*, ii. 702–04 (Edinburgh, 1909), he presents an interesting hypothesis by which Yima's successive openings of the world to cultivation would appear to allude to Aryan migrations. It has seemed to me that this story has, rather, a mythical character, in conformity with my interpretation of Yima's personality; but in any event a single case would not alter our general conclusions regarding the course of the evolution of mythology in Persia.

Another point of interest presented by Iranian mythology is that it collects and unites into a coherent system legends from two sources which are intimately connected with the two great racial elements of our civilization. The Aryan myths of the Vedas appear in Iran, but are greatly modified by the influence of the neighbouring populations of the valleys of the Tigris and the Euphrates — Sumerians, Assyrians, etc. Occasional comparisons of Persian stories with Vedic myths or Babylonian legends have accordingly been introduced into the account of Iranian mythology to draw the reader's attention to curious coincidences which, in our present state of knowledge, have not yet received any satisfactory explanation. In a paper read this year before the American Oriental Society I have sought to carry out this method of comparison in more systematic fashion, but studies of such a type find no place in the present treatise, which is strictly documentary and presentational in character. The use of hypotheses has, therefore, been carefully restricted to what was absolutely required to present a consistent and rational account of the myths and to permit them to be classified according to their probable nature. Due emphasis has also been laid upon the great number of replicas of the same fundamental story. Throughout my work my personal views are naturally implied, but I have sought to avoid bold and hazardous hypotheses.

It has been my endeavour not merely to assemble the myths of Iran into a consistent account, but also to give a readable form to my *exposé*, although I fear that Iranian mythology is often so dry that many a passage will seem rather insipid. If this impression is perhaps relieved in many places, that happy result is largely due to the poetic colouring of Darmesteter's translation of the Avesta and of the Warners' version of the *Shāhnāmah*. The editor of the series has also employed his talent in versifying such of my quotations from the Avesta as are in poetry in the original. In so doing he has, of course, adhered to the metre in which these portions of the Avesta are written, and which is familiar to English readers as being that of Longfellow's *Hiawatha*, as it is also that of the Finnish *Kalevala*. Where prose is mixed with verse in these passages Dr. Gray has reproduced the original commingling. While, however, I am thus indebted to him as well as to Darmesteter, Mills, Bartholomae, West, and the Warners for their meritorious translations, these versions have been compared in all necessary cases with the original texts.

My hearty gratitude is due to Professor A. V. Williams Jackson, who placed the library of the Indo-Iranian Seminar at Columbia University at my disposal and gave me negatives of photographs taken by him in Persia and used in his *Persia Past and Present*. It is this hospitality and that of the University of Pennsylvania which have made it possible for me to pursue my researches after the destruction of my library in Louvain. Dr. Charles J. Ogden of New York City also helped me in many ways. For the colour-plates I am indebted to the courtesy of the Metropolitan Museum of Art, New York, where the Persian manuscripts of the *Shāhnāmah* were generously placed at my service; and the Open Court Publishing Company of Chicago has permitted the reproduction of four illustrations from their issue of *The Mysteries of Mithra*.

A. J. CARNOY.

University of Pennsylvania,
1 November, 1916.

# TRANSCRIPTION AND PRONUNCIATION

THE transcription of Avesta, Pāhlavī, and Persian adopted in this study is of a semi-popular character, for it has been felt that the use of the strictly technical transliterations—*x* for *kh*, *γ* for *gh*, *θ* for *th*, etc., and the employment of "superior" letters to indicate spurious diphthongs, as *va*$^{i}$*rya* for *vairya*—would confuse readers who are not professed Iranists. This technical transcription is of value for philologists, not for mythologists.

The vowels have in general the Italian value and are short or long, the latter being indicated by the macron. The vowel *ə*, which, except in a few technical passages in the Notes, is here written *e*, is pronounced with the dull sound of the "neutral vowel," much as *e* in English *the man*, when uttered rapidly; *ã* is a nasalized vowel, roughly like the French nasalized *am* or *an*; *āo* has the sound of *a* in English *all* (in strict transcription *āo* should be written *āə*); *āi* and *āu* are pronounced as in English *aisle* and Latin *aurum*; in *aē*, *ao*, *eu*, *ēu* (properly *əu*, *ə̄u*), and *ōi* both components are sounded; *ere* (properly *ərə*) represents the vocalic *r*, as in English *better* (*bettṛ*). Sometimes the metre shows that a diphthong is to be monophthongized or that a single long vowel is to be resolved into two short ones (cf. Ch. V, Note 54, Ch. V, Note 13); this depends chiefly on etymology, and no rule can be given to govern all cases of such occurrences.

The consonants are pronounced in general as in English. The deviations are: *c* is pronounced like English *ch* in *church* or Italian *c* in *cicerone*; *g* is always hard; *ṭ* stands midway between *t* and *d*; *zh* is like *z* in English *azure* or like French *j* in *jour*; *khv* represents the Scottish or German *ch* + *v*; *kh*, *gh*, *th*, *dh*, *f*, and *w* are pronounced as in Scottish *loch* or German *ach*, German *Tag*, English *thin*, *this*, *far*, and *win* respectively.

In the quotations from the *Shāhnāmah* the Arabic letters *ḍ*, *ḥ*, and *q* occur; *ḍ* and *ḥ* are pronounced very emphatically, and *q* is a *k* produced deep in the throat. The transcription employed in the Warner translation of Firdausī differs somewhat, but not sufficiently to cause confusion, as when, for instance, following the Persian rather than the Arabic pronunciation, they write Zahhák instead of Dahhāk, etc. They also use the acute accent instead of the macron to denote long vowels, as *í* instead of *ī*, etc.

# INTRODUCTION

ETHNOLOGICALLY the Persians are closely akin to the Aryan races of India, and their religion, which shows many points of contact with that of the Vedic Indians, was dominant in Persia until the Muhammadan conquest of Iran in the seventh century of our era. One of the most exalted and the most interesting religions of the ancient world, it has been for thirteen hundred years practically an exile from the land of its birth, but it has found a home in India, where it is professed by the relatively small but highly influential community of Parsis, who, as their name ("Persians") implies, are descendants of immigrants from Persia. The Iranian faith is known to us both from the inscriptions of the Achaemenian kings (558–330 B.C.) and from the Avesta, the latter being an extensive collection of hymns, discourses, precepts for the religious life, and the like, the oldest portions dating back to a very early period, prior to the dominion of the great kings. The other parts are considerably later and are even held by several scholars to have been written after the beginning of the Christian era. In the period of the Sassanians, who reigned from about 226 to 641 A.D., many translations of the Avesta and commentaries on it were made, the language employed in them being not Avesta (which is closely related to the Vedic Sanskrit tongue of India), but Pāhlavī, a more recent dialect of Iranian and the older form of Modern Persian. A large number of traditions concerning the Iranian gods and heroes have been preserved only in Pāhlavī, especially in the *Būndahish*, or "Book of Creation." Moreover the huge epic in Modern Persian, written by the great poet Firdausī, who died about 1025 A.D., and known under the name of *Shāhnāmah*, or "Book of the Kings," has likewise rescued a great body of traditions and legends which would otherwise have passed into oblivion; and though in the epic these affect a more historical guise, in reality they are generally nothing but humanized myths.

This is not the place to give an account of the ancient Persian religion, since here we have to deal with mythology only. It will suffice, therefore, to recall that for the great kings as well as for the priests, who were followers of Zoroaster (Avesta Zarathushtra), the great prophet of Iran, no god can be compared with Ahura Mazda, the wise creator of all good beings. Under him are the Amesha Spentas, or "Immortal Holy Ones," and the Yazatas, or "Venerable Ones," who are secondary deities. The Amesha Spentas have two aspects. In the moral sphere they embody the essential attainments of religious life: "Righteousness" (Asha or Arta), "Good Mind" (Vohu Manah), "Desirable Kingdom" (Khshathra Vairya), "Wise Conduct" and "Devotion" (Spenta Ārmaiti), "Perfect Happiness" (Haurvatāt), and "Immortality" (Ameretāt). In their material nature they preside over the whole world as guardians: Asha is the spirit of fire, Vohu Manah is the protector of domestic animals, Khshathra Vairya is the patron of metals, Spenta Ārmaiti presides over earth, Haurvatāt over water, and Ameretāt over plants.

The Amesha Spentas constitute Ahura Mazda's court, and it is through them that he governs the world and brings men to sanctity. Below Ahura Mazda and the Amesha Spentas come the Yazatas, who are for the most part ancient Aryan divinities reduced in the Zoroastrian system to the rank of auxiliary angels. Of these we may mention Ātar, the personification of that fire which plays so important a part in the Mazdean cult that its members have now become commonly, though quite erroneously, known as "Fire-Worshippers"; and by the side of the genius of fire is found one of water, Anāhita.

Mithra is by all odds the most important Yazata. Although

# PLATE XXXII

## Iranian Deities on Indo-Scythian Coins

### 1. Mithra

The Iranian god of light with the solar disk about his head. From a coin of the Indo-Scythian king Huviṣka. After Stein, *Zoroastrian Deities on Indo-Scythian Coins*, No. I. See pp. 287–88.

### 2. Apām Napāt

The "Child of Waters." The deity is represented with a horse, thus recalling his Avestic epithet, *aurvaṭ-aspa* ("with swift steeds"). From a coin of the Indo-Scythian king Kaniṣka. After Stein, *Zoroastrian Deities on Indo-Scythian Coins*, No. III. See pp. 267, 340.

### 3. Māh

The moon-god is represented with the characteristic lunar disk. From a coin of the Indo-Scythian king Huviṣka. After Stein, *Zoroastrian Deities on Indo-Scythian Coins*, No. IV. See p. 278.

### 4. Vāta or Vāyu

The wind-god is running forward with hair floating and mantle flying in the breeze. From a coin of the Indo-Scythian king Kaniṣka. After Stein, *Zoroastrian Deities on Indo-Scythian Coins*, No. V. See pp. 299, 302.

### 5. Khvarenanh

The Glory, here called by his Persian name, Farro, holds out the royal symbol. From a coin of the Indo-Scythian king Huviṣka. After Stein, *Zoroastrian Deities on Indo-Scythian Coins*, No. VI. See pp. 285, 304–05, 311, 324, 332–33, 343.

### 6. Ātar

The god of fire is here characterized by the flames which rise from his shoulders. From a coin of the Indo-Scythian king Kaniṣka. After Stein, *Zoroastrian Deities on Indo-Scythian Coins*, No. VII. See pp. 266–67.

### 7. Vanainti (Uparatāt)

This goddess, "Conquering Superiority," is modelled on the Greek Nike ("Victory"), and seems to carry in one hand the sceptre of royalty, while with the other she proffers the crown worn by the Iranian kings. From a coin of the Indo-Scythian king Huviṣka. After Stein, *Zoroastrian Deities on Indo-Scythian Coins*, No. VIII.

### 8. Verethraghna

On the helmet of the war-god perches a bird which is doubtless the Vāreghna. The deity appropriately carries spear and sword. From a coin of the Indo-Scythian king Kaniṣka. After Stein, *Zoroastrian Deities on Indo-Scythian Coins*, No. IX. See pp. 271–73.

1

2

3

4

5

6

7

8

pushed by Zoroaster into the background, he always enjoyed a very popular cult among the people in Persia as the god of the plighted word, the protector of justice, and the deity who gives victory in battle against the foes of the Iranians and defends the worshippers of Truth and Righteousness (Asha). His cult spread, as is well known, at a later period into the Roman Empire, and he has as his satellites, to help him in his function of guardian of Law, Rashnu ("Justice") and Sraosha ("Discipline").

Under the gods are the spirits called Fravashis, who originally were the manes of ancestors, but in the Zoroastrian creed are genii, attached as guardians to all beings human and divine.

It is generally known that the typical feature of Mazdeism is dualism, or the doctrine of two creators and two creations. Ahura Mazda (Ormazd), with his host of Amesha Spentas and Yazatas, presides over the good creation and wages an incessant war against his counterpart Angra Mainyu (Ahriman) and the latter's army of noxious spirits. The Principle of Evil has created darkness, suffering, and sins of all kinds; he is anxious to hurt the creatures of the good creation; he longs to enslave the faithful of Ahura Mazda by bringing them into falsehood or into some impure contact with an evil being; he is often called Druj ("Deception"). Under him are marshalled the daēvas ("demons"), from six of whom a group has been formed explicitly antithetic to the Amesha Spentas. Among the demons are Aēshma ("Wrath, Violence"), Aka Manah ("Evil Mind"), Būshyāsta ("Sloth"), Apaosha ("Drought"), and Nasu ("Corpse"), who takes hold of corpses and makes them impure, to say nothing of the Yātus ("sorcerers") and the Pairikās (Modern Persian *parī*, "fairy"), who are spirits of seduction. The struggle between the good and the evil beings, in which man takes part by siding, according to his conduct, with Ahura Mazda or with his foe, is to end with the victory of the former at the great renovation of the world, when a flood of molten metal will, as an ordeal, purify all men and bring about the complete exclusion of evil.

Dualism, having impregnated all Iranian beliefs, profoundly influenced the mythology of Iran as well or, more exactly, it was in their mythology that the people of ancient Persia found the germ that developed into religious dualism.

# IRANIAN MYTHOLOGY

## CHAPTER I

## WARS OF GODS AND DEMONS

THE mythology of the Indians and the Iranians has given a wide extension to the conception of a struggle between light and darkness, this being the development of myths dating back to Indo-European times and found among all Indo-European peoples. Besides the cosmogonic stories in which monstrous giants are killed by the gods of sky or storm we have the myths of the storm and of the fire. In the former a heavenly being slays the dragon concealed in the cloud, whose waters now flow over the earth; or the god delivers from a monster the cows of the clouds that are imprisoned in some mountain or cavern, as, for example, in the legends concerning Herakles and Geryoneus or Cacus.[1] In the second class of myths the fire of heaven, produced in the cloud or in an aerial sea, is brought to earth by a bird or by a daring human being like Prometheus.

All these myths tell of a struggle against powers of darkness for light or for blessings under the form of rain. They were eminently susceptible of being systematized in a dualistic form, and the strong tendency toward symbolism, observable both in old Indian (Vedic) and old Iranian conceptions, resulted in the association of moral ideas with the cosmic struggle, thus easily leading to dualism.

The recent discoveries in Boghaz Kyoi and elsewhere in the Near East have shown that the Indo-Iranians were in contact with Assyro-Babylonian culture at an early date, and there are many reasons for believing that their religious ideas were influenced by their neighbours, especially as regards the group of gods known in India as the Ādityas, whose function is to be the guardians of the law (Sanskrit *ṛta* = Avesta *asha*) and of morality.[2]

Now, Babylonian mythology could only confirm the Indo-Iranians in their conceptions concerning the cosmic battle against maleficent forces or monstrous beings. Thus Assyro-Babylonian legends tell of the fight between Tiāmat, a huge monster of forbidding aspect, embodying primeval chaos, and Marduk, a solar deity. As Professor Morris Jastrow suggests,[3] the myth is based upon the annual phenomenon witnessed in Babylonia when the whole valley is flooded, when storms sweep across the plains, and the sun is obscured. A conflict is going on between the waters and storms on the one hand, and the sun on the other; but the latter is finally victorious, for Marduk subdues Tiāmat and triumphantly marches across the heavens from one end to the other as general overseer.

In other myths, more specifically those of the storm, the storm is represented by a bull,[4] an idea not far remote from the Indo-Iranian conception which identifies the storm-cloud with a cow or an ox. The storm-god is likewise symbolized under the form of a bird, a figure which we also find in Iranian myths, as when an eagle brings to the earth the fire of heaven, the lightning. Similarly in Babylonian mythology the bird Zu endeavours to capture the tablets of Fate from En-lil, and during the contest which takes place in heaven Zu seizes the tablets, which only Marduk can recover. Like the dragon who has hidden the cows, Zu dwells in an inaccessible recess in the mountains, and Ramman, the storm-god, is invoked to conquer him with his weapon, the thunderbolt.[5]

Among the Indo-Iranians, the poetic imagination of the Vedic Indians has given the most complete description of the conflict in the storm-cloud. With his distinctive weapon, the *vajra* ("thunderbolt"), Indra slays the demon of drought called

# PLATE XXXIII

1

## Typical Representation of Mithra

Mithra is shown sacrificing the bull in the cave. Beneath the bull is the serpent, and the dog springs at the bull's throat, licking the blood which pours from the wound. The raven, the bird sacred to Mithra, is also present. On either side of the god stands a torch-bearer, symbolizing the rising and the setting sun respectively, and above them are the sun and the moon in their chariots. This Borghesi bas-relief in white marble, now in the Louvre, was originally in the Mithraeum of the Capitol at Rome. After Cumont, *The Mysteries of Mithra*, Fig. 4.

2

## Scenes from the Life of Mithra

This bas-relief, discovered in 1838 at Neuenheim, near Heidelberg, shows in the border, round the central figure of the tauroctonous deity, twelve of the principal events in his life. Among them the clearest are his birth from the rock (top of the border to the left), his capture of the bull, which he carries to the cave (border to the right), and his ascent to Ahura Mazda (top border). The second scene from the top on the border to the left represents Kronos (Zarvan, or "Time") investing Zeus (Ahura Mazda) with the sceptre of the universe. After Cumont, *The Mysteries of Mithra*, Fig. 15.

1

2

Vṛtra ("Obstruction") or Ahi ("Serpent"). The fight is terrible, so that heaven and earth tremble with fear. Indra is said to have slain the dragon lying on the mountain and to have released the waters (clouds); and owing to this victory Indra is frequently called Vṛtrahan ("Slayer of Vṛtra"). The Veda also knows of another storm-contest, very similar to this one and often assigned to Indra, although it properly belongs to Trita, the son of Āptya. This mighty hero is likewise the slayer of a dragon, the three-headed, six-eyed serpent Viśvarūpa. He released the cows which the monster was hiding in a cavern, and this cave is also a cloud, because in his fight Trita, whose weapon is again the thunderbolt, is said to be rescued by the winds. He lives in a secret abode in the sky and is the fire of heaven blowing from on high on the terrestrial fire (*agni*), causing the flames to rise and sharpening them like a smelter in a furnace.[6] Trita has brought fire from heaven to earth and prepared the intoxicating draught of immortality, the soma that gives strength to Indra.[7]

In Iran, Indra is practically excluded from the pantheon, being merely mentioned from time to time as a demon of Angra Mainyu. Trita, on the other hand, is known as a beneficent hero, one of the first priests who prepared haoma (the Indian soma),[8] the plant of life, and as such he is called the first healer, the wise, the strong "who drove back sickness to sickness, death to death." He asked for a source of remedies, and Ahura Mazda brought down the healing plants which by many myriads grew up all around the tree Gaokerena, or White Haoma.[9] Thus, under the name of Thrita (Sanskrit Trita) he is the giver of the beverage made from the juice of the marvellous plant that grows on the summits of mountains, just as Trita is in India.[10]

Under the appellation of Thraētaona, son of Āthwya (Sanskrit Āptya), another preparer of haoma,[11] he smote the dragon Azhi Dahāka, three-jawed and triple-headed, six-eyed, with mighty strength, an imp of the spirit of deceit created by Angra

Mainyu to slaughter Iranian settlements and to murder the faithful of Asha ("Justice"), the scene of the struggle being "the four-cornered Varena," a mythical, remote region. Like the storm-gods and the bringers of fire, Thraētaona sometimes reveals himself in the shape of a bird, a vulture,[12] and later we shall see how, under the name of Farīdūn, he becomes an important hero in the Persian epic. His mythical nature appears clearly if one compares the storm-stories in the Veda with those in the Avesta. All essential features are the same on both sides. The myth of a conflict between a god of light or storm and a dragon assumes many shapes in Iran, although in its general outlines it is unchanging. In Thraētaona's struggle the victor was, as we have seen, connected with fire. Now fire itself, under the name of Ātar, son of Ahura Mazda, is represented as having been in combat with the dragon Azhi Dahāka:

"Fire, Ahura Mazda's offspring,
Then did hasten, hasten forward,
Thus within himself communing:
'Let me seize that Glory unattainable.'
But behind him hurtled onward
Azhi, blasphemies outpouring,
Triple-mouthed and evil-creedèd:
'Back! let this be told thee,
Fire, Ahura Mazda's offspring:
If thou holdest fast that thing unattainable,
Thee will I destroy entirely,
That thou shalt no more be gleaming
On the earth Mazda-created,
For protecting Asha's creatures.'
Then Ātar drew back his hands,
Anxious, for his life affrighted,
So much Azhi had alarmed him.
Then did hurtle, hurtle forward,
Triple-mouthed and evil-creedèd,
Azhi, thus within him thinking:
'Let me seize that Glory unattainable.'
But behind him hastened onward
Fire, Ahura Mazda's offspring,
Speaking thus with words of meaning:

'Hence! let this be told thee,
Azhi, triple-mouthed Dahāka:
If thou holdest fast that thing unattainable,
I shall sparkle up thy buttocks, I shall gleam upon thy jaw,[13]
That thou shalt no more be coming
On the earth Mazda-created,
For destroying Asha's creatures.'
Then Azhi drew back his hands,
Anxious, for his life affrighted,
So much Ātar had alarmed him.
Forth that Glory went up-swelling
To the ocean Vourukasha.
Straightway then the Child of Waters,
Swift of horses, seized upon him.
This doth the Child of Waters, swift of horses, desire:
'Let me seize that Glory unattainable
To the bottom of deep ocean,
In the bottom of profound gulfs.'" [14]

Although much uncertainty reigns as to the localization of the sea Vourukasha and the nature of the "Son of the Waters" (Apãm Napāt), the prevalent opinion is that they are respectively the waters on high and the fire above, which is born from the clouds.

The Avesta's most poetical accounts of the contest on high are, however, not the descriptions of battles with Azhi Dahāka, but the vivid pictures of the victory of Tishtrya, the dog-star (Sirius), over Apaosha, the demon of drought.[15] Drought and the heat of summer were the great scourges in Iranian countries, and Sirius, the star of the dog-days, was supposed to bring the beneficent summer showers, whereas Apaosha, the evil demon, was said to have captured the waters, which had to be released by the god of the dog-star. Accordingly we find the faithful singing:

"Tishtrya the star we worship,
Full of brilliancy and glory,
Holding water's seed and mighty,
Tall and strong, afar off seeing,
Tall, in realms supernal working,
. . . . . . . .

For whom yearn flocks and herds and men —
'When will Tishtrya be rising,
Full of brilliancy and glory?
When, Oh, when, will springs of water
Flow again, more strong than horses?'" [16]

Tishtrya listens to the prayer of the faithful, and being satisfied with the sacrifice and the libations, he descends to the sea Vourukasha in the shape of a white, beautiful horse, with golden ears and caparisoned in gold. But the demon Apaosha rushes down to meet him in the form of a dark horse, bald with bald ears, bald with a bald back, bald with a bald tail, a frightful horse. They meet together, hoof against hoof; they fight together for three days and nights. Then the demon Apaosha proves stronger than the bright and glorious Tishtrya and overcomes him, and he drives him back a full mile from the sea Vourukasha. In deep distress the bright and glorious Tishtrya cries out:

"Woe to me, Ahura Mazda!
Bane for you, ye plants and waters!
Doomed the faith that worships Mazda!
Now men do not worship me with worship that speaks my name. . . . If men should worship me with worship that speaks my name, . . .
For myself I'd then be gaining
Strength of horses ten in number,
Strength of camels ten in number,
Strength of oxen ten in number,
Strength of mountains ten in number,
Strength of navigable rivers ten in number." [17]

Hearing his lament, the faithful offer a sacrifice to Tishtrya, and the bright and glorious one descends yet again to the sea Vourukasha in the guise of a white, beautiful horse, with golden ears and caparisoned in gold. Once more the demon Apaosha rushes down to meet him in the form of a dark horse, bald with bald ears. They meet together, they fight together at the time of noon. Then Tishtrya proves stronger than Apaosha and overcomes him, driving him far from the sea Vourukasha and shouting aloud:

"Hail to me, Ahura Mazda!
Hail to you, ye plants and waters!
Hail the faith that worships Mazda!
Hail be unto you, ye countries!
Up now, O ye water-channels,
Go ye forth and stream unhindered
To the corn that hath the great grains,
To the grass that hath the small grains,
To corporeal creation." [18]

Then Tishtrya goes to the sea Vourukasha and makes it boil up and down, causing it to stream up and over its shores, so that not only the shores of the sea, but its centre, are boiling over. After this vapours rise up above Mount Ushindu that stands in the middle of the sea Vourukasha, and they push forward, forming clouds and following the south wind along the ways traversed by Haoma, the bestower of prosperity. Behind him rushes the mighty wind of Mazda, and the rain and the cloud and the hail, down to the villages, down to the fields, down to the seven regions of earth.

Not only does Tishtrya enter the contest as a horse, but he also appears as a bull, a disguise which reminds us of the Semitic myth in which the storm-god Zu fights under the shape of a bull, and which is an allusion to the violence of the storms and to the fertility which water brings to the world.

Finally Tishtrya is changed into a brilliant youth, and that is why he is invoked for wealth of male children. In this avatar he manifests himself

"With the body of a young man,
Fifteen years of age and shining,
Clear of eye, and tall, and sturdy,
Full of strength, and very skilful." [19]

This rain-myth was later converted into a cosmic story, and Tishtrya's shower was supposed to have taken place in primeval times before the appearance of man on earth, in order to destroy the evil creatures produced by Angra Mainyu as a counterpart of Mazda's creation. Tishtrya's co-operators were Vohu Manah, the Amesha Spentas, and Haoma, and he produced rain during ten days and ten nights in each one of the three forms which he assumed — an allusion to the dog-days that were supposed to be thirty in number. "Every single drop of that rain became as big as a bowl, and the water stood the height of a man over the whole of this earth; and the noxious creatures on the earth being all killed by the rain, went into the holes of the earth." Afterward the wind blew, and the water was all swept away and was brought out to the borders of the earth, and the sea Vourukasha ("Wide-Gulfed") arose from it. "The noxious creatures remained dead within the earth, and their venom and stench were mingled with the earth, and in order to carry that poison away from the earth Tīshtar went down into the ocean in the form of a white horse with long hoofs," conquering Apaosha and causing the rivers to flow out.[20]

In his function of collector and distributor of waters from the sea Vourukasha, Tishtrya is aided by a strange mythical being, called the three-legged ass. "It stands amid the wide-formed ocean, and its feet are three, eyes six, mouths nine, ears two, and horn one, body white, food spiritual, and it is righteous. And two of its six eyes are in the position of eyes, two on the top of the head, and two in the position of the hump; with the sharpness of those six eyes it overcomes and destroys. Of the nine mouths three are in the head, three in the hump, and three in the inner part of the flanks; and each mouth is about the size of a cottage, and it is itself as large as Mount Alvand [eleven thousand feet above the sea]. . . . When that ass shall hold its neck in the ocean its ears will terrify, and all the water of the wide formed ocean will shake with agitation. . . . When it stales in the ocean all the sea-water will become purified." Otherwise, "all the water in the sea would have perished from the contamination which the poison of the evil spirit has brought into its water." [21] Darmesteter thinks this ass is another incarnation of the storm-cloud, whereas West maintains that it is some foreign god tolerated by the Mazdean priests and fitted into their system.[22]

Zoroastrianism, being inclined to abstraction and to personifying abstractions, has created a genius of victory, embodying the conquest of evil creatures and foes of every description which the myths attribute to Thraētaona, Tishtrya, and other heroes. The name of this deity is Verethraghna ("Victory over Adverse Attack"), an expression reminding us of the epithet Vṛtrahan ("Slayer of Vṛtra") of the mighty Vedic conqueror-god Indra. The *vṛtra*, the "attack," is in the latter case made into the name of the assailing dragon Ahi, the Iranian Azhi.

Verethraghna penetrated into popular worship and even became the great Hercules of the Armenians, who were for centuries under the influence of Iranian culture and who called the hero Vahagn, a corruption of Verethraghna.[23] He was supposed to have been born in the ocean, probably a reminiscence of the sea Vourukasha, and he mastered not only the dragon Azhi, whom we know, but also Vishāpa, whose name in the Avesta is an epithet of Azhi, meaning "whose saliva is poisonous," and he fettered them on Mount Damāvand.[24] In a hymn of the Avesta [25] the various incarnations of Verethraghna are enumerated. Here he describes himself as "the mightiest in might, the most victorious in victory, the most glorious in glory, the most favouring in favour, the most advantageous in advantage, the most healing in healing." [26] He destroys the malice of all the malicious, of demons as well as of men, of sorcerers and spirits of seduction, and of other evil beings. He comes in the shape of a strong, beautiful wind, bearing the Glory made by Mazda that is both health and strength; [27] and next he conquers in the form of a handsome bull, with yellow ears and golden horns.[28]

Thirdly, he is a white, beautiful horse like Tishtrya, and then a burden-bearing camel, sharp-toothed and long-haired. The fifth time he is a wild boar, and next, once more like Tishtrya, he manifests himself in the guise of a handsome youth of fifteen, shining, clear-eyed, and slender-heeled.

The seventh time he appears

"In the shape of the Vāreghna,
Grasping prey with what is lower,
Rending prey with what is upper,[29]
Who of bird-kind is the swiftest,
Lightest, too, of them that fare forth.
He alone of all things living
To the arrow's flight attaineth,
Though well shot it speedeth onward.
Forth he flies with ruffling feathers
When the dawn begins to glimmer,
Seeking evening meals at nightfall,
Seeking morning meals at sunrise,
Skimming o'er the valleyed ridges,
Skimming o'er the lofty hill-tops,
Skimming o'er deep vales of rivers,
Skimming o'er the forests' summits,
Hearing what the birds may utter." [30]

Then Verethraghna comes as "a beautiful wild ram, with horns bent round," and again as "a fighting buck with sharp horns." That these are symbols of virility is shown by the next avatar, the tenth, in which he appears

"In a shining hero's body,
Fair of form, Mazda-created,
With a dagger gold-damascened,
Beautified with all adornment.

. . . . . . .

Verethraghna gives the sources of manhood, the strength of the arms, the health of the whole body, the sturdiness of the whole body, and the eyesight of the *kar*-fish, which lives beneath the waters and can measure a ripple no thicker than a hair, in the Rangha whose ends lie afar, whose depth is a thousand times the height of a man. . . . He gives the eyesight of the stallion, which in the dark and cloudy night can perceive a horse's hair lying on the ground and

## PLATE XXXIV

### Iranian Deities on Indo-Scythian and Sassanian Coins

1. Tishtrya

The god bears bow and arrows, and his representation as female is probably due to imitation of the Greek Artemis. From a coin of the Indo-Scythian king Huviṣka. After Stein, *Zoroastrian Deities on Indo-Scythian Coins*, No. X. See pp. 267–70.

2. Khshathra Vairya

The deity "Desirable Kingdom," who is also the god of metals, is appropriately represented in full metal armour. From a coin of the Indo-Scythian king Huviṣka. After Stein, *Zoroastrian Deities on Indo-Scythian Coins*, No. XI. See p. 260.

3. Ardokhsho

This goddess is evidently modelled on the Greek Tyche ("Fortune") and has been held to be the divinity Ashi. The name, as given on the coin, seems to mean "Augmenting Righteousness," and in view of the reference to Haurvatāt and Ameretāt as "the companions who augment righteousness" (*ashaokhshayantāo saredyayāo*, *Yasna*, xxxiii. 8–9), the Editor suggests that Ardokhsho may be one of these Amesha Spentas, probably Ameretāt, the deity of vegetation. From a coin of the Indo-Scythian king Huviṣka. After Stein, *Zoroastrian Deities on Indo-Scythian Coins*, No. XVI. See pp. 260, 281.

4. Asha Vahishta

In every respect except the name this deity is represented precisely like Mithra. From a coin of the Indo-Scythian king Huviṣka. After Stein, *Zoroastrian Deities on Indo-Scythian Coins*, No. XVII. See p. 260.

5. Ahura Mazda

The conventional representation of Ahura Mazda floats above what appears to be a fire temple, rather than an altar, from which rise the sacred flames. From a Parthian coin. After Drouin, in *Revue archéologique*, 1884, Plate V, No. 2.

6. Fire Altar

The altar here appears in its simplest form. From a Sassanian coin in the collection of the Editor.

7. Fire Altar

The altar is here much more elaborate in form. From a Sassanian coin in the collection of the Editor.

8. Fravashi

Of interest as showing the appearance of a Fravashi ("Genius") in the flame, and as representing the king as one of the guardians of the fire, although strictly only the priests are permitted to enter Ātar's presence. From a Sassanian coin. After Dorn, *Collection de monnaies sassanides de . . . J. de Bartholomaei*, Plate VI, No. 1. See pp. 261, 342.

1

2

3

4

5

6

7

8

knows whether it is from the head or from the tail. . . . He gives the eyesight of the golden-collared vulture, which from as far as the ninth district can perceive a piece of flesh no thicker than the fist, giving just as much light as a shining needle gives, as the point of a needle gives."[31]

Yet even this is not all, for we are also told that

> "Be they men or be they demons,
> Verethraghna, Ahura's creature,
>
> . . . . . . . .
>
> Breaketh battle-hosts in pieces,
> Cutteth battle-hosts asunder,
> Presseth battle-hosts full sorely,
> Shaketh battle-hosts with terror.
>
> . . . . . . . .
>
> Then, when Verethraghna, Ahura's creature,
> Bindeth fast the hands behind them,
> Teareth out the eyeballs from them,
> Maketh dull the ears with deafness
> Of the close battle-hosts of the confederated countries,
> Of the men false to Mithra [or, belying their pledges],
> They cannot maintain their footing,
> They cannot oppose resistance."[32]

The poetic inspiration of this hymn has made it interesting to quote it at some length, especially as it shows the concentration in the person of the genius of victory of many features belonging to the old myths of contests on high.

This story was apt to have many replicas. Beyond those mentioned here Persian mythology possessed several more, such as the story of Keresāspa, who smote the horny dragon or the golden-heeled Gandarewa,[33] and whose exploits have been made the subject of an extensive narrative in the *Shāhnāmah*, as will be set forth later on.

Iranian mythology, being essentially dualistic, contains numerous other contests, such as the overpowering of Yima, the king of the golden age, by Azhi Dahāka, the killing of the primeval bull by Mithra, the battle between Ahura Mazda and Angra Mainyu in the first times of creation, the war waged by Zarathushtra, the prophet, against the tenets of the demons, and the same struggle at the end of the world by the future prophet Saoshyant.

All this will be considered in subsequent chapters, and all this, according to certain mythologists like James Darmesteter, is the perpetual repetition (with some modifications) of the struggle in the storm-cloud between the light and the darkness. That conclusion is obviously exaggerated, although it is very likely, and very natural also, that features borrowed from the famous myth have penetrated into those other battles which are, each of them, incidents of the great dualistic war between the two creations. It is this conflict that we are now going to follow from the time of creation to the renovation of the world at the end of this period of strife.

# CHAPTER II

## MYTHS OF CREATION

THE Iranian legend of creation is as follows.[1] Ahura Mazda lives eternally in the region of infinite light, but Angra Mainyu, on the contrary, has his abode in the abyss of endless darkness, between them being empty space, the air. After Ahura Mazda had produced his creatures, which were to remain "three thousand years in a spiritual state, so that they were unthinking and unmoving, with intangible bodies," the Evil Spirit, having arisen from the abyss, came into the light of Ahura Mazda. Because of his malicious nature, he rushed in to destroy it, but seeing the Good Spirit was more powerful than himself, he fled back to the gloomy darkness, where he formed many demons and fiends to help him.

Then Ahura Mazda saw the creatures of the Evil Spirit, terrible, corrupt, and bad as they were, and having the knowledge of what the end of the matter would be, he went to meet Angra Mainyu and proposed peace to him: "Evil spirit! bring assistance unto my creatures, and offer praise! so that, in reward for it, thou and thy creatures may become immortal and undecaying." But Angra Mainyu howled thus: "I will not depart, I will not provide assistance for thy creatures, I will not offer praise among thy creatures, and I am not of the same opinion with thee as to good things. I will destroy thy creatures for ever and everlasting; moreover, I will force all thy creatures into disaffection to thee and affection for myself." Ahura Mazda, however, said to the Evil Spirit, "Appoint a period! so that the intermingling of the conflict may be for nine thousand years"; for he knew that by setting that time the Evil Spirit would be undone. The latter, unobservant and ignorant, was content with the agreement, and the nine thousand years were divided so that during three thousand years the will of Mazda was to be done, then for three thousand years there is an intermingling of the wills of Mazda and Angra Mainyu, and in the last third the Evil Spirit will be disabled.

Afterward Ahura Mazda recited the powerful prayer *Yathā ahū vairyā* [2] and, by so doing, exhibited to the Evil Spirit his own triumph in the end and the impotence of his adversary. Perceiving this, Angra Mainyu became confounded and fell back into the gloomy darkness, where he stayed in confusion for three thousand years. During this period the creatures of Mazda remained unharmed, but existed only in a spiritual or potential state; and not until this triple millennium had come to an end did the actual creation begin.

As the first step in the cosmogonic process Ahura Mazda produced Vohu Manah ("Good Mind"), whereupon Angra Mainyu immediately created Aka Manah ("Evil Mind"); and in like manner when Ahura Mazda formed the other Amesha Spentas, his adversary shaped their counterparts. After all this was completed, the creation of the world took place in due order — sky, water, earth, plants, animals, mankind.

In shaping the sky and the heavenly bodies Ahura Mazda produced first the celestial sphere and the constellations, especially the zodiacal signs. The stars are a warlike army destined for battle against the evil spirits. There are six million four hundred and eighty thousand small stars, and to the many which are unnumbered places are assigned in the four quarters of the sky. Over the stars four leaders preside, Tishtrya (Sirius) being the chieftain of the east, Haptōk Rīng (Ursa Major) of the north, Satavēs of the west, and Vanand of the south. Then he created the moon and afterward the sun.

In the meanwhile, however, the impure female demon Jahi had undertaken to rouse Angra Mainyu from his long sleep

— "Rise up, we will cause a conflict in the world," — but this did not please him because, through fear of Ahura Mazda, he was not able to lift up his head. Then she shouted again, "Rise up, thou father of us! for I will cause that conflict in the world wherefrom the distress and injury of Aūharmazd and the archangels will arise. . . . I will make the whole creation of Aūharmazd vexed."

When she had shouted thrice, Angra Mainyu was delighted and started up from his confusion, and he kissed Jahi upon the head and howled, "What is thy wish? so that I may give it thee?" And she shouted, "A man is the wish, so give it to me." Now the form of the Evil Spirit was a log like a lizard's body, but he made himself into a young man of fifteen years,[3] and this brought the thought of Jahi unto him.

Then Angra Mainyu with his confederate demons went toward the luminaries that had just been created, and he saw the sky and sprang into it like a snake,[4] so that the heavens were as shattered and frightened by him as a sheep by a wolf. Just like a fly he rushed out upon the whole creation and he made the world as tarnished and black at midday as though it were in dark night. He created the planets in opposition to the chieftains of the constellations, and they dashed against the celestial sphere and threw the constellations into confusion,[5] and the entire creation was as disfigured as though fire had burned it and smoke had arisen.

For ninety days and nights the Amesha Spentas and Yazatas contended with the confederate demons and hurled them confounded back into the darkness. The rampart of the sky was now built in such a manner that the fiends would no more be able to penetrate into it; and when the Evil Spirit no longer found an entrance, he was compelled to rush back to the nether darkness, beholding the annihilation of the demons and his own impotence.

Then as the second step in the cosmogonic process Ahura Mazda created the waters.[6] These converge into the sea

Vourukasha ("Wide-Gulfed"), which occupies one third of this earth in the direction of the southern limit of Mount Albūrz and is so wide that it contains the water of a thousand lakes. Every lake is of a particular kind; some are great, and some are small, while others are so vast that a man with a horse could not compass them around in less than forty days.

All waters continually flow from the source Ardvī Sūra Anāhita ("the Wet, Strong, and Spotless One"). There are a hundred thousand golden channels, and the water, warm and clear, goes through them toward Mount Hūgar, the lofty. On the summit of that mountain is Lake Urvis, into which the water flows, and becoming quite purified, returns through a different golden channel. At the height of a thousand men an open golden branch from that affluent is connected with Mount Aūsīndōm and the sea Vourukasha, whence one part flows forth to the ocean for the purification of the sea, while another portion drizzles in moisture upon the whole of this earth. All the creatures of Mazda acquire health from it, and it dispels the dryness of the atmosphere.

There are, moreover, three large salt seas and twenty-three small. Of the three, the Pūitika (Persian Gulf) is the greatest, and the control of it is connected with moon and wind; it comes and goes in increase and decrease because of her revolving. From the presence of the moon two winds continually blow; one is called the down-draught, and one the up-draught, and they produce flow and ebb.

The spring Ardvī Sūra Anāhita, which we have just mentioned, and from which all rivers flow down to the earth, is worshipped as a goddess. She is celebrated in the fifth *Yasht* of the Avesta as the life-increasing, the herd-increasing, the fold-increasing, who makes prosperity for all countries. She runs powerfully down to the sea Vourukasha, and all its shores are boiling over when she plunges foaming down, she, Ardvī Sūra, who has a thousand gulfs and a thousand outlets.

Not only does Anāhita bring fertility to the fields by her

waters, but she makes the seed of all males pure and sound, purifies the wombs of all females, causes them to bring forth in safety, and puts milk in their breasts.[7] She gave strength to all heroes of primeval times so that they were able to overcome their foes, whether the demons, the serpent Azhi, or the golden-heeled Gandarewa.

She is personified under the appearance of a handsome and stately woman.[8]

"Yea in truth her arms are lovely,
White of hue, more strong than horses;
Fair-adorned is she and charming;
. . . . . . . .
With a lovely maiden's body,
Very strong, of goodly figure,
Girded high and standing upright,
Nobly born, of brilliant lineage;
Ankle-high she weareth foot-gear
Golden-latcheted and shining.
. . . . . . . .
She is clad in costly raiment,
Richly pleated and all golden,
. . . . . . . .
For adornment she hath ear-rings
With four corners and all golden.
On her lovely throat a necklace
She doth wear, the maid full noble,
Ardvī Sūra Anāhita.
Round her waist she draws a girdle
That fair-formed may be her bosom,
That well-pleasing be her bosom.
On her brow a crown she placeth,
Ardvī Sūra Anāhita,
Eight its parts, its jewels a hundred,
Fair-formed, like a chariot-body,
Golden, ribbon-decked, and lovely,
Swelling forth with curve harmonious.
She is clad in beaver garments,
Ardvī Sūra Anāhita,
Of the beaver tribe three hundred."

This precise description points to the existence of representations of the goddess, a thing unusual in Persia in ancient times. But Anāhita, as Herodotus tells us, was at that period identified with the Semitic Ishtar, a divinity of fertility and fecundity, and a powerful deity invoked in battle and in war, both these functions being attributed to Anāhita in the hymn quoted above. Ishtar seems to have absorbed in Babylonia many of the attributes of Ea's consort Nīn Ella, the "Great Lady of the Waters," the "Pure Lady" of birth, whose name is the exact equivalent of Ardvī Sūra Anāhita; and it was Nīn Ella, more probably than Ishtar, who was the prototype of the Iranian goddess.

The Evil Spirit, however, also came to the water and sent Apaosha, the demon of drought, to fight against Tishtrya (Sirius), who bestows water upon the earth during the summer; the result of their encounter being the conflict that has been narrated above.

The third of the processes of creation was the shaping of the world. After the rain of Tishtrya had flooded the earth and purified it from the venom of the noxious creatures, and when the waters had retired, the thirty-three kinds of land were formed. These are distributed into seven portions: one is in the middle, and the others are the six regions (*kēshvars*) of the earth.

To counteract the work of Ahura Mazda, Angra Mainyu came and pierced the earth, entering straight into its midmost part; and when the earth shook, the mountains arose. First, Mount Albūrz (Hara Berezaiti) was created, and then the other ranges of mountains came into being; "for as Albūrz grew forth all the mountains remained in motion, for they have all grown forth from the root of Albūrz. At that time they came up from the earth, like a tree which has grown up to the clouds and its root to the bottom." The mountains stand in a row about Albūrz, which is the knot of lands and is the highest peak of all, lifting its head even to the sky. On one of its summits, named Taēra, the sun, the moon, and the stars rise, and from another of its heights, Hukairya, the water of

Ardvī Sūra Anāhita flows down, while on it the haoma, the plant of life, is set. What plant this haoma was we do not know, but its intoxicating qualities produced an exaltation which naturally caused it to be regarded as divine.

Next came the creation of the vegetable kingdom when Ameretāt, the Amesha Spenta who has plants under her guardianship, pounded them small and mixed them with the water which Tishtrya had seized. Then the dog-star made that water rain down over all the earth, on which plants sprang up like hair upon the heads of men. Ten thousand of them grew forth, these being provided in order to keep away the ten thousand diseases which the evil spirit produced for the creatures. From those ten thousand have sprung the hundred thousand species of plants that are now in the world.

From these germs the "Tree of All Seeds" was given out and grew up in the middle of the sea Vourukasha, where it causes every species of plant to increase. Near to that "Tree of All Seeds" the Gaokerena ("Ox-Horn") tree was produced to avert decrepitude. This is necessary to bring about the renovation of the universe and the immortality that will follow; every one who eats it becomes immortal, and it is the chief of plants.[9]

The Evil Spirit formed a lizard in the deep water of Vourukasha that it might injure the Gaokerena;[10] but to keep away that lizard Ahura Mazda created ten *kar*-fish, which at all times continually circle around the Gaokerena, so that the head of one of them never ceases to be turned toward the lizard. Together with the lizard those fish are spiritually fed, and till the renovation of the universe they will remain in the sea and struggle with one another.

The Gaokerena tree is also called "White Haoma." It is one of the manifestations of the famous haoma-plant, which has been mentioned many times, while its terrestrial form, the yellow haoma, is the plant of the Indo-Iranian sacrifice and the one which gives strength to men and gods. It is with this thought in mind that the sacrificer invokes "Golden Haoma":

"Thee I pray for might and conquest,
Thee for health and thee for healing,
Thee for progress and for increase,
Thee for strength of all my body,
Thee for wisdom all-adornèd.
. . . . . . .
Thee I pray that I may conquer,
Conquer all the haters' hatred,
Be they men or be they demons,
Be they sorcerers or witches,
Rulers, bards, or priests of evil,
Treacherous things that walk on two feet,
Heretics that walk on two feet,
Wolves that go about on four feet,
Or invading hordes deceitful
With their fronts spread wide for battle." [11]

Above all, however, Haoma is expected to drive death afar, to give long life,[12] and to grant children to women and husbands to girls.

"Unto women that would bring forth
Haoma giveth brilliant children,
Haoma giveth righteous offspring.
. . . . . . .
Unto maidens long unwedded
Haoma, quickly as they ask him,
Full of insight, full of wisdom,
Granteth husbands and protectors." [13]

The terrestrial haoma is said to grow on the summits of the mountains, especially on Albūrz (Hara Berezaiti), to which divine birds brought it down from heaven. It is collected in a box, which is placed in an iron vase, and after the priest has taken five or seven pieces of the plant from the box and washed them in the cup, the stalk of haoma is pounded in a mortar and filtered through the *vara*, the juice being then mixed with other sacred fluids and ritual prayers being recited.

The Haoma sacrifice is supposed to date back to primeval times, its first priests being Vīvanghvant, Āthwya, Thrita, and Pourushaspa, the heroes of ancient ages. The offering of it is an Indo-Iranian rite, and the same legends are found in the Veda, where *amṛta soma* ("immortal soma" [= *haoma*]) has been brought from heaven to a high mountain by an eagle. Swift as thought, the bird flew to the iron castle of the sky and brought the sweet stalks back.[14] It is actually an Indo-European myth closely associated with the fire-myths, for the fire of the sky (the lightning) is said to have been brought to earth either by a bird or by a daring human being (Prometheus), while exactly the same story is told of the earthly fire-drink, the honey-mead, the draught of immortality (*ἀμβροσία*). Curiously enough, the Babylonian epic also knows of a marvellous plant that grows on the mountains, the plant "of birth" belonging to Shamash, the sun-god. When the wife of the hero Etana is in distress because she is unable to bring into the world a child which she has conceived, Etana prays Shamash to show him the "plant of birth": "O Lord, let thy mouth command, and give me the plant of birth. Reveal to me the plant of birth, bring forth the fruit, grant me offspring"; and an eagle then helps Etana to obtain the plant.[15] The Etana-myth is also related to the story of Rustam's birth, as will be narrated in a subsequent chapter.

When Angra Mainyu, the destroyer, came to the plants, he found them with neither thorn nor bark about them; but he coated them with bark and thorns and mixed their sap with poison, so that when men eat certain plants, they die.[16] There was also a beautiful tree with a single root. Its height was several feet, and it was without branches and without bark, juicy and sweet; but when the Evil Spirit approached it, it became quite withered.[17]

In Iranian mythology the creation of fire constitutes, to all intents, a subdivision of the creation of the vegetable world, the close connexion between fire and plants in Indo-Iranian conceptions being due to the fact that it was the custom of those peoples to obtain flame by taking a stick of hard wood, boring it into a plank or board of softer wood (that of a lime-tree, for instance), and turning it round and round till fire was produced by the friction.[18] For this reason the Veda declares that Fire (Agni) is born in wood, is the embryo of plants, and is distributed in plants. But fire has likewise a heavenly origin, for it is the son of the sky-god (Dyaus) and was born in the highest heavens, whence it was brought to earth, as already narrated, though it is also described as having its origin in the aerial waters. Owing to his divine births, Agni in India is often regarded as possessing a triple character and is *triṣadhastha* ("having three stations or dwellings"), his abodes being heaven, earth, and the waters. The fire of the hearth has been held in very great veneration among all Indo-Europeans. It was adored as Hestia in Greece and as Vesta in Rome, while in India the domestic Agni is called Gṛhapati ("Lord of the House"). It is also the guest (*atithi*) in human abodes, for it is an immortal who has taken up his home among mortals; it is Viśpati ("Lord of the Settlers"), their leader, their protector. It is the friend, the brother, the nearest kinsman of man;[19] it is the great averter of evil beings, just as it keeps off wild animals in the forest at night.

The second aspect under which fire is subservient to humanity is the part that it plays as the messenger who brings to the gods the offerings of men. It is the sacrificial fire, and as such it is called Narāśaṁsa ("Praise of Men") in India.[20]

As is well known, fire enjoys quite a special veneration in Iran, and under its first guise, as a representative of divine essence on earth, it dwells in the home of each of the faithful. Particular reverence is given to the sacred flame which is maintained with wood and perfumes in the so-called fire temples, two kinds of which are distinguished: the great temple for the Bahrām fire and the small shrine, or *ādarān*. The Bahrām fire, whose preparation lasts an entire year, is constituted out of sixteen different kinds of fire and concentrates in itself the essence and the soul of all fires.[21] It is maintained by means of six logs of sandal-wood and is placed in the sacred room,

# PLATE XXXV

## Ancient Fire Temple near Iṣfahān

The structure, originally domed, is built of unburnt bricks. Its height is about fourteen feet, and its diameter about fifteen; octagonal in plan, its eight doors face the eight points of the compass; the inner sanctuary is circular. It apparently dates at least from the Sassanian period, and its shape may be compared with what seems to be a fire temple as pictured on Parthian coins (see Plate XXXIV, No. 5). For the history of the shrine, so far as known, see Jackson, *Persia Past and Present*, pp. 256–61. After a photograph by Professor A. V. Williams Jackson.

vaulted like a dome, on a vase. Five times a day a *mobed*, or priest, enters the room. The lower part of his face is covered with a veil (Avesta *paitidāna*), preventing his breath from polluting the sacred fire, and his hands are gloved. He lays down a log of sandal-wood and recites three times the words *dushmata*, *duzhūkhta*, *duzhvarshta* to repel "evil thoughts, evil words, evil deeds."

As in India, so in Iran several kinds of fire are distinguished: Berezisavanh ("Very Useful") is the general name of the Bahrām fire, the sacred one which shoots up before Ahura Mazda and is kept in the fire temples; Vohu Fryāna ("Good Friend") is the fire which burns in the bodies of men and animals, keeping them warm; Urvāzishta ("Most Delightful") burns in the plants and can produce flames by friction; Vāzishta ("Best-Carrying") is the aerial fire, the lightning that purifies the sky and slays the demon Spenjaghrya; Spēnishta ("Most Holy") burns in paradise in the presence of Ahura Mazda.

Of these five fires, one drinks and eats, that which is in the bodies of men; one drinks and does not eat, that which is in plants, which live and grow through water; two eat and do not drink, these being the fire which is ordinarily used in the world, and likewise the fire of Bahrām (= Berezisavanh); one consumes neither water nor food, and this is the fire Vāishta.[22]

This classification enjoyed a very great success among the Talmudists, who took it from the Mazdeans in the second century A.D.[23] Besides these five fires, the Avesta knows of Nairyōsangha, who is of royal lineage and whose name reminds us of *narāśamsa*, the epithet of Agni ("the Fire") in India. Like Narāśaṁsa Agni, Nairyōsangha is the messenger between men and gods and he dwells with kings, inasmuch as they are endowed with a divine majesty. The emanation of divine essence in kings, however, is more often called *khvarenanh* (Old Persian *farnah*), which is a glory that attaches itself to monarchs as long as they are worthy representatives of divine power, as will be seen later in the story of Yima.

The fire was all light and brilliancy, but Angra Mainyu came up to it, as to all beings of the good creation, and marred it with darkness and smoke.[24]

The fifth creation was the animal realm. Just as there was a tree Gaokerena which had within itself all seeds of plants and trees, so Iranian mythology knows of a primeval ox in which were contained the germs of the animal species and even of a certain number of useful plants.

This ox, the sole-created animate being, was a splendid, strong animal which, though sometimes said to be a female,[25] is usually described as a bull. When the Evil Spirit came to the ox, Ahura Mazda ground up a healing fruit, called *bīnāk*, so that the noxious effects of Angra Mainyu might be minimized; but when, despite this, "it became at the same time lean and ill, as its breath went forth and it passed away, the ox also spoke thus: 'The cattle are to be created, their work, labour, and care are to be appointed.'" When Gēush Urvan ("the Soul of the Ox") came forth from the body, it stood up and cried thus to Ahura Mazda, as loudly as a thousand men when they raise a cry at one time: "With whom is the guardianship of the creatures left by thee, now that ruin has broken into the earth, and vegetation is withered, and water is troubled? Where is the man of whom it was said by thee thus: 'I will produce him, so that he may preach carefulness?'" Ahura Mazda answered: "You are made ill, O Gōshūrvan! you have the illness which the evil spirit brought on; if it were proper to produce that man in this earth at this time, the evil spirit would not have been oppressive in it." Gēush Urvan was not satisfied, however, but walked to the vault of the stars and cried in the same way, and his voice came to the moon and to the sun till the Fravashi[26] of Zoroaster was exhibited to it, and Ahura Mazda promised to send the prophet who would preach carefulness for the animals, whereupon the soul of the ox was contented and agreed to nourish the creatures and to protect the animal world.

From every limb of the ox fifty-five species of grain and

twelve kinds of medicinal plants grew forth, their splendour and strength coming from the seminal energy of the ox. Delivered to the moon, that seed was thoroughly purified by the light of the moon and fully prepared in every way, and then two oxen arose, one male and one female, after which two hundred and eighty-two pairs of every single species of animal appeared upon the earth. The quadrupeds were to live on the earth, the birds had their dwelling in the air, and the fish were in the midst of the water.

Another myth ascribes the killing of the primeval ox to the god Mithra.

The legend concerning the birth and the first exploits of Mithra runs thus.[27] He was born of a rock on the banks of a river under the shade of a sacred fig-tree, coming forth armed with a knife and carrying a torch that had illumined the sombre depths. When he had clothed himself with the leaves of the fig-tree, detaching the fruit and stripping the tree of its leaves by means of his knife, he undertook to subjugate the beings already created in the world. First he measured his strength with the sun, with whom he concluded a treaty of friendship — an act quite in agreement with his nature as a god of contracts — and since then the two allies have supported each other in every event.

Then he attacked the primeval ox. The redoubtable animal was grazing in a pasture on a mountain, but Mithra boldly seized it by the horns and succeeded in mounting it. The ox, infuriated, broke into a gallop, seeking to free itself from its rider, who relaxed his hold and suffered himself to be dragged along till the animal, exhausted by its efforts, was forced to surrender. The god then dragged it into a cave, but the ox succeeded in escaping and roamed again over the mountain pastures, whereupon the sun sent his messenger, the raven, to help his ally slay the beast. Mithra resumed his pursuit of the ox and succeeded in overtaking it just at the moment when it was seeking refuge in the cavern which it had quitted. He seized it by the nostrils with one hand and with the other he plunged his hunting-knife deep into its flank. Then the prodigy related above took place. From the limbs and the blood of the ox sprang all useful herbs and all species of animals, and "the Soul of the Ox" (Gēush Urvan) went to heaven to be the guardian of animals.

The myths relating to the primeval ox contain traces of several older Indo-European myths. First, the conception of the production of various beings out of the body of a primeval gigantic creature is a cosmogonic story, fairly common in the mythology of many nations and reproduced in the Eddic myth of the giant Ymir, who was born from the icy chaos and from whose arm sprang both a man and a woman. He was then slain by Odhin and his companions, and of the flesh of Ymir was formed the earth, of his blood the sea and the waters, of his bones the mountains, of his teeth the rocks and stones, and of his hair all manner of plants.[28]

Many features recall to us, on the other hand, the contests on high between a light-god and some monster who detains the rain which is the source of life for terrestrial beings and which is often personified under the shape of a cow. The kine are concealed in caves or on mountains, or the monster is hidden in a mountain cavern and escapes, as is the case with Verethraghna and Azhi in the Armenian myth. In the birth of Mithra traces of solar myths may also be detected. The raven is the messenger of the sun because, like the bird Vāreghna,

> "Forth he flies with ruffling feathers
> When the dawn begins to glimmer." [29]

Here, then, we are dealing with a secondary myth.

As regards the various species of animals produced from the ox, the Mazdean books speak first of mythical beings, such as the three-legged ass that has been described above, the lizard created by Angra Mainyu to destroy the tree Gaokerena, and the *kar*-fishes that defend it. They know, moreover, of an ox-

## PLATE XXXVI

1

### Mithra Born from the Rock

The deity, bearing a dagger in one hand and a lighted torch in the other, rises from the rock. From a bas-relief found in the Mithraeum which once occupied the site of the church of San Clemente at Rome. After Cumont, *The Mysteries of Mithra*, Fig. 30.

2

### Mithra Born from the Rock

The divinity, lifting a cluster of grapes in his right hand, emerges from the rock, on which he rests his left hand. On the rock are sculptured a quiver, arrow, bow, and dagger. On either side of Mithra stand the two torch-bearers, Caut and Cautopat (whose names, in the opinion of the Editor, mean "the Burner" and "He Who Lets His Burned [Torch] Fall"), doubtless symbolizing the rising and the setting sun, as Mithra is the sun at noonday. From a white marble formerly in the Villa Giustiniani, Rome, but now lost. After Cumont, *The Mysteries of Mithra*, Fig. 31.

1

2

fish that exists in all seas; when it utters a cry, all fishes become pregnant, and all noxious water creatures cast their young. There is also an ox, called Hadhayōsh or Sarsaok in Pāhlavī, on whose back men in primeval times passed from region to region across the sea Vourukasha. Many mythical birds are known in the Mazdean mythology. We have already seen the raven as an incarnation of Verethraghna ("Victory") and as a messenger of the sun to Mithra. The most celebrated bird, however, is Saēna, the Sīmurgh of the Persians, whose open wings are like a wide cloud and full of water crowning the mountains.[30] He rests on the tree of the eagle, the Gaokerena, in the midst of the sea Vourukasha, the tree with good remedies, in which are the seeds of all plants. When he rises aloft, so violently is the tree shaken that a thousand twigs shoot forth from it; when he alights, he breaks off a thousand twigs, whose seeds are shed in all directions.

Near this powerful bird sits Camrōsh, who would be king of birds, were it not for Saēna. His work is to collect the seed which is shed from the tree and to convey it to the place where Tishtrya seizes the water, so that the latter may take the water containing the seed of all kinds and may rain it on the world.[31] When the Turanians invade the Iranian districts for booty and effect devastation, Camrōsh, sent by the spirit Berejya, flies from the loftiest of the lofty mountains and picks up all the non-Iranians as a bird does corn.[32]

The bird Vāregan, Vārengan, or Vāreghna (sometimes translated "raven") is the swiftest of all and is as quick as an arrow. We have already seen[33] that he is one of Verethraghna's incarnations, and under his shape the kingly Glory (*Khvarenanh*) of Yima left the guilty hero and flew up to heaven.[34] He is essentially a magic bird with mysterious power. Thus Zoroaster is represented as asking Ahura Mazda what would be the remedy "should I be cursed in word or thought." Ahura Mazda answers: "Thou shouldst take a feather of the wide-feathered bird Vārengan, O Spitama Zarathushtra. With that feather thou shouldst stroke thy body, with that feather thou shouldst conjure thy foe. Either the bones of the sturdy bird or the feathers of the sturdy bird carry boons.

> Neither can a man of brilliance
> Slay or rout him in confusion.
> It first doth bring him reverence, it first doth bring him glory.
> Help to him the feather giveth
> Of the bird of birds, Vārengan." [35]

The same thing is recorded of Saēna (the Sīmurgh) in the *Shāhnāmah*. When Zāl leaves the nest of the Sīmurgh, who has brought him up, his foster-father gives him one of his feathers so that he may always remain under the shadow of his power.

> "Bear this plume of mine
> About with thee and so abide beneath
> The shadow of my Grace. Henceforth if men
> Shall hurt or, right or wrong, exclaim against thee,
> Then burn the feather and behold my might." [36]

When the side of Rūdābah, Rustam's mother, is opened to allow the child to be brought into the world, Zāl heals the wound by rubbing it with a feather of the Sīmurgh, and when Rustam is wounded to death by Isfandyār, he is cured in the same way.[37]

The bird Karshiptar has a more intellectual part to play, for he spread Mazda's religion in the enclosure in which the primeval king Yima had assembled mankind,[38] as will be narrated below. There men recited the Avesta in the language of birds.[39]

The bird Ashō-zushta also has the Avesta on his tongue, and when he recites the words the demons are frightened.[40] When the nails of a Zoroastrian are cut, the faithful must say: "O Ashō-zushta bird! these nails I present to thee and consecrate to thee. May they be for thee so many spears and knives, so many bows and eagle-winged arrows, so many sling-stones against the Māzainyan demons." [41] If one recites this formula, the fiends tremble and do not take up the nails, but if the

## PLATE XXXVII

### The Sīmurgh

The Sīmurgh, flying from its mountain home, restores the infant Zāl to his father Sām, who had caused the child to be abandoned because it had been born with white hair. In his hand the prince carries the ox-headed mace as a symbol of royalty. The painting shows marked Perso-Mongolian influence. From a Persian manuscript of the *Shāhnāmah*, dated 1587–88 A.D., now in the Metropolitan Museum of Art, New York. See also pp. 330–31.

parings have had no spell uttered over them, the demons and wizards use them as arrows against the bird Ashō-zushta and kill him. Therefore, when the nails have had a charm spoken over them, the bird takes them and eats them, that the fiends may do no harm by their means.[42] Ashō-zushta is probably the theological name of the owl.[43]

The part played by birds as transmitters of revelation leads in later literature to the identification of the Sīmurgh with Supreme Wisdom.[44] As we have said more than once, the conception of mythical birds dates back to Indo-Iranian — even Indo-European — times, and often those birds are incarnations of the thunderbolt, the sun, the fire, the cloud, etc. In the *Ṛgveda* the process is seen in operation. The soma is often compared with or called a bird; the fire (*agni*) is described as a bird or as an eagle in the sky; and the sun is at times a bird, whence it is called *garutmant* ("winged"). The most prominent bird in the Veda, however, is the eagle, which carries the soma to Indra and which appears to represent lightning.[45] So in Eddic mythology the god Odhin, transforming himself into an eagle, flies with the mead to the realm of the gods. Besides these mythical birds there are one hundred and ten species of winged kind, such as the eagle, the vulture, the crow, and the crane, to say nothing of the bat, which has milk in its teat and suckles its young, and is created of three races, bird, dog, and musk-rat, for it flies like a bird, has many teeth like a dog, and dwells in holes like a musk-rat.

Other beasts and birds were formed in opposition to noxious creatures: the white falcon kills the serpent with its wings; the magpie destroys the locust; the vulture, dwelling in decay, is created to devour dead matter, as do the crow — the most precious of birds — and the mountain kite.[46] So it is also with the quadrupeds, for the mountain ox, the mountain goat, the deer, the wild ass, and other beasts devour snakes. Dogs are created in opposition to wolves and to secure the protection of sheep; the fox is the foe of the demon Khava; the ichneumon destroys the venomous snake and other noxious creatures in burrows; and the great musk-animal was formed to counteract ravenous intestinal worms. The hedgehog eats the ant which carries off grain; when the grain-carrying ant travels over the earth, it produces a hollow path; but when the hedgehog passes over it, the track becomes level. The beaver is in opposition to the demon which is in the water.

The cock, in co-operation with the dog, averts demons and wizards at night and helps Sraosha in that task, and the shepherd's dog and the watch-dog of the house are also indispensable creatures and destroyers of fiends. The dog likewise annihilates covetousness and disobedience, and when it barks it destroys pain, while its flesh and fat are remedies for averting decay and anguish from man. Ahura Mazda created nothing useless whatever; all these animals have been formed for the well-being of mankind and in order that the fiends may continually be destroyed.[47]

## CHAPTER III

## THE PRIMEVAL HEROES

THE culmination of Iranian cosmogony was the creation of the human race. For the Mazdeans the first man was Gaya Maretan ("Human Life"),

> "Who first of Ahura Mazda
> Heard the mind and heard the teachings,
> From whom, too, Ahura Mazda
> Formed the Aryan countries' household
> And the seed of Aryan countries." [1]

He was the first man, as Saoshyant will be the last,[2] and his bones will rise up first of all at the resurrection.[3] His spirit lived three thousand years with the spirit of the ox during the period when creation was merely spiritual, and then Ahura Mazda formed him corporeally. He was produced brilliant and white, radiant and tall, under the form of a youth of fifteen years, and this from the sweat of Ahura Mazda.[4] In the meantime, however, the demons had done their work, and when Gaya Maretan issued from the sweat he saw the world dark as night and the earth as though not a needle's point remained free from noxious creatures; the celestial sphere was revolving, and the sun and moon remained in motion, and the creatures of evil were fighting with the stars. The Evil Spirit sent a thousand demons to Gaya Maretan, but the appointed day had not yet come, for Gaya was to live thirty years and was able to repel the fiends and to kill the dreadful demon Arezūra.[5] When at length the time had come for his immolation, Jahi induced Angra Mainyu to pour poison on the body of Gaya, whom he further burdened with need, suffering, hunger, disease, and the plagues of the wicked Būshyāsta (the demon of sloth), of Astō-Vīdhōtu, and of other destroying beings. Gaya died, and his body became molten brass,[6] while other minerals arose from his members: gold, silver, iron, tin, lead, quicksilver, and adamant. Gold was Gaya's seed, which was entrusted to the earth and carefully preserved by Spenta Ārmaiti, the guardian of earth. After forty years it brought forth the first human pair, Māshya and Māshyōī, under the appearance of a *rīvās*-plant (*Rheum ribes*) with one stem and fifteen leaves, because the human couple were intimately united and were born at the age of fifteen years.[7]

The parallelism between this myth accounting for the production of human beings and the ox-story explaining how animals were created is very striking and is intentional, and in the Avesta the primeval man and the primeval ox are invoked together.[8] The same parallelism, curiously enough, exists in the cosmogony of the Scandinavians, in which it is reported that the cow Audhubla was produced at the same time as the giant Ymir.[9] The primeval giant is an Indo-European conception. We find it also in India in a form more similar to the Iranian version, for in primordial times Puruṣa ("Male") was alone in the world, but differentiated himself into two beings, husband and wife.

Besides this myth, the Indians knew of another explanation for the origin of the human race. The first man is Manu, son of Vivasvant, or Yama, son of Vivasvant. Yama and his sister Yamī were twins, and after the latter had overcome the scruples of the former, they produced mankind,[10] a similar story being told of Māshya and Māshyōī in Iran, as will be set forth later on. Moreover, Yama and Yamī exist in Persia under the names of Yima and Yimāka (Pāhlavī Yim and Yimak), though they have been changed into a king and a queen of legendary but no longer primeval times. In Iran Yima is the son of Vīvanghvant, the same being as the Indian Vivasvant, and both are mythical priests who offered the

Soma sacrifice. They are heavenly beings in connexion with the Aśvins (the evening and the morning star) and have been taken by several scholars for the bright morning sky or the rising sun. Although this is uncertain, the latter myth seems to ascribe to man a heavenly origin, so that Darmesteter wonders whether the youth of fifteen who is the first man is not identical with the hero who in the contest on high slays the demon Azhi or other storm-dragons. The question is, of course, hardly answerable in our present state of knowledge, but it seems at least probable that a certain contamination between the storm-myth and the story of the first man has taken place. We may observe that the first man is said to be white and brilliant, that he slays a demon before being overcome by the powers of darkness, and that he is born from sweat, etc.

A Manichean narrative of the creation and life of the primeval man [11] is still more like a storm-myth: "The first man was created by the Lord of Paradise to fight against darkness. He had five divine weapons: warm breeze, strong wind, light, water, and fire. He dressed himself with the warm breeze, put light above it, and then water, wrapped himself in the frightfulness of winds, took fire as a spear, and rushed forward to the battle. The demon was assisted by smoke, flame, burning fire, darkness, and clouds. He went to meet the first man, and after fighting for twenty years he proved victorious, stripped his adversary of his light, and wrapped him in his elements."

As to Māshya and Māshyōī, who grew up under the form of a tree, they give an illustration of another myth of man's origin, the equivalents of which are found in many national traditions. In Greece the Korybantes were born as trees, and other legends speak of the birth of Attis from an almond-tree and of Adonis from a myrtle, while Vergil mentions a similar story of Italic origin.[12]

Coming back to the Iranian myth, we must narrate the

deeds of Māshya and Māshyōī. In their *rīvās*-plant they were united in such a manner that their arms rested behind on their shoulders, while the waists of both of them were brought close and so connected that it was impossible to distinguish what belonged to one and what to the other, although after a time they changed from the shape of a plant into that of human beings and received a soul. Meanwhile the tree had grown up and brought forth fruit that were the ten varieties of man. Now Ahura Mazda spoke to Māshya and Māshyōī thus: "You are man, you are the ancestry of the world, and you are created perfect in devotion by me; perform devotedly the duty of the law, think good thoughts, speak good words, do good deeds, and worship no demons!" Then they thought that since they were human beings, both of them, they must please one another and they went together into the world.[13] The first words that they exchanged were that Mazda had created water and earth, plants and animals, stars, moon, and sun, and all the good things which manifest His bounty and His justice.

Then, however, letting the Spirit of Deceit penetrate into their intellects, they said that it was Angra Mainyu who had formed water, earth, etc.; and this lie gave much enjoyment to the Druj ("Deceit, Lie") because they had become wicked, and they are his prey until the renovation of the world.

For thirty days they had gone without food, covered with clothing of herbage. After thirty days they went forth into the wilderness, and coming to a white-haired goat, they milked the milk from the udder with their mouths. Then Māshya said, "I was happy before I had drunk that milk, but my pleasure is much greater now that I have enjoyed its savour." This, however, was an impious word,[14] and as a punishment they were deprived of the taste of the food, "so that out of a hundred parts one part remained."

Thirty days later they came to a sheep, fat and white-jawed, which they slaughtered. Extracting fire from the wood of a lote-plum (a kind of jujube) and a box-tree, they stimulated the flame with their breath and took as fuel dry grass, lotus, date-palm leaves, and myrtle. Making a roast of the sheep, they dropped three handfuls of the meat into the fire, saying, "This is the share of the fire"; and one piece of the remainder they tossed to the sky, saying, "This is the share of the Yazatas," whereupon a vulture advanced and carried some of it away as a dog eats the first meat.

At first Māshya and Māshyōī had covered themselves with skins, but afterward they made garments from a cloth woven in the wilderness. They also dug a pit in the earth and found iron, which they beat out with a stone. Thus, though they had no forge, they were able to make an edged tool, with which they cut wood and prepared a shelter from the sun.

All those violations of the respect which they had to entertain for the creatures of Ahura Mazda made them more completely the prey of the impure demons so that they began to quarrel with each other, gave each other blows, and tore one another's hair and cheeks. Then the fiends shouted to them from the darkness, "You men, worship Angra Mainyu, so that he may give you some respite!" Thereupon Māshya went forth, milked a cow, and poured the milk toward the northern part of the sky, for the powers of evil dwell in the north; and this made them the slaves of the demon to such an extent that during fifty winters they were so ill that they had no mind to have any intercourse with one another. After this, however, desire arose in Māshya and then in Māshyōī, and they satisfied their impulses and reflected that they had neglected their duty for fifty years. Thus after nine months a pair of children were born to them, but such was their tenderness for their infants that the mother devoured one and the father one; wherefore Ahura Mazda, seeing this, took tenderness for offspring from them.[15] They then had seven other pairs, male and female, from every one of whom children were born in fifty years, while the parents themselves died at the age of a hundred.[16] The story of the first human pair seems to have been influenced by theological conceptions and probably also by the traditions of Semitic people, perhaps even by the Jews, since we have only a late redaction of the myth.

Of these seven pairs one was Sīyākmak and Nashāk, who had as children another pair, Fravāk and Fravākaīn. From them fifteen pairs were born who produced the seven races of men, and since then there has been a constant continuance of the generations in the world. Nine races, owing to the increase of population, proceeded on the back of the ox Sarsaok through the sea Vourukasha and settled in the regions on the other side of the water, while six races remained in Khvanīras, among them being the pair Tāzh and Tāzhak who went to the plain of Arabia, whence the Persians call the Arabs Tāzīs. The Iranians are the descendants of Haoshyangha (Pāhlavī Hōshang) and of Gūzhak.

Besides the fifteen races issued from the lineage of Fravāk, son of Sīyākmak, there are ten varieties of mythical men, grown on the tree from which Māshya and Māshyōī were detached, these being "such as those of the earth, of the water, the breast-eared, the breast-eyed, the one-legged, those also who have wings like a bat, those of the forest, with tails, and who have hair on the body."

In the Persian epic Gaya Maretan has become the first king of the Iranians, and Siyāmak is his son, but some old features are preserved in the very much adulterated legend. Thus Gayōmart (=Gaya Maretan) is said to have dwelt at first on a mountain whence his throne and fortune arose, a detail which may date back to the period when, according to Darmesteter's supposition, the first man was said to have been born in the mountains of the clouds. His subjects wore leopards' skins, just as Māshya and Māshyōī were first clad in the fells of animals. Gayōmart reigned thirty years over the world, while Gaya Maretan was supposed to have lived on earth the same length of time; and just as Gaya Maretan was "white and brilliant," Gayōmart was "on his throne like a sun or a full moon over a lofty cypress" — another feature which supports Darmesteter's hypothesis.

The account of the struggle between Angra Mainyu and the first man is reduced in Firdausī's narrative to a war between Siyāmak, son of Gayōmart, and the wicked king Ahriman (=Angra Mainyu), in which the superb youth was killed.

> "When Gaiúmart heard this the world turned black
> To him, he left his throne, he wailed aloud
> And tore his face and body with his nails;
> His cheeks were smirched with blood, his heart was broken,
> And life grew sombre." [17]

The victory of darkness has thus become the overcoming of Gayōmart by a moral gloom. Siyāmak, however, had left a son Hōshang — who in the older legend is his grandson — and he attacked the devilish foe, cut off his monstrous head, and trampled him in scorn.

In the traditions of the Iranians the story of Gaya Maretan is immediately followed by that of Hōshang, who is the old Iranian hero Haoshyangha, mentioned several times in the Avesta and referred to in the *Būndahish* as the son of Fravāk, son of Sīyākmak. The name of this mythical ruler seems to mean "King of Good Settlements," [18] and he often receives the epithet *paradhāta* (Pāhlavī *pēshdāṭ*), or "first law-giver." He is the Numa of the Iranians, the first organizer of the Iranian nation, and is, moreover, supposed to have introduced the use of fire and metals.

The old tradition concerning him simply says that he was a man who was brave (*takhma*) and lived according to justice (*ashavan*). Thanks to the sacrifice which he offered on the top of Hara Berezaiti, the great iron mountain celebrated in all Iranian myths, he obtained divine protection; he invoked Ardvī Sūra Anāhita, the goddess who, as already stated, lets her beneficent waters flow down from this height; and he also addressed a prayer to Vāyu, the god of wind. "He sacrificed a hundred stallions, a thousand oxen, and ten thousand lambs" [19] while seated "on a golden throne, on a golden cushion, on a golden carpet, with *baresman* [20] outspread, with hands overflowing," [21] and he obtained the favour that the awful kingly Glory, the *Khvarenanh*, clave to him

"For a time of long duration,
So that he ruled over the earth sevenfold,
Over men and over demons,
Over sorcerers and witches,
Rulers, bards, and priests of evil,
Who slew two-thirds
Of the demon hordes Māzainyan
And the lying fiends of Varena." [22]

Making them bow in fear, they fled down to darkness,[23] and on account of his exploits his Fravashi ("Genius") is invoked to withstand the evil done by the daēvas.[24]

The Persian writings have nothing but praise to tell of Hōshang, who was a just and upright sovereign, civilizing the world and filling the surface of the earth with justice, so that during his reign men reposed "in the gardens of content and quiet, in the bowers of undisturbed security; Prosperity drew the bloom of happiness from the vicinity of his imperial pavilion; and Victory borrowed brilliancy of complexion from the violet surface of his well-tempered sword." [25]

Whereas early tradition said that he had offered a sacrifice on the top of an iron mountain, Firdausī tells us that he won the iron from the rock by craft and was the first to deal with minerals, besides inventing blacksmithing and making axes, saws, and mattocks. His civilizing activity extended even further, for he taught the human race how to dig canals to irrigate a dry country, so that men turned to sowing, reaping, and planting. Moreover he trained greyhounds for the chase and showed how to make garments from the skins of sables or foxes, instead of taking leaves for that purpose. Like all heroes, he was a smiter of daēvas — tradition had already attributed to him the slaying of two-thirds of the demons — and, as usual, that kind of exploit took place on a mountain.

"One day he reached a mountain with his men
And saw afar a long swift dusky form
With eyes like pools of blood and jaws whose smoke
Bedimmed the world. Húshang the wary seized
A stone, advanced and hurled it royally.
The world-consuming worm escaped, the stone
Struck on a larger, and they both were shivered.
Sparks issued and the centres flashed. The fire
Came from its stony hiding-place again
When iron knocked. The worldlord offered praise
For such a radiant gift. He made of fire
A cynosure. 'This lustre is divine,'
He said, 'and thou if wise must worship it.'" [26]

In this story it is not difficult to recognize a storm-myth thinly disguised: a hero on a mountain (= cloud) smites a large dragon bedimming the earth; he sends a stone (= thunderbolt); he causes fire (= lightning) to appear and illuminate the world; and, finally, he takes fire from its hiding-place and gives it to men. The mythical nature of the legend is the more evident in that it is an explanation to account for the feast of Sadah because

"That night he made a mighty blaze, he stood
Around it with his men and held the feast
Called Sada."

Hōshang is also said to have been the first to domesticate oxen, asses, and sheep, and to train dogs for guarding the flocks.

"'Pair them,' he said, 'use them for toil, enjoy
Their produce, and provide therewith your taxes.'" [27]

On the other hand, he issued orders for the destruction of beasts of prey. After forty years he left the throne to his heir Ṭahmūrath, the Takhma Urupi of the Avesta, whom he had brought up in the principles of justice and righteousness.

The Avestic tradition gives Takhma Urupi as the successor of Haoshyangha, but does not make him a son of the latter, as Firdausī does; in the early texts he is held to be a son of

Vīvanghvant and a brother of Yima, and is almost a doublet of Haoshyangha. He also has made a sacrifice to Vāyu ("Wind") and has been empowered to conquer all daēvas and men, all sorcerers and witches, etc., although he has not been able to secure a permanent mastery over them, as his predecessor did. After having reigned thirty years and subdued Angra Mainyu so as to ride him, turned into a horse, all around the earth from one end to the other, he was betrayed by his wife, who revealed to the Evil Spirit the secret of her husband's power. The demon, we are told, could attempt nothing against him so long as he betrayed no alarm, and accordingly Angra Mainyu instigated the wife of his conqueror to ask Takhma Urupi if he never was afraid to mount his swift black horse. Thereupon Ṭahmūrath confessed that he had no fear either on the summits or in the valleys, but that on Hara Berezaiti he was deeply alarmed when the horse rushed with lowered head, so that he used to raise his heavy noose, shouting aloud and giving the beast a blow on the head to make it pass hastily the dangerous spot. Having been promised incomparable presents by Angra, the woman revealed this secret to him, and when the horse was on the fatal mountain the following day, he opened his huge mouth and swallowed his rider.

Fortunately Yima managed to recover his brother's corpse from the body of Angra Mainyu, thereby rescuing the arts and civilization which had disappeared along with Takhma Urupi.[28] During that operation he had his hands defiled, but he was able to cleanse them by an infusion of the all-purifying *gōmēz* ("bull's urine").[29] This story also is scarcely unlike a storm-myth, and Darmesteter [30] compares it with the Scandinavian legend in which Odhin is swallowed by the wolf Fenrir, the demoniacal cloud-wolf "whose eyes and nostrils vomit fire, whose immense mouth reaches the sky with one jaw and the earth with the other." It should be noted that the scene of all those contests is Mount Hara Berezaiti.

Another story connected with Takhma Urupi is reported in

## PLATE XXXVIII

### Tahmūrath Combats the Demons

The hero, mounted on his charger and swinging his mace (a characteristic Persian weapon), struggles with four demons, whose forms are a combination of human and animal shapes. A touch of Chinese influence is discernible in the two human figures. From a Persian manuscript of the *Shāhnāmah*, dated 1605–08 A.D., now in the Metropolitan Museum of Art, New York.

the *Būndahish.*[31] "In the reign of Takhmōrup, when men continually passed, on the back of the ox Sarsaok [a curious parallel with the king's horse], from Khvanīras to the other regions, one night amid the sea the wind rushed upon the fireplace — the fireplace in which the fire was, such as was provided in three places on the back of the ox — which the wind dropped with the fire into the sea; and all those three fires, like three breathing souls, continually shot up in the place and position of the fire on the back of the ox, so that it becomes quite light, and the men pass again through the sea." The meaning of this myth is not altogether clear, although Darmesteter thinks that the ox is another incarnation of the cloud.[32]

In later narratives Takhma Urupi is represented as having a reign similar to that of his predecessor. He also teaches men how to clothe themselves, but instead of skins he gives them garments made by spinning the wool of sheep. As a rider of the devilish horse he was predestined to be the tamer of swift quadrupeds and to make them feed on barley, grass, and hay; moreover he taught the jackal to obey him and began to tame the hawk and the falcon.

Firdausī tells us further that when Ṭahmūrath had conquered the daēvas, binding most of them by charms and quelling the others with his massive mace, the captives, fettered and stricken, begged for their lives.

> "'Destroy us not,' they said, 'and we will teach thee
> A new and useful art.' He gave them quarter
> To learn their secret. When they were released
> They had to serve him, lit his mind with knowledge
> And taught him how to write some thirty scripts." [33]

This is evidently a later addition to the legend which makes Takhma Urupi fetter the daēvas, and the exploits of Ṭahmūrath have been further amplified by the historians of the Arab period, particularly as they have identified him with the Biblical Nimrod.

# CHAPTER IV

## LEGENDS OF YIMA

IN Iranian tradition the short reigns of Gayōmart, Hōshang, and Ṭahmūrath were followed, Firdausī says, by a period of seven hundred years during which Jamshīd ruled the Iranian world. Jamshīd is the Persian form of Yima Khshaēta ("Yima the Brilliant"), the name of a very ancient hero of the Indo-Iranians, and his epithet of "brilliant," which is also applied to the sun, corresponds not only to the early but also to the later conception of this monarch. Firdausī says that he "wore in kingly wise the crown of gold" and that on his jewelled throne he

> "sat sunlike in mid air.
> The world assembled round his throne in wonder
> At his resplendent fortune." [1]

In the Avesta Yima is the son of Vīvanghvant, who first offered the haoma to Ahura Mazda. Continuing, the poet describes him as

> "Brilliant, and with herds full goodly,
> Of all men most rich in Glory,
> Of mankind like to the sunlight,
> So that in his kingdom made he
> Beasts and men to be undying,
> Plants and waters never drying,
> Food invincible bestowing.
> In the reign of valiant Yima
> Neither cold nor heat was present,
> Neither age nor death was present,
> Neither envy, demon-founded.
> Fifteen years of age in figure
> Son and father walked together
> All the days Vīvanghvant's offspring,
> Yima, ruled, with herds full goodly." [2]

Thanks to the Glory which long accompanied him, Yima subjugated the daēvas and all their imps, taking from them riches and advantage, prosperity and herds, contentment and renown;[3] and Firdausī has faithfully preserved this tradition, declaring that for three hundred years of Yima's reign

> "Men never looked on death;
> They wotted not of travail or of ill,
> And dīvs like slaves were girt to do them service;
> Men hearkened to Jamshīd with both their ears,
> Sweet voices filled the world with melody."[4]

The golden age of Yima is an essential element of Zoroastrian chronology. The period between Angra Mainyu's invasion and Zarathushtra's religious reform is divided into three millenniums. The first was the reign of Yima, during which the good creation prevailed, and then came the dominion of Azhi Dahāka (Daḥḥāk), when demons ruled over the world, this being followed by a period of struggle up to Zarathushtra, whose birth Iranian tradition places in 660 B.C.[5]

Firdausī is obviously wrong in making Jamshīd reign seven hundred years only, for it is quite clear that the reigns of Jamshīd and Daḥḥāk are in complete parallelism and must last a thousand years each.[6] For the Zoroastrians, who conceived illness, death, cold, etc., as the direct products of the Evil Spirit, it was quite natural to admit the existence at the beginning of the world of a period in which the good creation had not yet felt Angra Mainyu's deleterious influence; and the Iranian climate, moreover, was likely to lead to such a conception, since after a glorious and luxuriant spring it offers the drought of summer and the cold of winter.[7]

In the *Shāhnāmah* Jamshīd says that he is both king and archimage,[8] and this seems to have been the old tradition. Yima had been both the material and the spiritual educator of mankind, but the Zoroastrians wished to emphasize that the religious teacher of the Iranians was Zarathushtra, and so they made Yima say to Ahura Mazda:

"I was neither made nor tutored
To receive the faith and spread it";

whereupon Ahura Mazda replies:

"If thou, Yima, art not ready
To receive the faith and spread it,
then further my creatures, then increase my creatures,
then show thyself ready to be both the protector and the guardian and the watcher of my creatures." [9]

Accordingly Yima introduces men into their earthly abode like a king of settlers opening new countries to his people each time they fall short of ground to cultivate. He receives from Ahura Mazda a golden arrow and a scourge inlaid with gold, and he undertakes to secure to his subjects a delightful abode with neither cold nor wind, full of flocks and herds, men, dogs, and birds. Three fires protected that beautiful land, the Frōbak on the mountain in Khvārizm, the fire Gūshasp on Mount Asnavand, and the fire Būrzhīn Mitrō on Mount Rēvand,[10] but under such favourable conditions flocks and men increased so much that after three hundred years had passed away, there was no longer room for them. Then Ahura Mazda warned Yima:

"'Yim, Vīvanghvant's beauteous offspring,
Earth in sooth is overflowing
Both with small beasts and with great beasts,
Men, and dogs, and flying creatures,[11]
And with ruddy fires red blazing.
Nor indeed can they find places,
small beasts and great beasts and men.'
Then at noon Yima went forward to the light, in the direction of the path of the sun,
And earth's surface he abraded
With the arrow, made all golden,
With the scourge he stroked it over,
thus speaking:
'O thou holy, dear Ārmaiti,[12]
Go thou forward, stretch thyself out
to bear small beasts and great beasts and men.'

Then Yima made this earth stretch itself apart a third larger than it was before. There small beasts and great beasts and men roved

Just as was their will and pleasure,
Howsoever was his pleasure." [13]

But a time came when the earth was even thus too small, so that Yima had once more to perform the same rite; and he did this yet again, making the earth increase in size by one third on each occasion, so that after nine hundred years the surface of the world became double what it had been at first.

"Then Ahura Mazda, the Creator, convened an assembly with the spiritual Yazatas [14] in the famous Airyana Vaējah, at the goodly Dāitya.[15] Then Yima the Brilliant, with goodly flocks, convened an assembly with the best men in the famous Airyana Vaējah, at the goodly Dāitya. Then Ahura Mazda spake to Yima: 'O beauteous Yima, son of Vīvanghvant! On the evil material world the winters are about to fall, wherefore there shall be strong, destructive winter; on the evil material world the winters are about to fall, wherefore straightway the clouds shall snow down snow from the loftiest mountains into the depths of Ardvī [Sura Anāhita].[16] Only one-third of the cattle, Yima, will escape of those who live in the most terrible of places,[17] of those who live on the tops of mountains, of those who live in the valleys of the rivers in permanent abodes.[18]

Till the coming of that winter
Shall the land be clad in verdure,
But the waters soon shall flood it
When the snow hath once been melted,

and, Yima, it will be impassable in the material world where now the footprints of the sheep are visible. Therefore make an enclosure (*vara*) long as a riding-ground (*caretu*) on every side of the square; gather together the seed of small cattle and of great cattle, of men and dogs and birds and red, blazing fires. Then make the enclosure long as a riding-ground on every side of the square to be an abode for men, long as a riding-ground on every side of the square as a stall for cattle.

> In their course make thou the waters
> There flow forth, in width a *hāthra;*
> And there shalt thou place the meadows
> where unceasingly the golden-coloured, where unceasingly the invincible food is eaten.
> And there shalt thou place the mansions
> with cellars and vestibules, with bastions and ramparts.

"'Gather together the seed of all men and women that are the greatest and the best and the finest on this earth; gather together the seed of all kinds of cattle that are the greatest and the best and the finest on this earth; gather together the seed of all plants that are the tallest and the sweetest on this earth; gather together the seed of all fruits that are the most edible and the sweetest on this earth. Bring these by pairs to be inexhaustible so long as these men shall stay in the enclosure. There will be no admittance there for humpback or chicken-breast, for *apāvaya*,[19] lunacy, birth-mark, *daiwish*,[19] *kasvīsh*,[19] mis-shapenness, men with deformed teeth or with leprosy that compels seclusion, nor any of the other marks which are the mark of Angra Mainyu laid upon men. In the largest part of the place thou shalt make nine streets, in the middle six, and in the smallest three. In the streets of the largest part gather a thousand seeds of men and women, in those of the middle part six hundred, in those of the smallest part three hundred. With thy golden arrow thou shalt mark thine enclosure,

> And bring thou to the enclosure
> a shining door, on its inner side shining by its own light.'"[20]

At this Yima was much at a loss and wondered how he could ever make such an enclosure. Ahura Mazda, however, told him to stamp the earth with his heels and to knead it with his hands, as people do when now they knead potter's clay; and then Yima made exactly what Ahura Mazda had commanded. When all was ready, Ahura Mazda provided the *vara* with special lights, because only once a year can they who dwell there see sun, moon, and stars rising and setting, so that they think that a year is but one day. Every fortieth year a male and female are born to each human pair, and thus it is for every sort of animal. These men live a happy life in the enclosure of Yima, but since Zarathushtra, the prophet, had no access to it, the religion was brought thither by the bird Karshiptar.[21]

The Avesta does not give any precise indication as to the time of the coming of the winter predicted by Mazda, and though it looks as if that scourge afflicted mankind in ancient times, later books show that this was not the case. The fatal and destructive winter is to occur in the last period of the world. Three hundred years before the birth of Ukhshyaṭ-nemah (one of the sons of Zarathushtra who are to be born in the last millennium of the world) the demon Mahrkūsha will destroy mankind by snow and frost within the space of three years, after which Yima's enclosure will be opened and the earth will again be populated. The name of this demon Mahrkūsha means "Destroyer, Devastator," and is of Iranian formation, but in later times it was confused with the Aramaic word *malqôs*, "autumnal rain," so that in more recent texts the idea of the fatal freezing winter was abandoned for that of the deluging rain of Malqôs.[22]

A tradition which dates from very ancient days represents Yima as diverging at a certain moment from the path of justice. He commits a fault, and from that instant he loses his Glory and his kingdom and finally is put to death, while a devilish being named Ḍaḥḥāk (the old Avestic dragon Azhi Dahāka) extends his power over the world of the Aryans.

As to the nature of Yima's sin some uncertainty prevails in the tradition. Nevertheless, there are certain hints that this fault consisted in having rendered his subjects immortal by giving them forbidden food to eat, and in the *Gāthās* of Zoroaster the poet prays to Ahura Mazda in order to avoid such sins as that of Yima, who gave men meat to eat in small pieces, as it was offered to the gods in sacrifice.[23] A late book, on the other hand, relates that Yima unwittingly gave meat to a daēva,[24] although the most current form of the legend is that Yima

"In his mind began to dwell on
Words of falsehood and of untruth." [25]

Firdausī explains that Yima's lie was in reality a sin of presumption.

"One day contemplating the throne of power
He deemed that he was peerless. He knew God,
But acted frowardly and turned aside
In his ingratitude. He summoned all
The chiefs, and what a wealth of words he used!
'The world is mine, I found its properties,
The royal throne hath seen no king like me,
For I have decked the world with excellence
And fashioned earth according to my will.
From me derive your provand, ease, and sleep,
Your raiment and your pleasure. Mine are greatness
And diadem and sovereignty. Who saith
That there is any great king save myself?
Leechcraft hath cured the world, disease and death
Are stayed. Though kings are many who but I
Saved men from death? Ye owe me sense and life:
They who adore me not are Âhrimans.
So now that ye perceive what I have done
All hail me as the Maker of the world.'" [26]

Another story of Yima's sin is connected with the fact that he had a sister Yimak who, as is the case with all primeval pairs, was also his wife. Various moral considerations regarding the incestuous union of this twin pair have been made for Yama and Yamī in India as well as for Yima and Yimāka in Iran. In India a Vedic hymn [27] records a conversation between the twins in which Yama refuses to do what the sages at that time condemned as a grave sin, whereas in the Pāhlavī books the union of Yim and Yimak is given as an example of the

# PLATE XXXIX

1

## Ḍaḥḥāk (Azhi Dahāka)

The tyrant is seated on his throne, surrounded by his courtiers. From his shoulders spring the serpents. From a Persian manuscript of the *Shāhnāmah*, dated 1602 A.D., now in the Metropolitan Museum of Art, New York.

2

## Jamshīd on His Throne

The king administers justice and is attended not merely by human servitors, but also by *dīvs* ("demons") in monstrous guise, *murghs* ("birds"), and *parīs* ("fairies"). The figures show a mixture of Indian and Chinese influence, and it has been conjectured that the miniatures in this manuscript are the work of a Mongolian or Turkistān artist well acquainted with Persia, but living in northern India. From a Persian manuscript of the *Shāhnāmah*, dated 1602 A.D., now in the Metropolitan Museum of Art, New York.

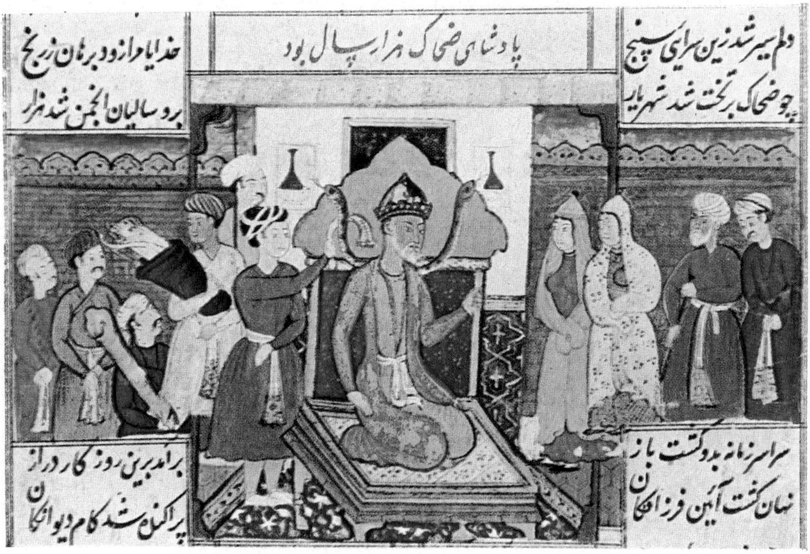
پادشاهی ضحاک هزار سال بود
دلم سیر شد زین سرای سپنج
خدایا مرا زود برهان ز رنج
چو ضحاک بر تخت شد شهریار
برو سالیان انجمن شد هزار
سراسر زمانه بدو گشت باز
برآمد برین روزگار دراز
نهان گشت آیین فرزانگان
پراکنده شد کام دیوانگان

I

پادشاهی جمشید هفتصد سال بود
گرانمایه جمشید فرزند اوی
کمر بست یکدل پر از پند اوی
بیامد بدان تخت فرخ پدر
برسم کیان بر سرش تاج زر
کمر بست با فر شاهنشهی
جهان گشت سرتاسر او را رهی
زمانه برآسود از داوری
به فرمان او دیو و مرغ و پری
جهان را فزوده بدو آبروی
فروزان شده تخت شاهی بدو

2

*Khvētōk-dās*, or incestuous marriage, which was recommended by the Mazdeans at one period in their history. In the *Būndahish*[28] Yima is said to have given his sister to a demon after he had been blinded by folly at the end of his reign, and to have himself married a demoness, these unions resulting in monstrous and degenerate beings, such as tailed apes.

Whatever Yima's sin may have been, the king soon received his punishment, for the Glory (*Khvarenanh*), an emanation of divine radiancy that gave prestige to the Iranian monarchs, deserted him immediately and left him trembling, confounded, and defenceless before his foes. The first time that the Glory departed from Yima, it was in the shape of a Vāreghna bird, and Mithra, the lord of broad pastures, whose ear is quick to hear, and who has a thousand senses, seized it. The second time that the Glory departed from Yima the Brilliant, it was seized by Thraētaona, the victorious hero who after a thousand years was to take from the devilish Ḍaḥḥāk (Azhi Dahāka) the realm which Yima lost. The third time it was the manly-minded Keresāspa who seized the Glory, and who also was to be a valiant and victorious ruler of the Iranians.[29]

Yima, deprived of the Glory that made his power, was overcome by a being of decidedly mythical nature, the famous serpent Azhi Dahāka, whom we have seen to be an incarnation of the storm-cloud. In later texts this monster is called by a Semitic name, Ḍaḥḥāk ("the Man with a Sarcastic Laugh"), but this is merely a popular etymology, a pun on his real appellation. He is now an Arab king, living in Babylon, and in the Avesta itself we read that Azhi Dahāka, the triple-mouthed, offered sacrifice to Ardvī Sūra in the land of Bawrī (Babylon), wishing to become the ruler of the world and to make the seven regions of earth empty of men. Although his prayer was not granted to such an extent, he overcame Yima and made captives of his two sisters, Sanghavak and Arenavak.[30] If in the Avesta Azhi Dahāka still has three mouths like the dragon, in the *Shāhnāmah* he is completely a man, though he has two snakes springing from his shoulders, where they grew through a kiss of Angra Mainyu, a legend which recurs in Armenia.

In the presence of this monstrous fiend Yima

> "fled, surrendering crown, throne and treasure,
> Host, power and diadem. The world turned black
> To him, he disappeared and yielded all." [31]

For a hundred years he hid himself, but then appeared one day in the Far East, on the shores of the Chinese sea, where his foe, informed of the fact, gave him no respite, and sawing him asunder, freed the world from him. In the older texts it is Spityura, a brother of Yima, who sawed Yima in twain.[32] Sometimes it is explained that he was in a hollow tree, where he had concealed himself; but by the command of Ḍaḥḥāk the stem of the tree was severed by the saw, and with it the man inside.[33]

The story of Yima is the most interesting and the only extensive myth of the Iranians, and it is certain that the legend dates back to Aryan, or at least to Indo-Iranian, times.

As the Avesta knows of Yima, son of Vīvanghvant, so the Veda speaks of Yama, son of Vivasvant. As Yima is the chief of a remote kingdom, a marvellous realm where there is neither cold nor suffering, so Yama is the ruler of the fathers, the departed souls, with whom he revels in a huge tree. Just as Yima's *vara* is concealed either on a mountain or in some recess where sun and moon are not seen, Yama's dwelling is in the remote part of the sky. While Yima calls a gathering of men to assemble them in his *vara*, Yama collects the people and gives the dead a resting-place. Yima has opened the earth for mankind; Yama is "lord of the settlers" (*viśpati*) and "father." Yima has found new countries, following a road toward the sun; Yama has a path for the dead to lead them to their abode, being the first to die and having discovered "a way for many." A bird brings messages into Yima's *vara;* Yama has the owl or the pigeon as his envoy.

In spite of these points in common, there is an important discrepancy. Yama is the first mortal being and is clearly associated with death and with a kingdom of the departed, whereas Yima is simply a monarch of ancient times, his reign is a golden age for mankind, and his enclosure has no clear location.

This divergency is explained by the fact that the Iranians had another legend for the first man: the story of Gaya Maretan, which dates back to the Aryan period. Thus, owing to the desire of the Iranians for a more coherent system of mythology, the concurrent legend of Yima has been transferred into later, though still primeval, times, although Yima has remained — and this is very eloquent — the first sacrificer, the patriarchal lord of mankind at the dawn of history.

The story of Yama as it is in India [34] is clearly a legend accounting for the origin of man, but the primitive shape of the story is probably an elemental myth. Several scholars have endeavoured to show that Yama originally was the sun, and although this has never been conclusively demonstrated, there is much to be said in favour of the hypothesis.

It is certain that in the Veda Yama is often treated as a god. He is the friend of Agni and sometimes is identified with him. He is the son of the deity Vivasvant ("Whose Light Spreads Afar"), who most probably was at first the rising sun [35] and who was also father of the Aśvins (the morning and the evening star).

The evidence concerning Yama-Yima is, on the whole, that he is the setting sun. He follows the path of the sun to go to a remote recess, whither he leads all men with him. The path of the sun was a very natural symbol of the path of human life, the same words were used in Sanskrit for the death of men and for the sunset,[36] and Indian literature declares that the sun is the sure retreat. The sun is a bird or has birds as its messengers, like Yama; and like a sun-god Yama has two steeds, golden-eyed and iron-hoofed.

In Iran the solar nature of Yima is rather more accentuated than in India, and the old epithets of Yima are striking in this respect. He is commonly called *khshaēta* ("brilliant"), an adjective which is at the same time the regular epithet of the sun (*hvare khshaēta*, Persian *khurshīd*); and moreover he is *khvarenanguhastema* ("the most glorious, the most surrounded with light") and *hvare-daresa* ("who looks like the sun, the sun-like one"). These epithets, which are very natural as a survival if Yima had once been the sun, would be incomprehensible if he was originally the first man and nothing more. He is also *hvăthwa* ("with goodly herds"), an adjective that very possibly alludes to the stars following the setting sun in his retreat, especially as stars are said in Vedic literature to be the lights of virtuous men who go to the heavenly world,[37] so that they would thus form the natural flock of Yima. Yima's golden arrow reminds us strikingly of a similar missile in the hands of his father Vivasvant in the Veda, by means of which he sends men to the realm of the dead.[38] Other luminous gods, like Apollo, show the same features, and it seems not improbable that these arrows are the rays of the sun.

The brilliancy of Yima was so deeply rooted in tradition that Firdausī is still more definite about it. As we have already seen, Jamshīd sits like the sun in mid air, his fortune and his throne are resplendent, and the royal Glory shines brightly from him. That this dates back to ancient sources is proved by the fact that Firdausī has a very curious sentence about Yima which is not at all in keeping with the nature of Jamshīd as a worldly king; he puts in the monarch's mouth the words, "I will make for souls a path toward the light." This is taken from the passage already quoted from the *Vendīdād* in which Yima goes toward the path of the sun to open earth for men, and it shows that this typical action of Yima may originally have been meant for the dead: Yima used to lead the departed toward the sun, on the way of the sun that is the path of Yima.

The end of Yima is also very characteristic. When his brilliancy quits him, the world turns black to him and he vanishes. When he appears again, it is in the distant east, where the sun rises.

A solar year-myth seems likewise to have been involved in the story, for Yima is the founder of the feast of Naurūz, the New Year's Day that with the Persians occurs in March at the beginning of the radiant spring. Yima's vernal kingdom is destroyed by the demon of cold and frost (Mahrkūsha), yet the sun and life do not disappear forever from the world, but are kept in reserve for the next spring, like the beings in Yima's *vara*. As we have seen, the legend of Yima as told in the *Vendīdād* expressly says that in the *vara* one year is one day. The disappearance of the sun in winter is thus assimilated to its daily departure to the remote recess in the world of darkness, and the story of Yima's century of concealment until he reappears in the East is very much in the same spirit.

The connexion of Yima with a tree reminds us of Yama's abode in a high tree, and in the *Atharvaveda* an arboreal dwelling-place is the home of the gods in the third heaven.[39]

No doubt other stories have come to be mixed up with the solar myths of the departed souls. Thus the legend of Yima's defeat by a storm-cloud monster, Azhi Dahāka, is probably borrowed from the very prolific storm-myth of which we have heard so many times. The abduction of Yima's two fair sisters and their release by the storm-god Thraētaona is a mere variation of the release of the imprisoned cows by this god,[40] although the sisters are at the same time, possibly, a reminiscence of Yama's two brilliant steeds.

The description of the monster's victory over Yima in Firdausī has many features of a storm-myth:

> "The king of dragon-visage came like wind
> . . . . . . . . . . .
> And having seized the throne of Sháh Jamshíd
> Slipped on the world as 't were a finger-ring." [41]

The palace of the dragon, which is called *kvirinta*, is compared to a bird with large wings.[42]

Finally, the story of Yima and Yama is closely related to that of the twins Yama-Yamī or Yima-Yimak, who after much hesitation agree to have intercourse with one another and become the parents of mankind. In Iran the tradition is a doublet of the legend of Māshya and Māshyōī, in which similar hesitations occur. It seems clear enough that such a story has been invented to account for the propagation of human beings from one single pair.

Since the word "Yama" means "twin," it is fairly probable that this story belongs originally to Yama, although it is also possible, as several scholars admit, that Yamī has been invented later and that Yama was primarily the twin of another being, perhaps Agni (fire of earth and fire on high), or that he was the soul of the departed considered as the *alter ego* of the living man.[43] It might seem preferable, however, to abide by the most natural explanation and admit that Yama is the male twin of Yamī. Now the twin pair had to come from some pre-existent being, as was the case with Māshya and Māshyōī, who sprang from Gaya Maretan's seed. In the legend of Yima, some traces are left of a story that made the first pair arise from the violent division of one being. Yima is sawn asunder — a curious feature which is much in the spirit of mythical stories among people of fairly elementary culture. Among the Indo-Europeans we know of the Indian first man Puruṣa, who differentiated himself into two beings, husband and wife. On the other hand, the Slavonic people tell the story that the moon, the wife of the sun, separated herself from him and fell in love with the morning star, whereupon she was cut in two by the sword of Perkúnas. Comparing this myth with the Iranian legend that the seed of the primeval ox was preserved in the moon, one wonders if there are no traces of that Indo-European tradition in the story of Yima. At all events it is clear that Yima's legend combines several conceptions concerning the first man and the dead. The old myth of the pair issued from the first giant became mixed with a more poetic conception which made the setting sun the first departed, the father of the fathers, as well as with a myth of winter, and possibly with a moon-myth accounting for the division of the moon into quarters and a storm-myth in its classical tenure. The idea of Yima's sin is so very Zoroastrian in its form that it can scarcely be regarded as belonging to the original story. In the primitive myth Yima obviously fell a victim in a struggle with a dragon of darkness (cloud or night). There was, however, perhaps a tradition of a fault committed by the first men, accounting for the evils reigning on earth, a conception which is, as a matter of fact, very widely spread, quite independently of any Semitic or Christian influence.

Before relating the stories concerning other legendary kings of Iran, we should point to the large development which Yima's story received in later times. All kinds of great deeds were attributed to King Jamshīd, especially his institution of castes, his medical knowledge, and his works as a constructor.

"Then to the joy of all he founded castes
For every craft; it took him fifty years.
Distinguishing one caste as sacerdotal
To be employed in sacred offices,
He separated it from other folk
And made its place of service on the mountains
That God might be adored in quietude.
Arrayed for battle on the other hand
Were those who formed the military caste;
They were the lion-men inured to war —
The Lights of armies and of provinces —
Whose office was to guard the royal throne
And vindicate the nation's name for valour.
The third caste was the agricultural,
All independent tillers of the soil,
The sowers and the reapers — men whom none
Upbraideth when they eat. . . .
The fourth caste was the artizans. They live
By doing handiwork — a turbulent crew." [44]

This tradition of Yima's activity is probably fairly ancient. He was indeed the material organizer of mankind, and the castes were already in existence in the days of Zoroaster, for the *Gāthās* know of a caste of priests, of nobles or warriors, and of farmers. The location of priests on the mountains curiously recalls the fact that the heroes of ancient times are represented in the Avesta as offering their sacrifices on the mountain-tops, and Herodotus reports the same thing concerning the Persians in his day: "It is their wont to perform sacrifices to Zeus, going up to the most lofty of the mountains; and the whole circle of the heavens they call Zeus." [45]

Regarding the farmers Firdausī says, in the passage from which we have just quoted, that,

> "Though clothed in rags,
> The wearers are not slaves, and sounds of chiding
> Reach not their ears. They are free men and labour
> Upon the soil safe from dispute and contest.
> What said the noble man and eloquent?
> ''T is idleness that maketh freemen slaves.'"

This high appreciation of the agricultural caste is also very much in the spirit of Zoroastrianism.

As regards his medical skill, Jamshīd is said to have known

> "Next leechcraft and the healing of the sick,
> The means of health, the course of maladies." [46]

Moreover he made use of his marvellous power to search among the rocks for precious stones, he knew the arts of navigation, and his wisdom brought to light the properties of all things. It is doubtful, however, whether his functions as a healer were primitive, for the medical art is more properly ascribed to Farīdūn (Thraētaona) or to Īrmān (Airyaman).

Yima's works as a constructor were better known, and many an old ruin today is still ascribed to him by the Persians. This fame is, Firdausī continues, a result of his subjugation of the demons, whom he instructed how to

"Temper earth with water
And taught them how to fashion moulds for bricks.
They laid foundations first with stones and lime,
Then raised thereon by rules of art such structures
As hot baths, lofty halls, and sanctuaries."

Even more is ascribed to Jamshīd by the writers of Muhammadan times. As a wise king of great brilliancy he was assimilated to Solomon, while as a primeval monarch and probably as the builder of the enclosure against the destructive winter he was confused with Noah. Either on account of this or because his wisdom brought to light the properties of things he was supposed to have discovered wine. Mirkhond tells an anecdote about this.[47] Having tried the taste of the juice of grapes, the king observed a sensation of bitterness and conceived aversion for it, thinking that it was a deadly poison. A damsel of the palace, seized with violent pain in her head, longed for death and accordingly resolved to drink of the juice that was deemed poisonous. She did not die, however, but drank so much of it that she fell into a beneficent sleep which lasted an entire day and night. On awaking she found herself restored to perfect health, and for this reason the monarch ordered the general use of wine.

## CHAPTER V

## TRADITIONS OF THE KINGS AND ZOROASTER

THE serpent-like dragon of the storm-cloud described as the three-headed monster in Indo-European myths has often appeared in our account of Iranian mythology. We have seen how the cloud was forgotten for the serpent, and how the serpent became a human monster, the conqueror of Yima. Of his dragon nature he preserves a dragon-like face and two snakes on his shoulders, the fruit of Angra Mainyu's kisses. As we find the legend in Firdausī in a completely anthropomorphized shape, it retains many features of the myth in the form in which it appears in its most complete version in Armenian books: the monstrous dragon Azhdak (Azhi Dahāka), with serpents sprung from his shoulders and served by a host of demons, is conquered by Vahagn (Verethraghna), the hero who replaces Farīdūn (Thraētaona) in Armenian Mazdean mythology, and the demon is fettered in a gorge on Mount Damāvand, the serpents sprung from his shoulders being fed on human flesh. We find all these features in Firdausī's account. Ḍaḥḥāk every night sent to his cook two youths who were slaughtered so that their brains might feed the snakes. Two high-born Persians disguised as cooks devised a scheme to rescue one youth from each pair doomed to death, and when the young men who escaped, thanks to their contrivance, fled to the mountains,

> "Thus sprang the Kúrds, who know no settled home,
> But dwell in woolen tents and fear not God." [1]

Like the dragon of old, Ḍaḥḥāk is a coward who lives in constant terror because his death at the hand of Farīdūn has been predicted in a dream which he had one night when he was sleeping with one of Jamshīd's sisters. Like the serpent of early myth, who roared at the blows of the storm-god, he yells with fright through fear of Farīdūn.

Ḍaḥḥāk is not merely a wicked and maleficent being, but is also the personification of tyranny and barbarity in contrast with Iranian civilization. Like rude tribes at war in all times, he knows only massacre, pillage, and arson. In his kingdom oppression reigns, and like all tyrants he desires the best of his subjects to give official excuse to his abuses.

"He called the notables from every province
To firm the bases of his sovereignty,
And said to them: 'Good, wise, illustrious men!
I have, as sages wot, an enemy
Concealed, and I through fear of ill to come
Despise not such though weak. I therefore need
A larger host — men, dívs, and fairies too —
And ask your aid, for rumours trouble me;
So sign me now a scroll to this effect: —
"Our monarch soweth naught but seeds of good,
He ever speaketh truth and wrongeth none."'
Those upright men both young and old subscribed
Their names upon the Dragon's document,
Against their wills, because they feared the Sháh." [2]

All this is in complete contrast to the Iranian ideal of order, truth, and wisdom, and accordingly Ḍaḥḥāk is the type of the *dregvant*, the man of the Lie and the king of madmen.

"Zahhák sat on the throne a thousand years
Obeyed by all the world. Through that long time
The customs of the wise were out of vogue,
The lusts of madmen flourished everywhere,
All virtue was despised, black art esteemed,
Right lost to sight, disaster manifest;
While dívs accomplished their fell purposes
And no man spake of good unless by stealth." [3]

As if by a natural instinct of justice, the tyrant in his abuses is pursued by fear of punishment. After the dream which we have already mentioned Ḍaḥḥāk runs about the world, quarrelling and slaughtering men and nations to anticipate the attack of him who is to satisfy the popular conscience by causing his ruin. He has an army of spies, among them being Kundrav, a very ancient mythical creature of the Indo-Iranians (Sanskrit Gandharva, Avesta Gandarewa), who appears in the Avesta as a dragon killed by Keresāspa. Kundrav manages to penetrate into Farīdūn's tent when he is at table, and having gained his confidence, he notes all his preparations against Ḍaḥḥāk, after which, escaping from the hero's camp, he makes a full report to the tyrant. Ḍaḥḥāk endeavours to avert his destined ruin, but in vain, for he is opposed by Farīdūn, endowed with the kingly Glory of Yima, and tall and firm like a cypress.[4] Ābtīn (i.e. Thrita Āthwya), the father of Farīdūn (Thraētaona), had been killed by Ḍaḥḥāk to feed the serpents, and his son planned revenge for this ignominious murder, another task being the release of the two sisters of Jamshīd (Yima), who had been surrendered to the monster when their brother fell.

"Trembling like a willow-leaf,
. . . . . . . . .
Men bore them to the palace of Zahhák
And gave them over to the dragon king,
Who educated them in evil ways
And taught them sorcery and necromancy." [5]

After Farīdūn had taken possession of Ḍaḥḥāk's palace,

"Then from the women's bower he brought two Idols
Sun-faced, dark-eyed; he had them bathed, he purged
The darkness of their minds by teaching them
The way of God and made them wholly clean;
For idol-worshippers had brought them up
And they were dazed in mind like drunken folk.
Then while the tears from their bright eyes bedewed
Their rosy cheeks those sisters of Jamshíd
Said thus to Farídún: 'Mayst thou be young

> Till earth is old! What star was this of thine,
> O favoured one! What tree bore thee as fruit,
> Who venturest inside the Lion's lair
> So hardily, thou mighty man of valour?'" [6]

It is curious to see the old myth of the release of the women of the clouds transformed into a merely romantic episode, and one wonders whether the bath which the women must undergo is not a remnant of their sojourn in the waters on high.

Farīdūn then assails Ḍaḥḥāk with a lasso made of lion's hide, and while the dragon king, blinded by jealousy at the sight of

> "dark-eyed Shahrinâz,
> Who toyed bewitchingly with Farídún," [7]

rushed about like a madman, the hero bound him around the arms and waist with bonds that not even a huge elephant could snap. He conveyed the captive to Mount Damāvand, where he fettered him in a narrow gorge and studded him with heavy nails, leaving him to hang, bound by his hands, to a crag, so that his anguish might endure. He is not killed by the hero because in myth the storm-dragon does not die, but often escapes from the hold of the light-god.

Tradition knows little of Farīdūn outside of his healing power and his victory over the dragon. Nevertheless the *Dīnkarṭ* [8] mentions the division of his kingdom between his sons Salm, Tūr, and Īraj; and the *Būndahish* [9] explains that the two former killed the latter, as well as his posterity, with the exception of a daughter who was concealed by Farīdūn and who bore the hero Manushcithra, or Minūcihr, the successor of Farīdūn. The legends concerning these princes thus date back to a fairly ancient period, although it is doubtful whether they had the amplitude and the character which they assume in Firdausī's epic. These stories are not mythical, but merely epic, and they centre about the jealousy of two older brothers who, envious of the younger son of Farīdūn because he was braver and more beloved by his father, treacherously put him to death. Manushcithra, grandson of the unfortunate Īraj, was to be the avenger of his grandfather, aided by Keresāspa (Garshāsp), an ancient hero, who occupies a very secondary position in the *Shāhnāmah*, but is, nevertheless, one of the greatest figures of old Iranian tradition. Keresāspa, whose name means "with slender horses," is another son of Thrita Āthwya, the father of Farīdūn (Thraētaona) and seems originally to have been a doublet of the latter, especially as his main exploit is also the slaying of dragons.

With his strength and his club Keresāspa is the Hercules of Iran, and it is not in the least remarkable that he is supposed to have slain many foes both human and demoniacal, among them being not only Gandarewa and Srvara, but also Vareshava, Pitaona, Arezō-shamana, the sons of Nivika and of Dāshtayāni, the nine sons of Pathana, Snāvidhka, and the nine sons of Hitāspa, the murderer of his brother Urvākhshaya.[10] Moreover he is one of the heroes who, at the end of time, when Azhi Dahāka (Ḍaḥḥāk) will escape from the place of concealment where Thraētaona (Farīdūn) has fettered him, will slay the dragon and free the world.

He has accomplished his exploits under the protection of a third part of Yima's Glory (*Khvarenanh*) and he is, therefore, worshipped by the warriors to obtain strength "to withstand the dreadful arm and the hordes with wide battle array, with the large banner, the flag uplifted, the flag unfolded, the bloody flag; to withstand the brigand havoc-working, horrible, man-slaying, and pitiless; to withstand the evil done by the brigand." [11]

Among Keresāspa's feats some are described in the Avesta and in the Pāhlavī books.[12] His most dreadful fight was with the dragon Srvara ("Horned"),

"Which devoured men and horses,
Which was venomous and yellow,
Over which a flood of venom
Yellow poured, its depth a spear's length,

On whose back did Keresāspa [13]
Cook food in an iron kettle
As the sun drew nigh the zenith.
Heated grew the fiend and sweaty,
Forth from 'neath the kettle sprang he
And the boiling water scattered.
To one side in terror darted
Manly-minded Keresāspa."

The Pāhlavī sources further inform us that the dragon's teeth were as long as an arm, its ears as great as fourteen blankets, its eyes as large as wheels, and its horn as high as Ḍaḥḥāk. Undismayed, Keresāspa sprang on its back and ran for half a day on it, and, notwithstanding his alarm, finally contrived to smite its neck with his famous club, thus slaying the monster with a single blow.

In the case of Gandarewa the victory was no less brilliant. The personality of this demon is very interesting, for he is an Indo-Iranian spirit of the deep.[14] In India his abode is generally in the regions of the sky, where he hovers as a bright meteor, though he often appears likewise in the depths of the waters, where he courts the aqueous nymphs, the Apsarases, so that he becomes a genius of fertility. In Iran Gandarewa is a lord of the abyss who dwells in the waters and is the master of the deep. Sometimes he is a beneficent being who brings the haoma, but more often he withholds the plant as its jealous guardian. He is decidedly a fiend, although he has preserved the epithet "golden-heeled" to remind us of his previous brilliancy. He is a dragon like Azhi Dahāka or Srvara,[15] rushing on with open jaws, eager to destroy the world of the good creation. As Keresāspa went to meet him, he saw dead men sticking in Gandarewa's teeth, and when the monster had seized the hero's beard, both began to fight in the sea. After a conflict of nine days and nights Keresāspa overcame his adversary, and grasping the sole of his foot, he flayed off his skin up to his head and bound him hand and foot, dragging him to the shore of the sea. Even so, the fiend was not wholly subjugated, but slaughtered and ate Keresāspa's fifteen horses and pushed the hero himself blinded into a dense thicket. Meanwhile he carried off the hero's wife and family, but Keresāspa quickly recovered, went out to the sea, released the prisoners, and slew the fiend.[16]

Of Snāvidhka it is recorded that he used to kill men with his nails, and that his hands were like stones. To all he shouted:

> "'I am immature, not mature;
> But if I attain to manhood,
> Of the earth a wheel I'll make me,
> Of the sky I'll make a chariot;
> I'll bring down the Holy Spirit
> From the House of Praise [17] all radiant,
> Angra Mainyu I'll make fly up
> From the hideous depths of Hades;
> And they twain shall draw my chariot,
> Both those spirits, good and evil,
> if the manly-minded Keresāspa slay me not.' The manly-minded Keresāspa slew him." [18]

Arezō-shamana was a more sympathetic adversary, brave and valiant, always on his guard, and supple in his mode of fighting. Hitāspa was the murderer of Keresāspa's brother Urvākhshaya, a "wise chief of assemblies," and to avenge this crime the hero smote Hitāspa and bore him back on his chariot.[19]

Moreover the Iranian Hercules purged the land of highwaymen, who were so huge that the people used to say, "Below them are the stars and moon, and below them moves the sun at dawn, and the water of the sea reaches up to their knees." [20] Since Keresāspa could stretch no higher, he smote them on their legs, and falling, they shattered the hills on the earth.

A gigantic bird named Kamak, which overshadowed the earth and kept off the rain till the rivers dried up, eating up men and animals as if they were grains of corn, was also killed by Keresāspa, who shot arrows at it constantly for seven days and nights.[21] This story is evidently the adulterated form of an old myth of storm or rain.

A wolf called Kapūṭ or Pēhīn likewise fell, together with its nine cubs, at the hand of Keresāspa,[22] who was also compelled to fight even with the elements of nature, the wind being tempted to assail him when the demons said, "See, Keresāspa despises thee and resists thee, more than anyone else." Aroused by the taunt, the wind came on so strongly that every tree and shrub in its path was uprooted, while by its breath the whole earth was reduced to powder, and a dark cloud of dust arose. When it came to Keresāspa, however, it could not even move him from the spot, and the hero, seizing the spirit of the wind, overthrew him until he promised to go again below the earth.[23]

Unfortunately, the conqueror of so many foes was himself conquered by a woman, a witch (*pairikā*) called Khnāthaiti, who was in the court of Pitaona, a prince whom Keresāspa had also killed.[24] Under the influence of his wife he became addicted to Turanian idolatry and completely neglected the maintenance of the sacred fire. On account of this grievous sin Ahura Mazda permitted him to be wounded during his sleep by one of the Turks with whom he lived in the plain of Pēshyānsaī, and though he was not killed, he was brought into a state of lethargy.[25] Since that moment he has lain there in slumber, protected by the kingly Glory which he took from Yima and by nine thousand nine hundred and ninety-nine Fravashis, or guardian spirits.[26] Thus he will remain till the end of the world, when Ḍaḥḥāk (Azhi Dahāka), fettered by Farīdūn on Mount Damāvand, will be released by the powers of evil, who will rally for the last struggle against good. Freed from his chains, Ḍaḥḥāk will rush forth in fury and swallow everything on his way: a third of mankind, cattle, and sheep. He will smite the water, fire, and vegetation, and will commit all possible abuses. Then the water, the fire, and the vegetation will lament before Ahura Mazda and pray that Farīdūn may be revived to slay Ḍaḥḥāk, else fire declares that it will not heat, and water that it will flow no more. Then Mazda will send Sraosha to rouse Keresāspa, whom he will call three times. At the fourth summons the hero will wake and go forth to encounter Ḍaḥḥāk, and smiting him on the head with his famous club, will slay him, the death of the arch-fiend marking the beginning of the era of happiness.

Till then, however, as long as Keresāspa is asleep, his soul must make its abode either in paradise or in hell, but since the heinous offence which he committed against the fire made entrance into paradise very difficult for him in spite of all his exploits, he was sent to hell, though Zarathushtra obtained the promise that he would be summoned by Ahura Mazda. He complained at the hideous sights which he saw in the realm of punishment and said that he did not deserve such misery, for he had been a priest in Kābul, but Ahura Mazda with great severity reminded him of the fire, his son, which had been extinguished by him. He then implored Mazda's pardon, reciting all the deeds which he had performed: "If Srvara, the dragon, had not been killed by me, all thy creatures would have been annihilated by it. If Gandarewa had not been slain by me, Angra Mainyu would have become predominant over thy creatures"; but Mazda was inflexible: "Stand off, thou soul of Keresāspa! for thou shouldst be hideous in my eyes, because the fire, which is my son, was extinguished by thee." Nevertheless, when the spirits in heaven heard of Keresāspa's valorous feats, they wept aloud, and Zarathushtra intervened, so that after a discussion between him and the spirit of fire, who pleaded against Keresāspa, Gēush Urvan made supplication unto Mazda, while Zarathushtra, to propitiate Ātar's wrath, vowed that he would provide that the sanctity of the fire should be maintained on earth, wherefore the hero's soul was finally admitted into Garōṭmān ("House of Praise," "Paradise").[27]

As has already been said, no fair place is granted to the great national hero in the *Shāhnāmah*, his personality being divided by splitting the name Sāma Keresāspa Naire-manah into several personalities. In this way Sām became the grandfather, and

## PLATE XL

### Rustam and the White Demon

Entering the cavern where the demon lurks, the hero hews him limb from limb and finally slays him. In this miniature the sole traces of the animal nature of the demon are the horns springing from his head. From a Persian manuscript of the *Shāhnāmah*, dated 1605–08 A.D., now in the Metropolitan Museum of Art, New York.

Narīmān the great-grandfather, of Rustam, who took the place of Keresāspa as the Hercules of Iran, whereas Garshāsp, the tenth Shāh, who bears Keresāspa's name, is little more than a shadowy personality.[28]

Garshāsp appears for the first time as a prince who helped Minūcihr (Manushcithra) to take revenge for the death of his grandfather Īraj at the hands of his two brothers. Firdausī does not make it quite clear whether this Garshāsp is identical with the one who reigned as the tenth Shāh, but it seems more than likely that the two Garshāsps are the remnants of a hero who has been stripped of his exploits by the popularity of the new comer Rustam and his family, the deeds of the Rustamids being the central subject of Firdausī's epic throughout the reigns of several Shāhs, beginning with Minūcihr.

Minūcihr himself seems to be a faded personality. His name, Manushcithra, appears in the Avesta [29] and means "offspring of Manu" (the Vedic name of the first man), whereas in Pāhlavī literature it was held to signify "born on Mount Mānūsh." [30] Besides his punishment of his grandfather's murderers, the *Būndahish* records that he mounted a sheep of the kind called *kūrishk*, which was as high as a steed. He had a prosperous reign during which he made canals to regulate the course of the rivers, but for twelve years he was a captive of the Turanian king Afrāsiyāb (Pāhlavī Frāsīyāv, the Frangrasyan of the Avesta), who confined him in a mountain gorge and kept him there in misery till Aghrēraṭ (Avesta Aghraēratha, Persian Ighrīrath) saved him from his distress and consequently was slain by the tyrant.[31] This is not much, but is more than is told by the *Shāhnāmah*, which, indeed, devotes its account of Minūcihr's reign to the facts in connexion with Rustam's birth.

Sām is the most prominent vassal of Minūcihr. He is, as already noted, a fragment of Keresāspa's personality and betrays his origin in telling stories of dragons slain by him with a club that weighed three hundred *mans*.[32] His adversary was

"Like some mad elephant, with Indian sword
In hand. Methought, O Sháh! that e'en the mountains
Would cry to him for quarter! He pressed on,
. . . . . . . . . .
Then like a maddened elephant I dashed him
Upon the ground so that his bones were shivered."

More striking still is the slaying of the dragon which haunted the river Kashaf:

"That dragon cleared the sky
Of flying fowl and earth of beast of prey.
It scorched the vulture's feathers with its blast,
Set earth a-blazing where its venom fell,
Dragged from the water gruesome crocodiles,
And swiftly flying eagles from the air.
Men and four-footed beasts ceased from the land;
The whole world gave it room.
. . . . . . . . .
I came. The dragon seemed a lofty mountain
And trailed upon the ground its hairs like lassos.
Its tongue was like a tree-trunk charred, its jaws
Were open and were lying in my path.
Its eyes were like two cisterns full of blood.
It bellowed when it saw me and came on.
. . . . . . . . .
When it closed
And pressed me hard I took mine ox-head mace
And in the strength of God, the Lord of all,
Urged on mine elephantine steed and smote
The dragon's head: thou wouldst have said that heaven
Rained mountains down thereon. I smashed the skull,
As it had been a mighty elephant's,
And venom poured forth like the river Nile.
So struck I that the dragon rose no more." [33]

All these details strikingly resemble the story of Srvara.

A son is born to Sām in his old age, but the white hair of the babe so disgusts the father that he commands the child to be carried to the famous mountain Albūrz (Hara Berezaiti). There, fortunately, it is found by the Sīmurgh, the mythical bird Saēna, which we have described above and which takes care of the infant until he becomes a tall and sturdy youth.

In the meanwhile Sām regrets his fault, and being told in a dream where the child is, he goes to Mount Albūrz and fetches home his son, to whom he gives the name of Zāl. Zāl falls in love with Rūdābah, the daughter of the prince of Kābul, a descendant of Ḍaḥḥāk; but though the maid is fair and graceful, the marriage is opposed first by her father and then by the Shāh because she is of the race of the devilish King. This is the subject of a tale which Firdausī narrates with much talent, but it is no mythology, although the love for an Ahrimanian woman recalls the errors of Keresāspa. Finally, of course, every obstacle is removed, and Zāl marries Rūdābah.

Before long the princess is found to be pregnant, but no deliverance comes, and Rūdābah suffers in vain. Then a thought occurs to Zāl. On his departure from the nest where he had spent his infant years the Sīmurgh had given him one of its pinions as a talisman, bidding him burn the feather in case of misfortune, whereupon the bird would immediately come to his rescue. He did so, and the Sīmurgh, arriving instantly, told him that the birth would be no natural one. It bade him bring

"A blue-steel dagger, seek a cunning man,
Bemuse the lady first with wine to ease
Her pain and fear, then let him ply his craft
And take the Lion from its lair by piercing
Her waist while all unconscious, thus imbruing
Her side in blood, and then stitch up the gash.
Put trouble, care, and fear aside, and bruise
With milk and musk a herb that I will show thee
And dry them in the shade. Dress and anoint
Rúdába's wound and watch her come to life.
Rub o'er the wound my plume, its gracious shade
Will prove a blessing." [34]

The mandate of the Sīmurgh was scrupulously obeyed, and when Rūdābah awoke and saw her babe, she joyously cried, "I am delivered" (*birastam*), which in Persian happens to be a pun on the name of the future hero, Rustam, the ancient form of which (if the word were extant) would be Raodhatakhma

("Strong in Growth").[35] When little more than a child the promising youth breaks the neck of an elephant with a single blow of his mace and with some companions takes possession of a stronghold on Mount Sipand. Henceforth Rustam will be the Roland or the Cid of the Persian epic and he puts his sword — or rather his club — at the disposal of all Iranian kings in succession. There are no traces of mythology in his adventures, which are of a warlike character *par excellence*, although occasionally they are at the same time romantic, as in the story of his son Suhrāb, who was brought up among the Turanians, and whom his father killed in single combat, not knowing that he was his son.[36] The feats performed by Rustam in the service of the Iranian kings against the Turanians are attributed in Pāhlavī literature to the monarchs themselves, and it is evident that Rustam is a personality whose importance has been made much greater in comparatively recent times. He is the hero of Seistān and has clearly taken the place of Keresāspa and other Persian or Median heroes.

If Rustam is the Roland of Firdausī, Afrāsiyāb plays the part of the Emir Marsile, the chief of the Saracens in the French epic; he is the arch-unbeliever, the leader of the Turanian hordes.

In the Avesta he is known as Frangrasyan and has a much more mythical character than Rustam. Judging from the episode of his fight with Uzava, in which he is said to have detained the rivers so as to desolate Iran by drought, he belonged originally to a rain-myth. Ancient legend says that he lived in a stronghold (*hankana*) in the depths of the earth, where he offered an unsuccessful sacrifice to Ardvī Sūra Anāhita in the desire of seizing the kingly Glory of the Aryans which had departed from Yima and, escaping Azhi Dahāka, had taken refuge in the midst of the sea Vourukasha.[37]

The treacherous Turanian king tried to seize it, but though he stripped himself naked and swam to catch it, the Glory fled

## PLATE XLI

### The Death of Suhrāb

The figure of the king, bending over the son whom he has unwittingly slain, is full of pathos. Rustam's famous steed, Rakhsh, stands in the upper background. From a Persian manuscript of the *Shāhnāmah*, dated 1605–08 A.D., now in the Metropolitan Museum of Art, New York.

زدش بر زمین بر بکردار شیر — بدانست کو هم نماند بزیر
سبک تیغ تیز از میان برکشید — بر شیر بیدار دل بردرید
بپیچید سهراب و یک آه کرد — ز نیک و بد اندیشه کوتاه کرد
بدو گفت کین بر من از من رسید — زمانه بدست تو دادم کلید
تو زین بی‌گناهی که این گوژپشت — مرا برکشید و بزودی بکشت
ببازی بگویند همسال من — بخاک اندر آمد چنین یال من
نشان داد مادر مرا از پدر — ز مهر اندر آمد روانم بسر
همی جستمش تا ببینمش رو — بدادم کنون جان بدین آرزو
کنون گر تو در آب ماهی شوی — و یا چون شب اندر سیاهی شوی
وگر چون ستاره شوی بر سپهر — ببری ز روی زمین پاک مهر
بخواهد هم از تو پدر کین من — چو بیند که خشتست بالین من
ازین نامداران و گردنکشان — کسی هم برد سوی رستم نشان

away, and an arm of the sea, called lake Haosravah, resulted from the movement of the water. Twice again he renewed his effort, but each time a new gulf was formed, and all was in vain. Then the crafty Turanian rushed out of the sea, with evil words on his lips, uttering a curse and saying: "I have not conquered that Glory of the Aryan lands, born and unborn, and of righteous Zarathushtra.

> Both will I confound together,
> All things that are dry and fluid,
> Both great and good and beautiful;
> Sore distressed, Ahura Mazda
> Formeth creatures that oppose him."

Thus, according to this legend, he became a maleficent fiend, a drought-demon, who was made prisoner by Haoma and finally killed by Haosravah.[38] All these elements are preserved in Firdausī's legend, but the story has become a regular conflict between two nations or, at least, between two dynasties. This warfare is the kernel of the Iranian epic material, the struggle being divided into several episodes.

The first is the defeat of Naotara (Persian Naudhar), a son of Manushcithra (Persian Minūcihr). Although Firdausī places the event after Minūcihr's death, the older tradition [39] connects the facts with the reign of the latter king. The Iranians are made prisoners in the mountains of Padashkhvārgar (Ṭabaristān), but though Afrāsiyāb afflicts them with starvation and disease, his brother Aghraēratha (Persian Ighrīrath) sympathizes with the captives and releases them, whereupon Afrāsiyāb, in anger, kills his brother. Aghraēratha, although living among unbelievers, was a pious man, and after his death was placed among the immortals. Under the name of Gōpatshah [40] he dwells in the region of Saukavastān, near Airyana Vaējah, his form being that of a bull from his feet to his waist and of a man from his waist to his head. His home is on the sea-shore, where he continually pours holy water into the sea for the worship of God. Thus he kills innumerable noxious creatures, but if he should cease doing so, all those maleficent beings would fall on earth with the rain.[41]

The second episode is the battle between Afrāsiyāb and Uzava Tumāspana (Persian Zav), this hero being a nephew of Naotara, and his mother being the daughter of Afrāsiyāb's sorcerer. Afrāsiyāb had invaded Iran, stopped the course of all the rivers, and by his witchcraft prevented rain from falling, thus producing drought and starvation; [42] but Uzava, who, though a child, had the maturity and the strength of an adult,[43] frightened the sorcerers and their chief and caused rain to fall. In two myths, therefore, Afrāsiyāb inflicts starvation on the Iranians, and in the latter he does it by withholding the rain, so that his original nature as a rain-demon is scarcely open to question.

The third invasion is connected with the name of Kavi Kavāta (Persian Kai Qubād), the first king of the dynasty of the Kaiānians. In India the word *kavi* means "a sage," a respectable person in ancient days; in Iran it was applied to princes in olden times, and since those rulers originally were not Zoroastrians, *kavi* (Persian *kai*) in the Avesta often has the signification of "unbeliever," though this pejorative sense does not apply to the group of legendary kings who are regularly provided with that epithet and who, therefore, are called Kaiānians. Like Zāl, Kai Qubād is said to have been abandoned on Mount Albūrz at his birth, and there, protected only by a waist-cloth, he was freezing near a river when Zav perceived him and saved his life.[44] He remained on Albūrz until, Zav and his successor being dead, the Iranian throne was vacant; but meanwhile Afrāsiyāb had again invaded the country. Thereupon Zāl sent his son Rustam to Mount Albūrz to fetch Qubād and to make him the sovereign of all Iranian tribes; and then it was that Rustam, who had received Sām's club (i. e. the mace of Keresāspa), began to distinguish himself and to beat back the invaders.

The successor of Kavi Kavāta is Kavi Usan (Persian Kai

Kāūs), whose name has been compared with that of an ancient seer who is known as Kāvya Uśanas in the Vedas, where he is renowned for his wisdom. There he is said to have driven the cows on the path of the sun and to have fashioned for Indra the thunderbolt with which the god slew Vṛtra. The identification is not quite certain, however, because the character of Usan is completely altered in Iran into that of an ordinary king, although a trace of his quality of driver of cows may perhaps survive in the legend of his wonderful ox, to whose judgement all disputes were referred as to the boundary between Iran and Turan.[45] Yet Kai Kāūs was not really wise, for he was, at least according to Firdausī, an imperfect character, easily led astray by passion.[46] Legend has transferred wisdom to his minister Aoshnara, whose epithet is *pouru-jira*, "very intelligent."[47] While yet in his mother's womb, he taught many a marvel and at his birth he was able to confound Angra Mainyu by answering all the questions and riddles of Frācīh, the unbeliever.[48] This story is a replica of the legend of Yōishta, a member of the virtuous Turanian family of the Fryānas,[49] who preserved his town from the devastations of the ruffian Akhtya by resolving the ninety-nine riddles asked by that malicious spirit and by confounding the fiend with three other enigmas which he was unable to answer,[50] a tradition which reminds us of the legend of Œdipus. Aoshnara became the administrator of Usan's kingdom and taught many invaluable things to mankind, but unfortunately the inconstant monarch at last became tired of his minister's wisdom and put him to death.

Kai Kāūs was not only inconstant but presumptuous, for he ascended Mount Albūrz, where he built himself seven dwellings, one of gold, two of silver, two of steel, and two of crystal. He then endeavoured to restrain the Māzainyan daēvas, or demons of Māzandarān, only to be led into a trap by one of these evil beings who tempted him by making him discontented with his earthly sovereignty and by flattering him so as to induce him to aim at the sovereignty of the heavenly regions. Yielding to the tempter, he sought to reach the skies by means of a car supported by four eagles, and he also began to display insolence toward the sacred beings to such a degree that he lost his Glory. His troops were then defeated, and he was compelled to flee to the Vourukasha, where Nairyōsangha, the messenger of Ahura Mazda, was about to slay him when the Fravashi of Haosravah, yet unborn, implored that his grandfather might be spared on account of the virtues of the grandson.[51]

During this expedition — or during one to Hāmāvarān, which is only a duplicate of the other — the land of Iran, being abandoned by its ruler, was laid desolate by a fiend called Zainigāv, who had come from Arabia and in whose eye was such venom that he killed any man on whom he gazed. So dire was the calamity that the Iranians called their enemy Afrāsiyāb into their country to rid them of Zainigav, and for that task the Turanian received the kingly Glory which had abandoned the frivolous king Kai Kāūs. Afrāsiyāb, however, abused his power, and the Iranians had once more to be saved by Rustam, who released Kai Kāūs and expelled the Turanians.

Kai Kāūs had married a Turanian woman named Sūdābah, a vicious creature who made shameful propositions to Syāvarshan (Persian Kai Siyāvakhsh), who was the son of a previous wife of her husband and a superb youth. Since, however, the pious young man rejected her love, she calumniated him to Kai Kāūs, so that Syāvarshan had to flee to Afrāsiyāb, who received him well and even gave him his daughter in marriage; but the honour with which he was welcomed roused the jealousy of Keresavazdah (Persian Garsīvaz), the brother of Afrāsiyāb, who by false accusations persuaded the king to put Siyāvakhsh to death.

To avenge this deed was the life-task of his son Haosravah (Persian Kai Khusrau), the greatest king of the Kaiānian dynasty. His name means "of good renown, glorious," and perhaps he was originally the same person as the Vedic hero

## PLATE XLII

### KAI KĀŪS ATTEMPTS TO FLY TO HEAVEN

The ambitious king fastens four young eagles to the corners of his throne, making them fly upward by attaching raw meat to four spears. As he rises through the clouds, the animals on the mountain-top look at him with amazement. The king's features have been obliterated by some pious Muhammadan who was offended by the transgression of the prohibition against portraying living creatures (cf. Plate XLIV). From a Persian manuscript of the *Shāhnāmah*, dated 1587–88 A. D., now in the Metropolitan Museum of Art, New York.

Suśravas, who helped Indra to crush twenty warriors mounted on chariots.[52] It is, indeed, a striking coincidence that in the Avesta the gallant Haosravah, who united the Aryan nations into one kingdom, begs of Ardvī Sūra as a boon, not only that he may become the sovereign lord of all countries, but also

> "That of all the yokèd horses
> I may drive my steeds the foremost
> O'er the long length of the racecourse;
> That we break not through the pitfall
> Which the foe, with treacherous purpose,
> Plots against me while on horseback."[53]

The war waged by Haosravah against Afrāsiyāb is a long one, full of incidents of a fine epic character as we find them in the *Shāhnāmah*, but all this has been grafted on the old legend of Frangrasyan's death, which originally was in close connexion with the story of the vain attempts of the impious king to seize the Glory of the Aryan monarchs. As we have already seen, Frangrasyan, enraged by his failure, was swearing, cursing, and blaspheming in his subterranean abode; but at that very moment he was overheard by Haoma (probably the "White Haoma," the tree of all remedies, which grows in the sea Vourukasha), who managed to fetter the Turanian murderer and to drag him bound to King Haosravah.

> "Kavi Haosravah then slew him
> Within sight of Lake Caēcasta,
> Deep and with wide spreading waters,
> Thus avenging the foul murder
> Of his father, brave Syāvarshan."[54]

In this contest, being helped by the fire of warriors that was burning on his horse's mane, so that he could see in the subterranean darkness where the Turanian was living and where he had his idols,[55] Haosravah destroyed everything and then established the fire on Mount Asnavand. The intervention of

Haoma (the drink of the gods when they fight the demons), and the presence of a supernatural fire, of the white steed, and of the cavern, as well as the location of the contest on a lake, point to some natural myth as the origin of the story, though it is too adulterated to admit of any convincing interpretation. Firdausī, of course, introduces still more profound alterations. Instead of being in his own subterranean palace, Afrāsiyāb is supposed to have taken refuge in a cavern after having been completely beaten by Kai Khusrau and having taken to flight, while Haoma has become the hermit Hūm, who overhears him bewailing his defeat and tries to capture the fugitive, who escapes by plunging into the lake. Kai Khusrau is called immediately and seizes Garsīvaz (Keresavazdah), the murderer of Siyāvaḳḥsh. To compel Afrāsiyāb to emerge from his retreat his beloved brother Garsīvaz is tortured, and finally both brothers are put to death.[56]

Having achieved the greatest exploit of the epic and having avenged his father, Haosravah fears that he may lapse into pride and meet the same end as Yima. He becomes melancholy, resolves to resign the throne to Aurvaṭ-aspa (Persian Luhrāsp), and finally rides with his paladins into the mountains, where he disappears. A few knights follow him till the end, but are lost in the snow, so that he alone, guided by Sraosha, arrives alive in heaven, where, in a secret place and adorned with a halo of glory, he sits on a throne until the renovation of the world.[57]

This very noteworthy legend of the retirement of the mighty king and warrior has been compared by Darmesteter [58] with an episode of the *Mahābhārata*, the great Indian epic, where the hero Yudhiṣṭhira, weary of the world, designated his successors and with his four brothers set out on a journey northward toward the mountains and the deserts of Himavant (the Himālayas). One after the other all his companions expired exhausted on the way, but he with his faithful dog, who was Dharma ("Righteousness") in disguise, entered heaven, not having tasted death. Unless the story has been borrowed from the Indians, it is Indo-Iranian, the latter explanation being the more probable since the immortality of Haosravah is already known in the Avesta.[59]

Among the companions of Haosravah who died on the way were Gīv, son of Gūdarz, both gallant heroes who played an important part in the war against Afrāsiyāb, and Ṭūs, son of Naotara (Persian Naudhar), the last monarch of the Pīshdādian dynasty. He had been barred from his realm by the accession of the Kaiānian kings because he was too frivolous, but after having been the competitor of Haosravah, he became his friend. An epic of Naotara's sons seems to have existed in which Ṭūs was the conqueror of the sons of Vaēsaka (Persian Vīsah), the uncle of Afrāsiyāb, for he is said to have besieged them in the pass of Khshathrō-Suka on the top of the holy and lofty Mount Kangha;[60] and as a reward for his exploits and after his death he will be among the thirty who will help Saoshyant at the end of the world.[61]

His brother Vīstauru ("Opposed to Sinners"[62]) is famed for having obtained from Ardvī Sūra, when he was pursuing idolators, the power to cross the River Vītanguhaiti.

> "'This is true, in sooth veracious,
> Ardvī Sūra Anāhita,
> that as many demon-worshippers have been slain by me as I have hairs on my head. Therefore do thou, Ardvī Sūra Anāhita, provide me a dry crossing[63]
> O'er the good Vītanguhaiti.'
> Ardvī Sūra Anāhita hastened down
> With a lovely maiden's body,
> Very strong, of goodly figure,
> Girded high and standing upright,
> Nobly born, of brilliant lineage,
> Wearing golden foot-gear shining
> And bedecked with all adornment.
> Certain waters made she stand still,
> Others caused she to flow forward,
> And a crossing dry provided
> O'er the good Vītanguhaiti."[64]

After the reign of Kai Khusrau the scene of Firdausī's epic shifts toward Balkh in Bactria, and the military character of the poem yields to more religious interests. We have, indeed, arrived at the point where legends, which are for the most part of a mythical character, are brought into connexion with traditions concerning the origins of the Zoroastrian religion, of Zoroaster himself, and of the persons around him.

In Firdausī's view the successor of Kai Khusrau is Luhrāsp, the Aurvaṭ-aspa of the Avesta, who is renowned only as the father of Vīshtāspa, the first Zoroastrian king, and of Zairivairi ("Golden-Breastplated"; Persian Zarīr). The deeds of the latter are of much the same kind as those of other Iranian heroes. He is a slayer of Turanians, and near the river Dāitya he killed Humayaka, a demon-worshipper who had long claws and lived in eight caverns, and he also did to death the wicked Arejaṭ-aspa,[65] but was treacherously assassinated by the wizard Vīdrafsh and avenged by his son Bastvar.[66] All this savours pretty much of a combat with dragons.

In the Greek author Athenaeus [67] Zairivairi appears under the name Zariadres and is said to be a son of Adonis and Aphrodite. This is a truly mythic genealogy, for Aphrodite is the usual Greek translation of Anāhita, the goddess of the waters, and her most natural lover is Apãm Napāt, "the Child of the Waters," whose name the Greek writer here renders by Adonis, the habitual paramour of Aphrodite. A very frequent epithet of Apãm Napāt is *aurvaṭ-aspa* ("with swift steeds"), which is precisely the name of Zairivairi's father. Accordingly, Darmesteter thinks [68] that Zairivairi is a mythical being and extends the conclusion to his brother Vīshtāspa and even to the prophet Zarathushtra. This opinion is rejected by Orientalists of the present day, who, not without reason, think that Zarathushtra actually existed; but nevertheless it is possible that Zairivairi has been introduced into Vīshtāspa's family by a contamination of legends or by a similarity of names, such as has produced many errors concerning Vīshtāspa himself. Zairivairi

## PLATE XLIII

### Gushtāsp Kills a Dragon

The hero slays a dragon in serpent form. The representation of the desert scene is very well done, and Perso-Mongolian influence is strongly marked. From a Persian manuscript of the *Shāhnāmah*, dated 1587–88 A.D., now in the Metropolitan Museum of Art, New York.

اژدها کشتن گشتاسب در ولایت روم

is the hero of a romantic adventure, which is attributed to his brother Gushtāsp (Vīshtāspa) in the *Shāhnāmah*.[69] He was the handsomest man of his time, just as Odatis, the daughter of King Omartes, was the most beautiful woman among the Iranians. They saw one another in a dream and fell in love, but when the princess was invited to a great feast at which she had to make her choice and throw a goblet to the young noble who pleased her, she did not see Zairivairi. Leaving the room in tears, she perceived a man in Scythian attire at the door of the palace and recognized the hero of her dream. It was Zairivairi, who had come in haste, knowing the intentions of Omartes, and the lovers fled together.[70]

Vīshtāspa himself is known for heroic exploits. He defeated some unbelievers, like Tāthryavant, Peshana, and Arejaṭaspa (Persian Arjāsp), king of the Hyaonians, although it is difficult to say whether these are more or less historical facts in connexion with the protector of Zoroaster or are mythical exploits attributed to some other Vīshtāspa who became identified with the prophet's patron. The old tradition concerning the latter reports that he was the husband of Hutaosa, a name which is the same as that of Darius's wife Atossa. He had in his possession the Iranian Glory, which he is said to have taken to Mount Rōshan, where it still is; and he was converted to the new faith after having imprisoned Zoroaster, who had been falsely accused by priests of the old religion, but had proved his innocence by miraculously curing the favourite horse of the king.[71] In Vīshtāspa's court was the important family of the Hvōgvas, containing Jāmāspa, the minister of Vīshtāspa, who became the husband of Zoroaster's daughter Pourucista and who was one of the prophet's first protectors; while his brother Frashaoshtra was the father-in-law of Zoroaster through the latter's marriage to Hvōvī.

Zoroaster (Zarathushtra), of the Spitama family, was the son of Pourushaspa, who is said to have been the fourth priest of Haoma,[72] but we know very little about him from the Avesta itself. Later literature, on the other hand, concocted a life of Zoroaster which is full of marvels and in which the prophet is in continual intercourse with Ahura Mazda and the Amesha Spentas, achieving all manner of prodigious deeds. These legends appear comparatively late in Mazdeism, centuries after Zoroaster's life, and probably contain very few historical elements, although they have accumulated stories borrowed from various sources and even include pious forgeries. The Avesta knows of an intervention of divine beings only at Zoroaster's birth. A plant of haoma contained the prophet's Fravashi, or pre-created soul, which Pourushaspa, the father of Zoroaster and a priest of Haoma, happened to absorb. He married Dughdhōva, who had received the *khvarenanh* which has been so frequently mentioned, and thus the Glory of Yima himself was transferred to Zoroaster. The daēvas repeatedly sought to kill the prophet both before and after his birth, and the adorers of idols persecuted him, but in vain. Ahura Mazda then entered into communion with him and revealed the religion to him. For ten years he had only one disciple, his cousin Maidhyōi-māongha, but at last he won converts in Vīshtāspa's court among the members of the Hvōgva family, the king himself becoming a believer through the insistence of his wife Hutaosa. A long war followed between Vīshtāspa and Arejaṭ-aspa, king of the Hyaonians, who was determined to suppress Zoroastrianism, and though the prophet's brothers Zairivairi (Persian Zarīr) and Spentōdāta (Persian Isfandyār) fought gallantly, Zoroaster was slain by the Turanian Brāṭrō-rēsh, one of the *karapans* (idolatrous priests) who had tried to kill him at his birth.

Zoroaster has left three germs in this world, and they are like three flames which Nairyōsangha, the messenger of the gods and a form of Agni,[73] has deposited in Lake Kãsu (the Hāmūn Swamp in Seistān), where they are watched by ninety-nine thousand nine hundred and ninety-nine Fravashis. Near that lake is a mountain inhabited by faithful Zoroastrians,

# PLATE XLIV

## Sculpture Supposed to Represent Zoroaster

Parsi tradition seeks to identify this figure with Zoroaster, and the conventional modern pictures of the Prophet are of this general type. The identification is by no means certain, for the figure has also been held to represent Ahura Mazda or — with much greater probability — Mithra. Ahura Mazda regularly appears as a bearded man in a winged disk (see Plate XXXIV, No. 5); identification with Mithra is favoured by the sunflower on which the figure stands and by the mace which he holds (cf. *Yasht*, vi. 5, x. 96). The face is mutilated, probably by the early Arab conquerors, who, as strict Muhammadans, objected to representations of living beings (cf. the similar mutilations in miniature paintings, Plate XLII). From a Sassanian sculpture at Takht-i-Bustān, Kirmānshāh. After a photograph by Professor A. V. Williams Jackson.

and once in each millennium a maiden, bathing in the waters, will receive one of those germs. Thus three prophets (Saoshyants, "They Who Will Advantage") will be born in succession: first Ukhshyaṭ-ereta (Hūshēṭar), then Ukhshyaṭ-nemah (Hūshēṭar-māh), and finally Astvaṭ-ereta, the Saoshyant *par excellence*. They will reveal themselves in periods when evil will be prevalent and will put an end to wickedness. The last Saoshyant will come when Ḍaḥḥāk will have desolated the world after having broken his fetters on Mount Damāvand; but Keresāspa, as we have seen,[74] will slay him at the very instant when Saoshyant appears with the kingly Glory (*Khvarenanh*), and when he will definitely conquer the Druj (the principle of falsehood), Angra Mainyu, and the evil creation.

# CHAPTER VI

# THE LIFE TO COME

THE account of the Saoshyants, the future sons of Zoroaster, brings us to the theme of Iranian eschatology. Like Odysseus in Greece, or Dante in the *Divina Commedia*,[1] Arṭā Vīrāf, a wise and virtuous Mazdean, is supposed in a late Pāhlavī book to have visited the other world, and it will be interesting to follow him in his journey to see what were the Mazdean conceptions of heaven and of hell.

When the soul of Vīrāf went forth from its body, the first thing which it beheld was the Cinvat Bridge (the bridge of "the Divider") which all souls must cross before they pass to the future world. There he saw before him a damsel of beautiful appearance, full-bosomed, charming to heart and soul; and when he asked her, "Who art thou? and what person art thou? than whom, in the world of the living, any damsel more elegant, and of more beautiful body than thine, was never seen by me," she replied that she was his own religion (*daēna*) and his own deeds — "it is on account of thy will and actions, that I am as great and good and sweet-scented and triumphant and undistressed as appears to thee."

Then the Cinvat Bridge became wider, and with the assistance of Sraosha ("Obedience to the Law") and Ātar ("Fire") Vīrāf could easily cross. Both Yazatas promised to show him heaven and hell, but before entering the kingdom of the blest, he had to pass through Hamīstakān, the resting-place of those whose good works and sins exactly counterbalance. There they await the renovation of the world, their only sufferings being from cold and heat.

Passing from Hamīstakān, Vīrāf ascended the three steps of "good thought, good word, good deed," which are the abodes of the souls of those who did not practise the specific Mazdean virtues, although they were righteous men. These steps lead to Garōtmān (Avesta Garō Nmāna, "House of Praise"), and there dwell the souls of men who constantly practised the Zoroastrian precepts: the liberal, who walk adorned in all splendour; those who chanted the *Gāthās* (the "Hymns" of Zoroaster), in gold-embroidered raiment; those who contracted next-of-kin marriages,[2] illuminated by radiance from above; those who killed noxious creatures; the agriculturists; the shepherds. All of them are brilliant and walk about in great pleasure and joy. Then the pilgrims came to a river which souls were endeavouring to cross, some being able to do this easily, and others failing utterly. In reply to Vīrāf's questions Ātar explained that the river came from the tears which men shed from their eyes in unlawful lamentation for the departed, and that those who could not cross were the souls for whom their relatives made an exaggerated and irreligious display of grief. Ātar also showed a lake whose water was the sap of wood which had been placed on the sacred fire without being quite dry.

Returning to the Cinvat Bridge, Vīrāf and his guides followed the soul of a wicked man, just arrived from earth. In its first night of hell it must endure as much misfortune as a man can bear in a whole unhappy life. A dry and stinking cold wind comes to meet that man, and he sees his vile life under the shape of a profligate woman, naked, decayed, gaping, and bandy-legged. Descending the three steps of "evil thought, evil word, evil deed," the soul of the wicked arrives at the greedy jaws of hell, which is a most frightful pit, where the darkness is so thick that the hand can grasp it, and where the stench makes every one stagger and fall. Each of the damned thinks, "I am alone," and when three days and three nights have elapsed, he wails, "The nine thousand years are completed, and they will not release me!" Everywhere are noxious creatures, the smallest of them as high as mountains, and they tear and worry the souls of the wicked as a dog does a bone.

For special crimes there are special punishments. The woman who has been unfaithful to her husband is suspended by her breasts, and scorpions seize her whole body, the same creatures biting the feet of those who have polluted the earth by walking without shoes. The woman who has insulted her husband is suspended by her tongue. A wicked king must hang in space, flogged by fifty demons. The man who has killed cattle unlawfully suffers in his limbs, which are broken and separated from one another. The miser is stretched upon a rack, and a thousand demons trample him. The liar sees his tongue gnawed by worms. The unjust man who did not pay the salary of his workmen is doomed to eat human flesh. The woman who has slain her own child must dig into a hill with her breasts and hold a millstone on her head. The bodies of impostors and deceivers fall in rottenness. The man who has removed the boundary stones of others so as to make his own fields larger must dig into a hill with his fingers and nails. The breaker of promises and contracts, whether with the pious or with the wicked — since Mithra is both for the faithful and the unbelievers — is tortured by pricking spurs and arrows. Under the Cinvat Bridge there is an abyss for the most heinous sinners, this pit being so deep and so stinking that if all the wood of the earth were burned in it, it would not even emit a perceptible smell. There the souls of the wicked stand, as close as the ear to the eye, and as many as the hairs on the mane of a horse, and they also are submitted to various torments according to their different offences. At the very bottom of the abyss is Angra Mainyu (Ahriman), the Evil Spirit, who ridicules and mocks the wicked in hell, saying, "Why did you ever eat the bread of Ahura Mazda, and do my work? and thought not of your own creator, but practised my will?"

It would be interesting to know how much in Arṭā Vīrāf's

visions was influenced by the conceptions of other religions, including Judaism and Christianity. That the Semites influenced Iranian thought in some measure is obvious—the myth of the attempt of Kai Kāūs to fly to heaven, for instance, shows a remarkable parallelism to the Babylonian story of Etana, who sought to ascend on an eagle's back to the sky that he might secure the "plant of life."[3] The close association of Jews and Persians in the Exilic and post-Exilic periods seems to have caused some interchange of religious concepts, though the precise degree of this influence is still *sub judice*.[4]

# CHAPTER VII

# CONCLUSION

THE special interest presented to the mythologist by the study of Iranian myths lies in the fact that they show with ideal clearness the various stages in the evolution of myth toward historical legend.

As is well known, a myth originally is an effort toward accounting for some phenomenon. The attempt is made, of course, with the mental tendencies of people of a fairly elementary culture, but it is clear enough that primitive man does not only aim at giving an explanation, but at making it picturesque and appealing to his imagination; and it is equally obvious that he desires to stimulate the fancy of his fellow men by using symbols, testing their ingenuity by transferring one order of facts to another. This tendency generates parable, moral fiction, and riddle, and it is difficult to doubt that myth is one more aspect of that same turn of mind when we compare old riddles with old myths.

Otto Schrader has collected [1] several Indo-European riddles that are very instructive in this regard, and an episode of the *Shāhnāmah* also illustrates this explanation of myth. Thus, in Firdausī's epic [2] Minūcihr tests Zāl by hard questions, concocted by the shrewd priests, who formulate a series of riddles that are very much of the same kind as those which are found among people of primitive culture and which Schrader considers to be a source of myths. Zāl is asked what are a dozen cypresses with thirty boughs on each, and he finds them to be the twelve moons of every year, each moon having thirty days. Two horses, one white and one black, moving rapidly to catch each other, but in vain, prove to be day and night. A lofty pair of cypresses in which a bird nests, on the one at morning and on the other at evening, represents the two portions of the sky, and the bird which flies between them is the sun. The turn of mind which generated such stories would readily produce myths.

In the *Ṛgveda*, where we have found so many names of gods and heroes of Iranian mythology, mythical symbolism is rife and in full operation. Not only does the singer in his prayers remind his god of the myths that are current about him, but he makes new ones and gives another turn to mythical interpretations of facts because he is conscious that they are myths. For that reason the *Ṛgveda* makes us live in an atmosphere that is truly mythic, but, on the other hand, it presents such a free treatment of the various stories that it is much more difficult to give a clear account of the old Indian myths than of the Iranian legends. Vedic mythology is more fluid; the singer deals freely with the stories, mixes them, makes new combinations with the traditional elements, and even goes so far as to invent myths which are entirely new.

If we compare the Iranian situation with the Vedic, which, of course, at one time was the Indo-Iranian status, we observe that the Mazdean Iranians have plenty of myths, but that, to a great extent, the creative tendency has been checked. Their myths appear rather as survivals of prior times, and, consequently, they are more clearly delineated than in the Veda. In addition to this, they have been systematized according to the general tendency of Mazdeism, and the necessity of fitting them into the dualistic scheme accounts for the monotonous character of these myths, in which a good being is always at war with some evil one. The good beings are pretty much identical with one another, and the fiends are almost the same throughout. A sure proof that the real meaning of the myths has faded is the great number of epithets and details that are quite clear in the original form of the story, but are often meaningless and merely traditional in Mazdean lore.

The special evolution of myths in Iran assumes three forms. (a) The myth, being no longer understood as such, becomes a mere tale and, as is the case with tales, is apt to be subdivided into several stories or to be reproduced many times with different names. This has especially been the case with the storm-myth. The dragon is Azhi, Srvara, Zainigav, Apaosha, Gandarewa, etc.; the youthful and godlike victor is Thraētaona, Keresāspa, Raodhatakhma (Rustam), Haosravah, etc.

Myths are duplicated. Besides Yima-Yimak, we find Māshya-Māshyōī. Kavi Usan is twice a prisoner; Kavi Keresavazdah has been calumniated twice; Urupi and Keresāspa both ride on a demon; Kavi Kavāta and Zāl are both abandoned on Mount Albūrz at their birth; Thraētaona and Vīstauru both cross a river in a miraculous way; Yōishta and Aoshnara both answer the riddles of a sphinx. All heroes marry Turanian girls, and all stories take place on Mount Hara Berezaiti (Albūrz) or in the sea Vourukasha, etc., etc.

(b) On the other hand, several myths coalesce into one story, the most complete instance being the legend of Yima, which unites a story of primeval twins, a winter-myth, a myth comparing sunset to the death of man, a story of women captured by a fiend, etc.

(c) There is a gradual anthropomorphization of the myths. On the one hand, the mythical contest is changed into a moral one, the cloud-dragons, imprisoners of water, becoming heretics or enemies of the Zoroastrian religion. A curious instance of this is Farīdūn's conversion of Jamshīd's daughters, who had been brought up in vice and pagan lore by Ḍaḥḥāk, this being a transformation of the traditional story of the storm-god releasing the women of the cloud, i.e. the imprisoned waters. In Yima's story a moral motive has been introduced into the darkening of the sun by the cloud-dragon.

On the other hand, the mythical material becomes historical or, at least, epic. Monsters, dragons, etc., become Turanians, and the gods are transformed into kings of a purely human character, so that in many cases in the *Shāhnāmah* it is impossible to determine whether we are dealing with some historical event, more or less embellished by legend, or with a nature-myth that has been humanized. Ḍaḥḥāk is an Arabian king; Farīdūn is an audacious soldier; haoma, the draught of immortality, becomes a hermit in the story of Afrāsiyāb, etc.

In the legend of Yima we see all successive stages. First we have the setting sun, and then the setting sun, showing the path to the departed, becomes their sire, and his solar quality fades away. He is thus evolved into the first mortal or the king of the dead, and finally becomes an ordinary Iranian monarch of ancient times.

This transformation has, it is true, deprived the Iranians of the great source of Indian poetry, but has resulted, on the other hand, in providing them with a rich epic material, the direction in which their literature has been developed. They were also creative in this domain, for they wove many legends around their real kings, their prophet, etc. Both sources of inspiration have been so blended that in the *Shāhnāmah* Rustam's mace, which was originally the thunderbolt of Indra, is swung against the castellan bishops of the Syrian Church,[3] and that Zairivairi, a son of Apãm Napāt, is the lover of the daughter of the Emperor of Byzantium.

# NOTES

# INDIAN

## Chapter I

1. *Original Sanskrit Texts*, v. 356, note.
2. This is what F. Max Müller (*Ancient Sanskrit Literature*, London, 1859, pp. 526 ff.) called "henotheism."
3. *Original Sanskrit Texts*, v. 64, note.
4. See M. Bloomfield, *Religion of the Veda*, pp. 12, 126 ff. For the Iranian Asha see *infra*, pp. 260, 264.
5. For the Iranian conceptions of Ahura Mazda and Mithra see *infra*, pp. 260–61, 275 ff., 287–88, 305 ff.
6. For Ouranos see *Mythology of All Races*, Boston, 1916, i. 5–6, and for Moira see *ib.* pp. 283–84.
7. See H. Winckler, in *Mitteilungen der deutschen Orientgesellschaft*, No. 35 (1907); E. Meyer, "Das erste Auftreten der Arier in der Geschichte," in *Sitzungsberichte der königlich-preussischen Akademie der Wissenschaften*, 1908, pp. 14–19, and *Geschichte des Altertums*, I. ii. 651 ff. (3rd ed., Berlin, 1913); H. Jacobi, in *JRAS* 1909, pp. 721 ff., H. Oldenberg, ib. pp. 1095 ff., J. H. Moulton, *Early Zoroastrianism*, London, 1913, pp. 6 ff.
8. For the Amesha Spentas see *infra*, p. 260.
9. R. T. H. Griffith, *Hymns of the Rigveda*, ii. 87.
10. See *infra*, pp. 282, 294, 304.
11. See M. Bloomfield, in *American Journal of Philology*, xvii. 428 (1896), from *vi*+*snu* (cf. *sānu*, "back").
12. See *Mythology of All Races*, Boston, 1916, i. 26–27, 246–47.
13. See *Mythology of All Races*, Boston, 1916, i. 245–46.
14. See A. Hillebrandt, *Vedische Mythologie*, iii. 157 ff.
15. See *Shāhnāmah*, tr. J. Mohl, Paris, 1876–78, i. 69–70.
16. See *infra*, pp. 267, 340.
17. The word *śiva* means "auspicious."
18. See L. von Schroeder, *Mysterium und Mimus im Rigveda*, pp. 47 ff., 124 ff.

## Chapter II

1. See A. Hillebrandt, *Vedische Mythologie*, ii. 122–23.
2. Cf. *Mythology of All Races*, Boston, 1916, i. 208–09, 298.

3. See M. Bloomfield, in *JAOS* xvi. 1 ff. (1894); H. Usener, in *Rheinisches Museum*, lx. 26 ff. (1905).

4. See *infra*, pp. 265, 282.

5. See A. A. Macdonell and A. B. Keith, *Vedic Index*, ii. 434–37.

6. R. T. H. Griffith, *Hymns of the Rigveda*, iv. 355–56.

7. See J. Rhys, *Lectures on the Origin and Growth of Religion as illustrated by Celtic Heathendom*, London, 1888, pp. 114–15.

8. See L. R. Farnell, *Cults of the Greek States*, Oxford, 1896–1908, iii. 50 ff.

9. This expression denotes first five tribes famous in Vedic history, and then all men generally.

10. See A. Hillebrandt, *Vedische Mythologie*, iii. 418–19.

11. See A. B. Keith, in *JRAS* 1915, pp. 127 ff.

12. See *infra*, pp. 325–26.

13. See L. von Schroeder, *Mysterium und Mimus im Rigveda*, pp. 304–25.

14. See L. von Schroeder, *op. cit.* pp. 52, 63.

15. See *infra*, pp. 306–09.

16. *Indische Studien*, iv. 341 (1858).

17. Hence *iṣṭāpūrta*, "sacrifice and baksheesh," go together; see M. Bloomfield, *Religion of the Veda*, pp. 194 ff.

18. R. T. H. Griffith, *Hymns of the Rigveda*, iv. 133.

## Chapter III

1. See A. Hillebrandt, *Vedische Mythologie*, iii. 430 ff. Unlike M. Haug (*Essays on the Sacred Language, Writings, and Religion of the Parsis*, 3rd ed., London, 1884, pp. 287 ff.), Hillebrandt places the hostile contact with Iran after the period of the *Ṛgveda* and associates it with an older form of Iranian religion, not with Zarathushtra's teaching.

2. In Videgha Māthava V. Henry (*La Magie dans l'Inde antique*, 2nd ed., p. xxi.) sees the Indian Prometheus.

3. See A. B. Keith, in *JRAS* 1911, pp. 794–800.

4. Kubera appears as king of the Rakṣases in *Śatapatha Brāhmaṇa*, XIII. iv. 3. 10; cf. *Atharvaveda* VIII. x. 28.

## Chapter IV

1. See *Mythology of All Races*, Boston, 1916, i. 17–18.

2. Apparently each of these years is equal to 360 years of man; so Manu, i. 69, and the *Purāṇas* (cf. H. H. Wilson, *Viṣṇu Purāṇa*, ed. F. Hall, i. 49–50, and E. W. Hopkins, in *JAOS* xxiv. 42 ff. [1903]).

3. See B. C. Mazumdar, in *JRAS* 1907, pp. 337–39; Sir R. G.

Bhandarkar, *Vaiṣṇavism, Śaivism, and Minor Religious Systems*, pp. 113–15.

4. *Religions of India*, pp. 465 ff.

5. *Indien und das Christentum*, pp. 215 ff.; for another view see Bhandarkar, *op. cit.* p. 12.

6. See A. B. Keith, in *JRAS* 1908, pp. 172 ff., 1912, pp. 416 ff., 1915, pp. 547–49, 1916, pp. 340 ff., and in *ZDMG* lxiv. 534–36 (1910).

7. *Das Rāmāyaṇa*, pp. 127 ff. For a different view see J. von Negelein, in *WZKM* xvi. 226 ff. (1902).

## Chapter V

1. This story forms the subject of a Vedic imitation, the *Suparṇādhyāya* (edited by E. Grube, Berlin, 1875); cf. J. Hertel, in *WZKM* xxiii. 299 ff. (1909), and H. Oldenberg, in *ZDMG* xxxvii. 54–86 (1893).

2. See J. Charpentier, in *ZDMG* lxiv. 65–83 (1910), lxvi. 44–47 (1912).

3. This is a new element in the tale and gives the best ground for regarding the narrative as Babylonian in origin; see M. Winternitz, in *Mitteilungen der anthropologischen Gesellschaft in Wien*, xxxi. 321 ff. (1901).

4. See W. Caland, *Über das rituelle Sūtra des Baudhāyana*, Leipzig, 1903, p. 21; A. B. Keith, in *JRAS* 1913, pp. 412–17.

5. See G. A. Grierson, in *ZDMG* lxvi. (1912) 49 ff.

6. This idea is based on a popular etymological connexion with Sanskrit *yam*, "to restrain"; but as a matter of fact the word Yama means "Twin."

## Chapter VI

1. This explanation is based on a purely fanciful etymology of *mām*, "me," and *dhā*, "to suck."

2. Cf. J. F. Fleet, in *JRAS* 1905, pp. 223–36; R. Garbe, *Indien und das Christentum*, pp. 131 ff.

3. See Sir G. A. Grierson, in *JRAS* 1913, p. 144.

4. See A. B. Keith, in *JRAS* 1908, pp. 172–73.

5. Sir R. G. Bhandarkar (*Vaiṣṇavism, Śaivism, and Minor Religious Systems*, pp. 35 ff.) seeks (though without success) to show that Kṛṣṇa as a cowherd is late.

6. See C. Lassen, *Indische Alterthumskunde*, ii. 811, 1107 ff. A. Barth (*Religions of India*, p. 200, note), while doubting this view, points out that the androgynous form of Śiva was known to Bardesanes (in Stobaeus, *Ecl. phys.* i. 56).

7. Sir R. G. Bhandarkar (*Vaiṣṇavism, Śaivism, and Minor Religious Systems*, pp. 147–49) ascribes the growth of a single deity to the period about the sixth century A. D. The Vināyakas, who appear reduced to one in Gaṇapati, or Gaṇeśa, are found in the *Mānava Gṛhya Sūtra* (ii. 14), and the *Mahābhārata* (xiii. 151. 26) mentions Vināyakas and Gaṇeśvaras as classes. Cf. M. Winternitz, in *JRAS* 1898, pp. 380–84.

8. See Sir R. G. Bhandarkar, *Vaiṣṇavism, Śaivism, and Minor Religious Systems*, pp. 153–55; R. Chanda, *The Indo-Aryan Races*, Rajshahi, 1916, pp. 223 ff.

## Chapter VII

1. Pāli is the term used to describe the language in which the Buddhist texts are preserved. It is a literary dialect whose origin is uncertain, but which is certainly not the language spoken by the Buddha, being much later than his time.

2. *Vaiṣṇavism, Śaivism, and Minor Religious Systems*, pp. 8 ff.

3. *Indien und das Christentum*, pp. 215 ff.

4. Cf. *Mythology of All Races*, Boston, 1916, i. 174–75.

5. See L. de la Vallée Poussin, *Bouddhisme, Opinions sur l'histoire de la dogmatique*, p. 239.

6. The phrase in question is *chaddanta;* see J. S. Speyer, in *ZDMG* lvii. 308 (1903).

7. See H. Lüders, in *Nachrichten von der königlichen Gesellschaft der Wissenschaften zu Göttingen*, 1901, p. 50; A. Foucher, in *Mélanges d'indianisme . . . offerts à M. Sylvain Lévi*, Paris, 1911, pp. 246–47, for very clear cases of a difference in date.

8. This conception is often ascribed to Iranian influence, i.e. the concept of the Fravashis; see A. Grünwedel, *Buddhistische Kunst*, 2nd ed., pp. 169 ff.

9. See *infra*, pp. 261, 300, 336.

10. See *infra*, pp. 327, 338.

## Chapter VIII

1. *SBE* xxii., p. xxxi., note, Oxford, 1884.

2. Cf., however, J. Charpentier, in *JRAS* 1913, pp. 669–74, who would connect the Ājīvikas with the Śaivite sects.

3. Cf. W. H. Schoff, in *JAOS* xxxiii. 209 (1913).

4. See M. Winternitz, in *JRAS* 1895, pp. 159 ff. Nejameṣa is also obviously to be read for Nejameya in *Baudhāyana Gṛhya Sūtra*, ii. 2, as in W. Caland, *Über das rituelle Sūtra des Baudhāyana*, Leipzig,

1903, p. 31. This passage, however, with its invocation of "mothers" (apparently the diseases of children), is evidently late.

## Chapter IX

1. See G. A. Grierson, in *JRAS* 1907, pp. 311 ff.; R. Garbe, *Indien und das Christentum*, pp. 271 ff.

2. The name of the river means "destroying (the merit of good) works."

3. On this mythological figure see I. Friedländer, "Khiḍr," in *Encyclopædia of Religion and Ethics*, vii. 693–95, Edinburgh, 1915.

# IRANIAN

## Chapter I

1. On this cycle of legends see M. Bréal, "Hercule et Cacus," in his *Mélanges de mythologie et de linguistique*, Paris, 1877, pp. 1–161, and cf. *Mythology of All Races*, Boston, 1916, i. 86–87, 303.

2. See *supra*, pp. 23–24.

3. *Religion of Babylonia and Assyria*, Boston, 1898, pp. 429, 432.

4. ib. p. 537.

5. ib. p. 541.

6. A. A. Macdonell, *Vedic Mythology*, Strassburg, 1897, p. 67.

7. For all these myths see *supra*, pp. 33, 35–36, 87–88, 93, 133.

8. *Yasna*, ix. 7.

9. *Vendīdād*, xx. 2–4.

10. Thrita, whose name means "third," was the third man who prepared the haoma, according to *Yasna*, ix. 9.

11. *Yasna*, ix. 7.

12. *Yasht*, v. 61.

13. This line, *frā thwãm zadanha paiti uzukhshāne zafarə paiti uzraocayeni*, well illustrates the extent to which much of the Avesta in its present form has suffered interpolation. It is obvious, from the parallelism with Azhi Dahāka's speech, that the line should read simply *frā thwãm paiti uzukhshāne* ("thee will I besprinkle wholly" [i. e. with fire]). The same thing occurs below in the last line of the translation from *Yasht*, viii. 24, where the parallelism with *dasanãm gairinãm aojo* ("strength of mountains ten in number") shows that the word *nāvayanãm* ("navigable") is interpolated in the line *dasanãm apãm nāvayanãm aojo*, which should read *dasanãm apãm aojo* ("strength of rivers ten in number").

14. *Yasht*, xix. 47–51. The "Child of Waters" is mentioned in magic Mandean inscriptions as "Nbat, the great primeval germ which the Life hath sent" (H. Pognon, *Inscriptions mandaïtes des coupes de Khouabir*, Paris, 1898, pp. 63, 68; cf. also p. 95).

15. G. Hüsing (*Die traditionelle Ueberlieferung und das arische System*, p. 53) thinks that Apaosha means "Coverer," "Concealer" (from *apa + var*).

16. *Yasht*, viii. 4–5.

17. *Yasht*, viii. 23–24.
18. *Yasht*, viii. 29.
19. *Yasht*, viii. 13. Fifteen was the paradisiac age to the Iranian mind.
20. *Būndahish*, vii. 4–7 (tr. E. W. West, in *SBE* v. 26–27).
21. *Būndahish*, xix. 1–10.
22. J. Darmesteter, *Ormazd et Ahriman*, p. 148; E. W. West, in *SBE* v. 67, note 4.
23. M. Ananikian, "Armenia (Zoroastrianism in)," in *Encyclopædia of Religion and Ethics*, i. 799, Edinburgh, 1908.
24. J. Darmesteter, *Zend-Avesta*, ii. 559.
25. *Yasht*, xiv.
26. Cf. the healing functions of Thrita and Thraētaona, *supra*, p. 265, and *infra*, p. 318.
27. Cf. the story of Ātar, *supra*, pp. 266–67.
28. Cf. the legend of Tishtrya, *supra*, p. 269.
29. Namely, seizing its prey with its talons and rending it with its beak. The bird Vāreghna is apparently the raven.
30. *Yasht*, xiv. 19–21. The comparison of the lightning to a bird is of frequent occurrence.
31. *Yasht*, xiv. 27–33.
32. *Yasht*, xiv. 62–63.
33. *Yasna*, ix. 11.

## Chapter II

1. Adapted from E. W. West's translation of *Būndahish*, i–iii, and *Selections of Zāṭ-Sparam*, i–ii, in *SBE* v. 1–19, 156–63.
2. "As the best lord"; the opening words of *Yasna*, xxvii. 13, and a formula frequently used in prayers. Cf. L. H. Mills, in *JRAS*, 1910, pp. 57–68, 641–57.
3. A reminiscence of the myths of Tishtrya and Verethraghna; cf. *supra*, pp. 269, 272.
4. A reminiscence of the storm-myths of Azhi, etc.; cf. *supra*, pp. 266–67.
5. The planets are evil beings since they do not follow the regular course of the stars.
6. *Būndahish*, xiii.
7. *Yasht*, v. 1–4.
8. *Yasht*, v. 7, 64, 126–129.
9. *Būndahish*, ix; *Selections of Zāṭ-Sparam*, viii.
10. *Būndahish*, xviii.
11. *Yasna*, ix. 17–18.
12. *Yasna*, ix. 19–20.

13. *Yasna*, ix. 22–23. It is scarcely necessary to note that the word "Haoma" is dissyllabic.

14. A. A. Macdonell, *Vedic Mythology*, Strassburg, 1897, p. 111.

15. M. Jastrow, *Religion of Babylonia and Assyria*, Boston, 1898, pp. 520–21.

16. *Būndahish*, xxvii. 1.

17. *Selections of Zāṭ-Sparam*, ii. 5.

18. O. Schrader, "Aryan Religion," in *Encyclopædia of Religion and Ethics*, ii. 39, Edinburgh, 1910.

19. A. A. Macdonell, *Vedic Mythology*, Strassburg, 1897, p. 88 ff.

20. See *supra*, pp. 44–45.

21. J. Darmesteter, *Zend-Avesta*, i. pp. lix ff.

22. *Būndahish*, xvii. 1–4.

23. J. Darmesteter, *Zend-Avesta*, i. 150.

24. *Būndahish*, iii. 24; *Selections of Zāṭ-Sparam*, ii. 11.

25. *Selections of Zāṭ-Sparam*, ii. 6.

26. Namely, his spiritual prototype, his supra-terrestrial self or guardian spirit. For this account of Gēush Urvan see *Būndahish*, iii. 17–18, iv. 1–5.

27. F. Cumont, *The Mysteries of Mithra*, Chicago, 1903, p. 131 ff.

28. See P. D. Chantepie de la Saussaye, *Religion of the Teutons*, Boston, 1902, p. 341.

29. *Yasht*, xiv. 19.

30. *Yasht*, xiv. 41.

31. *Maīnōg-ī-Khraṭ*, lxii. 40–42 (tr. E. W. West, in *SBE* xxiv. 112).

32. *Būndahish*, xix. 13.

33. *Supra*, p. 272.

34. *Yasht*, xix. 35.

35. *Yasht*, xiv. 34–36.

36. J. Darmesteter, *Zend-Avesta*, ii. 571, note 51; *Shāhnāmah*, tr. A. G. and E. Warner, i. 246.

37. *Shāhnāmah*, i. 320–22.

38. *Vendīdād*, ii. 42.

39. *Būndahish*, xix. 16.

40. J. Darmesteter, *Ormazd et Ahriman*, p. 189.

41. *Vendīdād*, xvii. 9.

42. *Būndahish*, xix. 19.

43. C. Bartholomae, *Altiranisches Wörterbuch*, col. 259.

44. J. Darmesteter, in *SBE* xxiii. 203, note 4.

45. A. A. Macdonell, *Vedic Mythology*, Strassburg, 1897, p. 152; see also *supra*, pp. 47, 62.

46. *Būndahish*, xix. 21–25.

47. *Būndahish*, xix. 36.

## Chapter III

1. *Yasht*, xiii. 87.
2. *Yasna*, xxvi. 10.
3. *Būndahish*, xxx. 7.
4. *Būndahish*, xxiv. 1.
5. *Maīnōg-ī-Khraṭ*, xxvii. 14.
6. *Maīnōg-ī-Khraṭ*, xxvii. 18; J. Darmesteter, *Ormazd et Ahriman*, p. 159.
7. F. Windischmann, *Zoroastrische Studien*, p. 216.
8. *Yasht*, xiii. 86; *Yasna*, lxviii. 22; *Visparad*, xxi. 2.
9. J. Darmesteter, *Ormazd et Ahriman*, p. 159.
10. See *supra*, p. 68.
11. J. Darmesteter, *Ormazd et Ahriman*, p. 159, note 4.
12. F. Windischmann, *Zoroastrische Studien*, p. 215.
13. The Pāhlavī text is very uncertain in this place.
14. The nature of this sin is not clear. It seems, however, that they were required to respect all the creatures of Ahura Mazda.
15. This whole passage is very uncertain.
16. *Būndahish*, xv. 1–24.
17. *Shāhnāmah*, i. 120.
18. F. Justi, *Iranisches Namenbuch*, p. 126.
19. *Yasht*, v. 21.
20. The bundle of twigs which the Iranian priest holds in his hand during the sacrifice.
21. *Yasht*, xv. 7.
22. *Yasht*, xix. 26. The metre shows that the last word of the second line, *haptaithyām* ("sevenfold"), should be omitted, so that it should read *yaṭ khshayata paiti būmīm* ("so that o'er the earth he governed"). Mazana is probably the modern Māzandarān, and Varena seems to have corresponded to Gīlān (see L. H. Gray, "Māzandarān," in *Encyclopædia of Religion and Ethics*, viii. 507, Edinburgh, 1916).
23. *Yasht*, xvii. 25.
24. *Yasht*, xiii. 137.
25. Mirkhond, *History of the Early Kings of Persia*, tr. D. Shea, p. 68.
26. *Shāhnāmah*, i. 123; cf. also L. H. Gray, "Festivals and Fasts (Iranian)," in *Encyclopædia of Religion and Ethics*, v. 873–74, Edinburgh, 1912.
27. *Shāhnāmah*, i. 124.
28. J. Darmesteter, in *SBE* xxiii. 252, note 1.
29. J. Darmesteter, *Zend-Avesta*, ii. 266, note 49.
30. J. Darmesteter, *Ormazd et Ahriman*, p. 169.

31. xvii. 4.
32. J. Darmesteter, *Ormazd et Ahriman*, p. 167.
33. *Shāhnāmah*, i. 127.

## Chapter IV

1. *Shāhnāmah*, i. 131, 133.
2. *Yasna*, ix. 4–5.
3. *Yasht*, xix. 31–32.
4. *Shāhnāmah*, i. 134.
5. E. W. West, in *SBE* xlvii. p. xxix.
6. J. Darmesteter, *Zend-Avesta*, ii. 18.
7. J. Ehni, *Der vedische Mythus des Yama*, Strassburg, 1890, p. 171.
8. *Shāhnāmah*, i. 131.
9. *Vendīdād*, ii. 3–4. The second and fourth lines of verse read, more literally, "to remember and carry the religion." In the first line of Ahura Mazda's speech *mē* ("my") has been omitted as unmetrical both in Avesta and in English.
10. *Būndahish*, xvii. 5–8. Cf. the enumeration of the fires, *supra*, p. 285.
11. This line is unmetrical in the original (*mashyānãmca sūnãmca vayãmca*). The second or third word (probably the latter) apparently should be omitted.
12. Goddess of the earth.
13. *Vendīdād*, ii. 9–11.
14. Worshipful beings.
15. A mythical land, at one time identified with the valley of the Aras in Transcaucasia.
16. The river-goddess; cf. *supra*, p. 278.
17. The deserts (C. Bartholomae, *Altiranisches Wörterbuch*, col. 1799).
18. In stalls (C. Bartholomae, *Altiranisches Wörterbuch*, col. 819).
19. The meaning of these terms is unknown. The Editor suggests that *kasvīsh* may mean "dwarfishness" (cf. Avesta *kasu*, "small," *kasvika* "trifling").
20. *Vendīdād*, ii. 21–31.
21. *Vendīdād*, ii. 31–42.
22. *Dīnkarṭ*, XII. ix. 3 (tr. E. W. West, in *SBE* xlvii. 108).
23. *Yasna*, xxxii. 8; cf. J. H. Moulton, *Early Zoroastrianism*, p. 149; C. Bartholomae, *Altiranisches Wörterbuch*, col. 1866.
24. *Ṣad-Dar*, xciv. (tr. T. Hyde, *Historia religionis veterum Persarum*, p. 485).
25. *Yasht*, xix. 33.

26. *Shāhnāmah*, i. 134.
27. *Ṛgveda*, X. x; cf. *supra*, p. 68.
28. *Būndahish*, xxiii. 1.
29. *Yasht*, xix. 34–38.
30. *Yasht*, v. 29–34.
31. *Shāhnāmah*, i. 140.
32. *Yasht*, xix. 46.
33. Mirkhond, *History of the Early Kings of Persia*, tr. D. Shea, p. 120.
34. See *supra*, pp. 68–69; cf. also pp. 99–100, 159–61, 214–15.
35. A. A. Macdonell, *Vedic Mythology*, Strassburg, 1897, p. 43.
36. J. Ehni, *Die ursprüngliche Gottheit des vedischen Yama*, Leipzig, 1896, p. 8.
37. A. A. Macdonell, *Vedic Mythology*, Strassburg, 1897, p. 167; cf. *Ṛgveda*, X. lxviii. 11, "the manes have adorned the sky with constellations, like a black horse with pearls."
38. *Ṛgveda*, X. lxv. 6.
39. *Ṛgveda*, X. cxxxv. 1 (cf. A. A. Macdonell, *Vedic Mythology*, Strassburg, 1897, p. 167); *Atharvaveda*, V. iv. 3.
40. J. Darmesteter, *Ormazd et Ahriman*, p. 107.
41. *Shāhnāmah*, i. 139–40.
42. J. Darmesteter, *Études iraniennes*, ii. 210–12.
43. E. H. Meyer, *Indogermanische Mythen*, Berlin, 1883–87, i. 229.
44. *Shāhnāmah*, i. 132.
45. i. 132.
46. *Shāhnāmah*, i. 133.
47. Mirkhond, *History of the Early Kings of Persia*, tr. D. Shea, p. 103.

## Chapter V

1. *Shāhnāmah*, i. 147.
2. *Shāhnāmah*, i. 154–55.
3. *Shāhnāmah*, i. 145.
4. On his way to Ḍaḥḥāk's capital, Gang-i-Dizhhūkht (which Firdausī identifies with Jerusalem) Farīdūn was checked for an instant by a river, and a curious legend preserved in the Avesta (*Yasht*, v. 61–65) is related to the episode. Since the ferryman Pāurva was unwilling to row him across, he, having a complete knowledge of magic, assumed the shape of a vulture and flung the man high in air, so that for three days he went flying toward his house, but could not turn downward. When the beneficent dawn came at the end of the third night, Pāurva prayed to Ardvī Sūra Anāhita, who hastened to his rescue, seized him by the arm, and brought him safely home.
5. *Shāhnāmah*, i. 146.

6. *Shāhnāmah*, i. 162.
7. *Shāhnāmah*, i. 167.
8. VIII. xiii. 9 (tr. E. W. West, in *SBE* xxxvii. 28).
9. *Būndahish*, xxxi. 10.
10. *Yasht*, xix. 38–44 (cf. *Yasna*, ix. 11, *Yasht*, v. 38, xv. 28).
11. *Yasht*, xiii. 136.
12. *Yasna*, ix. 11 = *Yasht*, xix. 40, Pāhlavī *Rivāyat*, tr. E. W. West, in *SBE* xviii. 374.
13. The metre of the original shows that Keresāspa is to be pronounced Kṛsa-aspa.
14. *Supra*, pp. 58–59, 94–95, 143.
15. The author is not convinced by the arguments advanced by G. Hüsing (*Die traditionelle Ueberlieferung und das arische System*, pp. 135–39) to prove that Gandarewa was originally a bird.
16. *Yasht*, xix. 41, Pāhlavī *Rivāyat*, tr. E. W. West, in *SBE* xviii. 375.
17. Heaven.
18. *Yasht*, xix. 43–44. The metre of the original is not wholly correct.
19. *Yasht*, xv. 28, xix. 41.
20. Pāhlavī *Rivāyat* (tr. E. W. West, in *SBE* xviii. 376).
21. E. W. West, in *SBE* xviii. 378, note 1.
22. *Maīnōg-ī-Khraṭ*, xxvii. 50.
23. Pāhlavī *Rivāyat* (tr. E. W. West, in *SBE* xviii. 376–77).
24. *Yasht*, xix. 41, *Vendīdād*, i. 9.
25. *Būndahish*, xxix. 7.
26. *Yasht*, xiii. 61.
27. Pāhlavī *Rivāyat* (tr. E. W. West, in *SBE* xviii. 373–80).
28. *Shāhnāmah*, i. 174.
29. *Yasht*, xiii. 131.
30. *Būndahish*, xii. 10.
31. *Būndahish*, xxxi. 21–22.
32. A Persian weight of widely varying values.
33. *Shāhnāmah*, i. 291, 296–97.
34. *Shāhnāmah*, i. 320–22.
35. On the story of Rustam cf. G. Hüsing, *Beiträge zur Rustamsage*, Leipzig, 1913.
36. *Shāhnāmah*, ii. 119–87; for the *motif* in saga-cycles see M. A. Potter, *Sohrab and Rustam: The Epic Theme of a Combat between Father and Son*, London, 1902.
37. *Yasht*, v. 41–43.
38. *Yasna*, xi. 7; *Yasht*, ix. 18–22, xix. 56–64.
39. *Būndahish*, xxxi. 21; J. Darmesteter, *Zend-Avesta*, ii. 400.
40. *Būndahish*, xxix. 5.

41. *Maīnōg-ī-Khraṭ*, lxii. 31–36. This seems to be a reminiscence of the man-headed bulls in Babylonian art (L. C. Casartelli, *Philosophy of the Mazdayasnian Religion under the Sassanids*, § 182).

42. J. Darmesteter, *Zend-Avesta*, ii. 400.

43. *Dīnkart*, VII. i. 31 (tr. E. W. West, in *SBE* xlvii. 1–12).

44. *Būndahish*, xxxi. 24.

45. *Dīnkart*, VII. ii. 62–63 (tr. E. W. West, in *SBE* xlvii. 31–32).

46. *Shāhnāmah*, ii. 26.

47. *Yasht*, xiii. 131; *Afrīn-ī-Zartusht*, 2.

48. *Dinkarṭ*, VII. i. 36 (tr. E. W. West, in *SBE* xlvii. 13).

49. *Yasna*, xlvi. 12; *Yasht*, v. 81–83.

50. J. Darmesteter, *Zend-Avesta*, ii. 386; cf. the Pāhlavī text as ed. and tr. by E. W. West, in *The Book of Arda Viraf*, Bombay, 1872.

51. *Dīnkarṭ*, IX. xxii. 4–12 (tr. E. W. West, in *SBE* xxxvii. 220–23).

52. A. A. Macdonell, *Vedic Mythology*, Strassburg, 1897, p. 64.

53. *Yasht*, v. 50.

54. *Yasht*, ix. 17–18. Haosravah and Caēcasta are trisyllabic.

55. J. Darmesteter, *Zend-Avesta*, i. 154.

56. *Shāhnāmah*, iv. 264–69.

57. *Dīnkarṭ*, VII. i. 40 (tr. E. W. West, in *SBE* xlvii. 14).

58. J. Darmesteter, *Zend-Avesta*, ii. 661, note 29; see also *supra*, pp. 149–50.

59. *Afrīn-ī-Zartusht*, 7.

60. *Yasht*, v. 54.

61. J. Darmesteter, *Zend-Avesta*, ii. 380.

62. C. Bartholomae, *Altiranisches Wörterbuch*, col. 1459.

63. The prose line *āaṭ mē tūm arədvī sūre anāhite hush(k)əm pəshum raēcaya* should probably read,

> *āaṭ hush(k)əm pəshum raēcaya*
> *arədvī sūre anāhite*
> ("So a crossing dry provide thou,
> Ardvī Sūra Anāhita").

64. *Yasht*, v. 77–78.

65. *Yasht*, v. 113.

66. J. Darmesteter, *Études iraniennes*, ii. 230. The chief Pāhlavī source for Zairivairi, the *Yāṭkar-ī-Zarīran*, has been edited by Jamaspji Minocheherji Jamasp-Asana (Bombay, 1897) and translated by Jivanji Jamshedji Modi (Bombay, 1899).

67. *Deipnosophistae*, xiii. 35 (p. 575).

68. J. Darmesteter, *Zend-Avesta*, iii. p. lxxxii.

69. *Shāhnāmah*, iv. 318 ff.

70. J. Darmesteter, *Zend-Avesta*, iii. p. lxxxi; cf. E. Rohde, *Der griechische Roman*, 2nd ed., Leipzig, 1900, pp. 47–55.

71. F. Rosenberg, *Le Livre de Zoroastre* (*Zarâtusht Nâma*), pp. 47–55.
72. *Yasna*, ix. 13.
73. See *supra*, pp. 44, 284–85.
74. See *supra*, pp. 327–28.

## Chapter VI

1. Cf. also E. J. Becker, *A Contribution to the Comparative Study of the Medieval Visions of Heaven and Hell*, Baltimore, 1899.
2. Cf. L. H. Gray, "Marriage (Iranian)," in *Encyclopædia of Religion and Ethics*, viii. 456–59, Edinburgh, 1916.
3. See *supra*, pp. 283, 336.
4. Cf. the literature cited in the Bibliography (V), p. 402.

## Chapter VII

1. "Aryan Religion," in *Encyclopædia of Religion and Ethics*, ii. 39, Edinburgh, 1910.
2. *Shāhnāmah*, i. 308–11.
3. *Shāhnāmah*, i. 378.

# BIBLIOGRAPHY

# INDIAN

## I. ABBREVIATIONS

| | |
|---|---|
| *ASS* . . . | Ānandāśrama Sanskrit Series. |
| *BI* . . . . | Bibliotheca Indica. |
| *JAOS* . . | Journal of the American Oriental Society. |
| *JRAS* . . | Journal of the Royal Asiatic Society. |
| *SBE* . . . | Sacred Books of the East. |
| *WZKM* . | Wiener Zeitschrift für die Kunde des Morgenlandes. |
| *ZDMG* . . | Zeitschrift der deutschen morgenländischen Gesellschaft. |

## II. GENERAL WORKS


Barth, A., *The Religions of India.* London, 1882.

Benfey, T., in J. S. Ersch and J. G. Gruber, *Allgemeine Encyklopädie der Wissenschaften und Künste*, II. xvii. 158–213. Leipzig, 1840.

Colebrooke, H. T., *Essays.* Revised ed. by W. D. Whitney. 2 vols. London, 1871–72.

Coleman, C., *Mythology of the Hindus.* London, 1832.

Coomaraswamy, A. K., *Mediaeval Sinhalese Art.* London, 1908.

——— *The Arts and Crafts of India and Ceylon.* London, 1913.

Eggeling, H. J., "Brahman," in *Encyclopædia Britannica*, 11th ed., iv. 378–79.

——— "Brahmanism," in *Encyclopædia Britannica*, 11th ed., iv. 381–87.

——— "Hinduism," in *Encyclopædia Britannica*, 11th ed., xiii. 501–13.

Fergusson, J., *Tree and Serpent Worship.* 2nd ed. London, 1873.

——— *History of Indian and Eastern Architecture.* London, 1878. Revised ed. by J. Burgess and R. Phené Spiers. 2 vols. London, 1910.

Frazer, R. W., *Indian Thought Past and Present.* London, 1915.

Garbe, R., *Indien und das Christentum.* Tübingen, 1914.

Griswold, H. DeWitt, *Brahman: A Study in the History of Indian Philosophy.* New York, 1900.

Havell, E. B., *Indian Sculpture and Painting.* London, 1908.

——— *The Ideals of Indian Art.* London, 1911.

——— *The Ancient and Medieval Architecture of India.* London, 1915.

Hopkins, E. W., *The Religions of India.* Boston, 1895.

——— *India Old and New.* New York, 1901.

——— "The Sacred Rivers of India," in *Studies in the History of Religions Presented to Crawford Howell Toy,* pp. 213–29. New York, 1912.

Lassen, C., *Indische Alterthumskunde.* 4 vols. Bonn and Leipzig, 1847–61. 2nd ed. of i–ii. Leipzig, 1867–73.

Lehmann, E., "Die Inder," in P. D. Chantepie de la Saussaye, *Lehrbuch der Religionsgeschichte,* ii. 4–161. 3rd ed. Tübingen, 1905.

Lyall, A. C., *Asiatic Studies.* 2 series. London, 1882–99.

Macdonell, A. A., *Sanskrit Literature.* London, 1900.

MacNicol, N., *Indian Theism.* Oxford, 1915.

Monier-Williams, Sir M., *Brahmanism and Hinduism.* 4th ed. London, 1891.

——— *Indian Wisdom.* 4th ed. London, 1893.

Moor, E., *The Indian Pantheon.* London, 1810. New ed. by W. O. Simpson. Madras, 1897.

Moore, G. F., *History of Religions,* chh. xi–xiv. Edinburgh, 1913.

Muir, J., *Original Sanskrit Texts on the Origin and History of the People of India, their Religion and Institutions.* 5 vols. London, 1858–72. 3rd ed. of i, London, 1890; 2nd ed. of ii, 1871; 2nd ed. of iii, 1868; 2nd ed. of iv, 1873; 3rd ed. of v, 1884.

Müller, F. Max *Lectures on the Origin and Growth of Religion.* London, 1878.

——— *Contributions to the Science of Mythology.* 2 vols. London, 1897.

Noble, M. E., and Coomaraswamy, A. K., *Myths of the Hindus and Buddhists.* London, 1913.

Oldham, C. F., *The Sun and the Serpent.* London, 1905.

Oltramare, P., *L'Histoire des idées théosophiques dans l'Inde.* Paris, 1906.

Oman, J. C., *The Brahmans, Theists and Muslims of India.* London, 1907.

ORELLI, C. VON, "Indische Religionen," in *Allgemeine Religionsgeschichte*, ii. 4–140. 2nd ed. Bonn, 1911–13.

SCHROEDER, L. VON, *Indiens Literatur und Kultur*. Leipzig, 1887.

SMITH, V. A., *History of Fine Art in India and Ceylon*. London, 1911.

SPIEGEL, F., *Die arische Periode*. Leipzig, 1881.

VODSKOV, H. S., *Sjæledyrkelse og naturdyrkelse*, i. Copenhagen, 1897.

WARD, W., *A View of the History, Literature and Mythology of the Hindoos*. 5th ed. Madras, 1863.

WHITNEY, W. D., *Oriental and Linguistic Studies*. 2 vols. New York, 1873–74.

WILKINS, W. J., *Hindu Mythology*. 2nd ed. Calcutta, 1882.

WILSON, H. H., *Works*, ed. R. Rost. 7 vols. London, 1861–62.

WINTERNITZ, M., *Geschichte der indischen Litteratur*. 2 vols. Leipzig, 1905–13.

WURM, P., *Geschichte der indischen Religion*. Basel, 1874.

## III. THE VEDIC PERIOD

### (*a*) *Texts and Translations*

#### (α) *Saṁhitās*

1. *Ṛgveda*. Ed. T. Aufrecht, 2 vols., Bonn, 1877; with Sāyaṇa's commentary, ed. F. Max Müller, 4 vols., London, 1890–92; tr. H. Grassmann, 2 vols., Leipzig, 1876–77, A. Ludwig, 5 vols., Prague, 1876–88 (with an elaborate introduction — vol. iii — and notes), R. T. H. Griffith, 2 vols., Benares, 1896–97, F. Max Müller (hymns to the Maruts, Rudra, Vāyu, and Vāta), in *SBE* xxxii. (1891), H. Oldenberg (hymns to Agni from Books i–v), in *SBE* xlvi. (1897); commentary by H. Oldenberg, 2 vols., Berlin, 1909–12.

2. *Sāmaveda*. Ed. and tr. T. Benfey, Leipzig, 1848; ed. Satyavrata Sāmaśrami, Calcutta, 1873; tr. R. T. H. Griffith, Benares, 1893. See also W. Caland, *Die Jaiminīya Saṁhitā*, Breslau, 1907.

3. *Yajurveda*. (i) *Kāṭhaka Saṁhitā*. Ed. L. von Schroeder, 3 vols., Leipzig, 1900–10. (ii) *Taittirīya Saṁhitā*. Ed. *BI* 1860–99, A. Weber, in *Indische Studien*, xi–xii (1871–72); tr. A. B. Keith, 2 vols., Cambridge, Mass., 1914. (iii) *Maitrāyaṇī Saṁhitā*. Ed. L. von Schroeder, 4 vols., Leipzig, 1881–86. (iv) *Vājasaneyi Saṁhitā*. Ed. A. Weber, Berlin and London, 1852; tr. R. T. H. Griffith, Benares, 1899. The first three texts belong to the "Black" division of the *Yajurveda*, and the fourth to the "White."

4. *Atharvaveda.* Ed. R. Roth and W. D. Whitney, Berlin, 1856; tr. R. T. H. Griffith, 2 vols., Benares, 1897, M. Bloomfield (selected hymns), in *SBE* xlii. (1897), W. D. Whitney and C. R. Lanman, 2 vols., Cambridge, Mass., 1905. See M. Bloomfield, *The Atharvaveda*, Strassburg, 1899.

### (β) *Brāhmaṇas*

1. Attached to the *Ṛgveda.* (i) *Aitareya Brāhmaṇa.* Ed. T. Aufrecht, Bonn, 1879; ed. and tr. M. Haug, 2 vols., Bombay, 1863. (ii) *Kauṣītaki Brāhmaṇa.* Ed. B. Lindner, Jena, 1887.

2. Attached to the *Sāmaveda.* (i) *Pañcaviṁśa Brāhmaṇa.* Ed. A. Vedāntavāgīśa, in *BI* 1869–74. (ii) *Ṣaḍviṁśa Brāhmaṇa.* Ed. Jībānanda Vidyāsāgara, Calcutta, 1881.

3. Attached to the *Yajurveda.* (i) *Taittirīya Brāhmaṇa.* Ed. Rājendralāla Mitra, in *BI* 1855–70, N. Godabole, in *ASS* 1898. (ii) *Śatapatha Brāhmaṇa.* Ed. A. Weber, Berlin and London, 1855; tr. J. Eggeling, in *SBE* xii, xxvi, xli, xliii, xliv (1880–1900). There are no separate *Brāhmaṇas* for the *Kāṭhaka* and the *Maitrāyaṇī Saṁhitās*, but these texts include *Brāhmaṇa* portions.

4. Attached to the *Atharvaveda. Gopatha Brāhmaṇa.* Ed. Rājendralāla Mitra, in *BI* 1872.

### (γ) *Āraṇyakas and Upaniṣads*

1. Attached to the *Ṛgveda.* (i) *Aitareya Āraṇyaka*, including the *Aitareya Upaniṣad.* Ed. and tr. A. B. Keith, Oxford, 1909. (ii) *Śāṅkhāyana Āraṇyaka.* Tr. A. B. Keith, London, 1908. (iii) *Kauṣītaki Upaniṣad.* Ed. E. B. Cowell, in *BI* 1861.

2. Attached to the *Sāmaveda.* (i) *Jaiminīya Upaniṣad Brāhmaṇa.* Ed. and tr. H. Oertel, in *JAOS* xvi. 79–260 (1894). (ii) *Chāndogya Upaniṣad.* Ed. and tr. O. Böhtlingk, Leipzig, 1889.

3. Attached to the *Yajurveda.* (i) *Kāṭhaka Upaniṣad.* Ed. and tr. O. Böhtlingk, Leipzig, 1890. (ii) *Taittirīya Āraṇyaka.* Ed. H. N. Apte, in *ASS* 1898. (iii) *Taittirīya Upaniṣad.* Ed. Poona, 1889. (iv) *Maitrāyaṇī Upaniṣad.* Ed. E. B. Cowell, in *BI* 1870. (v) *Bṛhadāraṇyaka Upaniṣad.* Ed. and tr. O. Böhtlingk, Leipzig, 1889. (vi) *Īśā Upaniṣad.* Ed. *ASS* 1888. (vii) *Śvetāśvatara Upaniṣad* (attributed, though without much reason, to the Black *Yajurveda*). Ed. *ASS* 1890.

4. Attached to the *Atharvaveda.* (i) *Muṇḍaka Upaniṣad.* Ed. *ASS* 1889. (ii) *Praśna Upaniṣad.* Ed. and tr. O. Böhtlingk, Leipzig, 1890. (iii) *Māṇḍūkya Upaniṣad.* Ed. and tr. Bombay, 1895.

There are many other *Upaniṣads*, but they are of less importance and of doubtful age. The principal *Upaniṣads* are translated by F.

Max Müller, in *SBE* i (2nd ed., 1900), xv (1884), and by P. Deussen, *Sechzig Upanishads des Veda*, 2nd ed., Leipzig, 1905 (see also his *Philosophy of the Upanishads*, tr. A. S. Geden, London, 1906, and A. E. Gough, *The Philosophy of the Upanishads*, London, 1882).

(δ) *Ritual Literature*

The most important source for mythology in the ritual literature is furnished by the *Gṛhya Sūtras*, of which those of Āśvalāyana, Śāṅkhāyana, Pāraskara, Khādira, Āpastamba, Hiraṇyakeśin, and Gobhila are translated by H. Oldenberg, in *SBE* xxix, xxx (1886). The *Kauśika Sūtra* of the *Atharvaveda*, the chief text on Vedic magic, is edited by M. Bloomfield, New Haven, 1890, and translated in large part by W. Caland, *Altindisches Zauberritual*, Amsterdam, 1900, who has also edited the *Pitṛmedha Sūtra* (on ancestor-worship) of Gautama, Baudhāyana, and Hiraṇyakeśin. Of the *Dharma Śāstras*, or law-books, those of Āpastamba, Gautama, Vasiṣṭha, and Baudhāyana are translated by G. Bühler, in *SBE* ii (2nd ed., 1897), xiv (1882), who has also translated the later *Manu Smṛti*, in *SBE* xxv (1886).

(*b*) *General Treatises*

Bergaigne, A., *La Religion védique.* 4 vols. Paris, 1878–83.

Bloomfield, M., *The Religion of the Veda.* New York, 1908.

Colinet, P., "Le Symbolisme solaire dans le Rig-Veda," in *Mélanges Charles de Harlez*, pp. 86–93. Leyden, 1896.

Deussen, P., *Philosophie des Veda* (*Allgemeine Geschichte der Philosophie mit besonderer Berücksichtigung der Religionen*, i, part 1). 3rd ed. Leipzig, 1915.

Hardy, E., *Die vedisch-brahmanische Periode der Religion des alten Indiens.* Münster, 1893.

Henry, V., *La Magie dans l'Inde antique.* 2nd ed. Paris, 1909.

Hillebrandt, A., *Vedische Mythologie.* 3 vols. Breslau, 1891–1902.

Hopkins, E. W., "Henotheism in the Rig-Veda," in *Classical Studies in Honour of Henry Drisler*, pp. 75–83. New York, 1894.

——— "The Holy Numbers of the Rig-Veda," in *Oriental Studies: A Selection of the Papers Read before the Oriental Club of Philadelphia*, pp. 141–59. Boston, 1894.

Kaegi, A., *Der Rigveda.* 2nd ed. Leipzig, 1881. English translation by R. Arrowsmith. Boston, 1886.

Kuhn, A., *Die Herabkunft des Feuers und des Göttertranks.* 2nd ed. Gütersloh, 1886.

LÉVI, S., *La Doctrine du sacrifice dans les brāhmaṇas*. Paris, 1898.

MACDONELL, A. A., *Vedic Mythology*. Strassburg, 1897.

MACDONELL, A. A., and KEITH, A. B., *Vedic Index of Names and Subjects*. 2 vols. London, 1912.

OLDENBERG, H., *Die Religion des Veda*. Berlin, 1894.

PISCHEL, R., and GELDNER, K., *Vedische Studien*. 3 vols. Stuttgart, 1889–1901.

ROTH, R., "Die höchsten Götter der arischen Völker," in *ZDMG* vi. 67–77 (1852).

SANDER, F., *Rigveda und Edda*. Stockholm, 1893.

SCHROEDER, L. VON, *Indiens Literatur und Kultur*. Leipzig, 1887.

——— *Mysterium und Mimus im Rigveda*. Leipzig, 1908.

SIEG, E., *Die Sagenstoffe des Ṛgveda*. Stuttgart, 1902.

DE LA VALLÉE POUSSIN, L., *Le Védisme*. Paris, 1909.

——— *Le Brahmanisme*. Paris, 1910.

WEBER, A., "Vedische Beiträge," in *Sitzungsberichte der königlich preussischen Akademie der Wissenschaften*, 1894–1901.

### (*c*) *Treatises on Special Points*

#### 1. Cosmology

SCHERMAN, L., *Philosophische Hymnen aus der Ṛig- und Atharva-Veda-Sanhitâ*. Strassburg, 1887.

WALLIS, H. F., *Cosmology of the Rigveda*. London, 1887.

#### 2. Dyaus

BRADKE, P. VON, *Dyâus Asura, Ahura Mazdâ und die Asuras*. Halle, 1885.

HOPKINS, E. W., "Dyāus, Viṣṇu, Varuṇa, and Rudra," in *Proceedings of the American Oriental Society*, 1894, pp. cxlv–cxlvii.

#### 3. Varuṇa

BOHNENBERGER, K., *Der altindische Gott Varuṇa*. Tübingen, 1893.

FOY, W., *Die königliche Gewalt nach den altindischen Rechtsbüchern*, pp. 80–86. Leipzig, 1895.

HILLEBRANDT, A., *Varuṇa und Mitra*. Breslau, 1877.

OLDENBERG, H., "Varuṇa und die Ādityas," in *ZDMG* l. 43–68 (1896).

4. Mitra

Eggers, A., *Der arische Gott Mitra.* Dorpat, 1894.

Meillet, A., "Le Dieu indo-iranien Mitra," in *Journal asiatique*, X. i. 143–59 (1907).

5. Pūṣan

Perry, E. D., "Notes on the Vedic Deity Pūṣan," in *Classical Studies in Honour of Henry Drisler*, pp. 240–43. New York, 1894.

Siecke, E., *Pūṣan.* Leipzig, 1914.

6. Ādityas

Oldenberg, H., "Varuṇa und die Ādityas," in *ZDMG* xlix. 177–78 (1895), l. 50–54 (1896).

7. Savitṛ

Oldenberg, H., "Noch einmal der vedische Savitar," in *ZDMG* lix. 253–64 (1905).

8. Aśvins

Myriantheus, L., *Die Aśvins oder arischen Dioskuren.* Munich, 1876.

9. Uṣas

Brandes, E., *Uṣas.* Copenhagen, 1879.

10. Indra

Hopkins, E. W., "Indra as the God of Fertility," in *JAOS* xxxvi. 242–68 (1917).

Perry, E. D., "Indra in the Rigveda," in *JAOS* xi. 117–208 (1885).

11. Trita

Bloomfield, M., "Trita, the Scape-Goat of the Gods, in Relation to Atharva-Veda, vi. 112 and 113," in *Proceedings of the American Oriental Society*, 1894, pp. cxix–cxxiii.

Macdonell, A. A., "The God Trita," in *JRAS* 1893, pp. 419–96.

12. Rudra and the Maruts

Charpentier, J., "Über Rudra-Śiva," in *WZKM* xxiii. 151–79 (1909).

——— "Bemerkungen über die Vrātyas," in *WZKM* xxv. 355–68 (1911).

Keith, A. B., "The Vrātyas," in *JRAS* 1913, pp. 155–60.

Schroeder, L. von, "Bemerkungen zu Oldenberg's Religion des Veda," in *WZKM* ix. 233–52 (1895).

Siecke, E., *Indra's Drachenkampf (nach dem Rig-Veda)*. Berlin, 1905.

13. Aditi

Colinet, P., "Étude sur le mot Aditi," in *Muséon*, xii. 81–90 (1893).

Hillebrandt, A., *Ueber die Göttin Aditi*. Breslau, 1876.

Oppert, G., "Über die vedische Göttin Aditi," in *ZDMG* lvii. 508–19 (1903).

14. Saraṇyū

Bloomfield, M., "Contributions to the Interpretation of the Veda," in *JAOS* xv. 172–88 (1893).

15. Gandharvas

Meyer, E. H., *Gandharven-Kentauren*. Berlin, 1883.

Schroeder, L. von, *Griechische Götter und Heroen*, i. 23–39. Berlin, 1887.

16. Apsarases

Siecke, O., *Die Liebesgeschichte des Himmels*. Strassburg, 1892.

17. Ṛbhus

Ryder, A. W., *Die Ṛbhus im Ṛgveda*. Gütersloh, 1901.

18. Animal Worship

Hopkins, E. W., "Notes on Dyāus, Viṣṇu, Varuṇa, and Rudra," in *Proceedings of the American Oriental Society*, 1894, p. cliv.

Keith, A. B., "Some Modern Theories of Religion and the Veda," in *JRAS* 1907, pp. 929–49.

Winternitz, M., *Der Sarpabali*. Vienna, 1888.

19. Asura

Macdonell, A. A., "Mythological Studies in the Rigveda," in *JRAS* 1895, pp. 168–77.

20. Namuci

Bloomfield, M., "Contributions to the Interpretation of the Veda," in *JAOS* xv. 143–63 (1893).

21. Dadhikrā

Henry, V., "Dadhikrā-Dadhikrāvan et l'euhémérisme en exégèse védique," in *Album Kern*, pp. 5–12. Leyden, 1903.

22. Piśācas

Charpentier, J., *Kleine Beiträge zur indoiranischen Mythologie*, pp. 1–24. Upsala, 1911.

23. Mātariśvan

Charpentier, J., *Kleine Beiträge zur indoiranischen Mythologie*, pp. 69–83. Upsala, 1911.

24. Bṛhaspati

Strauss, O., *Bṛhaspati im Veda*. Leipzig, 1905.

25. Manu

Lindner, B., "Die iranische Flutsage," in *Festgruss an Rudolf von Roth*, pp. 213–16. Stuttgart, 1903.

Müller, F. Max, *India, What can it teach us?*, pp. 133–38. London, 1883.

Weber, A., "Zwei Sagen aus dem Çatapathabrāhmaṇa über Einwanderung und Verbreitung der Arier in Indien," in *Indische Studien*, i. 161–232 (1851).

26. Eschatology

Boyer, A. M., "Étude sur l'origine de la doctrine du saṁsāra," in *Journal asiatique*, IX. xviii. 451–99 (1901).

Caland, W., *Altindischer Ahnencult*. Leyden, 1893.

——— *Die altindischen Todten- und Bestattungsgebräuche*. Amsterdam, 1896.

Ehni, J., *Der vedische Mythus des Yama*. Strassburg, 1890.

——— *Die ursprüngliche Gottheit des vedischen Yama*. Leipzig, 1896.

Geldner, K., "Yama und Yamī," in *Gurupūjākaumudī, Festgabe . . . Albrecht Weber*, pp. 19–22. Leipzig, 1896.

Keith, A. B., "Pythagoras and the Doctrine of Transmigration," in *JRAS* 1909, pp. 569–606.

Scherman, L., *Materialien zur Geschichte der indischen Visionslitteratur*. Leipzig, 1892.

Windisch, E., *Buddha's Geburt*, pp. 57–76. Leipzig, 1908.

## IV. THE EPIC

### (*a*) *Texts and Translations*

#### (α) *Mahābhārata*

The *Mahābhārata* has been edited several times in India: at Calcutta in 1834–39 and 1894, at Madras in 1855–60, at Bombay in 1863, 1888, and 1890. An edition based on the South Indian manuscripts, which vary greatly from those in Northern India, was published at Bombay in 1906–11. There are two complete English translations, one made at the expense of Pratāpa Chandra Rāy, Calcutta, 1882–94, and one by M. N. Dutt, Calcutta, 1895–1904.

The *Bhagavadgītā*, which has been edited repeatedly, is translated by K. T. Telang in *SBE* viii (2nd ed., 1898) (together with the *Anugītā* and *Sanatsujātīya*), R. Garbe, Leipzig, 1905, P. Deussen and O. Strauss, in *Vier philosophische Texte des Mahābhāratam, Sanatsujāta-Parvan-Bhagavadgītā-Mokṣadharma-Anugītā*, Leipzig, 1906 (the *Bhagavadgītā* separately, Leipzig, 1911).

#### (β) *Rāmāyaṇa*

The *Rāmāyaṇa*, which exists in three different recensions, has often been edited: by G. Gorresio, Turin, 1843–67, K. B. Parab, 3rd ed., Bombay, 1909, and T. R. Krishnacharya and T. R. Vyasacharya, Bombay, 1911. It has been translated by R. T. H. Griffith, Benares, 1895, M. N. Dutt, Calcutta, 1892–93, and A. Roussel, Paris, 1903–09.

### (*b*) *Treatises*

Bühler, G., *Indian Studies*, ii. Vienna, 1892.

Dahlmann, J., *Das Mahābhārata als Epos und Rechtsbuch*. Berlin, 1895.

——— *Genesis des Mahābhārata*. Berlin, 1899.

——— *Die Sāṁkhya Philosophie*. Berlin, 1902.

Fausböll, V., *Indian Mythology according to the Mahābhārata in Outline*. London, 1902.

Feer, L., "Vṛtra et Namuci dans le Mahābhārata," in *Revue de l'histoire des religions*, xiv. 291–307 (1886).

Garbe, R., *Indien und das Christentum*, pp. 209–71. Tübingen, 1914.

Holzmann, A., *Agni*. Strassburg, 1878.

——— *Arjuna*. Strassburg, 1879.

——— "Indra," in *ZDMG* xxxii. 290–340 (1878).

HOLZMANN, A., "Die Apsarasen," in *ZDMG* xxxiii. 631–44 (1879).
——— "Agastya," in *ZDMG* xxxiv. 589–96 (1880).
——— "Brahman," in *ZDMG* xxxviii. 167–234 (1884).
——— *Das Mahābhārata.* 4 vols. Kiel, 1892–95.
HOPKINS, E. W., *The Great Epic of India.* New York, 1901.
——— *India Old and New.* New York, 1901.
——— "Mythological Aspects of Trees and Mountains in the Great Epic," in *JAOS* xxx. 347–74 (1910).
——— "Sanskrit Kabăiras or Kubăiras and Greek Kabeiros," in *JAOS* xxxiii. 55–70 (1913).
——— *Epic Mythology.* Strassburg, 1915.
JACOBI, H., *Das Rāmāyaṇa.* Bonn, 1893.
——— *Das Mahābhārata.* Bonn, 1903.
KEITH, A. B., "The Child Kṛṣṇa," in *JRAS* 1908, pp. 169–75.
KENNEDY, J., "The Child Kṛṣṇa," in *JRAS* 1907, pp. 951–92.
LUDWIG, A., *Ueber das Verhältnis des mythischen Elementes zu der historischen Grundlage des Mahābhārata.* Prague, 1884.
——— *Ueber das Rāmāyaṇa und die Beziehungen desselben zum Mahābhārata.* Prague, 1894.
ROUSSEL, A., *Idées religieuses et sociales de l'Inde ancienne d'après les légendes du Mahābhārata.* Fribourg, 1911.
SCHOEBEL, C., *Le Rāmāyaṇa au point de vue religieux, philosophique et moral.* Paris, 1888.
SÖRENSEN, S., *Index to the Mahābhārata.* London, 1904 ff.
SPEIJER, J. S., "Le Mythe de Nahusha," in *Acten des sechsten internationalen Orientalisten-Congresses*, iii. 81–120 (Leyden, 1885).
VAIDYA, C. V., *The Riddle of the Rāmāyaṇa.* Bombay and London, 1906.
WEBER, A., *Ueber das Rāmāyaṇa.* Berlin, 1870.

## V. THE PURĀṆAS AND TANTRAS

The following eighteen texts are generally recognized as the *Purāṇas par excellence:*

1. *Brahma Purāṇa.* Ed. *ASS* 1895.
2. *Padma Purāṇa.* Preserved in two recensions, the first as yet unedited, the second ed. N. N. Mandlick, in *ASS* 1894.
3. *Viṣṇu Purāṇa.* Ed. Jībānanda Vidyāsāgara, Calcutta, 1882; tr. H. H. Wilson, London, 1840 (2nd ed. by F. Hall, in Wilson's *Works*, vi–ix, London, 1864–77), M. N. Dutt, Calcutta, 1896; Book

v, on the life of Kṛṣṇa, by A. Paul, *Krischnas Weltengang*, Munich, 1905.

4. *Vāyu Purāṇa.* Ed. Rājendralāla Mitra, in *BI* 1880–88, *ASS* 1905.

5. *Bhāgavata Purāna.* Ed. Bombay, 1904, 1910; ed. and tr. E. Burnouf, M. Hauvette-Besnault, and P. Roussel, 5 vols., Paris, 1840–98. See also P. Roussel, *Cosmologie hindoue d'après le Bhāgavata Purāṇa*, Paris, 1898, *Légendes morales de l'Inde*, Paris, 1900.

6. *Nārada* (or *Nāradīya* or *Bṛhannāradīya*) *Purāṇa.* Ed. Hṛṣīkeśa Śāstrī, in *BI* 1891.

7. *Mārkaṇḍeya Purāṇa.* Ed. K. M. Banerjea, in *BI* 1862, Jībānanda Vidyāsāgara, Calcutta, 1879; tr. F. E. Pargiter, in *BI* 1888–1905, M. N. Dutt, Calcutta, 1897.

8. *Agni Purāṇa.* Ed. *BI* 1870–79, *ASS* 1900; tr. M. N. Dutt, Calcutta, 1903–04.

9. *Bhaviṣya Purāṇa.* Ed. Bombay, 1897. (An interpolated and in part untrustworthy text; see T. Aufrecht, in *ZDMG* lvii. 276–84 [1903].)

10. *Brahmavaivarta* (or *Brahmakaivarta*) *Purāṇa.* Ed. Calcutta, 1888.

11. *Liṅga Purāna.* Ed. Bombay, 1857, Jībānanda Vidyāsāgara, Calcutta, 1885.

12. *Varāha Purāṇa.* Ed. Hṛṣīkeśa Sāstrī, Calcutta, 1887–93.

13. *Skanda Purāṇa.* The original is lost, but various texts claim to be parts of it: *Sūtasaṁhitā*, ed. *ASS* 1893; *Śahyādrikhaṇḍa*, ed. T. G. da Cunha, Bombay, 1877; *Kāśīkhaṇḍa*, ed. Benares, 1868, Bombay, 1881.

14. *Vāmana Purāṇa.* Ed. Calcutta, 1885.

15. *Kūrma Purāṇa.* Ed. Nīlmaṇi Mukhopādhyāya Nyāyālaṁkāra, Calcutta, 1886–90.

16. *Matsya Purāṇa.* Ed. Jībānanda Vidyāsāgara, Calcutta, 1876, *ASS* 1907.

17. *Garuḍa Purāṇa.* Ed. Jībānanda Vidyāsāgara, Calcutta, 1890, Bombay, 1903; tr. in *Sacred Books of the Hindus*, ix, Allahabad, 1911.

18. *Brahmāṇḍa Purāṇa.* Not extant as a whole; a part, *Adhyātmarāmāyaṇa* ed. Bombay, 1891, 1907.

Of the *Upapurāṇas*, or minor texts of this type, the *Kālikā Purāṇa*, which contains an important chapter on the victims offered to Durgā, was published at Bombay in 1891; the *Saura Purāṇa* is edited in *ASS* 1889, and summarized and partially translated by W. Jahn, Strassburg, 1908.

Much information on the contents of the *Purāṇas* is given by H. H. Wilson in his translation of the *Viṣṇu Purāṇa* and in his *Essays on*

*Sanskrit Literature* (*Works*, iii. 1–155), by E. Burnouf in the preface to his edition and translation of the *Bhāgavata Purāṇa*, by T. Aufrecht in his *Catalogus codicum mss. Sanscriticorum . . . in Bibliotheca Bodleiana*, Oxford, 1859, and by J. Eggeling in his *Catalogue of the Sanskrit Manuscripts in the Library of the India Office*, vi, London, 1899. See also A. Holzmann, *Das Mahābhārata*, 4 vols., Kiel, 1892–95 (especially vol. iv.).

The Tantric texts are now being made accessible by a series of translations, etc., by "Arthur Avalon," Calcutta and London, 1913 ff. Those which have thus far appeared are as follows: *Tantra of the Great Liberation* (*Mahānirvāṇatantra*), with introduction and commentary; *Hymns to the Goddess* (*Tantrābhidhāna*), Sanskrit text and English translation; *Ṣaṭcakranirūpaṇa*, Sanskrit text and English translation; *Principles of Tantra*, part 1, *The Tantratattva of Śrīyukta Śiva Chandra Vidyārṇava Bhattāchārya Mahodaya*, with introduction and commentary; *Prapañcasāra Tantra*, ed. Tārānātha Vidyāratna; *Kulacūḍāmaṇi Tantra*, ed. Girīśa Candra Vedāntatīrtha. These texts are intended to bring out the philosophic meaning of the belief in the female principle as the Supreme Being.

## VI. BUDDHISM

### (*a*) *Texts and Translations*

Of the texts of the Southern canon, preserved in Pāli and at the present time current in Ceylon, the most important for mythology is the sixteenth *Sutta* of the *Dīgha Nikāya*, the *Mahāparinibbānasutta*, tr. T. W. Rhys Davids, *Dialogues of the Buddha*, London, 1910, K. E. Neumann, *Die letzten Tage Gotamo Buddho's*, Munich, 1911. The tales of the *Jātakas* pertain to folk-lore rather than mythology proper.

Of works which, while belonging frankly to the Hīnayāna, show a tendency to the doctrines of the Mahāyāna the chief is the *Mahāvastu*, ed. É. Sénart, 3 vols., Paris, 1882–97.

Of those of Mahāyānistic tendency the most notable are: *Lalitavistara*, ed. S. Lefmann, 2 vols., Halle, 1902–08; tr. P. E. Foucaux, in *Annales du Musée Guimet*, vi, xix (Paris, 1884–94; this may originally have been a Hīnayāna text); *Buddhacarita* by Aśvaghoṣa, ed. E. B. Cowell, Oxford, 1893; tr. E. B. Cowell, in *SBE* xlix (1894) (it dates perhaps from about 100 A. D.); *Saundarānanda Kāvya* by Aśvaghoṣa, ed. Haraprasāda Śāstrī, in *BI* 1910; *Sūtrālaṁkāra* by Aśvaghoṣa, of which only a Chinese translation exists, tr. E. Huber, Paris, 1908; *Mahāyānaśraddhotpāda* by an author whose identity is uncertain, tr. from Chinese by Teitaro Suzuki, *Aśvaghosha's Discourse on the Awakening of Faith in the Mahāyāna*, Chicago, 1900; *Jātaka-*

*māla* by Āryaśūra (of the school of Aśvaghoṣa), ed. H. Kern, Cambridge, Mass., 1891; tr. J. S. Speyer, London, 1895; *Avadānaśataka*, ed. J. S. Speyer, Petrograd, 1902–09; tr. L. Feer, in *Annales du Musée Guimet*, xviii (Paris, 1891); *Divyāvadāna*, ed. E. B. Cowell and R. A. Neil, Cambridge, 1886 (in the main Hīnayāna of the second or third century A. D.).

The following *Sūtras* are strictly Mahāyānistic: *Saddharmapuṇḍarīka*, ed. H. Kern and Bunyiu Nanjio, Petrograd, 1908 ff.; tr. H. Kern, in *SBE* xxi (1884); *Kāraṇḍavyūha*, prose version ed. Satyavrata Sāmaśramī, Calcutta, 1873; *Sukhāvatīvyūha*, ed. F. Max Müller and Bunyiu Nanjio, Oxford, 1883; tr. F. Max Müller, in *SBE* xlix (1894); *Amitāyurdhyānasūtra*, tr. from Chinese by J. Takakusu, in *SBE* xlix (1894); *Laṅkāvatāra*, ed. Calcutta, 1900; *Rāṣṭrapālapraipṛcchā*, ed. L. Finot, Petrograd, 1901.

Of the Buddhist Tantric literature the *Pañcakrama* is edited by L. de la Vallée Poussin, *Études et textes tantriques*, Ghent and Louvain, 1896; *Bodhicaryāvatāra* by Śāntideva, tr. L. de la Vallée Poussin, Paris, 1907.

### (*b*) *Indian Buddhism*

Burnouf, E., *Introduction à l'histoire du bouddhisme indien*. 2nd ed. Paris, 1876.

Copleston, R. S., *Buddhism, Primitive and Present, in Magadha and Ceylon*. 2nd ed. London, 1908.

Dahlmann, J., *Nirvāṇa*. Berlin, 1896.

——— *Buddha*. Berlin, 1898.

——— *Indische Fahrten*. Freiburg, 1908.

——— *Die Thomas-Legende*. Freiburg, 1912.

Eklund, J. A., *Nirvana*. Upsala, 1900.

Foucher, A., *Étude sur l'iconographie bouddhique de l'Inde*. 2 vols. Paris, 1900–05.

——— *L'Art gréco-bouddhique du Gandhāra*. Paris, 1905.

——— *The Beginnings of Buddhist Art and other Essays in Indian Archaeology*. London, 1915.

Getty, A., *The Gods of Northern Buddhism*. Oxford, 1914.

Gogerly, D. J., *Ceylon Buddhism*. New ed. Colombo, 1908.

Grünwedel, A., *Buddhistische Kunst in Indien*. 2nd ed. Berlin, 1900; English translation, with additions, by T. Burgess and Mrs. Gibson. London, 1901.

Hackmann, H., *Buddhism as a Religion*. London, 1910.

Hardy, E., *Der Buddhismus*. Münster, 1890.

Hardy, R. S., *Manual of Buddhism*. 2nd ed. London, 1880.

KERN, J., *Der Buddhismus und seine Geschichte in Indien* (tr. H. Jacobi). 2 vols. Leipzig, 1882–84.

——— *Manual of Indian Buddhism.* Strassburg, 1896.

KOEPPEN, C. F., *Die Religion des Buddha.* 2nd ed. Berlin, 1906.

LEHMANN, E., *Der Buddhismus.* Tübingen, 1910.

MONIER-WILLIAMS, SIR M., *Buddhism.* London, 1889.

NAGENDRA NATH VASU, *The Northern Buddhism and its Followers in Orissa.* Calcutta, 1911.

OLDENBERG, H., *Buddha, sein Leben, seine Lehre und seine Gemeinde.* 5th ed. Berlin, 1906. English tr. of 1st ed., London, 1882.

PISCHEL, R., *Leben und Lehre des Buddha.* 2nd ed. Leipzig, 1910.

RHYS DAVIDS, T. W., *History of Indian Buddhism.* 3rd ed. London, 1897.

——— *Buddhism, its History and Literature.* London, 1904.

——— "Buddha," in *Encyclopædia Britannica,* 11th ed., iv. 737–42.

——— "Buddhism," in *Encyclopædia Britannica,* 11th ed., iv. 742–49.

SÉNART, É., *Essai sur la légende du Bouddha.* 2nd ed. Paris, 1882.

SUZUKI, TEITARO, *Outlines of Mahāyāna Buddhism.* London, 1907.

DE LA VALLÉE POUSSIN, L., *Bouddhisme, Études et materiaux.* Brussels, 1897.

——— *Bouddhisme, Opinions sur l'histoire de la dogmatique.* Paris, 1909.

WINDISCH, E., *Māra und Buddha.* Leipzig, 1895.

——— *Buddha's Geburt.* Leipzig, 1908.

WINTERNITZ, M., *Geschichte der indischen Litteratur,* ii, part 1. Leipzig, 1913.

### (*c*) *Tibetan Buddhism*

FRANCKE, A. H., *Antiquities of Indian Thibet,* i. Calcutta, 1914.

GRÜNWEDEL, A., *Mythologie des Buddhismus in Thibet und der Mongolei.* Leipzig, 1900.

——— *Bericht über archäologische Arbeiten in Idikutschari und Umgebung im Winter 1902–1903.* Munich, 1906.

——— *Alt-buddhistische Kulturstätten in Chinesisch-Turkestan.* Berlin, 1912.

PANDER, E., *Das Pantheon des Tschangtscha Hutuktu; ein Beitrag zur Iconographie des Lamaismus.* Ed. A. Grünwedel, in *Veröffentlichungen aus dem königlichen Museum für Völkerkunde in Berlin,* 1890.

RHYS DAVIDS, T. W., "Lāmāism," in *Encyclopædia Britannica*, 11th ed., xvi. 96–100.

ROCKHILL, W. W., *The Land of the Lamas*. London, 1891.

SCHLAGINTWEIT, E., *Buddhism in Thibet*. Leipzig and London, 1863.

WADDELL, L. A., *The Buddhism of Thibet*. London, 1895.

(*d*) *Buddhism, Hinduism, and Christianity*

AIKEN, C. F., *The Dhamma of Gotama the Buddha and the Gospel of Jesus the Christ*. Boston, 1900.

CLEMEN, C., *Religionsgeschichtliche Erklärung des Neuen Testaments*. Giessen, 1909.

EDMUNDS, A. J., *Buddhist and Christian Gospels*. 4th ed. by M. Anesaki. 2 vols. Philadelphia, 1908–09.

FABER, G., *Buddhistische und Neutestamentliche Erzählungen*. Leipzig, 1913.

GARBE, R., *Indien und das Christentum*. Tübingen, 1914.

GRAY, L. H., "Brahmanistic Parallels in the Apocryphal New Testament," in *American Journal of Theology*, vii. 308–13 (1903).

HASE, K. VON, *Neutestamentliche Parallelen zu buddhistischen Quellen*. Berlin, 1905.

HOPKINS, E. W., *India Old and New*. New York, 1902.

KUHN, E., "Buddhistisches in den apokryphen Evangelien," in *Gurupūjākaumudī, Festgabe . . . Albrecht Weber*, pp. 116–19. Leipzig, 1896.

PFLEIDERER, O., *Die Entstehung des Christentums*. 2nd ed. Munich, 1907.

SEYDEL, R., *Das Evangelium von Jesu in seinen Verhältnissen zu Buddha-Sage und Buddha-Lehre*. Leipzig, 1882.

——— *Die Buddha-Legende und das Leben Jesu nach den Evangelien*. 2nd ed. Weimar, 1897.

SÖDERBLOM, N., "The Place of the Christian Trinity and of the Buddhist Triratna amongst Holy Triads," in *Transactions of the Third International Congress for the History of Religions*, pp. 391–410 (London, 1912).

DE LA VALLÉE POUSSIN, L., "L'Histoire des religions de l'Inde et l'apologétique," in *Revue des sciences philosophiques et théologiques*, vi. 490–526 (1912).

VAN DEN BERGH VAN EYSINGA, A., *Indische Einflüsse auf evangelische Erzählungen*. 2nd ed. Göttingen, 1909.

WEBER, A., *Über Kṛshṇa's Geburtsfest, Kṛshṇajanmāshṭamī.* Berlin, 1868.

WECKER, O., *Christus und Buddha.* 3rd ed. Münster, 1910.

## VII. JAINISM

### (a) *Texts and Translations*

The sacred texts of the Jains have been published in Indian editions, usually with Sanskrit commentaries and vernacular explanations. The following have been edited or translated in Europe, being classed either as *Aṅgas* or *Upāṅgas: Nirayāvaliyāsuttam, een Upanga der Jaina's*, ed. S. J. Warren, Amsterdam, 1879; *Ācārāṅga Sūtra*, ed. H. Jacobi, London, 1882; tr. H. Jacobi, in *SBE* xxii (1884); *Uttarādhyayana Sūtra*, ed. Calcutta, 1879; tr. H. Jacobi, in *SBE* xlv (1895); *Sūtrakṛtānga Sūtra*, ed. Bombay, 1880; tr. H. Jacobi, in *SBE* xlv (1895); *Upāsakadaśā Sūtra*, ed. and tr. A. F. R. Hoernle, in *BI* 1888–90; *Aupapātika Sūtra*, ed. E. Leumann, Leipzig, 1883; *Daśavaikālika Sūtra*, ed. E. Leumann, in *ZDMG* xlvi. 581–613 (1892); *Antakrtadaśā Sūtra* and *Anuttaraupapātika Sūtra*, ed. Calcutta, 1875; tr. L. D. Barnett, London, 1907.

Of the many later canonical and non-canonical texts by far the most important is the *Kalpasūtra* by Bhadrabāhu, ed. H. Jacobi, Leipzig, 1879; tr. H. Jacobi, in *SBE* xxii (1884). Jacobi has also edited and translated the following: *Bhaktāmarastotra* and *Kalyāṇamandirastotra*, in *Indische Studien*, xiv. 359–91 (1876), *Caturviṁśatijinastuti*, in *ZDMG* xxxii. 509–34 (1878), *Sthavirāvalīcarita* or *Pariśiṣṭaparvan* by Hemacandra, in *BI* 1891, *Tattvārthādhigama Sūtra* by Umāsvāti, in *ZDMG* lx. 287–325, 512–51 (1906). Other noteworthy texts are *Ṛṣabhapañcāśikā* by Dhanapāla, ed. and tr. J. Klatt, in *ZDMG* xxxiii. 445–83 (1879); *Yogaśāstra* by Hemacandra, ed. and tr. E. Windisch, in *ZDMG* xxviii. 185–262, 678–79 (1874); *Śryādīśvaracarita* by Hemacandra, ed. Narmadāśaṅkaraśarman, Bombay, 1905; *Prabandhacintāmaṇi* by Merutuṅga, tr. C. H. Tawney, in *BI* 1899; *Kathākośa*, tr. C. H. Tawney, London, 1895; *Kalpasūtra*, ed. and tr. W. Schubring, Leipzig, 1905; *Jīvavicāra* by Śāntisūri, ed. and tr. A. Guérinot, in *Journal asiatique*, IX. xix. 231–88 (1902).

### (b) *Treatises*

BHANDARKAR, R. G., *Report on the Search for Sanskrit Manuscripts in the Bombay Presidency for the Year 1883–4.* Bombay, 1887.

BÜHLER, G., *Ueber die indische Secte der Jaina.* Vienna, 1887.

Burgess, J., "Note on Jaina Mythology," in *Indian Antiquary*, xxx. 27–28 (1901).

——— "Digambara Jaina Iconography," in *Indian Antiquary*, xxxii. 459–64 (1903).

——— "Jaina Mythology," in his translation of G. Bühler, *On the Indian Sect of the Jains*. London, 1903.

Feer, L., "Nātaputta et les Nigaṇṭhas," in *Journal asiatique*, VIII. xii. 209–52 (1888).

Guérinot, A., "La Doctrine des êtres vivants dans la religion jaina," in *Revue de l'histoire des religions*, xlvii. 34–50 (1903).

——— *Essai de bibliographie jaina*. Paris, 1906.

——— *Répertoire d'épigraphie jaina, précédé d'une esquisse de l'histoire du jainisme d'après les inscriptions*. Paris, 1908.

Hoernle, A. F. R., "Jainism and Buddhism," in *Proceedings of the Asiatic Society of Bengal*, 1898, pp. 39–55.

Jacobi, H., "Ueber die Entstehung der Çvetāmbara und Digambara Sekten," in *ZDMG* xxxviii. 1–42 (1884), xl. 92–98 (1886).

——— "Die Jaina Legende von dem Untergange Dvāravatī's und von dem Tode Kṛishṇa's," in *ZDMG* xlii. 493–529 (1888).

——— "Ueber den Jainismus und die Verehrung Krischna's," in *Berichte des VII internationalen Orientalisten-Congresses*, pp. 75–77 (Vienna, 1889).

Jaini, J., *Outlines of Jainism*. Cambridge, 1916.

Jhaveri, J. L., *First Principles of Jaina Philosophy*. Bombay, 1912.

Karbhari, B. F., *The Jain Philosophy collected and edited*. Bombay, 1912.

Leumann, E., "Die alten Berichte von den Schismen der Jaina," in *Indische Studien*, xv. 91–135 (1885).

——— *Die Avaśyaka-Erzählungen*. Leipzig, 1897.

Milloué, L. de, *Essai sur la religion des Jains*. Louvain, 1884.

——— "Étude sur le mythe de Vṛišabha," in *Annales du Musée Guimet*, x. 413–43 (1887).

Mironow, N., *Die Dharmaparīkṣa des Amitagati*. Leipzig, 1903.

Pullé, F. L., "La Cartografia antica dell' India," part 1, in *Studi italiani di filologia indo-iranica*, iv. 14–41 (1901).

Stevenson, Mrs. Sinclair, *Notes on Modern Jainism*. Oxford, 1910.

——— *The Heart of Jainism*. Oxford, 1915.

Warren, S. J., *Over die godsdienstige en wijsgeerige begrippen der Jainas*. Amsterdam, 1875.

WEBER, A., *Ueber das Çatrunjaya Māhātmyam.* Leipzig, 1858.

——— *Ueber ein Fragment der Bhagavatī.* 2 parts. Berlin, 1866–67.

——— "Ueber die Sūryaprajñapti," in *Indische Studien*, x. 256–316 (1868).

——— *Pañcadaṇḍachattraprabandha.* Berlin, 1877.

——— "Ueber die heiligen Schriften der Jaina," in *Indische Studien*, xvi. 211–479, xvii. 1–90 (1883–85). English translation by H. W. Smyth, in *Indian Antiquary*, xvii–xxi (1888–92).

——— *Ueber die Samyaktakaumudī.* Berlin, 1889.

## VIII. MODERN HINDUISM

BHANDARKAR, SIR R. G., *Vaisṇavism, Śaivism and Minor Religious Systems.* Strassburg, 1913.

BIRDWOOD, SIR G. C. M., *The Industrial Arts of India.* London, 1880.

CAMPBELL, A., *Santal Folk Tales.* Pokhuria, 1891.

CAMPBELL, J. S., *Notes on the Spirit Basis of Belief and Custom.* Bombay, 1885.

CARNEGY, P., *Notes on the Races, Tribes and Castes inhabiting the Province of Oudh.* Lucknow, 1868.

CROOKE, W., *North Indian Notes and Queries.* 6 vols. Allahabad, 1891–96.

——— *Tribes and Castes of the North-Western Provinces and Oudh.* 4 vols. Calcutta, 1896.

——— *Popular Religion and Folk-Lore of Northern India.* 2 vols. Westminster, 1896.

DALTON, E. T., *Descriptive Ethnology of Bengal.* Calcutta, 1872.

DAY, L. B., *Folk-Tales of Bengal.* London, 1883.

DUBOIS, J. A., *Hindu Manners and Customs.* 3rd ed. by H. K. Beauchamp. Oxford, 1906.

ELMORE, W. T., *Dravidian Gods in Modern Hinduism.* Lincoln, Neb., 1915.

FARQUHAR, J. N., *Modern Religious Movements in India.* New York, 1915.

GANGOOLY, O. C., *South Indian Bronzes.* Calcutta, 1915.

GOPINATHA RAO, T. A., *Elements of Hindu Iconography.* Madras, 1914.

GRIERSON, G. A., *Bihar Peasant Life.* Calcutta, 1885.

GROWSE, F. S., *Rāmāyan of Tulasi Dās.* 4th ed. Allahabad, 1887.

Growse, S. F., *Mathura, a District Memoir.* Allahabad, 1885.

Ibbetson, D. C. J., *Panjab Ethnography.* Calcutta, 1883.

Jackson, A. M. T., and Enthoven, R. E., *Folklore Notes,* i (Gujarāt). Bombay, 1914.

Kittel, F., *Ueber den Ursprung des Lingakultus in Indien.* Mangalore, 1876.

Knowles, J. H., *Folk-Tales of Kashmir.* 2nd ed. London, 1893.

Lévi, S., *Le Népal,* i. Paris, 1905.

McCulloch, W., *Bengali Household Tales.* London, 1912.

Nāṭeśa Śāstrī, *Folklore of Southern India.* 3 parts. Bombay, 1884–88.

Parker, H., *Village Folk-Tales of Ceylon.* 3 vols. London, 1910–14.

Ralston, W. R. S., *Tibetan Tales.* London, 1906.

Risley, H. H., *Tribes and Castes of Bengal.* Calcutta, 1891.

——— *The People of India.* 2 vols. 2nd ed. London, 1915.

Rivers, W. H. R., *The Todas.* London, 1906.

Russell, R. V., *The Tribes and Castes of the Central Provinces of India.* 4 vols. London, 1916.

Sherring, M. A., *The Sacred City of the Hindus.* London, 1868.

——— *Hindu Tribes and Castes.* 3 vols. Calcutta, 1872–81.

Sleeman, W. H., *Rambles and Recollections of an Indian Official.* London, 1893.

Srinivas Aiyangar, M., *Tamil Studies.* Madras, 1914.

Swynnerton, C., *Indian Nights' Entertainment.* London, 1892.

——— *Romantic Tales from the Panjâb.* Westminster, 1903.

Temple, R. C., *Panjab Notes and Queries.* 4 vols. Allahabad, 1883–86.

——— *Wide-Awake Stories.* Bombay, 1884.

——— *Legends of the Panjâb.* 3 vols. Bombay, 1884–1900.

Thurston, E., *Omens and Superstitions of Southern India.* London, 1912.

Thurston, E., and Rangachari, K., *Castes and Tribes of Southern India.* 7 vols. Madras, 1909.

Tod, J., *Annals and Antiquities of Rajasthan.* Rev. ed. with preface by D. Sladen. 2 vols. London, 1914.

Whitehead, H., *The Village Gods of South India.* London, 1916.

Wilkins, W. J., *Modern Hinduism.* 2nd ed. London, 1900.

Ziegenbalg, B., *Genealogy of the South Indian Gods.* English tr. Madras, 1869.

Valuable information as to Hindu religion and mythology is given in the fragments of the Greek embassador to India, Megasthenes (early part of the third century B. C.), translated by J. W. McCrindle, *Ancient India as Described by Megasthenes and Arrian*, London, 1877. Still more importance attaches to the writings of the Chinese Buddhist pilgrims Fa Hien and Sung Yun (400 and 518 A. D. respectively), translated by S. Beal, London, 1869 (Fa Hien also by J. Legge, Oxford, 1886), Hsüan Tsang (629–45 A. D.), translated by S. Beal, new ed., London, 1906, and by T. Watters, 2 vols., London, 1904–06, and I Tsing (671–95 A. D.), translated by E. Chavannes, Paris, 1894, and J. Takakusu, Oxford, 1897. The account of India by al-Bīrūnī (about 1030 A. D.), translated by E. Sachau, new ed., London, 1906, contains much on mythology, as does the Persian *Dabistān*, written in the seventeenth century (tr. D. Shea and A. Troyer, Paris, 1843, ii. 1–288). Some incidental material may be gleaned from the old travellers in India, such as Pietro della Valle (early seventeenth century; ed. E. Grey, 2 vols., London, 1892), and from the earlier missionary material, notably A. Roger, *Open-Deure tot het verborgen Heydendom*, Leyden, 1651 (new ed. by W. Caland, The Hague, 1915; French tr. Amsterdam, 1670; German tr. Nuremberg, 1663), and an anonymous Roman Catholic Portuguese missionary of the early seventeenth century partly translated by L. C. Casartelli, in *Babylonian and Oriental Record*, viii. 248–59, 265–70, ix. 41–46, 63–67 (1900–01) and *Anthropos*, i. 864–76, ii. 128–32, 275–81, iii. 771–72 (1906–08) (the author is believed by H. Hosten, in *Anthropos*, ii. 272–74 [1907], to have been Fr. Francis Negrone). For the problem of the relations between India and the Greeks see A. Weber, "Die Griechen in Indien," in *Sitzungsberichte der königlich preussischen Akademie der Wissenschaften*, 1890, pp. 901–33; G. d'Alviella, *Ce que l'Inde doit à la Grèce*, Paris, 1897; S. Lévi, *Quid de Græcis veterum Indorum monumenta tradiderint*, Paris, 1890, H. G. Rawlinson, *Intercourse between India and the Western World from the Earliest Times to the Fall of Rome*, Cambridge, 1916. Reference may also be made to M. Reinaud, *Mémoire géographique, historique et scientifique sur l'Inde . . . d'après les écrivains arabes, persans et chinois*, Paris, 1849.

## IX. PRINCIPAL ARTICLES ON INDIAN RELIGION IN THE ENCYCLOPÆDIA OF RELIGION AND ETHICS (VOLS. I–VIII)

ALLAN, J., "Māyā," viii. 503–05.

ANDERSON, J. D., "Assam," ii. 131–38.

ANESAKI, M., "Docetism (Buddhist)," iv. 835–40.

Bloomfield, M., "Literature (Vedic and Classical Sanskrit)," viii. 106–13.

Bolling, G. M., "Divination (Vedic)," iv. 827–30.

——— "Dreams and Sleep (Vedic)," v. 38–40.

Crooke, W., "Aghorī," i. 210–13.

——— "Ahīr," i. 232–34.

——— "Baigā," ii. 333.

——— "Banjāṛa," ii. 347–48.

——— "Bengal," ii. 479–501.

——— "Bhangi," ii. 551–53.

——— "Bhīls," ii. 554–56.

——— "Bombay," ii. 786–91.

——— "Death and Disposal of the Dead (Indian, non-Aryan)," iv. 479–84.

——— "Demons and Spirits (Indian)," iv. 601–08.

——— "Dosādh, Dusādh," iv. 852–53.

——— "Dravidians (North India)," v. 1–21.

——— "Gangā, Ganges," vi. 177–79.

——— "Gurkhā, Gorkhā," vi. 456–57.

——— "Hinduism," vi. 686–715.

——— "Images and Idols (Indian)," vii. 142–46.

——— "Kandh, Khond," vii. 648–51.

Deussen, P., "Ātman," ii. 195–97.

Frazer, R. W., "Dravidians (South India)," v. 21–28.

——— "Literature (Dravidian)," viii. 91–92.

Garbe, R., "Bhagavad-Gītā," ii. 535–38.

Geden, A. S., "Buddha, Life of the," ii. 881–85.

——— "Devayāna," iv. 677–79.

——— "Fate (Buddhist)," v. 780–82.

——— "God (Buddhist)," vi. 269–72.

——— "God (Hindu)," vi. 282–90.

——— "Images and Idols (Buddhist)," vii. 119–27.

——— "Inspiration (Hindu)," vii. 352–54.

Grierson, Sir G. A., "Bhakti-Mārga," ii. 539–51.

——— "Dards," iv. 399–402.

——— "Gāṇapatyas," vi. 175–76.

Gurdon, P. R. T., "Āhoms," i. 234–37.

——— "Khāsis," vii. 690–92.

Hillebrandt, A., "Brahman," ii. 796–99.
——— "Death and Disposal of the Dead (Hindu)," iv. 475–79.
Hodson, T. C., "Lushais," viii. 197–98.
Hoernle, A. F. R., "Ājīvikas," i. 259–68.
Hopkins, E. W., "Festivals and Fasts (Hindu)," v. 867–71.
Jacobi, H., "Agastya," i. 180–81.
——— "Ages of the World (Indian)," i. 200–02.
——— "Blest, Abode of the (Hindu)," ii. 698–700.
——— "Brāhmanism," ii. 799–813.
——— "Chakravartin," iii. 336–37.
——— "Cosmogony and Cosmology (Indian)," iv. 155–61.
——— "Cow (Hindu)," iv. 224–26.
——— "Daitya," iv. 390–92.
——— "Death and Disposal of the Dead (Jain)," iv. 484–85.
——— "Digambaras," iv. 704.
——— "Divination (Indian)," iv. 799–800.
——— "Durgā," v. 117–19.
——— "Heroes and Hero-Gods (Indian)," vi. 658–61.
——— "Incarnation (Indian)," vii. 193–97.
——— "Jainism," vii. 465–74.
Jolly, J., "Fate (Hindu)," v. 790–92.
Lyall, Sir C. J., "Mikirs," viii. 628–31.
Macdonell, A. A., "Hymns (Vedic)," vii. 49–58.
——— "Indian Buddhism," vii. 209–16.
——— "Literature (Buddhist)," viii. 85–89.
——— "Magic (Vedic)," viii. 311–21.
Rhys Davids, T. W., "Anāgata Vaṁsa," i. 414.
——— "Hīnayāna," vi. 684–86.
Rose, H. A., "Life and Death (Indian)," viii. 34–37.
——— "Magic (Indian)," viii. 289–93.
Russell, R. V., "Central Provinces," iii. 311–16.
Scott, Sir J. G., "Burma and Assam (Buddhism in)," iii. 37–44.
Sieg, E., "Bhṛgu," ii. 558–60.
Stevenson, M., "Festivals and Fasts (Jain)," v. 875–79.
Temple, Sir R. C., "Fetishism (Indian)," v. 903–06.
De la Vallée Poussin, L., "Ādibuddha," i. 93–100.
——— "Ages of the World (Buddhist)," i. 187–90.
——— "Avalokiteśvara," ii. 256–61.

De la Vallée Poussin, L., "Blest, Abode of the (Buddhist)," ii. 687–89.

——— "Bodhisattva," ii. 739–53.

——— "Cosmogony and Cosmology (Buddhist)," iv. 129–38.

——— "Death and Disposal of the Dead (Buddhist)," iv. 446–49.

——— "Incarnation (Buddhist)," vii. 186–88.

——— "Karma," vii. 673–76.

——— "Magic (Buddhist)," viii. 255–57.

——— "Mahāyāna," viii. 330–36.

——— "Mañjuśrī," viii. 405–06.

——— "Māra," viii. 406–07.

Waddell, L. A., "Death and Disposal of the Dead (Tibetan)," iv. 509–11.

——— "Demons and Spirits (Buddhist)," iv. 571–72.

——— "Demons and Spirits (Tibetan)," iv. 635–36.

——— "Divination (Buddhist)," iv. 786–87.

——— "Festivals and Fasts (Tibetan)," v. 892–94.

——— "Jewel (Buddhist)," vii. 553–57.

——— "Lāmaism," vii. 784–89.

Winternitz, M., "Jātaka," vii. 491–94.

# IRANIAN

## I. TEXTS AND TRANSLATIONS

1. *Avesta*. Ed. N. L. Westergaard, Copenhagen, 1852–54, F. Spiegel (incomplete), 2 vols., Vienna, 1853–58, K. F. Geldner, 3 vols., Stuttgart, 1885–96; the *Gāthās* only ed. and tr. M. Haug, 2 vols., Leipzig, 1858–60, L. H. Mills, Oxford, 1892–94; tr. Anquetil du Perron, 2 vols., Paris, 1771, F. Spiegel, 3 vols., Leipzig, 1852–63 (English tr. by A. Bleeck, 3 vols., Hertford, 1864), C. de Harlez, 2nd ed., Paris, 1881, J. Darmesteter and L. H. Mills, in *SBE* * iv (2nd ed., 1895), xxiii, xxxi (1883), J. Darmesteter, 3 vols., Paris, 1892–93, F. Wolff, Strassburg, 1910; the *Gāthās* only tr. L. H. Mills, Oxford, 1900, C. Bartholomae, Strassburg, 1904.

2. *Pāhlavī*. (i) *Artā-ī-Vīrāf*. Ed. and tr. E. W. West and M. Haug, Bombay, 1872; ed. K. J. Jamasp Asa, Bombay, 1902; tr. A. Barthelemy, Paris, 1887. (ii) *Bahman Yasht*. Ed. K. A. Nosherwān, Bombay, 1899; tr. E. W. West, in *SBE* v. 191–235 (1880). (iii) *Būndahish*. Ed. and tr. F. Justi, Leipzig, 1868; tr. E. W. West, in *SBE* v. 3–151 (1880). (iv) *Dīnkarṭ*. Ed. and tr. P. B. and D. P. Sanjana, Bombay, 1874 ff.; ed. D. M. Madan, 2 vols., Bombay, 1911; tr. (partial) E. W. West, in *SBE* xxxvii, xlvii. 1–130 (1892–97). (v) *Great Būndahish*. Ed. T. D. Anklesaria, Bombay, 1908. (vi) *Gujastak-ī-Abālish*. Ed. and tr. A. Barthelemy, Paris, 1887; tr. I. Pizzi, in *Bessarione*, II. iii. 299–307 (1902). (vii) *Maīnōg-ī-Khraṭ*. Ed. and tr. E. W. West, Stuttgart and London, 1871; ed. D. P. Sanjana, Bombay, 1895; tr. E. W. West, in *SBE* xxiv. 3–113 (1885). (viii) *Selections of Zāṭ-Sparam*. Tr. E. W. West, in *SBE* v. 155–87, xlvii. 133–70 (1880–97). (ix) *Yōsht-ī-Fryānō*. Ed. and tr. E. W. West, in *The Book of Arda Viraf*, pp. 207–66, Bombay, 1872; tr. A. Barthelemy, Paris, 1889.

3. *Persian and Arabic*. (i) *Dabistān*. Tr. D. Shea and A. Troyer, 3 vols., Paris, 1843 (only vol. i relevant here). (ii) *Firdausī, Shāhnāmah*. Ed. T. Macan, 4 vols., Calcutta, 1829; ed. and tr. J. Mohl, 7 vols., Paris, 1838–78 (translation separately, 7 vols., Paris, 1876–78); ed. J. A. Vullers and S. Laudauer, 3 vols., Leyden, 1877–84 (incomplete); tr. I. Pizzi, 8 vols., Turin, 1886–88, A. G. and E. Warner,

* For the abbreviations see those given in the Indian Bibliography, *supra*, p. 371.

London, 1905 ff. (iii) *Mas'ūdī, Les Prairies d'or.* Ed. and tr. C. Barbier de Meynard and Pavet de Courteille, 9 vols., Paris, 1861–77. (iv) *Mirkhond, History of the Early Kings of Persia.* Tr. D. Shea, London, 1832. (v) Mohl, J., *Fragmens relatifs à la religion de Zoroastre*, Paris, 1829 (German tr. by J. A. Vullers, Bonn, 1831). (vi) *Shahristānī, Kitāb al-Milal w'al-Niḥal.* Ed. W. Cureton, London, 1846; tr. T. Haarbrücker, 2 vols., Halle, 1850–51. (vii) *Ṭabarī, Chronique . . . sur la version persane de Bel'ami.* Ed. and tr. H. Zotenberg, 4 vols., Paris, 1867–74 (see also T. Nöldeke, *Geschichte der Perser und Araber zur Zeit der Sasaniden aus der arabischen Chronik des Tabari*, Leyden, 1879). (viii) *Tha'ālibī, Histoire des rois de Perse.* Ed. and tr. H. Zotenberg, Paris, 1900. (ix) *'Ulamā-i-Islām.* Ed. J. Mohl, *Fragmens relatifs à la religion de Zoroastre*, pp. 1–10, Paris, 1829; tr. J. A. Vullers, *Fragmente ueber die Religion des Zoroaster*, pp. 43–67, Bonn, 1831, E. Blochet, in *Revue de l'histoire des religions*, xxxvii. 23–49 (1899). (x) *Zarātushtnāmah.* Ed. and tr. F. Rosenberg, Petrograd, 1904.

## II. NON-IRANIAN SOURCES

Eznik of Kolb, *Against the Sects.* Tr. J. M. Schmid. Vienna, 1900.

Gelzer, H., "Eznik und die Entwicklung des persischen Religionssystems," in *Zeitschrift für armenische Philologie*, i. 149–63 (1903).

Gottheil, R. J. H., "References to Zoroaster in Syriac and Arabic Literature," in *Classical Studies in Honour of Henry Drisler*, pp. 24–51. New York, 1894.

Gray, L. H., "Zoroastrian . . . Material in the Acta Sanctorum," in *Journal of the Manchester Egyptian and Oriental Society*, 1913–14, pp. 37–55.

Hoffmann, G., *Auszüge aus syrischen Akten persischer Märtyrer.* Leipzig, 1880.

Kleuker, J. F., *Zend-Avesta*, Appendix, vol. ii, part 3. Leipzig and Riga, 1783.

Nöldeke, T., "Syrische Polemik gegen die persische Religion," in *Festgruss an Rudolf von Roth*, pp. 34–38. Stuttgart, 1893.

Rapp, A., "Die Religion und Sitte der Perser und übrigen Iranier nach den griechischen und römischen Quellen," in *ZDMG* xix. 1–89, xx. 49–204 (1865–66). English translation by K. R. Cama, 2 vols. Bombay, 1876–79.

Söderblom, N., "Theopompus and the Avestan Ages of the World," in *Dastur Hoshang Memorial Volume*, pp. 228–30. Not yet published.

THEODORE BAR KŌNĪ, *Liber Scholiorum*, tr. H. Pognon, *Inscriptions mandaïtes des coupes de Khouabir*, pp. 161–65. Paris, 1898.

TIELE, C. P., "Plutarchus over de Amšaspands," in *Feestbundel Prof. Boot*, pp. 117–19. Leyden, 1901.

## III. GENERAL TREATISES

AYUSO, F. G., *Los Pueblos iranios y Zoroastro*. Madrid, 1874.

BARTHOLOMAE, C., *Altiranisches Wörterbuch*. Strassburg, 1905.

BRISSON, B., *De regio Persarum principatu*, pp. 338–401. Ed. J. H. Lederlin. Strassburg, 1710.

CARNOY, A. J., *Religion of the Avesta*. London, no date.

——— "Le Nom des Mages," in *Muséon*, II. ix. 121–58 (1908).

——— "La Magie dans l'Iran," in *Muséon*, III. i. 171–88 (1916).

——— "The Moral Deities of India and Iran and their Origins," in *American Journal of Theology*, xxi. 58–78 (1917).

CASARTELLI, L. C., *Philosophy of the Mazdayasnian Religion Under the Sassanids*. English translation by F. Jamaspji. Bombay, 1889.

——— *The Religion of the Great Kings*. London, no date.

DARMESTETER, J., *Études iraniennes*, ii. 187–231. Paris, 1883.

DESAI, P. B., "Iranian Mythology: Comparison of a few Iranian Episodes with Hindu and Greek Stories," in *Spiegel Memorial Volume*, pp. 40–49. Bombay, 1908.

DHALLA, M. N., *Zoroastrian Theology*. New York, 1914.

EASTON, M. W., "The Divinities of the Gāthās," in *JAOS* xv. 189–206 (1891).

FRACHTENBERG, L. J., "Allusions to Witchcraft and Other Primitive Beliefs in the Zoroastrian Literature," in *Dastur Hoshang Memorial Volume*, pp. 399–453. Not yet published.

GEIGER, W., *Ostiranische Kultur in Altertum*. Erlangen, 1882. English translation by D. P. Sanjana. 2 vols. London, 1885–86.

GELDNER, K., "Zend-Avesta," in *Encyclopædia Britannica*, 11th ed., xxviii. 967–69.

——— "Zoroaster," in *Encyclopædia Britannica*, 11th ed., xxviii. 1039–43.

GELDNER, K., and CHEYNE, T. K., "Zoroastrianism," in *Encyclopædia Biblica*, coll. 5428–42. London, 1899–1903.

GILMORE, G. W., "Zoroaster, Zoroastrianism," in *New Schaff-Herzog Encyclopedia of Religious Knowledge*, xii. 522–35. New York, 1908–12.

Gorvala, R. F., "The Immortal Soul: Its Pre-Existence, Persistence after Death and Transmigration," in *Spiegel Memorial Volume*, pp. 99–124. Bombay, 1908.

Harlez, C. de, "Les Origines du zoroastrisme," in *Journal asiatique*, VII. xi. 101–34, xii. 117–76, xiii. 241–90, xiv. 89–140 (1878–79).

Haug, M., *Essays on the Parsis*. 3rd ed. London, 1884.

Henry, V., *Le Parsisme*. Paris, 1905.

Hovelacque, A., *L'Avesta, Zoroastre et le mazdéisme*. Paris, 1880.

Hüsing, G., *Die iranische Ueberlieferung und das arische System*. Leipzig, 1909.

Hyde, T., *Historia religionis veterum Persarum eorumque magorum*. Oxford, 1700.

Jackson, A. V. W., "Die iranische Religion," in *Grundriss der iranischen Philologie*, ii. 612–708. Strassburg, 1903.

Justi, F., *Iranisches Namenbuch*. Marburg, 1895.

——— "Die älteste iranische Religion und ihr Stifter Zarathustra," in *Preussische Jahrbücher*, lxxxviii. 55–86, 231–62 (1897).

Karaka, D. F., *History of the Parsis*. 2 vols. London, 1884.

Lehmann, E., "Die Perser," in P. D. Chantepie de la Saussaye, *Lehrbuch der Religionsgeschichte*, ii. 162–233. 3rd ed. Tübingen, 1905.

Lord, H., *Religion of the Parsees*. London, 1630.

Ménant, J., *Zoroastre. Essai sur la philosophie religieuse de la Perse*. 2nd ed. Paris, 1857.

Modi, J. J., *Catechism of the Zoroastrian Religion*. Bombay, 1911.

Moore, G. F., *History of Religions*, chh. xv–xvi. Edinburgh, 1913.

Moulton, J. H., "Zoroastrianism," in *Dictionary of the Bible*, iv. 988–94. Edinburgh, 1898–1904.

——— *Early Zoroastrianism*. London, 1913.

Orelli, C. von, *Allgemeine Religionsgeschichte*, ii. 140–87. 2nd ed. Bonn, 1911–13.

Rawlinson, G., *Five Great Monarchies of the Ancient Eastern World:* Third Monarchy (Media), ch. iv; Fifth Monarchy (Persia), ch. vi. London, 1862.

——— *Seventh Great Oriental Monarchy*, ch. xxviii. London, 1876.

Sanjana, R. E. P., *Zarathushtra and Zarathushtrianism in the Avesta*. Leipzig, 1906.

Söderblom, N., "Du Genie du mazdéisme," in *Mélanges Charles de Harlez*, pp. 298–302. Leyden, 1896.

SÖDERBLOM, N., "The Place of the Christian Trinity and of the Buddhist Triratna amongst Holy Triads," in *Transactions of the Third International Congress for the History of Religions*, pp. 391–410 (London, 1912).

SPIEGEL, F., *Eranische Alterthumskunde*. 3 vols. Leipzig, 1871–78.

——— "Zur Geschichte des Dualismus," in his *Arische Studien*, i. 62–77. Leipzig, 1874.

——— *Die arische Periode*. Leipzig, 1881.

——— "Die alten Religionen in Erân," in *ZDMG* lii. 187–96 (1898).

STEIN, M. A., "Zoroastrian Deities on Indo-Scythian Coins," in *Babylonian and Oriental Record*, 1887, pp. 155–66.

TIELE, C. P., *Geschichte der Religion im Altertum* (tr. G. Gerich), i. 1–187. Gotha, 1898.

WILHELM, E., *On the Use of Beef's Urine according to the Precepts of the Avesta*. Bombay, 1899.

——— "Analogies in Iranian and Armenian Folklore," in *Spiegel Memorial Volume*, pp. 65–83. Bombay, 1908.

WINDISCHMANN, F., *Zoroastrische Studien*. Berlin, 1863.

## IV. TREATISES ON SPECIAL POINTS

### 1. Zoroaster

JACKSON, A. V. W., *Zoroaster, The Prophet of Ancient Iran*. New York, 1899.

——— "Some Additional Data on Zoroaster," in *Orientalische Studien Theodor Nöldeke . . . gewidmet*, pp. 1031–38. Giessen, 1906.

JUSTI, F., "The Life and Legend of Zarathushtra," in *Avesta . . . Studies in Honour of . . . Peshotanji Behramji Sanjana*, pp. 117–58. Bombay, 1904.

KERN, J. H. C., "Over het woord Zarathustra en den mythischen persoon van dien naam," in *Verslagen en mededeelingen der koninklijke akademie van wetenschappen*, xi. 132–64 (1868).

YOHANNAN, A., "Some Passages in Persian Literature Relating to Zoroaster," in *Spiegel Memorial Volume*, pp. 150–55. Bombay, 1908.

### 2. Ahura Mazda and Angra Mainyu

BRADKE, P. VON, *Dyâus Asura, Ahura Mazdâ und die Asuras*. Halle, 1885.

DARMESTETER, J., *Ormazd et Ahriman*. Paris, 1877.

Jackson, A. V. W., "Ormazd, or the Ancient Persian Idea of God," in *The Monist*, ix. 161–78 (1899).

3. Haurvatāt and Ameretāt

Darmesteter, J., *Haurvatāṭ et Ameretāṭ*. Paris, 1875.

4. Khshathrya Vairya

Jackson, A. V. W., "Khshathra Vairya," in *Avesta . . . Studies in Honour of . . . Peshotanji Behramji Sanjana*, pp. 159–66. Bombay, 1904.

5. Spenta Ārmaiti

Carnoy, A. J., "Aramati-Ārmatay," in *Muséon*, II. xiii. 127–46 (1912).

6. Fravashi

Söderblom, N., *Les Fravashis*. Paris, 1899.

7. Verethraghna

Charpentier, J., *Kleine Beiträge zur indoiranischen Mythologie*, pp. 25–68. Upsala, 1911.

8. Anāhita

Windischmann, F., *Die persische Anâhita oder Anaïtis*. Munich, 1856.

9. Mithra

Cumont, F., *Textes et monuments figurés relatifs aux mystères de Mithra*. 2 vols. Brussels, 1896–99.

——— *Les Mystères de Mithra*. 2nd ed. Brussels, 1902. English tr. by T. J. McCormack. Chicago, 1903.

Eggers, A., *Der arische Gott Mitra*. Dorpat, 1894.

Gray, L. H., "Deux étymologies mithriaques," in *Muséon*, III. i. 189–92 (1916).

Meillet, A., "Le Dieu indo-iranien Mitra," in *Journal asiatique*, X. i. 143–59 (1907).

Modi, J. J., "St. Michael of the Christians and Mithra of the Zoroastrians," in his *Anthropological Papers*, pp. 173–90. Bombay, no date.

Windischmann, F., *Mithra*. Leipzig, 1857.

10. Sīmurgh

Casartelli, L. C., "Çyêna-Sîmurgh-Roc," in *Compte rendu du congrès scientifique international des catholiques . . . 1891*, vi. 79–87.

11. Khvarenanh

Wilhelm, E., "Khvareno," in *Sir Jamshetjee Jejeebhoy Madressa Memorial Volume*· Bombay, 1914.

12. Cosmology

Carnoy, A. J., "Iranian Views of Origins in Connection with Similar Babylonian Beliefs," in *JAOS* xxxvi, 300–20 (1917).

Darmesteter, J., "Les Cosmogonies aryennes," in his *Essais orientaux*, pp. 171–207. Paris, 1883.

13. Deluge

Lindner, B., "Die iranische Flutsage," in *Festgruss an Rudolf von Roth*, pp. 213–16. Stuttgart, 1903.

14. Eschatology

Brandt, W., "Schicksale der Seele nach dem Tode nach mandäischen und parsischen Vorstellungen," in *Jahrbücher für protestantische Theologie*, xviii. 405–38, 575–603 (1902).

Casartelli, L. C., "The Persian Dante," in *Dastur Hoshang Memorial Volume*, pp. 258–73. Not yet published.

Hübschmann, H., "Parsische Lehre vom Jenseits und jüngsten Gericht," in *Jahrbücher für protestantische Theologie*, v. 203–45 (1879).

Jackson, A. V. W., "The Ancient Persian Doctrine of a Future Life," in *Biblical World*, viii. 149–63 (1896).

Modi, J. J., "The Divine Comedy of Dante and the Virâf-nâmeh of Ardâi Virâf," in his *Asiatic Papers*, pp. 31–44. Bombay, 1905.

Söderblom, N., *La Vie future d'après le mazdéisme*. Paris, 1901.

## V. ZOROASTRIANISM, JUDAISM, CHRISTIANITY, AND MUHAMMADANISM

AIKEN, C. F., "The Avesta and the Bible," in *Catholic University Bulletin*, iii. 243–91 (1897).

BÖKLEN, E., *Verwandtschaft der jüdisch-christlichen mit der parsischen Eschatologie*. Göttingen, 1902.

CHEYNE, T. K., "Possible Zoroastrian Influences on the Religion of Israel," in *Expository Times*, ii. 202–08, 224–27, 248–53 (1891).

GOLDZIHER, I., "Islamisme et parsisme," in *Revue de l'histoire des religions*, xliii. 1–29 (1901).

GRAY, L. H., "Zoroastrian Elements in Muḥammadan Eschatology," in *Muséon*, II. iii. 153–84 (1902).

HAUPT, E., *Über die Berührungen des Alten Testaments mit der Religion Zarathustras*. Treptow, 1867.

JACKSON, A. V. W., "Zoroastrianism and the Resemblances between it and Christianity," in *Biblical World*, xxvii. 335–43 (1906).

KOHUT, A., *Jüdische Angelologie und Dämonologie in ihrer Abhängigkeit vom Parsismus*. Leipzig, 1866.

——— "Was hat die talmudische Eschatologie aus dem Parsismus aufgenommen?," in *ZDMG* xxi. 552–91 (1867).

KUHN, E., "Eine zoroastrische Prophezeiung in christlichem Gewande," in *Festgruss an Rudolf von Roth*, pp. 217–21. Stuttgart, 1893.

MILLS, L. H., *Zarathushtra (Zoroaster), Philo, the Achaemenids and Israel*. 2 vols. Chicago, 1906.

——— *Avesta Eschatology Compared with the Books of Daniel and Revelations*. Chicago, 1908.

——— *Our Own Religion in Ancient Persia*. Chicago, 1913.

MOULTON, J. H., "Zoroaster and Israel," in *The Thinker*, i. 406–08, ii. 308–15, 490–501 (1892).

——— "Zoroastrian Influences on Judaism," in *Expository Times*, ix. 352–58 (1898).

SPIEGEL, F., "Der Einfluss des Semitismus auf das Avesta," in his *Arische Studien*, i. 45–61. Leipzig, 1874.

STAVE, E., *Über den Einfluss des Parsismus auf das Judentum*. Haarlem, 1898.

## VI. PRINCIPAL ARTICLES ON IRANIAN RELIGION IN THE ENCYCLOPÆDIA OF RELIGION AND ETHICS (VOLS. I–VIII)

Ananikian, M., "Armenia (Zoroastrian)," i. 794–802.
Carnoy, A. J., "Magic (Iranian)," viii. 293–96.
Casartelli, L. C., "Dualism (Iranian)," v. 111–12.
Cumont, F., "Anāhita," i. 414–15.
Edwards, E., "Altar (Persian)," i. 346–48.
——— "God (Iranian)," vi. 290–94.
Gray, L. H., "Achæmenians," i. 69–73.
——— "Blest, Abode of the (Persian)," ii. 702–04.
——— "Cosmogony and Cosmology (Iranian)," iv. 161–62.
——— "Divination (Persian)," iv. 818–20.
——— "Fate (Iranian)," v. 792–93.
——— "Festivals and Fasts (Iranian)," v. 872–75.
——— "Fortune (Iranian)," vi. 96.
——— "Heroes and Hero-Gods (Iranian)," vi. 661–62.
——— "Life and Death (Iranian)," viii. 37.
——— "Light and Darkness (Iranian)," viii. 61–62.
——— "Literature (Pahlavi)," viii. 104–06.
Jackson, A. V. W., "Ahriman," i. 237–38.
——— "Amesha Spentas," i. 384–85.
——— "Avesta," ii. 266–72.
——— "Demons and Spirits (Persian)," iv. 619–20.
——— "Images and Idols (Persian)," vii. 151–55.
Jones, H. S., "Mithraism," viii. 752–59.
Ménant, D., "Gabars," vi. 147–56.
Mills, L. H., "Ahuna-Vairya," i. 238–39.
Mills, L. H., and Gray, L. H., "Barsom," ii. 424–25.
Modi, J. J., "Haoma," vi. 506–10.
Moulton, J. H., "Fravashi," vi. 116–18.
——— "Iranians," vii. 418–20.
——— "Magi," viii. 242–44.
Nicholson, R. A., "Mazdak," viii. 508–10.

Sayce, A. H., "Median Religion," viii. 514–15.
Söderblom, N., "Ages of the World (Zoroastrian)," i. 205–10.
——— "Incarnation (Parsi)," vii. 198–99.
Söderblom, N., and Gray, L. H., "Death and Disposal of the Dead (Parsi)," iv. 502–05.

8.23
Publisher
Feb. 1938

8.23.
Publisher
Feb. 1938